Regulatory Governance in Developing Countries

THE CRC SERIES ON COMPETITION, REGULATION AND DEVELOPMENT

Series Editors: Paul Cook, *Professor of Economics and Development Policy and* Martin Minogue, *Senior Research Fellow, Institute for Development Policy and Management, University of Manchester, UK*

Titles in the series include:

Leading Issues in Competition, Regulation and Development
Edited by Paul Cook, Colin Kirkpatrick, Martin Minogue and David Parker

The Politics of Regulation
Institutions and Regulatory Reforms for the Age of Governance
Edited by Jacint Jordana and David Levi-Faur

Regulating Development
Evidence from Africa and Latin America
Edited by Edmund Amann

Regulatory Governance in Developing Countries
Edited by Martin Minogue and Ledivina Cariño

Regulatory Governance in Developing Countries

Edited by

Martin Minogue

Senior Research Fellow, Institute for Development Policy and Management and Director of the Regulatory Governance Research Programme, Centre on Regulation and Competition (CRC), University of Manchester, UK

Ledivina Cariño

Professor, National College of Public Administration and Governance, University of the Philippines, Manila

THE CRC SERIES ON COMPETITION, REGULATION AND DEVELOPMENT

Edward Elgar

Cheltenham, UK • Northampton, MA, USA

Published by
Edward Elgar Publishing Limited
Glensanda House
Montpellier Parade
Cheltenham
Glos GL50 1UA
UK

Edward Elgar Publishing, Inc.
William Pratt House
9 Dewey Court
Northampton
Massachusetts 01060
USA

A catalogue record for this book is available from the British Library

Library of Congress Cataloging in Publication Data

Regulatory governance in developing countries / edited by Martin Minogue, Ledivina V. Cariño
p. cm. – (The CRC series on competition, regulation and development)
Includes bibliographical references and index.
1. Trade regulation–Developing countries. 2. Industrial policy–Developing countries. 3. Independent regulatory commissions–Developing countries. 4. Administrative agencies–Developing countries. I. Minogue, Martin. II. Cariño, Ledivina V. III. Series.
HD3616.D453R44 2006
352.809172′4–dc22 2006005894

ISBN-13: 978 1 84542 612 5 (cased)
ISBN-10: 1 84542 612 6 (cased)

Printed and bound in Great Britain by MPG Books Ltd, Bodmin, Cornwall

Contents

Contributors

Erwin M. Alampay is Associate Professor in the National College of Public Administration and Governance (NCPAG), University of the Philippines, Manila

Enrico L. Basilio is Director of the Transport and Logistics Unit, Centre for Research and Communication, Manila, the Philippines

Julia Brown is a Researcher in the Centre on Regulation and Competition (CRC) and the Institute for Development Policy and Management (IDPM), University of Manchester, UK

Ledivina Cariño is a Professor in the National College of Public Administration and Governance (NCPAG), University of the Philippines, Manila

Jocelyn C. Cuaresma is a Researcher in the National College of Public Administration and Governance (NCPAG), University of the Philippines, Manila

Derek Eldridge is Director of Capacity Building in the Centre on Regulation and Competition (CRC), and Senior Lecturer in the Institute for Development Policy and Management (IDPM), University of Manchester, UK

Brian Goulden is an Associate Research Fellow with the Centre on Regulation and Competition (CRC), University of Manchester, UK

Perla E. Legaspi is Associate Professor in the National College of Public Administration and Governance (NCPAG), University of the Philippines, Manila

Grant Mackintosh works for Emanti Management, an independent consultancy specialising in water services in South Africa

Giandomenico Majone is Emeritus Professor at the European University, Florence, Italy

Martin Minogue is Senior Research Fellow in the Institute for Development Policy and Management (IDPM) and Director of the Regulatory Governance Research Programme, Centre on Regulation and Competition (CRC), University of Manchester, UK

Kobus Müller is a Professor in the School of Public Management, University of Stellenbosch, South Africa

Anthony Ogus is Professor of Law, and Research Fellow in the Centre on Regulation and Competition (CRC), University of Manchester, UK

Nicola Phillips is Senior Lecturer in the Department of Government, University of Manchester, UK

Frederik Uys is a Lecturer in the School of Public Management, University of Stellenbosch, South Africa

Peter Vass is Director of the Centre for Regulated Industries (CRI) School of Management, University of Bath, UK

Philip Woodhouse is Head of Institute in the Institute for Development Policy and Management (IDPM), University of Manchester, UK

Qing Zhang is a Researcher in the Centre on Regulation and Competition (CRC) and the School of Law, University of Manchester UK

Preface

Issues of regulation and competition have long been matters of both public policy debate and academic research in developed economies, but until recently were relatively unexamined in relation to developing economies. The Centre on Regulation and Competition (CRC) of the University of Manchester, UK, has been conducting research into regulatory developments and competition issues since 2001, with a primary focus on changes and reforms in developing countries, working together with partners both in the UK and overseas in China, Ghana, India, Malaysia, the Philippines, South Africa and Sri Lanka. This work has been funded primarily by the UK's Department for International Development, with other support from the UK Foreign and Commonwealth Office's Global Opportunities Fund, and from the British Council. Other collaborating agencies include the Foreign Investment Advisory Service of the World Bank, and the Competition Division of the United Nations Committee on Trade and Development (UNCTAD).

This book series is one of the many ways in which the work of the CRC and its partners is disseminated, complementing conferences, workshops, journal publication and policy briefs. This latest addition brings together findings of the CRC's research in regulatory governance, a neglected and sparsely researched context for regulatory and competition reforms, but now regarded as crucial to the understanding and improvement of market-based economic reforms. A particular focus is on case studies from two partner countries, South Africa and the Philippines, which illustrate the limitations of such reforms in delivering essential goods and services to poor communities, and the need for proponents of these reforms to give due regard to the political, social and economic contexts which will determine their shape and outcomes.

Paul Cook and Martin Minogue
CRC, University of Manchester

PART I

Conceptualising regulation, governance and development

1. Introduction: regulatory governance in developing countries

Martin Minogue and Ledivina Cariño

This book examines the problems involved in analysing and assessing the regulatory reforms that are now on the economic reform agenda in many developing countries. In developed economies, such well-established reforms are generally regarded as belonging to the post-privatisation phase; but in developing economies, privatisation has itself been an incomplete and faltering process, so that associated regulatory reforms are either new, or poorly understood and conceived: often, privatisation and regulatory reforms will proceed piecemeal, without proper sequencing or coordination. Despite the assumption by influential aid donors such as the World Bank that such reforms will have the merit of taking bureaucrats out of business, many factors in developing country political and economic systems demonstrate a propensity for regulation *inside* government. Since poor governance is regarded by aid donors as a major obstacle to effective economic reforms, a concern with institutionalising regulatory governance is a crucial aspect of the regulatory reform agenda, and indeed of broader programmes of governance and public sector reforms.

A significant feature of the contemporary research agenda on competition and regulation in developing economies has therefore been the emphasis placed on the institutions and processes of governance surrounding and conditioning the progress of these economic policy reforms. This does no more than reflect one of the leading themes in the developed country literature on regulation, usually labelled as 'regulatory governance' and deploying a new concept of the 'regulatory state' to set against the more conventional categories of 'welfare' or 'provider' state. This corresponded clearly enough to the 'new public management' model of public action, which rested on a similar counterposition of the traditional state and the 'enabling' state. The thrust of recent work in this field has been to emphasise the significance of 'regulatory governance' as an essential context that may determine the prospects for regulatory policy success or failure, and to remind policy reformers that their proposals are not introduced into a contextless environment.

INTERPRETING REGULATORY GOVERNANCE

First, we need to recall what regulatory governance is, how it has emerged as a significant element in the literature and practice of regulation in developed countries, and what purchase it has in the rather different economic and political conditions of developing countries. It is possible to suggest at least tentative answers to these questions (tentative because many of the conceptual issues are 'contested' and because for developing country systems empirical research in this area remains sparse and patchy).

A starting point is to acknowledge that regulatory governance is now fully accepted as a significant part of the literature on regulation in general and on privatisation and post-privatisation regulatory reforms in particular. The traditional literature always had a strong institutional component focusing on the role of legal institutions and practices, in an approach which saw regulation as primarily rule-based and principally involving issues of compliance and accountability (Ogus, 2002). But the most recent literature on developed, and particularly European, countries has been dominated by analysts such as Majone, intent on expanding the range of analysis to include the interactions of legal and administrative systems with political institutions and processes (Majone, 1996, 1997); by political scientists such as Moran (2001, 2002), concerned to establish broader concepts of 'the regulatory state', 'regulatory capture' and 'regulatory space' as a way of bringing together the political and economic issues inherent in contemporary state–market debates; and Wilks (1996), who demonstrates the diversity of regulatory ideas and practice even within an ostensibly uniform European system. An important dimension emerged in formulations of self-regulation, resting on relations of trust, as a means of escaping from more formalistic regulatory overload and inadequate forms of political accountability (Ayres and Braithwaite, 1992). In the first place, then, the analysis of regulation must go beyond examination of the formal rules that govern relationships between the public and private sectors, to the broader framework of state–market relations, and drawing on disciplinary contributions that range across economics, law, politics, and public policy and management.

Correspondingly, since regulation can be categorised as a distinctive mode of policymaking, or of governance (Majone, 1999), it must be examined in relation to the general public policy process. Majone's focus is on the extensive delegation of policymaking powers to what he describes as non-majoritarian institutions, by which he means the various new regulatory bodies but also judiciaries, tribunals and other regulatory and adjudicative agencies intrinsic to the public sector. His concern is that these institutions may become dangerously independent of the political process and so lack accountability. On the other hand Majone locates this development in a political logic which demands of politicians that they 'achieve credible policy commitments' (Majone, 1999, p. 4). An important issue raised here is that 'democratically accountable principals can transfer policy making powers to non-majoritarian institutions, but they cannot transfer their own legitimacy', which may be a significant agency cost where in theory 'delegation is justified only if its benefits exceed agency costs' (Majone, 1999, p. 7). Perhaps, therefore, a key insight is that 'independence from political control does not mean independence from public accountability' (p. 11). Majone concludes that in designing an effective regulatory state the key variables are:

1. the extent to which decisions are delegated to an independent agent rather than taken by the political principal;
2. the nature of the structure of governance itself, particularly in determining the agent's degree of independence from the political process;
3. the rules that specify the procedural framework, e.g. reason-giving requirements, consultative processes;
4. the scope for political principals to overrule agency decisions;
5. the relative autonomy of financial resources;
6. the extent of ex post monitoring, e.g. legislative oversight, judicial review, citizen's complaints procedure.

What is striking here is the way Majone moves between the narrower conception of regulatory instruments and procedures, and the broader conception of politics in ways that underwrite the usefulness of the label 'regulatory governance'. This means looking behind the institutional façade to grasp the 'real world' of public action. The orthodox model, with its emphasis on legal rules, formal structures of organisation, rational policy choice and the assumed implementation of formal policies has serious limitations. It oversimplifies the complex processes from which policy debates and decisions emerge; and neglects the political discourse of rule-making and rule application, notably the interplay of ideas, interests and resources, and the ways in which these interactions determine outcomes. It therefore fails to explain either policy and organisational failures, or policy innovations and successes, and obscures both the significance of relations of power and influence, and the extent to which public policies and their results are determined by conflicts and bargains between conflicting stakeholders, whether internal or external to public bureaucracies.

Analysis based on process may be conducted in ways that focus on real decision scenarios; the factors that determine choice between policy options; the actions that define implementation outcomes, and deficits;

and the relations between key actors. Such analysis helps to identify stakeholder interests and networks, and to explain both failed and effective policy changes, in particular by identifying winners and losers; and assists more realistic and feasible policy design, which in turn should produce more predictable and effective policy outcomes. This analytical model can be applied to any field of policy, and therefore has obvious value as a tool for improving and evaluating regulatory policies, and asking the significant questions about the effectiveness of regulatory policies in achieving broader systemic objectives such as poverty reduction.

In sum, analysis of regulation involves analysis of ideas, institutions, processes, activities and actors, in all their myriad interrelationships in economic, social and political spheres. The conceptions of the regulatory state and regulatory space offer us the broadest possible analytical framework in direct contradiction to the narrow formulations favoured in the standard literature on regulation, so capably criticised by Black (2002) for its preoccupation with the correction of market failure, when wider issues of the management of a risk society, and the achievement of social justice, should be equally insistent concerns.

INTERPRETING POLICY TRANSFER

When we turn to the application of this analysis to regulatory reforms in developing countries, the contributions to this book demonstrate that problems can be identified associated with the strong tendency to transfer to developing countries 'best practice' models of regulation rooted in the different economic, social and political conditions of developed countries. These contributions focus first of all on conceptual issues and debates. Phillips, in Chapter 2, challenges the contention that the regulatory state model is a useful framework within which to develop an understanding of the evolution of the state in different parts of the world. Her argument is set out in three dimensions. First, empirically, a variety of differing states are simply slotted into the preconceived model rooted in industrial state systems and processes, but 'the regulatory state model has generally yielded little purchase on the processes of state transformation and the nature of contemporary states in the huge variety of institutional and national settings outside the "core" of the advanced industrialised economies' (p. 18). Second, analytical approaches are constrained by a preference for the construction of ideal types of the state in a globalising economy, with a consequently reductivist allocation of specific cases to one or other of these idealised models. Third, a highly functionalist account of the regulatory state obscures our understanding of the complex institutional and political landscapes characteristic of developing states, and the extent to which differing forms of governance exist alongside regulatory governance in most contexts. Her main conclusion is that these landscapes are 'characterised more by "regulation without a regulatory state" than with the sorts of institutional and strategic structures stipulated by the regulatory state model' (p. 35); and that while empirical reforms are being widely pursued and constructed, the institutional and political conditions for success are found in only very limited cases: 'the regulatory state model can often prove more of a hindrance than a help in the study of regulation, at least in the developing world' (p. 36).

Phillips concedes that much existing reform activity in developing countries is based on an ideal type of regulatory state, and that some of the relevant institutional reforms are taking place. Majone (Chapter 3), is interested in what he terms 'spontaneous regulatory convergence' (p. 41), created by the demands for legal, institutional and economic harmonisation emerging from global institutions and agreements. Much of the drive towards international regulatory convergence operates through the setting of uniform international standards, particularly in areas of science and the regulation of risk. Majone quotes a World Bank study which demonstrates that stringent rules designed to protect health in EU countries would seriously damage African export trade, and argues that it is in the interests of developing countries to ensure that they are able to participate in and shape adjustments of international policies and rules. While calling for attention to 'regulatory science' and procedural rationality in decision-making, he emphasises that this has significant political as well as technical implications, since regulatory independence and efficiency must be achieved within a framework of political and public accountability.

Discussing 'policy imitation' in these contexts, Majone suggests that models emanating from economically and politically powerful countries are most likely to be emulated, and that this process may demonstrate 'push and pull' tendencies. These are themes explored by Minogue (Chapter 4). This chapter draws attention to conceptual difficulties involved in analysis of regulatory governance reforms in developing countries. These difficulties relate to contested definitions of regulation, to the weakness of comparative frameworks of analysis, to poor data and information about the real impact of core governance reforms, and to disagreements about what constitutes the proper scope of regulation. Crucially, an idealised model rooted in developed country practice and aid donor preferences is transplanted with little attempt to modify it to fit the many and varied political and institutional contexts in a range of developing and transitional economies. Minogue argues that the core ideal of 'independent regulation' rests on a naive view of the political process and a misunderstanding of political priorities, which in developing country contexts often mean that economic governance cannot be insulated from overriding political considerations: 'aid donors . . . must learn to accept that local political cultures will shape and mediate externally-derived economic and managerial reforms, rather than being transformed by them' (p. 78).

This message is partly challenged by Vass, in Chapter 5. He suggests that, with due modification and adaptation, the UK model of regulatory governance can appropriately be emulated elsewhere, the prize to be gained being improved economic efficiency and more effective provision of public goods and services. Yet his survey of recent developments in regulatory reforms in the UK demonstrates how necessary it is to locate analysis of such reforms within the institutional and policy framework in which they are being formulated and applied. In the UK system, as Vass emphasises, this means giving considerable weight to the legal and constitutional settings that determine the forms and effectiveness of public accountability mechanisms. Doubtless the achievement of sound mechanisms of accountability is desirable in developing country governance too, but where these are deficient or weak, legal-constitutional models will have little real purchase until broader governance and public management reforms are introduced. But such reforms are open to similar objections of cultural inappropriateness and contested values.

INSTITUTIONAL REFORMS, CAPACITY AND CAPTURE

Specific cases of regulatory reform in developing countries illustrate some significant issues. Elsewhere Ogus has described the necessary legal institutions and structures that provide the essential foundation for effective regulatory practice (Ogus, 2002) and has identified the institutional and behavioural weaknesses in developing country legal systems that make regulatory reforms difficult to achieve (Ogus, 2004). Here, in Chapter 6, Ogus and Zhang use empirical evidence, largely from China, to argue the merits of deregulation where regulatory regimes seem to be serving other than regulatory purposes. Their discussion of licensing systems demonstrates that such systems at best are overelaborate and dysfunctional, and at worst are kept in place to support rent-seeking activities by political and bureaucratic elites. The reduction and streamlining of such processes would, it is argued, remove constraints damaging to enterprises and economic growth in developing countries. While this reverts to the conventional argument for deregulation, it is worth noting that such reforms will come up hard against the very logic they identify as causal to the problem in the first place: political and bureaucratic self-interest, and political values that favour governmental control of a wide range of economic activities and agencies.

Legaspi's study (Chapter 7) of regulation in the context of local economic development in two contrasting Philippine cities echoes some of the discussion in Ogus and Zhang. What is demonstrated here is that issues of regulation and competition frameworks are not to be confined to central government contexts, but are significant at decentralised levels of governance, where 'local government is placed at a focal point of relationships and linkages with the private sector' (p. 138). Legaspi argues that regulation of local businesses and economic activity is part of the 'social regulation' function of local governments acting in the public interest. But her cases reveal dysfunctions associated with over-regulation on the one hand, and related opportunistic corruption on the other. Regulation may then work in the private rather than the public interest. This situation is exacerbated by confused lines of authority and responsibility between national and local regulators, and a lack of appropriate resources and capacity for effective regulation at the local level. In short, regulation at local levels of governance is desirable, but too often flawed, and rarely 'independent'.

As guardians of the public interest, regulators should in principle have both technical capacity and independence. Most developing countries started with a single regulator for multiple sectors, given the original focus on economic regulation and the relatively simple technologies of the regulated industries. It was expected that a single body could guide the provision of such disparate services as power, water, communications and transportation. With rapid technical changes, the norm for regulators now is to specialise in one industry even as they tackle multiple goals of economic and social regulation, as well as the regulation of competition.

Regulators must (again, in principle) be abreast of the technological sophistication of the regulated industry, and have working knowledge of its needs. This would allow them to assess the capacity of firms to deliver required services, to evaluate their petitions for rate increases and to balance these against the demands of consumers and clients. Their lawyers and accountants must match the industry's own staff so that neither the state nor the public are misled by the arguments and figures produced by the regulated firms. In developing states, such technical capacity is scarce and is often best developed within the regulated industries themselves. Taking advantage of this, some regulated firms provide the equipment and training for their regulators or contrive the appointment of industry insiders as regulators (see Coronel, 1998, for examples of this in the Philippine telecommunications industry). Eldridge and Goulden (Chapter 14) emphasise that an important response to these problems of building organisational and managerial autonomy reside within regulatory agencies themselves. They elaborate a diagnostic model that, if sensitively applied and adapted to individual agency conditions, would, they argue, substantially improve the ability of agency staffs to identify their own capacity constraints, build their internal institutional capacity, and strengthen their performance and effectiveness as regulators, a necessary (though not sufficient) step towards genuine regulatory independence.

The 'independence' of a regulatory agency should mean relative insulation from both political and industry pressures. This may be aimed for through constitutional measures, judicial review arrangements, location outside the normal state bureaucratic system, or incentives to regulatory staff. Recognition by the state of the importance of such forms of insulation is essential. Representation of and consultation with different interests forestalls capture by any single one. Nevertheless, representation is not without problems: as shown in Brown and Woodhouse (Chapter 11) in their study of water management and regulation in a rural region in South Africa, representation of black communities did not ensure awareness by these communities of the issues and their own interests. They suggest that proxies like advocacy non-governmental organisations (NGOs) may voice black interests better, but acknowledge that these may also filter the needs of black communities through a particular lens. Meanwhile, commercial interests complain that their higher ability to pay is not rewarded with stronger representation in the regulatory system.

The importance of regulators to the state is shown in both their hierarchical position and their functions. Hierarchical placement may seem like a simple concept. The higher they are placed in the bureaucracy, the less regulators are subject to administrative checks. Independent commissions have more autonomy than those attached to cabinet departments or those placed lower in the hierarchy. But agency placement may be highly complex, as Müller and Uys show in their study of water services in South Africa (Chapter 10). The national level sets standards and provides the regulatory framework. This is largely the function of the Ministry of Water Affairs, but it has to work in conjunction with the Ministry of Finance relative to water tariffs, and it is 'the executive political office bearer' of the Department of Water Affairs and Forestry that acts as the overall regulator of water services. This picture is complicated by concurrent national and provincial functional areas, exclusive provincial areas, and local government functional areas all of which have offices assigned to each function. The allocation of domestic service provision to local government bodies seems to accord with the best principles of decentralised public services, but in practice runs into the same problems of local capacity and capture identified in Legaspi (Chapter 7). The lesson here seems to be that institutional reforms will not be worth the legislative paper they are written on unless supported by real changes in political attitudes, managerial practices and organisational competencies.

The importance given by the state to regulators is also shown by the functions it entrusts to them. However, having multiple functions does not necessarily strengthen regulation, as two Philippine cases demonstrate. Basilio (Chapter 8) depicts the problems of saddling the Philippines Ports Authority (PPA) with developmental and revenue-raising functions. As a result, the PPA has developed a partnership with the shipping, cargo handling and terminal operators it is supposed to regulate and has encouraged them to form a virtual monopoly. Because it shares in their income, the PPA has also allowed them to make excessive increases in their customers' fees. This study also warns that while it might seem appropriate for government officials to be tasked with obligations to protect the public interest, where the institutional conditions for regulatory independence are absent, this overlooks the weakness that government may itself be a party motivated by self-interest. In the case of the PPA, government's desire for revenues seemed to override the goals of efficiency and competitiveness.

A similar situation is described by Cuaresma in Chapter 12 in respect of regulation of water services, where the government regulatory office, being funded by the private concessionaires, is unable to control them. Both cases also show that capture may be so entrenched in the surrounding legislative and contractual arrangements that the regulators are either part of the system of capture, or are powerless to resist it. Capture may be written into the law and be beyond the regulator's power to prevent. Basilio (Chapter 8) shows pitfalls in the law governing the PPA, which is then used by a president to promulgate an Executive Order practically requiring the board to do away with competition.

Moreover, the promulgators of a regulation do not have to be private-regarding to write rules that can be justified more by private than by public interest. This is the lesson of Ogus and Zhang's study of licensing procedures in developing countries (Chapter 6). They compared licensing integrated in the set-up process (SL) and those independent of it (IL), finding SL regimes imposing more entry costs but not necessarily improving compliance, saving compliance costs or saving monitoring costs for officials. Instead, benefits may accrue more to the bureaucrats giving the licence, agencies responsible for subsequent checking procedures, existing suppliers and politicians. Some of the benefits will take place through resort to corruption.

These examples show that regulatory capture is not simply the ability of regulated firms to get regulators to decide regularly in their favour. It should also encompass the view that government is an interested party.

Moreover, laws and regulations, even those seemingly neutral, need to be analysed for their potential ability to tilt decisions in favour of private interests. Representation and participation, as means to ward off such capture, also need to be examined for their efficacy in giving voice to these previously excluded and to the general public. This is a reminder of the deeply political nature of regulatory policymaking in developing countries.

REGULATION, MARKETS AND POVERTY

A core objective of development policy, both for leaderships in developing countries, and for the aid agencies that are the principal funders and drivers of economic reforms, is to reduce poverty, in line with the Millennium Development Goals. It is no simple matter to trace the linkages between the overarching poverty reduction strategy, and specific economic reforms of the kind represented by market-oriented policies that promote privatisation, competition and regulation. The dominant philosophy is still rooted in the classical view that economic growth will, through an inevitable process of 'trickle down' of benefits, inexorably reduce poverty. But the process remains stubbornly opaque, and resistant to easy generalisation. Even if it is accepted that economic growth can, and has, lifted millions of people out of some officially designated level of poverty in many developing countries over the past three decades (notably in China), some vexed and contentious issues remain. One of these is inequality of distribution of the benefits of economic growth, not merely in terms of income, but in terms of what the poor are able to command in other equally significant ways. One such area is the degree to which the poor are able to ensure access to core resources such as water, energy, and transport and communications. Under the traditional 'development' or 'provider' state model, access for the poor to basic needs was protected by the public interest role defined for the state (and supported by aid agencies). But the shift to an 'enabling' state has switched the emphasis to market-driven provision of services. The question that arises, and is yet to be fully answered, is whether this will be beneficial or damaging to poor groups and communities.

Some cases explored in the last part of this book sketch, if not the answers to this question, at least the outlines of what must be examined in order to answer it. In the case of telecommunications, Alampay (Chapter 9) uses Amartya Sen's well known perspective on the ability of people to command 'substantive freedoms' to live the lives they choose, or their 'capabilities', to examine the significance of universal access to information and communication technologies (ICTs) for this kind of capability. This analysis is based on an empirical study in the large Philippine city of Puerto

Princesa. Alampay concludes that while new technologies provide new possibilities for government to improve the capabilities of poorer groups, it is evident that traditional socioeconomic and cultural barriers continue to impede these advances in communication and information, so that already privileged groups gain most of the associated benefits. Capabilities, in Sen's terms, are easily enough identified, but not so easily acquired by those with few resources, in the absence of protection from regulatory bodies tasked with social as well as technical objectives.

The discontinuity between the narrower economic and technical objectives of market-based competition and regulatory reforms and the broader social objectives that tend to be the province of state-centred policies emerges clearly from the case studies here of the water sector (three related to South Africa, one to the Philippines). In South Africa, substantive institutional reforms have been introduced by a government motivated by the pressing basic needs of large parts of its population and the strength of its own political commitment to meet these needs. Müller and Uys (Chapter 10) set the scene with a useful account of these institutional (and legislative-based) changes. They describe a complex array of instruments and agencies, with potential for a 'multitude of regulatory institutions' and related duplications, confusions and conflicts. Privatisation does not appear to be an issue in itself: 'the predominant issue in South Africa is less *who* delivers the service than *at what price*' (p. 222). While a political debate takes place broadly between proponents of marketisation or at least full cost recovery, and those who argue for the need to 'decommodify' what is a public good, the devil appears to be in the policy detail, with many uncertainties about how the reformed institutional structures will work in practice, or how competition for access to this scarce resource by different user groups will be played out.

These issues are illuminated by the account by Brown and Woodhouse (Chapter 11), based on research into the implementation of key provisions in the National Water Act of 1998, to realise the efficient management of water resources while also redressing past inequities in accessibility to water. Set in the Inkomati Water Management Area (one of 19 such areas in South Africa) their research focuses on the introduction of a catchment management agency system intended to integrate different demands for water use, and the related groups of water users. A major lesson is that in seeking to correct historical disadvantages in water use and access, decentralising and participatory strategies may well be less appropriate than firm and centralised political direction, and mediation between contesting groups. At the same time, central agencies seem to have limited capacity to intervene effectively at local and regional levels. Unsurprisingly, then, the protection and strengthening of weak stakeholders (such as black farmers, poor domestic users) intended by the national reforms has not yet been achieved. Brown and Woodhouse urge attention to improved participatory mechanisms based on appropriate alliances of 'weak' stakeholders, combined with pragmatic attention to the needs of commercial users through flexible incentive systems, so offering a 'third way' that avoids the more stark choices between 'commodification' or 'decommodification' models of water provision.

The problems that attend privatisation of water provision in the absence of strong regulatory safeguards are classically illustrated in Cuaresma's study of the operation of two private water concessions in Metro Manila, the Philippines (Chapter 12). Conceived as a response to service failures by government-owned water corporations, the concessionaire agreements establish no obligation on concessionaires to provide water services to the approximately 1.3 million poor Manila residents without access to piped water: blighted and poor communities are last in priority for water connection, but first to experience reduced water supply or reduced water pressure in times of water scarcity. Meanwhile prices have risen by 500 per cent since 1997, without any corresponding commitments on service targets to poor areas. Cuaresma identifies a range of regulatory deficits and makes sensible recommendations to repair these. But the inbuilt flaws in the concession agreements, and the political influence of the powerful local elites who dominate the concession consortia, suggest that the prospect for such reforms is realistically bleak. A general lesson seems to be that privatisation into a weak regulatory framework may attract private investment, but will not improve provision of water to the poor.

A leading issue is not just the supply of water, and its price, but also how safe drinking water is. Again, it is usually poor communities who are left with unsafe water, at tremendous cost in terms of health. Mackintosh and Uys, in Chapter 13, set out the public policy response to this issue in South Africa, where in the 1990s up to 18 million people were without adequate water supply and some 25 per cent of deaths in the one to five age group could be attributed to poor water and sanitation. The policy response was to put in place a 'water services ladder' that populations could climb progressively. This has brought substantial improvements in supply, with ten million people brought onto the first rung of the ladder in terms of a basic level of supply. But drinking water quality remains a concern, particularly in rural areas. Despite appropriate legislative rules, compliance by water services authorities (mainly local municipalities) is often low, with poor understanding of the legislation, of regulatory requirements, and an absence of appropriate financial and managerial resources and skills to service these requirements. Mackintosh and Uys demonstrate through rural case studies that major contamination problems can rapidly be identified and corrected through adherence to the existing national quality management programme, which aims to increase compliance with national standards; they also show the benefits of cooperative governance initiatives between provincial and local levels in the context of this regulatory setting, something germane to the situation analysed in Brown and Woodhouse (Chapter 11).

In the final chapter (14) Eldridge and Goulden address the problem of inadequate capacities in regulatory agencies. Starting from the assumption that good regulation depends on the effective and efficient management of people and processes within regulatory agencies, they construct a diagnostic model that can be used by agencies to identify their own capacity needs and may be used then to establish means to improve regulatory performance. Testing and modifying this model on the basis of research in ten telecommunications regulatory agencies in Southern Africa, they offer it as a helpful tool for regulatory agencies generally. They are careful (and surely right) to present this as a design based on 'good practice', with due attention to be paid, in any agency seeking effective reforms, not merely to the technical content of whatever is being regulated, but to systemic issues of administrative and political context, internal and more general organisational cultures, and to the appropriateness (or otherwise) of inserting into these significant governance contexts practices imported from external sources or based on external experiences. This considered and intelligent design of regulation in local contexts is the prize to be gained from a proper attention to, and understanding of, the broad principles of regulatory governance.

REFERENCES

Ayres, I. and J. Braithwaite (1992), *Responsive Regulation: Transcending the Regulation Debate*, Oxford: Oxford University Press.

Black, J. (2002), *Critical Reflections on Regulation* (Discussion Paper No. 4), London: Centre for Analysis of Risk and Regulation, London School of Economics and Political Science.

Coronel, S. (1998), *Pork and Other Perks: Corruption and Governance in the Philippines*, Manila: Philippine Centre for Investigative Journalism.

Majone, G. (1996), *Regulating Europe*, London: Routledge.

Majone, G. (1997), 'From the positive to the regulatory state: Causes and consequences of the changes in modes of governance', *Journal of Public Policy*, **17**(2), 139–67.

Majone, G. (1999), 'The regulatory state and its legitimacy problems', *West European Politics*, **22**(1), 1–24.

Moran, M. (2001), 'Not steering but drowning: Policy catastrophe and the regulatory state', *The Political Quarterly*, **72**(4), 414–27.

Moran, M. (2002), 'Understanding the regulatory state', *British Journal of Political Science*, **32**, 391–413.

Ogus, A. (2002), 'Regulatory institutions and structures', *Annals of Public and Cooperative Economics*, **73**(4), 627–48.
Ogus, A. (2004), 'The importance of legal infrastructure for regulation (and deregulation) in developing countries', Working Paper No. 66, CRC, University of Manchester, Manchester.
Wilks, S. (1996), 'Regulatory compliance and capitalist diversity in Europe', *Journal of European Public Policy*, **3**, 536–59.

2. States and modes of regulation in the global political economy

Nicola Phillips

Across the fields of political economy and public policy, the 'regulatory state' model has become central to the debates about contemporary states and the various processes of transformation that they are assumed to be undergoing. For comparative political economists, long preoccupied with the diverse forms that capitalism takes in particular national settings, the perceived secular shift of states' functions towards regulation cuts across all three of the models of capitalism that dominate this debate – the Anglo-American (neoliberal), continental European (welfare) and Asian (developmental) varieties of capitalism are depicted now as underpinned by institutional forms and policy orientations associated with regulatory states. In international political economy (IPE), the transformations occasioned by the demands of globalisation are likewise framed within a generalised drift towards primarily regulatory functions, as opposed to the planning or interventionist functions associated with developmental and welfare states, and indeed the 'minimalist' characteristics generally ascribed to neoliberal states. Likewise, the field of public policy has become tightly associated with the study of regulation and regulatory practices across a wide range of national and sectoral settings. And an increasing array of students of governance, global political economy, global business and international institutions have pushed forward a research agenda that loosens the nationalist and statist inclinations of much of the regulation debate and centres instead on matters of 'global' regulation – that is to say, with regulation as a new and overarching mode and mechanism of global governance. The regulatory state model, it would seem, has gained a currency in recent years that has permeated state debates across the various parts of the social sciences. As Michael Moran (2002, p. 10) put it, the regulatory state has become, at the very least, 'a sort of intellectual brazier around which we can all gather, to warm our hands and speak to each other, in a world of increasingly fragmented academic professionalism'.

To continue Moran's metaphor, this chapter considers how far the heat of this intellectual brazier extends and exactly how much space there is around it for us all to cluster and converse with each other. The answer proposed here is that it currently throws out sufficient heat to warm the hands of only those that are very closest to it, and there is little room in that small circle for people at the back or any latecomers to squeeze in and share in its benefits. To put this in rather plainer language: the central argument is that the regulatory state model is, in fact, of limited direct relevance or utility in studying the nature and functions of contemporary states across much of the world. The first dimension of this argument is, inevitably, empirical. As in the case of the triad of models that underpin the varieties of capitalism debate, the regulatory state framework was developed as a research agenda both for and about the advanced industrialised world, originating first in the study of regulation as the foundation of US capitalism and then being extended to the study of the UK and continental Europe. Inasmuch as it has been increasingly stretched to encompass the study of states in the developing world, the agenda has largely been one of identifying the extent to which such states can be 'slotted into' the model. Difference, where observed, is thus presented as 'deviation'. In other words, the debate about regulatory states in the developing world has, for the most part, failed to reflect on the highly context-specific characteristics of both the model and the underlying assumptions about political systems, institutions and modes of economic organisation on which it is premised. It has reflected even less on the analytical, empirical and ideological implications that this specificity carries. As a result, the regulatory state model has generally yielded little purchase on the processes of state transformation and the nature of contemporary states in the huge variety of institutional and national settings outside the 'core' of the advanced industrialised economies.

Yet there is also rather more at stake in this argument. The regulatory state model – like the various models of capitalism – can be (and is increasingly being) challenged for the extent to which it relies on an analytical method associated with the identification of 'ideal types'. That is, the 'models' of states and forms of capitalist organisation are lined up next to one another as theoretical and empirical 'types' and national cases are then assigned to whichever of these types they are deemed most closely to approximate. The problems with squeezing a wide variety of different systems together under a single label, associated particularly with analyses that posit only two ideal types (such as Albert, 1993; Hall and Soskice, 2001), have been noted frequently, with particular attention to the analytical deficiencies of a single category of 'coordinated' market economies. The analytical value of such a category for understanding the differences between the German, Swedish and Japanese models seems to be minimal, as indeed it also is, as Peter Katzenstein (2003, p. 26) has observed persuasively, for advancing any considered and illuminating analysis of the regulatory and constitutive aspects of institutions (see also Phillips, 2004, pp. 16–22; Crouch, 2005). Furthermore, empirical cases other than those for which the models were initially elaborated – that is, those clustered in the developing world – are customarily considered in the light of which of the available models they most resemble, and, as before, it is identifying the sources of what is seen as 'deviation' that becomes the central intellectual exercise.

This analytical approach is even more problematic in its obscuring of the ways in which elements of various 'models' can and do co-exist in particular national political economies. In our haste to set up contrasting models that we can use to distinguish between, for example, liberal market economies and coordinated market economies, or between regulatory and developmental states, and to identify the sources of relative levels of competitiveness on this basis, we end up with a form of theoretical and analytical parsimony that neglects a great deal of the complexity that exists *within* national states and political economies. The result is a wide-ranging theoretical and empirical deficiency in the study of both forms of state and models of capitalism. In this light, Colin Crouch (2005, p. 440) has helpfully reformulated our task as studying empirical cases 'not to determine to which (singular) of a number of theoretical types they should each be allocated, but to determine which (plural) of these forms are to be found within them, in roughly what proportions, and with what change over time'.

In this agenda we find a particularly useful resource for overcoming two of the most salient issues in considering the regulatory state model outside the particular context of the advanced industrialised world. The first is the degree of functionalism that pervades the regulatory state debate and, more broadly, state debates across the various fields of the social sciences in which they are conducted. The second is the degree to which transporting the regulatory state model to states in the developing world hampers our analysis and understanding of the various forms of *regulation* that exist and are evolving in these states. That is to say, the linkages between the study of regulation and the study of the regulatory state have become excessively tight, and consequently both theoretically and analytically disabling. Across much of the developing world, I suggest, we encounter situations of what we might call 'regulation without a regulatory state', which is only very tenuously captured in analyses that are excessively anxious to squeeze the study of developing states into the analytical straitjacket of the regulatory state model. By loosening a little the intellectual compact between these two – somewhat different – sets of questions, we can go much further towards not only understanding the varieties of regulatory practices that occur within particular political economies, but also, moreover, accommodating the key premise that these political economies, and the states with which they are associated, may feature complex combinations of institutional and policy orientations. So, rather than trying, for the most part too hard, to identify whether states in Asia have now shifted decisively from the developmental state model to the regulatory state model and concentrating on which name badge (singular) should now be pinned on them, or whether the Chilean state should be described as regulatory, developmental or neoliberal, we can thus begin to understand the combinations of these elements that exist within states, the manner of their interaction and the nature of the political economies that emerge therefrom.

These are the arguments that this chapter develops. The first and second sections below address the emergence of the regulatory state model, and place particular emphasis on the forms of analytical functionalism that have come to pervade the resulting framework. The third section develops more fully the arguments about the comparative applicability of the regulatory state model, seeking to demonstrate the limitations of its relevance in the study of states outside the core of the advanced industrialised world. The conclusions pull the strands of the discussion together.

GLOBALISATION, DEVELOPMENT AND THE RISE OF THE REGULATORY STATE MODEL

As is well known, for many years the energetic debates about globalisation in the social sciences have centred around the validity or otherwise of the hypothesis of 'convergence'. The enormous body of comparative research that has sought to challenge the contention that economies, states and societies now tend towards common forms, orientations and ideas has unquestionably injected into the debate a real recognition of the need for careful empirical investigation and more reflective, less homogenising theorisations of globalisation processes. Yet this impressive literature does not usually contradict the idea that there might be certain common trends in the processes by which states are adapting to the demands of development and competitiveness under these conditions. If there *are* any accepted generalisations to be made about the contemporary evolution of states, in this sense, they are neatly captured in Peter Evans' (1997, p. 85) idea that the new 'stateness' is of a 'leaner, meaner kind'.

This, for Evans, is pursued primarily as a means of addressing the 'capacity gap' generated by states' post-war assumption of unsustainable welfare commitments under the post-war regimes. The 'social compacts' between states and societies in which liberalism was embedded and made politically manageable – the core of John Ruggie's (1982) seminal concept of 'embedded liberalism' – were specific to the European context, this being the only part of the world in which meaningful welfare states emerged. But the notion of a capacity gap stemming therefrom is equally valid in, for example, the Latin American context of inward-looking industrialisation, in which states assumed very sizeable stakes in their countries' productive structures, the running of the national economy, and the corporatist management of sociopolitical relations, bequeathing highly politicised state structures and hugely bloated and inefficient public sectors. Equally, the argument goes, Asian developmental states have been subject to sustained pressures as a result of globalisation and the influence of market and institutional actors associated with the current policy orthodoxy. Whichever the specific context, the movement towards a 'leaner, meaner' form of state is thus a response to the demands of competitiveness in the global economy *and* a response to the 'overload' on states seen to derive from Keynesian experiments in Europe and inward-looking or developmentalist projects in Latin America or East Asia.

What is interesting, however, is that over the course of the 1990s there was a sustained shift in understandings, particularly in the international financial institutions (IFIs), of what this 'leaner, meaner' stateness involves and how it might be achieved. In the early 1990s, the neoliberal discourse was dominated by the notion of 'minimalism' as the byword for an effective, efficient and desirable state. This was driven and characterised by a range of ideological shifts from the 1970s onwards that yielded qualitatively different visions of the appropriate and desirable relationship between state and market from that which had prevailed over much of the post-war period. 'Effective' states were conceived in this ideological frame of reference as 'nightwatchmen' states, with little or no direct economic or social role, and the 'Washington consensus' was articulated as the blueprint for the achievement of this arrangement. As the 1990s unfolded, however, this neoliberal orthodoxy was jettisoned even by its initial champions as perceptions mounted of the failures of so-called 'first generation' reforms and, moreover, of minimalist forms of state in redressing many of the governance problems associated with developing economies (World Bank, 1989, 1992, 1997). Corruption continued to be pervasive; inefficiency and ineffectiveness continued to be characteristic of even the more rationalised bureaucratic structures; transparency and accountability remained in very short supply. Thus, as George Philip (1999a, p. 76) observed of Latin America, 'the problem is that a nightwatchman state can also be a biased state'. Recognition of these failures went together with the IFIs' growing acknowledgement, rather through gritted teeth, of the ways in which the 'East Asian Miracle' contradicted many of the dominant equations of economic growth with a minimal state (World Bank, 1993).

Around the mid-1990s, consequently, the IFIs' agenda of state reform was pushed around an important corner. The core concept to arise from this shift in thinking was that of 'good governance'. It embodied the new belief in significant parts of the international financial community that economic growth was dependent not solely on an observance of the 'rationalities' of markets but also on the *quality* of governance thus defined – put another way, a recognition that a 'quantitative reduction [of state apparatuses] might end up in qualitative deterioration' (Welsch and Carrasquero, 2000, p. 34). Perception of *actual* qualitative deterioration – that quantitative reduction had, in fact, resulted in this deterioration – was of course the key point of departure in this rethinking of the reform agenda. Its essence was consequently an acknowledgement of the centrality of national states and their importance in pushing forward the sorts of reforms deemed conducive to the improved governance of economies and societies. This inclusion of institutions and governance in the World Bank's reform agenda found clear expression in successive titles of its annual *World Development Report* – from *The State in a Changing World* in 1997 to *Building Institutions for Markets* in 2002.

In short, the emphasis came to fall on the construction of an 'effective' state rather than on a minimal one, with effectiveness now understood as involving, on the one hand, enhanced technical and institutional effectiveness, with a special place afforded here for the issue of judicial independence and the rule of law, and, on the other, a 'corresponding liberal public sphere' characterised by an increasingly empowered civil society (Williams and Youngs, 1994, pp. 93–4). Administrative, legal and institutional structures and practices thus had come to be seen as integral parts of the economic reform process, and state reform became oriented to the enhancement of states' abilities to discharge a range of governance-related functions, understood mostly as the provision of key public goods. The revamped reform agenda, and the measures included under its rubric, have been captured under the general heading of 'second generation' reforms. The distinction between the first and second generations lies not only in their substance but also, moreover, in evolving ideas about the appropriate role and structure of states and their appropriate relationship with markets. Put simply, the first generation of structural reforms in Latin America and elsewhere was about the reduction in size of national states and public sectors, the retraction of their involvement in economic activity, and the 'rationalisation' of their administrative and bureaucratic functions – entirely in tune with the 'anti-statist' logic of the neoliberal orthodoxy.

Second generation reforms were premised on a very different set of objectives captured in notions of 'rebuilding' national states, constructing functioning and viable institutions, and strengthening states' institutional and policy-related capacities.

The important point about this transition is that the Bank's formulation of its governance agenda was predicated on a continuing overriding concern with markets: that is, institutions are of interest purely for their functions in creating the economic conditions in which markets can flourish and investments prosper, and for their potential utility in deflecting political impediments to effective liberalisation and deregulation. The substance of the second generation reform agenda reflects this continuing economism in the Bank's approach to key development questions, and thus it continues to formulate its prescriptions primarily in technical terms that reflect a set of 'rational' criteria for the achievement of 'effective' and 'efficient' states. On this understanding, the objectives of so-called 'second generation' reform fall broadly into three categories (Pastor and Wise, 1999): (a) 'market-completing measures' that aim to carry forward and/or complete the liberalisation processes initiated by first generation reforms; (b) 'equity-oriented programmes' relating to redressing pervasive distributional problems; and (c) good governance-related 'institution-building initiatives' for the purposes of enhancing state and institutional capacities and drawing civil society into policy-making processes.

In more general terms, this new development agenda has come to adopt and deploy the regulatory state model as both a useful descriptor of the functions and roles of contemporary states, and an ideological statement about what those functions and roles should be. As noted earlier, the study of regulation and the regulatory state had by this time a distinguished pedigree in the US and European public policy literatures, and indeed regulation had long been central to Anglo-American capitalism. The overarching concept of regulation is usually accepted as attracting three principal meanings (Baldwin et al., 1998; also see Moran, 2002; Jordana and Levi-Faur, 2004). The first, and narrowest, refers to regulation as a very specific set of 'targeted rules', usually associated with a corresponding administrative agency. The second conceives of regulation as a wider form of governance that refers to the gamut of ways in which states intervene in and steer national economies. The third deems regulation to constitute an overarching and all-inclusive structure of governance that encompasses 'all mechanisms of social control' and in which states are only a part of the overall landscape of actors and structures that exercise this control. The regulatory state model per se clearly finds most expression in the first and second of these approaches, and is taken most frequently to embody a particular type of policy-making environment oriented to entrenching mechanisms of control and management of the national economy. In this sense, the emergence of the regulatory state refers to a process by which economic management becomes 'proceduralised': it is characterised by an increasingly rule-based, technocratic and juridical approach to economic governance, in which there is a greater emphasis on institutional self-regulation (the archetypal example being central bank independence).

In striking similarity to the language of the second generation reform agenda, the functions of such a state are largely seen to be two-fold: first, to underpin markets and second, to address market failures through the provision of various rights and goods (McGowan and Wallace, 1996, p. 562). As such, the notion of the regulatory state has been developed in order to understand a situation characterised not by complete deregulation but also by key areas of re-regulation, particularly of financial markets (Gamble, 2000, p. 114; Burnham, 1999, p. 46). A disengagement of states from direct administrative responsibility for certain economic functions is thus accompanied by an increase in their regulatory functions. The classic case in this respect is the United States, in which neoliberal forms of economic organisation are accompanied by an extensive and penetrating web of regulatory provision. The regulatory state is thus fundamentally an enabling – rather than a planning or overtly interventionist – one, but should not be mistaken for a minimal one. Indeed, it is entirely possible that a regulatory state will have interventionist characteristics, but the point is that these are likely to be oriented towards underpinning rather than 'replacing' markets (McGowan and Wallace, 1996, p. 563).

Burnham's concept of the 'depoliticisation of economic management' shares a good deal of common ground with the regulatory state model, but goes quite a way further towards considering the roots and the implications of such a trend, not just the basic attributes of this form of state. He suggests, in essence, that depoliticised economic management refers to a set of strategies that aim to 'place at one remove the political character of decision-making' (Burnham, 1999, p. 47). This is not to be confused with either the elimination of political influence over economic activity (along the lines envisaged in the crudest early 1990s neoliberal rhetoric), or the 'wholesale evacuation of politics from policy making' (Burnham, 1999, p. 44). Rather the act of depoliticisation itself is, as Burnham emphasises, highly political. State managers 'retain arms-length control over crucial economic processes whilst benefiting from the distancing effect of depoliticisation', the overall upshot being an increase in government control through its consequent protection from the effects of politics on its decision-making processes (p. 47). Thus Burnham envisages a model of depoliticised, or 'rules-based', management that has three key pillars which are worth citing directly as a framework for our discussion in the following pages:

1. The 'reordering or reassignment of tasks' from the party in office (operational independence; 'managerial state').
2. Increased accountability, transparency and external validation of policy (fiscal codes, International Monetary Fund Code of Good Practice).
3. Acceptance of binding 'rules' limiting government room for manoeuvre (European Exchange Rate Mechanism, World Trade Organization (WTO) Dispute Settlement Mechanism).

The resulting form of governance, in this sense, is consistent with the mode of regulation envisaged in the regulatory state model – that is, one that is fundamentally oriented to facilitating market operations and limiting states to regulatory activities designed to correct market failures and enhance economic performance. This form of state and mode of economic management are thus sharply differentiated from the post-war welfare states of continental Europe, post-war corporatism in Europe and Latin America, developmental states in Asia, and variations on the developmental theme elsewhere in the world (such as Brazil).

THE PITFALLS OF FUNCTIONALISM

As indicated earlier, there are two key issues that this chapter is concerned to raise about the regulatory state debate. The first is largely of a theoretical and conceptual nature – namely, the problem of the functionalist biases that permeate the manner in which the debate is conducted and the foundations of the regulatory state model (Phillips, 2005). This issue arises in the context of the debates concerning the impact of globalisation on national states, which are framed predominantly as debates about the evolution of state capacity. As is well known, these questions focus on the extent to which the policy-making autonomy of states is or is not constrained by globalised market forces and the demands of competitiveness these are assumed to imply. Yet these questions are approached in a way that privileges functional understandings of the forms of state that are forged by globalisation. In this context, state capacity is identified and judged according to outcomes: if a state achieves economic competitiveness, efficiency and robust economic performance levels, or indeed if its policy outputs deviate substantially from what are presumed to be the requirements of the global financial orthodoxy, it is considered to be possessed of high levels of capacity and autonomy. In matters relating to forms of state, both neoliberal and critical perspectives conceive of the state as undergoing a process of adaptation to the challenges of achieving global economic competitiveness; the resulting forms of state are understood in a functional sense as the consequence of that adaptation. For neoliberals, this is conceived as the achievement of economic efficiency and competitiveness; for critical international political economists, it is represented by consistency with the demands of 'market civilisation' and 'disciplinary neoliberalism' (Gill, 1995). Either way, states are defined as functional, or dysfunctional, according to the economic outcomes of their adaptation to the demands of the new global economy. Not only is functionality thereby 'selected for' (Hay, 2004), but states are also *theorised* primarily on the basis of their functionality, or lack of it.

Functional*ism* – that is, the (inherently circular) use of functional outcomes as *explanations* of the phenomena in question – is rather more implicit in these perspectives, but nevertheless runs through them as a notable undercurrent. In a sense, it arises somewhat 'by default' as a result of the generalised failure to consider or advance clear understandings of the processes by which outcomes are produced. Across the globalisation–state debate, the competitive outcomes of state adaptation to the demands of globalisation are the focus of analysis, and strikingly little has been offered in the way of explanations of how those outcomes are generated or achieved. Likewise, attempts to analyse the form of state (usually singular) that emerges from these processes concentrate virtually exclusively on identifying what that state form looks like, rather than the causes of it and the concrete processes by which it is forged. Much of the process of adaptation, particularly in neoliberal analysis, is presented apparently as automatic, as the state responds in a mechanistic and 'rational' manner to a set of external imperatives. There are, of course, very robust exceptions to this general functionalist tendency, and indeed the need to escape it has frequently been intoned. Layna Mosley (2003, p. 15), for example, is concerned directly with identifying the 'causal mechanisms underpinning government policy selection', and pays particular attention to the ways in which financial market participants evaluate government policies and make investment decisions on this basis. Colin Hay and Ben Rosamond (2002) have explored the ways in which *ideas* about globalisation lead to a 'discursive construction of economic imperatives' by policy-makers. Critical IPE theorists have also attempted more than many others to avoid this pitfall and to explain the political and social processes by which state forms evolve, notably in the identification of the 'conveyor belts' by which the dictates of disciplinary neoliberalism are transmitted to national states. Yet we are still aware of an underlying argument in these critical IPE currents that Evans's 'leaner, meaner' form of state emerges as a result of its functionality for global capitalism and the capitalist interests that represent it, and therefore is explained by and theorised on the basis of this functionality (Phillips, 2005).

These general arguments about the treatment of states are nowhere more evident than in the regulatory state debate and the model on which it is based. The emergence of regulatory states, as we have seen, is considered widely – one would say, by almost all of those clustered around Moran's intellectual brazier – to be at least in part associated with the particular demands of competitiveness implied by contemporary globalisation and the neoliberal world order. The shift from continental European welfarism to other forms of governance based primarily on regulation, the process of change deemed to have been unleashed in Asian developmental states, and the forms of regulation emerging in parts of Latin America are conceived widely as functional responses to the prevailing realities of the global economy. The debate swirling around the developmental state model affords perhaps the clearest illustration. The argument that the Asian model is in trouble has been around for a long time, as neoliberal observers, in particular, have sought to identify the differences in performance between the Anglo-American economies and the Japanese economy as lying primarily in the relatively higher levels of state intervention and the form of state that this intervention requires. Yet similar arguments have found much greater force, from both the left and the right, in the aftermath of the Asian financial crises. For example, Iain Pirie's (2005) recent analysis of the new Korean state has seen the 'new mode of regulation' that is consolidating there as 'driven by the changing dictates of international competitiveness', noting that in these circumstances 'it is difficult to maintain the claim that *dirigiste* economic strategies continue to offer the same prospect of success within the contemporary global economy' (Pirie, 2005, pp. 38–9). Moreover, the failure – or 'incapacity' – of certain states to respond in this manner and develop similar sorts of regulatory orientation is presented as an explanation for their problematic record of economic and developmental performance. He thus goes on to argue that 'the Japanese state simply failed over the course of the 1980s and 1990s to adapt fully to global structural change: a failure which led to prolonged economic stagnation' (Pirie, 2005, p. 39).

The veracity or otherwise of this claim is not entirely the point for our purposes here and would take up much more space than is available. The important point concerns the functionalist bias that it reveals in the study of contemporary regulation and, moreover, the manner in which the *theoretical* construct of the regulatory state – which we have seen to have gained dominant currency across the range of state debates – 'selects for' functionality. It is built on, and for, the theoretical understanding and empirical analysis of a relatively small handful of cases that are deemed to be functional; the resulting theoretical debates and empirical models clearly reflect this analytical selection for functionality, and are consequently of limited general utility in studying the diverse forms of state, and indeed of regulation, that currently exist and evolve in the global political economy. The issue of functional*ism* is equally important. The regulatory state debate is conducted almost entirely as the study of the regulatory outcomes and outputs of states, and, as such, is for the most part a debate about policy and forms of state intervention that has little to say about the institutional forms and political underpinnings of regulatory states. Using the case of the ongoing debate about Asian developmental states once again, the concern has been to observe the regulatory activities of states and the results of institutional reforms to support these, and to determine at what point the label 'regulatory state' can then legitimately be ascribed to these cases. Traces of the 'old' model can then be depicted as residual, dysfunctional and likely to be eradicated as the new mode of regulation becomes more fully consolidated.

MODES OF REGULATORY GOVERNANCE

The second key issue for our discussion of the regulatory state model is the spirit of generalised applicability in which it is customarily deployed. Outside the Anglo-American and European contexts, the framework has been applied explicitly to a number of Asian states (Jayasuriya, 2001, 2002, 2005; Pirie, 2005) and to others such as the Chilean case (Muñoz, 1996, 2000) and beyond. Recalling the framework we set out earlier, these and other cases, to a greater or lesser extent, yield evidence of the processes and strategies associated with the movement towards rules-based, proceduralised and juridical forms of economic governance – including, notably, Central Bank independence, anti-monopoly and competition legislation, financial regulation and banking supervision, and so on. Yet an argument of convergence on a model of a regulatory state per se is extremely hard to sustain, even when we take appropriate care to identify the various distinctive forms that such a model might take (Lodge, 2002). Of course, any model will stumble across exceptions to its criteria; an argument that the regulatory state model does not apply in all cases and contexts is a rather facile and simplistic one, not to mention distinctly uninspiring. But a consideration of why it should be applicable only in a narrow set of cases, despite the frequently generalising way that its tenets are presented in the literature, opens up a set of much more interesting questions that invite more careful consideration of key elements of the debate on the evolution of contemporary states in the context of globalisation.

Stated baldly, the argument here is that regulatory states can only emerge in contexts characterised by an existing level of state capacity and a type of existing institutional configuration amenable to the development of regulatory strategies. The study of regulation therefore needs to pay significantly more attention to the interface between regulatory strategies considered 'desirable' for achieving the aims outlined above and the political and institutional environments in which they are intended to take root. At the very least, an independent and effective judicial system is a clear prerequisite, and the development of regulatory capacity involves a process of institutional reorganisation that includes extensive institutional innovation. In systems not possessed of such a judicial system, and not equipped (politically or technically) to engage in appropriate processes of state reform, an emphasis on regulation as a key function of states in the current structural context is very often fruitless. At the same time, a focus on the presence or absence of the characteristics of regulatory states, and an anxiety to use the regulatory state model as our theoretical lens, lead us to overlook the ways in which the majority of states in regions such as Asia, Latin America, the Middle East, the Caribbean or parts of Africa are of a much more hybrid nature than their counterparts in the advanced industrialised world. The majority of these systems are characterised by precisely the combinations that Crouch drew our attention to, and it is to the nature and interactions of the various elements in these combinations that we most fruitfully direct our attention.

Let us try to put some flesh on these arguments by turning to the Latin American context. Perhaps the best way into this discussion is through an observation of experiences with the 'good governance'-related state reform agenda, itself oriented primarily to creating the relevant conditions for effective regulatory governance. In a nutshell, there has been a manifest and problematic breach between good governance-related visions of a desirable state and the historically entrenched characteristics of Latin American states, and consequently the externally propelled state reform agenda has travelled into this regional setting with distinct difficulty. In one sense, this is because the broad institutional requirements for the successful implementation of governance reforms as formulated by the IFIs are simply not in existence in the vast majority of Latin American states. This is not necessarily a function of the 'under'-development of state institutions, although in some cases this is manifestly a problem. The real issue lies in a central inconsistency in the good governance agenda: that its success depends on a level of institutional and political capacity that frequently is only available to precisely the sorts of state that the agenda aims to dismantle or reconfigure. Most Latin American states have shown themselves to lack the necessary levels of institutional and political capacity for successful judicial reform, for example, or labour reform, in contrast with the patterns of capacity deriving in Asia from forms of 'embedded autonomy'

(Evans, 1995). At the same time, 'state bias' (Philip, 2003) persists as their dominant and pervasive trait. Historically this bias has been essentially a 'pro-elite' one, which both reflects and stems from the other dominant characteristics of states in the region – clientelism as the organising principle of the institutional and political system, corruption, patronage politics, patrimonialism, personalism and presidentialism.

Apart from their consequences for fiscal resources and overall macroeconomic stability, these traits – which, it should be said, are consciously generalised for the moment – have consistently obstructed the construction of democratically accountable, technocratic states that conform to the criteria of effectiveness and efficiency contained in the World Bank's good governance agenda, and indeed to the types of regulatory state that are assumed to be of generalised applicability. They translate into the frequent absence of a technocratic reforming elite possessed of both the political capacity and the political will necessary to advance an agenda of this sort. The pro-elite bias, in other words, removes many of the incentives that would need to be present in order for there to take place a radical reorientation of the prevalent political culture – from a clientelistic, personalist and biased one to a technocratic, meritocratic and intrinsically accountable one. This feeds into the second key inconsistency in the good governance agenda: the sorts of state that have enjoyed higher degrees of reformist capacity in Latin America have usually been those possessed of a range of other attributes considered 'undesirable' in dominant understandings of what 'good' governance looks like, such as the very significant centralisation of power in the executive branch, corruption, clientelism, quasi-authoritarian styles of governance and the relegation of state institutions. In such systems the legislature is commonly marginalised, judicial independence is rare (as is Central Bank independence), and the development of transparent, accountable bureaucracies is significantly impeded. Put another way, any 'effectiveness' – understood as the capacity for the consistent implementation of reform initiatives – has traditionally derived precisely from conditions of institutional weakness. The historically and theoretically important result has been something of a trade-off in Latin America between a state capable of reform and regulation, on the one hand, and a democratically accountable one, on the other (Philip, 1999b, 2003). While state effectiveness and accountability might be conjoined in theory, and indeed are so in both the good governance agenda and often in elaborations of the regulatory state model, they are by no means unequivocally linked in the Latin American setting.

In such a context, regulation has been a distinctly absent feature of Latin American states and their adaptation to the demands of globalisation. The regulatory state model has something to offer in light of its closeness of fit with neoliberalism: the emergence of new regulatory regimes has been encouraged by the policies of expenditure reduction allied to neoliberal preferences for market solutions (Wilks, 1996, p. 541), and expenditure reduction has been vigorously pursued in the vast majority of neoliberal economies in the region. It is also somewhat helpful in light of the contention that the policy constraints of globalisation make regulation a more attractive policy framework than other forms of intervention (McGowan and Wallace, 1996, p. 564), and rhetoric in Latin America has indeed emphasised regulatory governance as a key aspiration. The problem, though, is that the implementation of neoliberal strategies in Latin American countries has both preceded and outstripped the development of regulatory regimes and capacities, reflecting pervasive institutional weakness. Privatisation generally took place without previous preparation of the state to assume the role of regulator of competition, and consequently the politics of post-privatisation constitute less an example of a decisive shift to regulatory governance (as in the European and UK cases) than an example of the 'chronic inability of Latin American states to fulfil a regulatory function' (Fleury, 1999, p. 76). This applies virtually across the board, with the possible exception of Chile. In Argentina, for example, mechanisms for the regulation of competition among privatised enterprises emerged only after the state had divested itself, in a notably rushed and haphazard manner, of its assets. Those regulatory bodies that did come into being only after privatisation had taken place were consequently burdened from their inception with myriad legal problems and litigation (Manzetti, 2002, p. 8). There are a couple of instances of fairly effective and transparent regulatory bodies in Argentina – notably the gas and electricity commissions – but the overall pattern has been one in which regulatory bodies are financed from sources laden with political connections, subject to intense lobbying by large firms, and with little autonomy from the executive branch, the latter intervening and trespassing frequently on the exclusive authority of regulatory agencies (Pastor and Wise, 1998, p. 16; Manzetti, 2002, pp. 8–9).

There have been some cases of more successful or 'pre-emptive' regulation, such as in the Uruguayan case, but here these have been largely as a substitute for privatisation due to widespread political opposition to eliminating public ownership. Governments in the 1990s sought instead to emphasise greater competition in the public sector, the budget law of 2001, for instance, providing for the demonopolisation of telecommunications and insurance, except for workers' compensation insurance and basic telephony, and establishing regulatory bodies in the telecommunications and electricity sectors (US Department of State, 2002). Yet overall there was little serious political impetus from the government to significant reform of the state and public sector. And in general, serious regulation through competition policy has been either non-existent (as in the smallest, most bureaucratically underdeveloped states such as Paraguay and Ecuador) or largely ineffective (as in Argentina).

With the exception of Chile, Central Banks have not been accorded significant independence. The institutional realignments and 'operational independence' associated with the depoliticisation of policy management thus find minimal expression. But the elements connected with external mechanisms of policy validation and the acceptance of binding rules for limiting government room for manoeuvre have been much more in evidence. Such mechanisms most obviously include agreements with multilateral and financial institutions. While these are important for establishing credibility as well as necessary financing, though, it should be noted that these mechanisms of external validation remain perceived more as signs of weakness than as signs of economic health or as manifestations of an overall 'depoliticisation' of economic governance. Mechanisms of external validation that have found rather firmer ground relate to the domestic implantation of a rules-based policy-making environment. Fiscal codes, for example, have been put in place in Mexico, Chile, Argentina, Brazil and elsewhere, but are certainly not universal in Latin America. Apart from being politically charged, of course, the implementation of such laws of fiscal responsibility is complicated by the aforementioned levels of institutional weaknesses: at the very least, the successful installation of such policies requires a strengthening of audit tribunals (and their increased independence), as well as further reforms in the areas of pensions and taxation (*The Economist*, 6 May 2000). All of these have been especially problematic throughout the region, except – yet again, but even so only up to a point – in Chile where pensions reform has been held up as a neoliberal beacon of best practice.

The fact that the Chilean case is exceptional in so many ways relates primarily to the exceptional (in a comparative sense) nature of its state, and this brings us back to the key argument outlined above. Despite the significant concentration of power in the executive branch, consistent with most Latin American political systems, various bureaucratic arrangements in the Chilean system have afforded it a notable degree of institutional strength, cohesion and coherence, and inter-agency cooperation, which set the Chilean state apart from the other cases in the region (see Phillips, 2004, Ch. 9). This is largely due to the strength of the General Secretariat of the Presidency which has been the principal mechanism of coordination within the executive branch and between the branches of government, largely through its Division of Inter-Ministerial Cooperation, and was granted ministerial status early in the 1990s. It also helps that there is a considerable degree of ideological consensus on the market model in the structures of the Chilean state, despite political problems in the 1990s in areas such as labour and tax reform. Despite the persistence of high levels of politicisation in the judicial system, furthermore, the judiciary is constitutionally and technically independent of both the executive and the legislature, and on matters of regulatory enforcement has been reasonably – although not fully – effective. The Chilean case has thus been characterised by a much more extensive and effective system of regulation than elsewhere in the region, maintaining, for example, a system of financial regulation and banking supervision from the time of the banking crisis in the early 1990s, a structure of capital controls from 1991 onwards, and a fairly effective regulation of competition in the private and public sectors.

Yet the Chilean state can only be described as a 'regulatory state' if the term is taken in its widest sense to refer to all aspects of state intervention. In the same ways as we have questioned the label 'coordinated' to refer to an enormous diversity of capitalist systems, the label 'regulatory' seems to lose its value and analytical purchase as its definition gets broader. Retaining a certain distinction between 'developmental' and 'regulatory' certainly offers important insights into Asian and Latin American political economies. If this is done, the Chilean case becomes an interesting combination of a state that has pursued neoliberal reform without conforming strictly to either the institutional ideal-type (as noted above) or to the policy orthodoxy (most notably in the system of capital controls), elements of regulation and some aspects of a regulatory state, and a developmentalist orientation – what Marcus Kurtz (2001) has called, in a similar manner to our formulation here, 'developmentalism without a developmental state' – that is clearly manifested in the web of export promotion strategies and associated institutions (Phillips, 2004, pp. 75–9).

The point about the centrality of the institutional and political context is equally salient in other regions. In China, for example, mechanisms of external validation and constraint have been gradually adopted – most notably in this case through WTO membership, which has created considerable pressure for more adequate regulation in services and financial sectors. Yet the prospects for the elaboration of this sort of regulation are extremely thin given the strength of provincial and local governments and their political autonomy from (and defiance of) central government.[1] The structure of local monopolies is extensive (at a very basic level making it difficult for producers to sell products in other regions of the country); provincial and local economies are utilised largely as the fiefdoms of provincial and local governments; state banks are used by the latter as key sources of what has been called 'parafiscal investment' (see Breslin, 2003). Thus pressure from the WTO for increased regulation in specific sectors of key concern runs immediately into fierce political opposition from the provinces and localities, and moreover into an absence of national and local institutional infrastructures appropriate for sustaining it. Central bank independence has not been a major issue in Chinese discussions about reform, and neither have privatisation nor the development of a judicial system capable of providing a basis for juridical forms of economic governance.

In other parts of Asia, however, the model has found a somewhat firmer footing, and Kanishka Jayasuriya's (1998, 2001) work has emphasised the movements towards Central Bank independence in such cases as Japan and Korea (also Pirie, 2005). Yet his work focuses almost entirely on central banks, and it would be a considerable stretch to claim that, even in the cases just mentioned, the other dimensions of the 'regulatory state' have been put in place. Again, mechanisms of external validation have become important in the East Asian economies – notably binding agreements with the International Monetary Fund (IMF), conformity with WTO regulations, and regional integration initiatives designed to entrench rules and procedures as the basis of economic management. Yet financial regulation and banking supervision remain lacking and most East Asian systems share with the Latin American region a prevalence of clientelism and presidentialism as the key features of their political systems, contrary to the stipulations and the aims of the regulatory state model. Moreover, strong elements of both developmentalism and developmental states remain pivotal to the particular political economy of development that prevails in these economies. A claim that the regulatory state framework should now be the terrain on which debates about Asian states and development are conducted – as Jayasuriya (2005) has elegantly contended – can be and is being challenged for the sense in which it overlooks the continued co-existence of both developmentalist and regulatory functions, and indeed is hasty in its extrapolation from a still rather limited set of institutional reforms (mainly in the financial sector) to the emergence of a genuinely regulatory state as an institutional construct (Weiss, 2005; Thurbon and Weiss, 2006).

These brief sketches of some empirical cases in the developing world indicate, then, significant problems with thinking about 'a' regulatory state model, on the one hand, but, on the other, significant problems with deploying the model as a general framework within which to analyse the contemporary evolution of states in the context of global restructuring. The final reservation concerning the applicability of this model that we need to highlight very briefly relates to the assumptions that a depoliticisation of economic management, along the lines described by Burnham, generates greater effectiveness, efficiency, accountability and transparency in policy-making systems. While a shift to regulatory governance may result in an increasing insulation of government and state agencies from the 'unpalatable consequences of politics' (Burnham, 1999, p. 44), these are not generally accompanied by a shielding of systems of regulation from other forms of political influence. That is, two situations have commonly prevailed in states outside the Anglo-American and European contexts that have moved towards some degree of regulation in economic management. The first is that the elaboration of regulatory policies has proceeded without the necessary institutional changes or institutional innovation, and thus regulatory strategies have remained in the hands of government and other non-independent agencies, as opposed to the sorts of independent, non-governmental state agencies or para-statal bodies that have been associated with regulation elsewhere. The second is that regulatory bodies have indeed been developed to oversee regulatory activity, but have remained highly vulnerable to political 'capture', especially by the executive branch, and highly politicised in their operations. Either way, it has frequently been the case that greater levels of regulation have not been accompanied by greater levels of accountability and transparency, and overall politicisation has meant that technical and technocratic efficiency levels have not been significantly increased.

CONCLUSIONS

This discussion of some of the issues associated with the study of states and regulation in the developing world has suggested that the regulatory state model is of very limited utility outside the contexts of advanced industrialised capitalism. We have seen that there are many cases in which elements of an ideal-type regulatory state appear and are emerging in developing countries, but the model and the strategic orientation it represents depend, it is suggested, on a very specific set of institutional and political conditions that are to be found in only very limited cases. What we have seen, nevertheless, is that many states across Asia and Latin America, in particular, are engaged in regulatory activity and that some of the relevant institutional reforms are taking place. What have been termed 'mechanisms of external validation' find perhaps the widest and most convincing expression, associated as they are with the range of trade agreements, agreements with international and multilateral institutions, regional integration processes, and so on. Furthermore, a sectoral study of regulation yields fertile ground for the examination of changing forms of governance in developing countries. What we have on our hands, then, is a landscape characterised more by 'regulation without a regulatory state' than by the sorts of institutional and strategic structures stipulated by the regulatory state model. The conclusion that suggests itself is that the regulatory state model can often prove more of a hindrance than a help in the study of regulation, at least in the developing world.

A loosening of the intellectual grip of the regulatory state model also allows us freer theoretical and empirical rein to capture the complexities of contemporary capitalist systems and modes of economic and social governance in the parts of the world with which we are concerned. A research agenda that derives its methodological and theoretical apparatus from a context-specific 'ideal-type' is increasingly recognised to offer little purchase on the elements of different varieties of capitalist organisation, policy orientation and institutional design that exist *within* national political economies. The study of regulatory governance, in this sense, needs to be considered alongside whichever other forms of governance co-exist with it in a given empirical case, and the central research questions concern the nature of the system that is thereby constituted, the manner in which it evolves over time, and the political and economic forces that shape the combination of elements in question. The study of regulation in the developing world both requires such a strategy and, in turn, throws up enormous resource and insight for the resulting debates.

NOTE

1. I am grateful to Shaun Breslin for this point.

REFERENCES

Albert, Michel (1993), *Capitalism against Capitalism*, London: Whurr.

Baldwin, Robert, Colin Scott and Christopher Hood (1998), 'Introduction', in Robert Baldwin, Colin Scott and Christopher Hood (eds), *A Reader on Regulation*, Oxford: Oxford University Press, pp. 1–55.

Breslin, Shaun (2003), 'Paradigm shifts and time-lags?: The politics of financial reform in the People's Republic of China', *Asian Business and Management*, **2**, 1–24.

Burnham, Peter (1999), 'The politics of economic management in the 1990s', *New Political Economy*, **4**(1), 37–54.

Crouch, Colin (2005), 'Models of capitalism', *New Political Economy*, **10**(4), 439–56.

Evans, Peter (1995), *Embedded Autonomy: States and Industrial Transformation*, Princeton; NJ: Princeton University Press.

Evans, Peter (1997), 'The eclipse of the state? Reflections on stateness in an era of globalization', *World Politics*, **50**, 62–87.

Fleury, Sonia (1999), 'Reforma del Estado en América Latina: ¿Hacia Dónde?', ('Whither state reform in Latin America?' trans.), *Nueva Sociedad*, **160**, 58–80.

Gamble, Andrew (2000), 'Economic governance', in Jon Pierre (ed.), *Debating Governance: Authority, Steering, and Democracy*, Oxford: Oxford University Press, pp. 110–37.

Gill, Stephen (1995), 'Globalisation, market civilisation, and disciplinary neoliberalism', *Millennium: Journal of International Studies*, **24**(3), 399–423.

Hall, Peter A. and David Soskice (eds) (2001), *Varieties of Capitalism: The Institutional Foundations of Comparative Advantage*, Oxford: Oxford University Press.

Hay, Colin (2004), 'Re-stating politics, re-politicising the state: Neoliberalism, economic imperatives and the rise of the competition state', in Tony Wright and Andrew Gamble (eds), *Restating the State?* Special Issue of *The Political Quarterly*.

Hay, Colin and Ben Rosamond (2002), 'Globalization, European integration and the discursive construction of economic imperatives', *Journal of European Public Policy*, **9**(2), 147–67.

Jayasuriya, Kanishka (1998), 'Globalization, law and the transformation of sovereignty: The emergence of global regulatory governance', *Indiana Journal of Legal Studies*, **6**(2), 425–55.

Jayasuriya, Kanishka (2001), 'Globalisation and the changing architecture of the state: Regulatory state and the politics of negative coordination', *Journal of European Public Policy*, **8**(1), 101–23.

Jayasuriya, Kanishka (2002), 'Authoritarian liberalism, governance and the emergence of the regulatory state in post-crisis East Asia', in Richard Robison, Mark Beeson, Kanishka Jayasuriya and Hyuk-Rae Kim (eds), *Politics and Markets in the Wake of the Asian Crisis*, London: Routledge, pp. 315–30.

Jayasuriya, Kanishka (2005), 'Beyond institutional fetishism: From the developmental to the regulatory state', *New Political Economy*, **10**(3), 381–7.

Jordana, Jacint and David Levi-Faur (2004), 'The politics of regulation in the age of governance', in Jacint Jordana and David Levi-Faur (eds), *The Politics of Regulation: Institutions and Regulatory Reforms for the Age of Governance*, Cheltenham; UK and Northampton, MA, USA: Edward Elgar, pp. 1–28.

Katzenstein, Peter (2003), 'Small states and small states revisited', *New Political Economy*, **8**(1), 9–30.

Kurtz, Marcus (2001), 'State developmentalism without a developmental state: The public foundations of the "free market miracle" in Chile', *Latin American Politics and Society*, **43**(2), 1–25.

Lodge, Martin (2002), *On Different Tracks: Designing Railways Regulation in Britain and Germany*, Westport, CT: Praeger.

McGowan, Francis and Helen Wallace (1996), 'Towards a European regulatory state', *Journal of European Public Policy*, **3**(4), 560–76.

Manzetti, Luigi (2002), 'The Argentine implosion', The North–South Agenda Papers, No. 59, North–South Center, University of Miami, November, pp. 1–24.

Moran, Michael (2002), 'Review article: Understanding the regulatory state', *British Journal of Political Science*, **32**(2), electronic version, pp. 1–14.

Mosley, Layna (2003), *Global Capital and National Governments*, Cambridge: Cambridge University Press.

Muñoz Gomá, Oscar (ed.) (1996), *Después de las Privatizaciones: Hacia el Estado Regulador*, (After privatisation: towards 'the regulatory state' trans.), Santiago: CIEPLAN / Dolmen Ediciones.

Muñoz Gomá, Oscar (ed.) (2000), *El Estado y el Sector Privado: Construyendo una Nueva Economía en los Años 90*, (The state and the private sector: building a new economy in the 1990s' trans.), Santiago: FLACSO / Dolmen Ediciones.
Pastor, Manuel Jr and Carol Wise (1998), 'Stabilization and its discontents: Argentina's economic restructuring in the 1990s', The North–South Agenda Papers, No. 31, North–South Center, University of Miami, May, pp. 1–32.
Pastor, Manuel Jr and Carol Wise (1999), 'The politics of second-generation reform', *Journal of Democracy*, **10**(3), 34–48.
Philip, George (2003), *Democracy in Latin America: Surviving Conflict and Crisis?* Cambridge: Polity Press.
Philip, George (1999a), 'Democracy and state bias in Latin America: Some lessons from Mexico, Peru and Venezuela', *Democratization*, **6**(4), 74–92.
Philip, George (1999b), 'The dilemmas of good governance: A Latin American perspective', *Government and Opposition*, **34**(2), 226–42.
Phillips, Nicola (2004), *The Southern Cone Model: The Political Economy of Regional Capitalist Development in Latin America*, London: Routledge.
Phillips, Nicola (2005), 'State debates in international political economy', in Nicola Phillips (ed.), *Globalizing International Political Economy*, Basingstoke: Palgrave, pp. 82–115.
Pirie, Iain (2005), 'The new Korean state', *New Political Economy*, **10**(1), 25–42.
Ruggie, John Gerard (1982) 'International regimes, transactions, and change: Embedded liberalism in the postwar economic order', *International Organization*, **36**(2), 379–415.
Thurbon, Elizabeth and Linda Weiss (2006) 'Investing in openness: The evolution of FDI strategy in South Korea and Taiwan', *New Political Economy*, **11**, 2.
US Department of State (2002), '2001 Reports on Economic Policy and Trade Practices' – Uruguay Report', Washington, DC, Bureau of Economic and Business Affairs, http://www.state.gov/documents/organization/8214.pdf.
Weiss, Linda (2005), 'The state-augmenting effects of globalisation', *New Political Economy*, **10**(3), 345–53.
Welsch, Friedrich J. and José V. Carrasquero (2000), 'Perceptions of state reform in Latin America', *International Social Science Journal*, **52**(163), 31–8.
Wilks, Stephen (1996), 'Regulatory compliance and capitalist diversity in Europe', *Journal of European Public Policy*, **3**(4), 536–59.
Williams, David and Thomas Youngs (1994), 'Governance, the World Bank and liberal theory', *Political Studies*, **42**(1), 84–100.
World Bank (1989), *Sub-Saharan Africa: From Crisis to Sustainable Growth: A Long-Term Perspective Study*, New York: Oxford University Press.
World Bank (1992), *Governance and Development*, Washington, DC: IBRD.
World Bank (1993), *The East Asian Miracle: Economic Growth and Public Policy*, New York: Oxford University Press.
World Bank (1997), *World Development Report 1997: The State in a Changing World*, New York: Oxford University Press.

3. The internationalization of regulation: implications for developing countries

Giandomenico Majone

INTRODUCTION

Any trade concessions can be nullified by imposing an offsetting set of domestic policies. For this reason no institutional arrangement that oversees trade liberalization, such as the World Trade Organization (WTO), can confine its attention to 'border' rules. This explains the shift of emphasis from shallow integration – based on the removal of barriers to trade at the border – to deeper integration, which is concerned with national regulatory measures that had previously not been subject to international scrutiny. Even legitimate regulations, such as standards to protect the health and safety of citizens, can create serious obstacles to international trade if they are not harmonized. A certain amount of harmonization takes place through market processes or various forms of self-regulation. When voluntary harmonization is impossible or undesirable, it is necessary to rely on the work of international standards organizations, for example the Codex Alimentarius Commission. Since 1995 this body has played an increasingly important role, in part because national regulations based on Codex standards are presumed to comply with WTO principles. International standards are thus becoming highly relevant to developing countries, as shown by several recent examples. It is in the interest of these countries to be active members of standard-setting organizations like the Codex, in order to influence the formulation and implementation of international rules. Science is going to play a central role in international risk regulation and the harmonization of technical barriers to trade. Thus the possibility of playing an active role in the relevant bodies presupposes a stock of available scientific talent. For a number of developing countries the problem is no longer the availability of scientific expertise as such. Rather the problem may be a scarcity of professionals trained in 'regulatory science', the logic of decision-making under uncertainty, and the design of efficient regulatory policies and institutions.

FROM 'SHALLOW' TO 'DEEP' INTEGRATION

The profound changes of the world trading system since the 1980s are reflected in the transition from 'shallow' to 'deeper' integration. Shallow integration is economic integration based on the removal of barriers to exchange at the border, and limited coordination of national policies. The General Agreement on Tariffs and Trade (GATT) and the International Monetary Fund (IMF) were the core global institutions in the management of shallow integration. The remarkable success achieved in the 1960s and the first half of the 1970s in removing tariffs and quantitative restrictions served to underscore the significance of non-tariff barriers (NTBs) to international trade. Economists had been aware for a long time of a 'principle of equivalence', according to which any trade concessions can be nullified by imposing an offsetting set of domestic policies. However, the practical significance of this principle was generally appreciated only in the late 1970s, when national governments reacted to the double threat of economic stagnation and inflation by increasing the level of protection of domestic industry by massive recourse to NTBs, in particular technical and health standards.

These developments could be observed not only in the world economy at large, but even in the European Community/European Union (EC/EU), where the abolition of internal tariffs, already achieved in the 1960s, was seriously impaired by the proliferation of national regulations and standards. It thus became clear that no institutional arrangement that oversees trade liberalization can afford to confine its rules and attention to 'border' measures. Hence the emergence of issues of deeper integration on the international agenda. These issues concern 'behind-the-border' policies that had previously not been subject to international scrutiny or negotiation. Instead of the older agenda of removing barriers that block exchange at the national borders, the new agenda items include conflicts over domestic regulatory regimes and perceived policy externalities (Kahler, 1995, p. 2). In the EC/EU the turn to deeper integration was signified by the internal market program, which was supposed to achieve a fully integrated European market by 1992. In the international trading system, concerns about the impact of domestic regulations on free trade led to the Tokyo and Uruguay Rounds Agreements on technical barriers to trade; to the Agreement on the Application of Sanitary and Phytosanitary Measures (SPS Agreement), also reached in the Uruguay Round; to agreements extending the scope and competence of the international trading rules by the inclusion of new subjects, such as agriculture and intellectual property rights; finally, to the transformation, in 1995, of the GATT into the World Trade Organization (WTO).

SPONTANEOUS REGULATORY CONVERGENCE

Concerns about the adverse effect of different national regulations and other NTBs on free trade usually lead to demands for harmonization. There are, however, many different types of harmonization, as is shown in the first part of this chapter. A first distinction is between spontaneous harmonization achieved through 'parametric adjustment' (see below), and harmonization achieved through multilateral agreements, usually with the help of formal international institutions.

A good deal of convergence of different national regulations occurs spontaneously – through market or other social processes, such as imitation, and the independent decisions of a multitude of individuals – rather than by the deliberate efforts by policy-makers and bureaucrats. In this section I review some of the most important strategies of spontaneous convergence. In the case of unilateral harmonization a country chooses to adapt its regulations to those of another country or group of countries. This strategy is particularly important to small countries whose economies are heavily dependent on international trade and which therefore tend to be 'regulation takers'. Like unilateral harmonization, policy imitation is an example of what Charles Lindblom calls parametric adjustment – a decision situation where decision-maker X adjusts his or her decision to Y's decisions, without seeking to induce a response from Y. Policy imitation affords relief from the necessity of searching for conscious innovations which, if wrong, expose the policy-maker to severe criticism. In a complex and uncertain environment the strategy of adopting successful foreign models may be rational – provided the timing is right and the two systems are not too dissimilar.

Models emanating from economically and politically powerful countries are most likely to be imitated. The force exerted by a foreign model can be of two types: push or pull. American influence on the development of antitrust policy in Germany and Japan at the end of World War II exemplifies the first type. On the other hand, American deregulatory policies of the 1970s and British privatization policies of the 1980s attracted the attention of policy-makers in developed and developing countries without direct pressures, except those transmitted through the markets. In practice, policy imitation is often the result of both push and pull forces.

Private legislation is a special case of the pull model of policy imitation. Private legislatures are organizations – often professional bodies – that draft laws in the hope that other bodies will adopt them. They do not purport to enact legislation themselves, but they often enjoy sufficient prestige to make their recommendations attractive to legislators. In the field of international trade, private legislatures have enjoyed substantial influence by promulgating model laws that many national legislatures have enacted. The greater the success of a particular proposal, the greater the pressure individual states face to adopt them. This is an instance of the effect of network externalities: once a model takes on the character of an international standard, states or private economic actors derive benefits from conforming to it that are independent of the intrinsic virtues of the particular rules contained in the law. Self-regulation may be regarded as a type of private legislation, but its special features and importance for international economic relations suggest it should be treated separately.

SELF-REGULATION

The present drive toward international regulatory harmonization rests in part on the belief that ex ante, top-down harmonization of product standards is a prerequisite for free and 'fair' trade. In fact, ex ante harmonization is less essential to international economic integration than it was once thought. Recent research shows not only that an initial difference in standards need not distort trade, but that it is trade itself that leads to their (ex post) convergence. This is because standards concerning environmental quality, risk control, or consumer protection are positively correlated with the standard of living. Thus, as wealth grows as a result of free trade, the endogeneous demand for higher standards grows as well. It follows that, paradoxically, the ex ante harmonization of standards as a precondition of free trade can be counterproductive since it may prevent or limit trade, and the wealth effects it produces (Casella, 1996).

Historical traditions may also militate against a full acceptance of self-regulation, since there is a strong historical link between standardization and the emergence of the sovereign territorial state (Spruyt, 1994). Views of standardization have changed radically, however, as a result of the development of technology and the advance of globalization. Standards are indeed public goods – in the sense that they fulfill specific functions deemed desirable by the community that shares them – but this does not mean that they must be established by government fiat. A good standard must reflect the preferences, levels of acceptable risk, resources, and technical constraints of the community of users, rather than some centrally defined vision of the 'public interest'. The fact that, in today's integrating world economy, the relevant community of standards users need not be territorially defined, distinguishes the contemporary from the traditional understanding of standards, in particular their nature as a special type of public goods known as 'club goods'.

The properties of joint supply – it does not cost anything for an additional individual to enjoy the benefits of a public good, such as air quality improvements – and non-excludability – it is impossible or inefficient to exclude individuals from the enjoyment of the public good – define what the literature of public finance refers to as 'pure public goods'. If only the joint supply property is retained, that is, we assume that exclusion is possible, we have 'club goods' (Buchanan, 1965). A voluntary association established to provide excludable public goods is a 'club'. If the preferences and the technologies for the provision of club goods are such that the number of clubs that can be formed in a society of given size is large, then an efficient allocation of these excludable public goods through the voluntary association of individuals into clubs is possible. With a large number of alternative clubs available, any effort to discriminate against an individual will induce his or her exit into a competing club, or the creation of a new one. If optimal club sizes are large relative to the population, however, discrimination is possible and stable equilibria may not exist. With an optimal club size of two-thirds of the population, for example, only one such club can exist (Mueller, 1989, pp. 150–54). In a non-competitive situation the normative concerns expressed in the past about the delegation of powers to self-regulatory organizations (SROs) – for example, the lack of internal democracy of these bodies, where industrial interests tend to be over-represented – are understandable. But these criticisms, developed in contexts where a few SROs are given near monopoly powers, lose much of their point where many 'clubs' are available. This tends to be the situation in expanding markets.

In fact, what happens to the number of standard-setting organizations as the size of the market expands, for example as a result of the merging of previously separate national markets? It has been shown (Casella, 1996) that under reasonable assumptions, the number of clubs increases as the size of the market increases. Two elements determine the optimal number of clubs. One is the cost of producing the standards ('club fees'); the other is the cost of an inappropriate standard. Notice that because a standard represents a public good, its cost is shared by the members of the corresponding club, while the cost of an inappropriate standard is borne separately by each club member. Now, as the market expands, the number of standards also expands because the increase in the variety of goods makes necessary a more finely tuned targeting of the public goods provided by the standards – product quality, safety, equipment compatibility, and so on. The standards required for transactions in a more diverse market are likely to be both more sophisticated and more costly. The higher cost of the standard, because of the larger size of the club, is shared over more members, but the standard is less precisely tailored to individual needs. Hence, for a sufficiently large increase in market size the optimal number of clubs must increase.

The general implication of Casella's model is that top-down harmonization is desirable only when the market is small and relatively homogeneous. In a large market, harmonization, especially technical harmonization, often is brought about not by a policy imposed from the top, but simply through the recognition of similar preferences or similar needs (for example, for producers in the same industry). This conclusion seems to be supported by empirical evidence. Thus, already some ten years ago, the Organisation for Economic Co-operation and Development (OECD) observed that all industrialized countries tend to converge towards a greater emphasis on self-regulation and non-mandatory standards – hence towards a greater variety of standards and standard-setting organizations. A large market like the United States is remarkable for the high decentralization of its standardization system. There are literally hundreds of organizations involved in the development of standards. The American National Standards Institute (ANSI), a private organization, coordinates private standards, approves standards as American National Standards, and represents the United States in international standards organizations. In practice, however, only about one-half of all standards developers participate in the ANSI system, and several organizations which do not participate, such as the American Society of Testing, are as well known internationally as ANSI.

INTERNATIONAL STANDARDS ORGANIZATIONS

International, or regional, bodies like the International Standards Organization (ISO), the Codex Alimentarius Commission, or the European standardization bodies CEN, CENELEC and ETSI, occupy an intermediate position between the private 'clubs' mentioned above, and public regulatory institutions. On the one hand, the standards produced by these international bodies are voluntary – they are not legally binding, and are generally produced by consensus of the participants. On the other hand, the influence of national governments is considerable, even if it is often exercised indirectly; that is, through the national standardization bodies. At any rate, the importance of these international organizations is growing continuously, and no government can afford to ignore them or to be a purely passive member. For example, the ISO – which we may take as a prototype of similar international organizations – is a worldwide federation of national standards bodies from 132 countries, of which 88 are full members, 35 are correspondent members, and 9 are subscriber members. The ISO achieved only modest results in its early years – it was created in 1947 from the union of two pre-existing organizations – but began to play a bigger role in the 1960s. It more than doubled the number of standards between 1968 and 1971, while the membership grew from 15 countries in 1947 to 70 in 1971. It also began in the 1970s to cooperate with several regional associations – notably with the European standards organizations – and made a particular effort to attract Japan and other Asian countries to the organization.

The technical work of ISO is highly decentralized, being carried out in a hierarchy of over 200 technical committees and subcommittees, and more than 2000 working groups. The main cost of standardization is borne by the member organizations: member firms in national bodies supply and support the experts who comprise the various committees. Some 30,000 experts participate annually in ISO standardization: the technical work is coordinated from the ISO central secretariat in Geneva, which has a full-time staff of some 165. ISO standards – which cover most technical fields with the exception of the electrotechnical domain, which falls under the responsibility of the International Electrotechnical Commission – are developed on the basis of consensus among the experts from the sectors that have expressed a requirement for a particular standard. Since ISO standards are voluntary, they are used only to the extent that people find them useful. In this sense, they are market-driven.

Of particular relevance to international regulation in the area of food safety – with which this chapter is particularly concerned – is the Codex Alimentarius Commission (CAC), an international organization set up in 1962 under the auspices of the Food and Agriculture Organization (FAO) and the World Health Organization (WHO). The role of the CAC – with a current membership of 165 member governments – is to promote international trade in food through the adoption of standards aimed at ensuring fair trade practices and the protection of consumers' health. Initially it was felt that Codex standards – which define the identity of the product and describe the basic composition and quality factors required for international trade, especially provisions on food additives, contaminants, and hygiene requirements – were being developed so as to assist developing countries by providing a ready-made standard they could adopt. Hence, developing countries tended to assume that, if they adopted Codex standards into their own legislation, they might gain access to the markets of the developed world. This did not happen since most Codex standards were not implemented by developed countries, which were unwilling to disrupt their long established system of controls.

The situation has changed, however. The CAC has played an increasingly important role in international trade since 1995, the year in which the World Trade Organization was established. Under WTO agreements (to be discussed in greater detail below) national measures that are based on international food standards are presumed to comply with WTO principles. The close connection between WTO rules and Codex (and other international) standards implies that the latter are now important also to developed countries. Thus Codex standards have been invoked in several trade disputes between the United States and the European Community/European Union (EC/EU). The following recent (2002) example is particularly interesting for the present discussion because it shows how a Codex standard helped protect the economic interest of a developing country – in this case, Peru – against a restrictive EC regulation.

The dispute, known as the Sardine case, involved an EC regulation reserving the name 'sardine' to certain fish species (*Sardine pilchardus*, to be found in the Mediterranean) to the exclusion of others (such as the Peruvian *Sardinops sagax*), thus precluding Peru from marketing its sardines under the name 'sardines' in the territory of the EC. The WTO Panel's finding that the European regulation violated Article 2.4 of the Agreement on Technical Barriers to Trade (TBT) is interesting because the Panel considered a Codex standard on sardines, adopted in 1978, as a 'relevant international standard'. This standard laid down common marketing standards for preserved sardines and it covered 20 sardine species, including both *pilchardus* and *Sardinops sagax*. The fact that the Codex recognized both species as 'sardines' also meant that the Peruvian product could be allowed to be marketed in Europe under that name. The WTO Panel found that the EC had not used the Codex standard as a basis for its own regulation. In other words, the EC regulation did not conform to the international standard since it had not taken the latter as 'the principal constituent or fundamental principle' of its technical standard. The EC appealed against this point of law, arguing that 'using a standard as a basis for a technical regulation' simply means that there must be a 'rational relationship' between the technical regulation and the standard. This was the case for the EC regulation since it used part of the international standard as a basis for the regulation. The Panel did not accept this argument, saying that 'something cannot be considered a "basis" for something else if the two are contradictory'. The EC regulation contradicted the Codex standard because it prohibited the use of the label 'sardine' for species other than *pilchardus*, while the Codex standard allowed *Sardinops sagax* to be marketed under the label 'sardines'. Thus it could not be maintained that the European regulation took the international standard as a basis.

It should be noted, however, that there are many instances of EC regulations that are based on Codex standards or incorporate its guidelines. Such standards are even appealed to in cases before the European Court of Justice. For instance, the Court has used reports of the Codex Commission to clarify the meaning of the terms 'hazard' and 'scientific risk assessment'. It also referred to Codex standards to determine the characteristic features of yogurt in a case on the labeling of foodstuffs, and in deciding whether a food additive presented a risk to public health or met a real need. Reference has also been made to Codex standards on the limits for lead and cadmium in certain foodstuffs.

VARIETIES OF REGULATORY HARMONIZATION

As the above discussion shows, a good deal of regulatory harmonization today is achieved by reference to international standards. It is important to realize, however, that the term 'harmonization' can apply to any aspect or stage of the regulatory process, not just to the final outcome; that is, a specific standard or regulation. Generally speaking, the purpose of harmonization, as the term is used in the present context, is to make the regulatory requirements or public policies of different jurisdictions more similar, if not identical. Regulatory regimes, and the political and institutional systems in which they are embedded, can differ in numerous aspects. Hence, several broad types of harmonization may be usefully distinguished (Leebron, 1996). First, specific rules or standards that prescribe the desired characteristics of the outputs of production processes, institutions, or transactions may be harmonized. For example, emission limits for polluting factories located in different countries may be made more similar. We could call this 'output harmonization' since the goal is to reduce pre-existing differences in certain characteristics of the relevant outputs or outcomes. Second, international regulatory harmonization may relate to certain governmental policy objectives – for example, the central banks of the G-7 countries attempt to keep inflation within agreed limits – or to general policy principles such as the polluter-pays and the precautionary principles.

Finally, harmonization of institutional structures, procedures or methodologies is often sought. Thus some of the provisions of the North American Free Trade Agreement (NAFTA; the reference here is to the NAFTA 'side agreement' on the environment) require that certain procedures for enforcement of domestic laws, including appellate review, be harmonized. Procedural harmonization often serves to reinforce other types of harmonization. If the aim is to harmonize decisional outcomes, both substantive criteria and decisional processes are implicated. Rules, policies and principles will generally not be truly harmonized unless the procedures and institutions for implementing them are made more similarly effective, and doing so may mean making them more similar (Leebron, 1996, p. 46). This, incidentally, is the reason why harmonization, for example in the environmental field, fails to produce identical, or at least very similar, results across the European

Union. European measures are typically implemented by national administrations, but the EU is not competent to harmonize national administrative procedures and processes. The problem has been recognized for some time, and certain directives attempt to harmonize not only national laws and policy objectives, but also the institutional design of the 'competent authorities' at national level (e.g. with respect to their independence in the case of telecommunications). The power of the EU in this area is, however, quite limited.

There are situations where procedural harmonization is not meant to reinforce other types of harmonization, but is the only type that is politically, economically, or technically feasible. For instance, in the case of the NAFTA environmental side-agreement it would have been impossible to impose on Mexico the same environmental standards used in Canada or the United States. Hence, Article 3 of the agreement recognizes 'the right of each Party to establish its own levels of domestic environmental protection . . .', while Article 5 requires that 'each Party shall effectively enforce its environmental laws and regulations through appropriate government action . . .'; and Article 6 requires that 'interested persons' be able to request a Party's regulatory authorities to investigate possible violations of domestic environmental laws and regulations.

An important example of procedural harmonization is provided by the already mentioned WTO Agreement on Sanitary and Phytosanitary (SPS) Measures. Harmonization is discussed in Article 3, which states, in part, that: (a) in order to harmonize SPS measures on as wide a basis as possible, member states shall base their measures on international standards, guidelines or recommendations, where they exist; (b) SPS measures that conform to international standards shall be deemed to be necessary to protect human, animal or plant life or health; (c) member states may, however, introduce or maintain SPS measures that result in a higher level of protection than would be achieved by measures based on the relevant international standards, provided there is 'scientific justification' for the stricter measures; and (d) member states are required to 'play a full part, within the limits of their resources, in the relevant international organizations and their subsidiary bodies', such as the Codex Alimentarius Commission.

This Article is noteworthy in several respects. First, nothing substantive is said about the level of the international standards, not even of a qualitative nature. By way of comparison, the NAFTA Agreement on Environmental Cooperation stipulates that 'each Party shall ensure that its laws and regulations provide for high levels of environmental protection and shall strive to continue to improve those laws and regulations'. At the same time, the Agreement recognizes 'the right of each Party to establish its own levels of domestic environmental protection'. Thus, at least according to a widely accepted interpretation, a member of NAFTA is permitted to set its own levels of protection, as long as those levels are 'high' by some more or less objective standard (see also Article 95(3) of the Treaty on the European Union, according to which 'The Commission, in its proposals . . . concerning health, safety, environmental protection and consumer protection, will take as a base a high level of protection').

By contrast, the approach of the WTO SPS Agreement is purely procedural, as shown also by the requirement that the member states play an active role in the activities of the international standardization bodies. Also the requirement that a country provide 'scientific justification' if it wishes to adopt a higher level of protection than that provided by international standards, goes in the same procedural direction. Given the uncertainty surrounding the scientific basis of risk regulation, 'scientific justification' can only mean that the relevant arguments should satisfy generally accepted rules of scientific methodology – an important point we elaborate in the following pages.

REGULATORY SCIENCE AND FREE TRADE

Increasingly, science is playing a significant role in the regulation of international trade. In particular, the SPS Agreement introduces a new science-based regime for disciplining health regulations which may affect international trade in agricultural products and foodstuffs. Annex A to the Agreement defines a sanitary or phytosanitary measure as any measure applied to protect animal or plant life or health from a variety of risks, including 'risks arising from additives, contaminants, toxins or disease-causing organisms in foods, beverages or feedstuffs'.

Article 2(2) of the Agreement states, inter alia, that members of the WTO shall ensure that any SPS measure 'is based on scientific principles and is not maintained without sufficient scientific evidence, except as provided for in paragraph 7 of Article 5'. Article 5 deals with risk assessment as a method for determining the appropriate level of health protection. Risk assessment is the standard by which SPS measures are to be judged as necessary and justified. In other words, for such measures to be necessary, based on scientific principles and not maintained without sufficient scientific evidence, they must be supported by a risk assessment conducted according to the criteria, and taking into account the factors, mentioned in Article 5. As interpreted by the WTO Appellate Body in the beef hormones case, this article says that there must be a rational relationship between the SPS measure and the risk assessment.

The exception provided by Article 5(7) applies to cases where relevant scientific evidence is insufficient, in which case a member state may *provisionally* adopt a measure 'on the basis of available pertinent information . . . Members shall seek to obtain the additional information necessary for a more objective assessment of risk and review the sanitary or phytosanitary measure accordingly *within a reasonable period of time*' (emphasis added). Article 5(7) is the only reference to a precautionary approach in the entire Agreement. I shall come back to this approach in a later section, after briefly discussing some of the conceptual and technical complexities surrounding the notions of 'scientific justification' and 'risk assessment' as they apply to regulatory measures.

The process of standard setting is at the core of risk regulation. If we understand the extent of scientific uncertainty in standard setting, we are in a good position to appreciate the problems of regulatory science. Extrapolation is a key element in the establishment of environmental and health standards, hence a good part of the uncertainty inherent in standard setting originates in various types of extrapolation processes. There is, first, the problem of extrapolating from animal experiments. A major issue in regulatory science is the determination of the animal species that best predicts the response in humans. There is little hope that one species could provide the broad range of predictive potential needed to assess the responses of a highly heterogeneous human population to different types of toxic substances. The heterogeneity of human populations leaves the public authorities with an almost impossible regulatory task. In an effort to find a way out of this dilemma, scientists have developed several mathematical models expressing the probability of a lifetime response, P, as a function of dosage D: $P = f(D)$. This is the dose–response function. Different choices of f lead to different models.

Regardless of the choice of model, however, one has always to extrapolate from data points at high doses (the type of data provided by animal experiments) to the low levels relevant to the regulation of risk to humans. However, the same data points are compatible with a variety of extrapolating functions (Calabrese, 1978). Thus under a threshold (non-linear) dose–response model it would be possible to establish a 'virtually safe' level of exposure, at the numerical value of the threshold, even though high doses produce adverse health effects. Instead, if one uses a linear dose–response relationship, adverse health effects are predicted at every level of exposure, so there is no obvious point at which a reasonable standard could be set.

It may be argued – as it is by many advocates of the precautionary principle – that if there is no firm scientific basis for choosing among different dose–response models, then one should opt for the safest or most conservative procedure. One problem with the conservatism argument is that it is not clear where one should stop. A no-threshold model is more conservative than one that admits the existence of thresholds for adverse health effects. But within the large class of no-threshold models many degrees of conservatism are possible. Again, in designing a toxicological experiment one could use the most sensitive species, the most sensitive strain within the species, and so on down to the level of the most sensitive animal. In short, it is difficult to be conservative in a consistent manner unless one is prepared to propose a zero-risk approach to regulation. This, in a nutshell, is the main conceptual problem with the precautionary principle.

Now, extrapolating from the high doses shown to cause harm in animal experiments or in epidemiological studies to the much lower exposures normally faced by humans is the essence of quantitative risk assessments. From what has been said above it follows that uncertainty is a pervasive characteristic of regulatory risk assessments. But the technique has been accepted and continues to be used because there are no better alternatives. Thus the United States Supreme Court in *AFL-CIO v. American Petroleum Institute* (448 US 607 (1980)) – the landmark benzene case – not only confirmed the legitimacy of quantitative risk assessment; it effectively made reliance on the methodology obligatory for all American agencies engaged in health regulation. In most subsequent disputes over regulatory decisions to protect human health, the question has not been whether a risk assessment was required but whether the assessment offered by the agency was plausible (Mashaw et al., 1998, pp. 823–5). This historical background may explain US advocacy of science-based risk assessment at the international level, as well as that country's opposition to the precautionary principle advocated by the EU. Today the methodology of risk assessment is used by regulators in all developed and in many developing countries. Moreover, as mentioned above, risk assessment is the standard by which trade-restricting health regulations are evaluated as being necessary and justified. As such, it plays a crucial role in the debate about the application of the precautionary principle at the international level.

THE PRECAUTIONARY PRINCIPLE AND THE WTO

The precautionary 'principle' is an idea (perhaps a state of mind) rather than a clearly defined concept, much less a guide to consistent decision-making under uncertainty. Not surprisingly, an authoritative and generally accepted definition is nowhere to be found. The principle is of German origin (*Vorsorge Prinzip*), and has been used in that country since the 1980s in order to justify a number of important developments in environmental law. However, an eminent legal expert has distinguished no less than 11 different meanings assigned to the precautionary principle within German policy discourse.

The German approach was taken up by other policy elites in Europe, including those that drafted the EC's Fourth Environmental Action Program, who sought to develop an approach to environmental policy that was preventive rather than reactive. In the EC Treaty the principle appears only in the Title on environment. Article 174 EC (ex Article 130(r)) provides that Community environmental policy 'shall be based on the precautionary principle and on the principles that preventive action should be taken, that environmental damage should as a priority be rectified at the source and that the polluter should pay'. No definition of the precautionary principle is provided in this article or anywhere else in the Treaty.

As mentioned above, there is an indirect reference to a precautionary approach (again undefined) in Article 5(7) of the WTO SPS Agreement. WTO member states are allowed to take measures unsupported by a risk assessment when the relevant scientific evidence is insufficient, but only provisionally. Perhaps the best known statement of the precautionary 'approach' (suggesting something more flexible and less binding than a 'principle') is provided by Principle 15 of the Declaration of the 1992 UN Conference on Environment and Development (Rio Declaration):

> In order to protect the environment, the precautionary approach shall be widely used by States according to their capabilities. Where there are threats of serious and irreversible damage, lack of full scientific certainty shall not be used as a reason for postponing cost-effective measures to prevent environmental degradation.

Since the precautionary principle lends itself to a wide range of interpretations, it would be instructive to see how the European Court of Justice (ECJ) and the Court of First Instance have dealt with it. A detailed discussion of relevant cases is of course beyond the scope of the present chapter, but a general inference from major decisions appears to be that in cases of scientific uncertainty, member states have considerable discretion in deciding to err on the side of caution. They must however provide some evidence of scientific uncertainty. They must adduce evidence of a specific, concrete risk and not merely of potential risks based on a general precautionary approach. Thus in the famous German Beer case (Case 178/84 [1987]) – where the German government wanted to prohibit the sale of any beer not brewed according to German standards – the ECJ refused to allow a ban on additives in beer, based on a generic principle of prevention. The national authorities must come up with more specific scientific evidence than a mere reference to the potential risks posed by the ingestion of additives in general.

As already mentioned, the EU is currently engaged in a major effort to have the precautionary principle adopted as a 'full-fledged and general principle' of international law (European Commission, 2000). While some progress has been made in the field of international environmental law, the EU's commitment to, and application of, the principle has been repeatedly questioned or opposed by the WTO, by the United States, and by many other developed and developing countries. Thus the proposals on the precautionary principle presented by the EU to the Codex Alimentarius Committee on General Principles in April 2000 were opposed by the US and many other third countries, which fear that the principle may be too easily misused for protectionist purposes. Such fears are fed by episodes like the proposed aflatoxin standards, to be discussed in the next section, and the beef hormones dispute which for years has opposed the EU to some of its major trading partners. The European Commission argued that the precautionary principle applies across the whole of the SPS Agreement as a general principle of international law. The WTO's Appellate Body specifically rejected this argument and stated that the principle must receive authoritative formulation before it can be raised to the status sought for it by the EU. The same body also observed that a precautionary approach has not been written into Article 5(7) of the SPS Agreement as a ground for justifying measures that are otherwise inconsistent with the obligations of the WTO set out in particular provisions of the Agreement.

FOOD SAFETY, THE PRECAUTIONARY PRINCIPLE, AND THE COST OF NON-HARMONIZATION

As mentioned above, the European Commission would like to interpret the entire SPS Agreement in the light of the precautionary principle, in order to be able to conclude that the EU is free to adopt the level of safety that it deems appropriate, regardless of the objections other countries may raise. However, the search for higher and higher levels of safety leads to the promulgation of standards so stringent that the regulatory action ultimately imposes high costs without achieving significant additional safety benefits. Perhaps we should not be too concerned if such costs were felt only by exporters in rich countries like the United States and Canada, and by affluent European consumers. But what if the cost is borne by some of the poorest countries in the world?

The EU and all its member states claim to be deeply committed to assist, financially and otherwise, developing countries, especially African ones. However, World Bank economists have estimated the impact on some of the poorest African countries of new and very strict standards for aflatoxins proposed by the Commission in 1997 in the name of the precautionary principle. Aflatoxins are a group of related toxic compounds that contaminate certain foods and have been associated with acute liver carcinogens in humans. Aflatoxin B1 is the most common and toxic of these compounds. It is generally present in corn and corn products, groundnuts and groundnuts products, and tree nuts. The proposed standards are significantly more stringent than those adopted by the US, Canada and Australia, and also stricter than the international standards established by the Codex Commission. Countries such as Brazil, Bolivia, India, Mexico, Uruguay, Australia, Argentina and Pakistan, in opposing the European measures, requested detailed risk assessments from the European Union used in setting the new standards. As a consequence of consultations with the trading partners about these concerns, the European Commission relaxed the proposed aflatoxin standard for cereals, dried foods and nuts. Even after this relaxation, aflatoxin standards for products intended for direct human consumption remain quite stringent: 4 parts per billion (ppb), and 2 ppb for B1, against an overall Codex standard of approximately 9 ppb.

Using trade and regulatory survey data for the member states of the EU and nine African countries between 1989 and 1998, World Bank economists estimated that the new standards would decrease African exports of cereals, dried fruits and nuts to the EU by 64 percent, relative to regulation set at the international standards (Otsuki et al., 2000). The total loss of export revenue for the nine African countries is estimated to be US$400 million under EU standards, compared to a gain of US$670 million if standards were adopted according to Codex guidelines. Are the costs imposed on some of the poorest countries in the world justified by the health benefits for EU citizens? According to studies conducted by the Joint FAO/WHO Expert Committee on Food Additives, the Community standard of 2 ppb for B1 aflatoxin would reduce deaths from liver cancer by 1.4 deaths per billion, that is, by less than one death per year in the EU. For the purpose of this calculation the Community standard is compared to a standard that follows the international (Codex) guideline of 9 ppb. Since about 33,000 people die from liver cancer every year in the EU, one can see that the health gain produced by the precautionary standard is indeed minuscule.

In a recent new study, Wilson and Otsuki (2003) extend the above analysis by estimating the effect of aflatoxin standards in 15 importing (of which 4 are developing) countries on exports from 31 (21 developing) countries. They estimate that world exports would rise by an impressive US$38.8 billion if an international (Codex) standard were adopted, compared to the current divergent national standards in place. On the other hand, world exports are estimated to decrease by US$3.1 billion if the world adopted the EU standard (that is, 2 ppb) compared to current national standards.

Thus harmonization of this food safety standard at a level more stringent than one suggested by international standards can severely limit developing countries' exports. The authors conclude that an initiative to encourage the adoption of international standards, along with mechanisms to directly assist developing countries in raising standards to international levels, merits serious consideration.

THE PRECAUTIONARY PRINCIPLE AND THE LOGIC OF DECISION-MAKING UNDER UNCERTAINTY

The preceding analysis reveals the serious implications, for world trade in general and developing countries in particular, of regulatory measures inspired by the precautionary principle. Hence, it seems useful to devote some time to a methodological critique of this principle. The critique is based on some key notions of probability and utility theory (for a more detailed treatment see Majone, 2003). As I have repeatedly suggested, the precautionary principle is seriously flawed as an aid to rational decision-making under uncertainty. Although a lack of precise definitions makes it difficult to develop a formal critique, the following considerations may help to grasp the principle's main theoretical shortcomings.

To begin with, recall that risk is a compound measure (more precisely, a product) of the probability of harm and its severity. Now, according to the fundamental theorem of decision theory, the only consistent rule for decision-making under uncertainty is to choose the alternative that minimizes the expected loss (or maximizes the expected utility). Consider a situation where there are various possible events (or 'states of nature') $E_1, E_2, \ldots, E_n$, with probabilities $p_1, p_2, \ldots, p_n$, alternative actions $A_1, A_2, \ldots, A_m$, and losses l_{ij} for each combination of alternative A_i and event E_j, $i = 1, 2, \ldots, m$; $j = 1, 2, \ldots, n$. The optimal decision consists in choosing the alternative that minimizes the expected loss, that is, the sum of the products of the losses by the corresponding probabilities (formally: the alternative that minimizes $\Sigma_j p_j l_{ij}$).

Any good textbook on decision theory (for example, Lindley, 1971) provides the proof that any other decision rule – and in particular any rule that does not use both the losses and the corresponding probabilities – can lead to inconsistent decisions. One such decision rule is the minimax principle, which in some respects is quite similar to the precautionary principle. The minimax approach to decision-making under uncertainty uses losses but not probabilities, either denying the existence of the latter, or claiming that the method is to be used when they are unknown (here is an important similarity with the precautionary principle). This approach makes sense in special situations – zero-sum games where the uncertainty is 'strategic', that is, part of the strategy of a rational opponent – but not in the general case, as may be seen from the following examples. Consider first the decision problem described in Example 1, where the entries indicate losses, for example extra deaths due to exposure to a toxic substance:

Example 1

	$E_1\,(p_1)$	$E_2\,(p_2)$
A_1	10	0
A_2	1	1

Following the minimax rule, for each row (that is, alternative) we select the maximum loss (10 for A_1 and 1 for A_2), and choose the alternative that has the minimum of these values. This is A_2 with value 1. Hence the minimax rule says: always choose A_2. The principle of expected loss would assign probabilities p_1 and p_2 to the uncertain events and choose A_2 if $1 < 10\,p_1$, that is, $p_1 > 1/10$, otherwise A_1 should be selected. To see which of the two rules is more reasonable, suppose that p_1 is quite small (say, $p_1 = 0.01$ or 0.001) so that $10\,p_1$ is much less than 1. The minimax rule would still choose A_2, even though it is almost certain that no extra deaths would occur under A_1. The result is even more striking in Example 2, where only the loss corresponding to the pair (A_1, E_1) has been changed:

Example 2

	$E_1\,(p_1)$	$E_2\,(p_2)$
A_1	1.1	0
A_2	1	1

The minimax rule would still choose A_2, even though the expected loss for A_1 is much smaller for all values of p_1 less than, say, 0.8. In short, the problem with the minimax rule is that it does not take account of all the information available to the decision-maker. The advantage of the expected loss rule is that it takes account of both losses and probabilities.

As noted above, one defense of the minimax is that it is to be used when probabilities are unknown (and perhaps unknowable). This argument is strongly reminiscent of the distinction made by the American economist Frank Knight (1971 [1921]) in the 1920s between 'risk' (when the events are uncertain, but their probabilities are known) and 'uncertainty' (where the probabilities are unknown). Knight attached great theoretical importance to this distinction, but modern analysis no longer views the two classes of events as different in kind. Probabilities may be known more or less precisely, they may be more or less 'subjective', but there are some logical difficulties involved in giving meaning to the statement that the probabilities are unknown. If we insist that we are 'completely ignorant' as to which of the events $E_1, \ldots, E_n$ will occur, it is hard to escape the conclusion that all the events are equally likely to occur. But this implies that the probabilities are in fact known, and that $P(E_i) = 1/n$ for all i: the well-known uniform distribution!

The point of this digression on decision theory is to identify with more precision than would otherwise be possible the logical problems raised by the application of the precautionary principle. Like the minimax principle, the principle of precaution tends to focus the attention of regulators on some particular events and corresponding losses, rather than on the entire range of possibilities. As a consequence, regulators will base their determinations on worst cases, rather than on the weighted average of all potential losses; that is, on the expected overall loss. The most serious conceptual flaw, however, is the artificial distinction between situations where scientific information is sufficient to permit a formal risk assessment, and those where scientific information is said to be insufficient, inconclusive or uncertain. In reality, these are two points on a knowledge–ignorance continuum rather than two qualitatively distinct situations. The same logic that leads to the rejection of Knight's distinction between risk and uncertainty, applies also here. As we saw, by its very nature regulatory science deals with uncertainties. For example, for most toxic substances it is still unknown whether the relevant model for standard setting is a threshold or a linear one. Most scientists favor the latter model, but this only complicates the regulator's problem, since it is unclear where a standard should be set above the zero level. Moreover, the continuous progress of science and technology produces increasingly precise measurements of toxicity (e.g. parts per billion) so that the search for safety becomes ever more elusive.

In short, regulatory problems are not solved but only complicated by appealing to different logics of decision-making, according to the available level of information. Especially in risk regulation, the normal state of affairs is neither scientific certainty nor complete ignorance. For this reason a sensible principle of decision-making is one that uses all the available information, weighted according to its reliability, instead of privileging some particular hypothetical risk.

The prescriptions of decision theory break down only in one case, namely when losses (or utilities) are unbounded. In such a case it is clearly impossible to calculate expected values. An example of potential unbounded loss is the threat of serious and irreversible damage – the situation envisaged by Principle 15 of the Rio Declaration mentioned above. In this and similar situations, the precautionary principle may be a useful tool of risk management. But to acknowledge such possibilities is to recognize that the principle has a legitimate but quite limited role in risk management.

CONCLUSIONS

Today developing countries are more fully integrated into the GATT/WTO system than ever before. This is as it should be. For such countries 'rule-oriented' trade diplomacy is greatly preferable to power-oriented diplomacy. In other words, settlement of international disputes with reference to rules to which both parties have previously agreed is better than settlement by negotiation with (more or less implicit) reference to the relative power status of the parties. In the latter case, a developing country would hesitate to challenge a major country on which its trade depends. In the case of reference to agreed rules, the negotiators would argue about the application of the relevant rule, knowing that an unsettled dispute would ultimately be resolved by impartial third-party judgments – such as those provided by the WTO dispute-settlement procedures – based on the agreed system of rules. Thus the negotiators would be negotiating with reference to their respective predictions as to the outcome of those judgments, and not with reference to potential retaliations or actions by the more powerful country (Jackson, 1999).

Neither the mere existence of rules, nor mere membership in international regulatory bodies is sufficient, however. It is in the interest especially of developing countries to be active members in order to be able to influence the formulation and application of international rules. The experience of the European Union shows that small countries, such as Denmark and the Netherlands – 3 and 5 votes, respectively, against the 29 votes of each of the four largest members of the EU – can have an influence on rule-making at European level that is out of proportion to their political power. What such countries lack in terms of power they make up, in areas of particular interest to them, by innovative policy ideas and the demonstrated capacity to translate those ideas into practice. As I have argued in the preceding pages, science is going to play an increasingly important role in the international regulation of risk and the harmonization of technical barriers to trade. Thus the possibility of influencing the formulation of international rules presupposes a stock of available scientific talent. For many developing countries this is not today a problem. The problem, rather, may be to have a sufficient number of able people trained in 'regulatory science'. Regulatory science differs from the more traditional variety in several important respects. First, unlike his or her colleagues in academia and research laboratories, the regulatory scientist generally cannot afford to postpone a decision simply because the evidence is insufficient. In this he or she is similar to the judge, who cannot refuse to decide a case because the facts are uncertain. The risk regulator always decides under conditions of great uncertainty and, hence, must be familiar not only with the relevant branch of science – chemistry, toxicology, microbiology, nuclear physics, and so on – but also with the basic logic of decision-making under uncertainty. In particular, knowledge of the elements of decision theory is necessary in order to perform risk analysis, which is required by WTO rules in case a country wishes to depart from international standards of food safety. This heavy reliance on the principles of decision-making under uncertainty is a second importance difference from the traditional scientist, who may be concerned with probabilities, but not, usually, with the optimization of the consequences of his conclusions.

As indicated above, the modern theory of decision-making under uncertainty cannot guarantee the substantive correctness of a given regulatory decision – no theory can do this – but it ensures that the decision is internally coherent. This means that by following this methodology one is sure that all factors that go into the decision process are clearly identified, and especially that they are put together in a consistent way. It is not sufficiently appreciated that this sort of 'procedural rationality' is important not only for technical reasons (for example, for producing a risk assessment that satisfies WTO criteria), but also politically, being a necessary condition of public accountability. Precisely because regulatory decisions of the type discussed here are ultimately based on subjective evaluations of risk, it is essential that the regulator be in a position to explain and justify each step in the decision process to political leaders and to the public at large.

Independence is the other side of accountability. The regulator cannot be held responsible for his or her decisions unless he or she is given the necessary resources, and protection from undue political interference. This is of course a problem for the political leaders rather than for the regulators. It is up to the political leaders to design regulatory institutions capable of providing a good accountability framework as well as adequate protection of the regulators' political independence. The design of independent and accountable regulatory institutions is a topic deserving a separate treatment, but its importance should at least be acknowledged here. On the other hand, the regulator must be aware that he or she is not operating in a political vacuum. Especially when the life and health of the citizens are concerned, science, technology or economics may not provide the only relevant criteria for decision-making. When basic values have to be traded-off (at the margin), the ultimate responsibility must be political. However, the decision to override the opinion of the expert regulator must follow a well defined and generally known procedure. The procedure should entail a political cost high enough to discourage unjustified interference with the regulator's decision. Specification of the conditions and methods for overruling agency decisions by the political authorities is a neglected but very important aspect of institutional design.

REFERENCES

Buchanan, J.M. (1965), 'An economic theory of clubs', *Economica*, **32**, 1–14.

Calabrese, E.J. (1978), *Methodological Approaches to Deriving Environmental and Occupational Health Standards*, New York/London: Wiley International.

Casella, A. (1996), 'Free trade and evolving standards', in J.N. Bhagwati and R.E. Hudec (eds), *Fair Trade and Harmonization*, Vol. 1, Cambridge, MA: MIT Press, pp. 119–56.

Commission of the European Communities (2000), *Communication on the Precautionary Principle*, Brussels: COM (2000) 1.

Jackson, J.H. (1999), *The World Trading System*, Cambridge, MA: MIT Press.

Kahler, M. (1995), *International Institutions and the Political Economy of Integration*, Washington, DC: The Brookings Institution.

Knight, F.H. (1971 [1921]), *Risk, Uncertainty and Profit*, Chicago, IL: University of Chicago Press.

Leebron, D.W. (1996), 'Lying down with procustes: An analysis of harmonization claims', in J.N. Bhagwati and R.E. Hudec (eds), *Fair Trade and Harmonization*, Vol. 1, Cambridge, MA: MIT Press, pp. 41–118.

Lindley, D. (1971), *Making Decisions*, New York and London: Wiley-Interscience.

Majone, G. (ed.) (2003), *Risk Regulation in the European Union: Between Enlargement and Globalization*, Florence: European University Institute.

Mashaw, J.L., R.A. Merrill and P.M. Shane (1998), *Administrative Law*, 4th edn, St Paul, MN: West Group.

Mueller, D.C. (1989), *Public Choice II*, Cambridge: Cambridge University Press.

Otsuki, T., J.S. Wilson and M. Sewadeh (2000), 'Saving two in a billion: A case study to quantify the trade effect of European food safety standards on African exports' (mimeo), Washington, DC: The World Bank.

Spruyt, H. (1994), *The Sovereign State and its Competitors*, Princeton, NJ: Princeton University Press.

Wilson, J.S. and T. Otsuki (2003), 'Food safety and trade: Winners and losers in a non-harmonized world', *Journal of Economic Integration*, **18**(2), 266–87.

4. Apples and oranges: comparing international experiences in regulatory reform

Martin Minogue[1]

This chapter considers the idea and practice of *policy transfer*; that is, the ways in which a model of policy practice (often labelled 'best practice') in one policy system is copied or borrowed by another policy system. This discussion can, of course, proceed on the basis of simple country comparisons (e.g. the USA and the UK, as in Dolowitz and Marsh, 1998) but the focus here is on how such transfers occur as between developed economy systems of governance and developing economy systems of governance. The specific field used to illustrate this issue is that of regulatory reform, though the discussion goes well beyond a narrow definition of what regulatory reform consists of into the wider area of governance and public management.

The area of study involved here is public policy and management, more specifically development policy and management. Both fields (public policy and management, and development studies) are difficult to pin down in disciplinary terms; and both can very profitably draw on the rich insights offered by several disciplines, outside as well as inside the social sciences. Making the link between regulation and the broader governance field immediately produces conceptual difficulties, as well as the usual problems that exist in making sense of undeveloped or half understood practice: notably such questions as the role of politics, the question of regulatory capture, what we think we mean by independent regulation, and the very idea of reform itself, with its inherent notion that there is a perfectible model, which can be converted into a best practice, if only we can agree on the model, and then implement it in practice.

These questions are increasingly at the centre of research into and analysis of regulatory reforms in developing economies. While existing literature has principally been in the economic arena there is a growing recognition of the significance of 'regulatory governance', not only as a limiting constraint on economic policy reforms in developing countries, but also as a necessary building block in constructing an appropriate and effective model for policy transfer in this field. Aid agencies that fund such reforms (World Bank, Asian Development Bank, UNCTAD, and bilateral agencies such as the UK's Department for International Development) are beginning to reflect on the reshaping of regulatory and competition reform policies in the light of developing research findings. Effective development policy is not just a matter of getting the practice right, but of getting the ideas right too; it is the combination of sound ideas and workable institutions based on those ideas that is needed for effective policy reforms. In attempting such analysis of regulatory reform in developing countries, it quickly becomes apparent that we face problems of definition, scope, comparison and measurement.

DEFINITIONS

In relation to regulatory reforms, there is a surprising lack of clarity about what constitutes sound ideas, not least because of a lack of clarity over accepted definitions of regulation: indeed, 'concepts of regulation are legion' (McGregor et al., 2000, p. 1). As Ogus makes clear (Ogus, 2002), much of the literature provides a formal and legalistic definition that focuses on the construction and application of rules, while for many economists, regulation is primarily the means by which private firms are constrained from anti-competitive behaviour. Corresponding to the legalistic approach is the traditional view of government as a command and control regime operating in a precisely defined public interest, while the second view leads to a focus on the way in which regulation creates the conditions for efficient markets. The definition offered by a leading analyst of European regulation of 'sustained and focused control exercised by a public agency, on the basis of a legislative mandate, over activities that are generally regarded as desirable to society' (Majone, 1996, p. 9) appears to take in both meanings, but is still too narrow since regulation is often derived from sources other than a legislative instrument, and because the definition still leaves a question mark about who makes formulations of what is regarded as desirable for society, that is, the public interest. Since 'regulation is seen both as a form of public policy and as a means of constituting markets' (Wilks, 1996, p. 536), we need an approach which on the one hand captures the multi-layered nature of institutionalised regulation, and on the other leads us into an exploration of the way in which 'the dark world of politics sullies the purity of markets' (McGregor et al., 2000, p. 2). Even the narrower approach concedes that 'because regulation redistributes resources and rents, politicians often use it to secure political gains rather than correct market failures' (Guasch and Hahn, 1999, p. 137).

At this point it is worth setting out in some detail an argument presented by Black (2002) because her analysis, while based on European and American literature and practice, raises many of the conceptual issues that this chapter seeks to assert as highly significant in dealing with regulatory frameworks and practice in developing countries. This also impinges on the policy transfer issues discussed later, for if there turns out to be considerable conceptual and indeed empirical variation in the treatment of regulation in developed economies, serious questions arise about the nature and viability of 'best practice' models of regulation based in those economies, but recommended for application in developing economies.

Black is primarily concerned with 'quite fundamental questions of the nature and understanding of regulation [and] . . . the consequent role of the state'. She judges that the answers given to these questions in the literature on regulation are 'at best contested and at worst incoherent', not least because 'once regulation is not seen as something tied exclusively or even predominantly to the state, it is not clear where its boundaries lie either as a social practice or as an academic discipline' (Black, 2002, p. 1). Black notes a range of meanings given to regulation, starting with 'the core understanding that many have' of control-and-command regulation, seen as 'regulation by the state through the use of legal rules backed by (often) criminal sanctions' (Black, 2002, p. 2). The well-known failures of this model are rehearsed: instrument failure, information and knowledge failure, implementation failure, motivation failure and capture failure. Black is concerned to counterpoint this model with one of 'decentred regulation', dependent on notions of 'complexity, fragmentation, interdependencies, ungovernability, and the rejection of a clear distinction between public and private' (Black, 2002, p. 3). The characteristics of this approach are that:

- Fragmentation of knowledge goes beyond 'information asymmetry' to the idea that 'no single actor has all the knowledge required to solve complex, diverse and dynamic problems' (Black, 2002, pp. 3–4). Moreover, information is itself a social construct, there are no objective social truths. Fragmentation of power implies that control and power are dispersed between a range of social actors, including the state. Therefore regulation will invariably produce unintended consequences.
- The form of regulation may depend on the attitude to compliance of those regulated.
- No single actor can dominate the regulatory process: all actors are restricted by the limits of knowledge and autonomy of others.

In short, regulation is a complex interactive process which is 'co-produced' (Offe, 1984, p. 310, cited in Black, 2002, p. 5). All actors have needs and capacities and 'solutions' emerge from a mutually dependent relationship. This complexity is further affected by changes in the public–private set of relationships so that 'Governance, and regulation, is seen by some to be the outcome of the interaction of networks . . . which operate in the absence of formal governmental or legal sanction' (Black, 2002, p. 6). A gloss here would be that this would often be the case, even in the presence of formal sanctions, since usually a whole set of interactive influences and relationships determines how formal authority is operated in practice.

Black, usefully for our purposes here, derives three 'textbook' definitions from the existing literature:

1. rules enforcement and monitoring, typically by a specialist public agency;
2. any form of direct state intervention in the economy;
3. all mechanisms of social control of behaviour.

Clearly the first two meanings involve state activities, and correspond to widely accepted meanings, although the majority of economists currently working on regulation would be caught under the first meaning. Equally clearly the third meaning is difficult to pin down because it has virtually no boundaries or restrictive limitations. Yet Black uses a telling illustration from the UK Better Regulation Task Force (an 'independent' advisory body linked to the UK Cabinet Office) which defines regulation as 'any government measure or intervention that seeks to change the behaviour of individuals or groups' (BRTF, undated, p. 1). In principle, this seems to cover almost any area of economic and social activity, both public and private, and it might be added here that the Regulatory Impact Unit of the Cabinet Office takes a wide view of its remit, covering both public and business sectors, the whole of European Union regulation, and a range of social activities such as health, education, policing and criminal justice (RIU, 2003).

But Black concedes that 'there is also frequently an implicit or explicit assumption that the target of regulation is an economic actor' (Black, 2002, p. 10) and argues that this is true even of the 'regulatory state' literature that is used to describe the shift in the style of governance from the direct provision of public services to their provision by others under government supervision. In contrast, other literatures broaden the social scope of regulation to 'any sphere of social action (for example, the family, reproduction) that employs a range of both state and non-state actors'; and to other factors such as social cultural norms. This 'opens up pretty much the whole of social science', and for regulation specialists 'a seemingly endless territory ripe for colonisation' (Black, 2002, p. 11). This raises the inter-related issues of intentionality and outcomes. Behind these lies the question: who regulates? By the narrower definitions of regulation, the main province is markets, and actors (including state actors) in the market. Black here alludes to Ogus's (1994) 'politico-economic' concept of regulation, and contrasts this with a 'politico-social' concept where forms of social behaviour are regulated (for example, dangerous dogs, dangerous doctors). She does not wish to go so far as to propose that 'social' or 'economic' forces of themselves 'regulate', but argues that these forces 'affect the outcome of the interactions that constitute regulation', and strongly endorses the benefits of a broad definition, commenting that the narrow economic-based definitions 'led to the . . . futile "regulation", "de-regulation" and "re-regulation" debates of the 1980s' (Black, 2002, p. 16). This dismissiveness might give pause for thought to those who are still conducting those debates.

Black approvingly cites Hood's 'cybernetics' approach (Hood, 1998) in which a regulatory system sets standards, gathers information and modifies behaviour. This applies whether design or intentionality exist or not. Social norms or culture are potentially as 'regulatory' as legal rules. Black interestingly suggests that the real test here is an empirical one; where regulation is effective, it exists; where it is ineffective it does not exist. Regulation ultimately has to be 'proved'. Functional definitions are merely 'de-contextualised, generalised abstractions', while what she terms a 'conventionalist' definition is 'embedded in current practices rather than abstracted from them' (Black, 2002, p. 19). Recognising that there is a danger that the broad approach to regulation may be so wide-ranging as to produce incoherence, Black now proposes a definition which re-introduces the notion of intentionality but decouples this from the state and from purely economic activity. Hence, 'regulation is the sustained and focused attempt to alter the behaviour of others according to defined standards or purposes with the intention of producing a broadly identified outcome or outcomes, which may involve mechanisms of standard-setting, information-gathering and behaviour-modification' (Black, 2002, p. 19). Black concludes that the question of intentionality differs according to how protagonists define the objectives of regulation. For economists the principal aim is the correction of market failure, but this discussion has now added in the management of a risk society and the achievement of social justice.

The problems created by confining regulation within a narrow definition are illustrated by an interesting comparison by Vogel (2001) of regulatory trends in the EU and the US over the past four decades. Vogel argues that EU regulation was relatively weak in the 1960s to 1980s, while US regulation was strong and authoritative; yet in the past two decades the positions have virtually reversed. Vogel suggests that the nature of regulatory politics, therefore, demonstrates convergence, with some borrowing by the EU of earlier American principles, and yet the two systems show diverse policy outcomes, largely because of differences in the two regulatory cultures about what constituted the types of risks to be regulated. For our purposes, two points need to be noted from Vogel's study. First, similar policy outcomes do not inevitably result from institutional convergence. Second, Vogel's study, focusing on two major arenas of regulatory policy and practice, gives relatively little weight to economic issues, but places considerable emphasis on a regulatory politics that reflects social concerns and values, as well as social perceptions (degrees of trust or mistrust) of government. This type of analysis lends support to Black's case for a broad rather than a narrow definition of regulation: the concerns and characteristics that dominate in Vogel's version of European regulation, for example, seldom appear in the literature on economic regulation. Yet the two have something in common: in both areas, the current pressures for regulatory reform emerge from past regulatory failures.

This review of definitions concludes, then, that there are alternative and therefore contested definitions. We are free to choose between these, but our choices are likely to be determined by disciplinary settings and preferences, rather than by some neutral process of agreeing on one 'best' definition. Economists will mainly choose a narrow definition that reduces the complexities to be handled and focuses almost exclusively on economic agents and economic outcomes. This leads to a stance on regulatory reform that deals primarily in ex ante interventions, since ex post interventions are much too complex to allow rigorous (read 'quantitative') analysis. Moreover, the focus will be overwhelmingly on economic policy issues rather than social policy issues, though it is no means easy to maintain such a clear distinction. For example, current regulation of GM crops in Europe is driven by social concern over food issues together with a public distrust of contemporary science. These values (together with other food related disasters such as BSE) have produced a political response that supports the most restrictive possible approach to regulation, that is, the precautionary principle. Economic concerns and priorities have been pushed well down the political pecking order (Moran, 2001).

This reminds us that political and social scientists interested in regulation can be expected to prefer the broader, more inclusive definition referred to earlier. This does not just mean that such an approach will restrict analysis to social issues such as health, welfare, protection against environmental risk and so on. Nor does it involve restriction to specific political arenas (the regulation of food, the regulation of medicine). If we take the most obviously economic form of regulation, for example the regulation of public utilities such as energy, water, and so on, the inclusive definition is still needed. At the policy level, the analysis of specific sectoral regulation, to be complete, requires consideration of the *processes* involved. Essentially, these are standard processes of public policy, which involve examination not only of policy design and decisions, but of implementation; while studies of implementation require consideration of *impact*, that is, of *results* and *outcomes*. Invariably, such studies demonstrate an implementation gap or deficit together with a range of unintended consequences that produce outcomes at variance with those expected or intended. In a textbook policy system an evaluative procedure would close these gaps and adjust policy objectives to learned experience; but in real policy systems this rarely happens. Generally a process of incremental adjustment takes place over quite long time-scales. As Hood (1976) long ago demonstrated, such adjustment is principally conditioned by political factors.

SCOPE

Recent literature on regulation in developed economies, more particularly in Europe, reflects this type of policy-based conceptualisation and has produced the prevailing terminology of 'regulatory governance', the 'regulatory state', and 'regulatory space' (see especially Majone, 1997, 1999; Hansher and Moran, 1989; Wilks, 1996; a more detailed survey of this literature is in Minogue, 2001). What are the implications here for the *scope* of studies of regulation? Put in the simplest way, regulation (within any of the meanings examined earlier) must operate within some sort of governance framework, which in turn becomes part of the necessary scope of enquiry. This framework will incorporate institutions and processes of both public and private decision-making, the assumption being that at many points the private domain is subject to control, intervention and influence by the public domain. This gives rise to some uncertainty about the precise scope of regulation itself, the problem being to distinguish it sufficiently clearly from the rest of what government does.

Hood and Scott coin the term 'the regulation of government' as one that links the 'regulatory state' and the 'new public management' state, defining a regulatory state as 'one that puts heavy emphasis on rule-making, monitoring and enforcement . . . rather than on subsidies, direct ownership or state operation' (Hood and Scott, 2000, p. 2). They concede that 'the link between "regulation" and other activities in government is admittedly a fine one' (p. 5), but assist us greatly by providing a definition of 'regulation inside government' as one that must satisfy three main criteria:

1. one public organisation (or part of it) is attempting to shape the behaviour of another public organisation (or part of it);
2. there is some form of arm's-length separation between the two (that is, there is no co-existing managerial or hierarchical relationship);
3. the regulating body has some formal authority for its regulatory oversight.

Hood and Scott suggest that the regulatory problems inside government are much the same as for independent regulation, particularly in terms of information asymmetries, relational distance, and compliance costs; but conclude that 'the effectiveness of that regulatory process will be a critical success factor for the working of a managerial state' (Hood and Scott, 2000, p. 13). Perhaps provocatively, they argue that this 'new managerial bargain' (p. 12) is not such a revolutionary change from traditional government as it appears at first to be: earlier structures may have been replaced but this 'has been in the direction of writing down the rules of the game and setting up more formal structures for applying them' (p. 17); and elsewhere they have pointed to the paradox that increasing regulation of the public sector has been accompanied by attempts to reduce the burden of regulation on the private sector (Hood et al., 1999).

Hood and Scott call for cross-national studies of regulation inside government, and have demonstrated the light that particular case studies might shed on the regulatory state in their analysis of the UK (Hood et al., 1999). Here regulation inside government is defined as 'arm's-length [denoting some degree of organisational separation] oversight involving the setting or monitoring of standards [shaping the activities of another department], and based on some element of authority [official mandate]' (Hood et al., 1999, p. 21). They point out that we are not used to thinking of government as 'regulating' itself, though in the last two decades, regulation inside UK government has become an expanding 'industry', as large as the institutions of regulation for the private sector. There has been an increase not only in size but also in formality, intensity and specialisation. Regulation inside government can be distinguished in five different ways: functionally, territorially, sectorally, institutionally and presentationally. It is functionally diverse since regulatory bodies belong to distinct regulatory 'families', oversee government activities in different dimensions, and use different toolkits. It is territorially and sectorally diverse since different regulators operate in different regions and different sectors. These regulators are diverse institutionally in terms of their mandated authority and according to whether they are rule-bound or formula-driven. They are presentationally different with respect to the degrees of limelight they enjoy in the media.

To sum up this section, regulatory reforms have created a new regulatory state, incorporating a range of new regulatory practices. All this includes regulation inside government, outside government, across national government boundaries, in hybrid institutions that cross the private–public divide, and mechanisms of self-regulation. If we add in the notion of regulatory space, with a focus on behaviour, motivations, activities, transactions, and relations of power and influence, we see that the scope of regulation is extraordinarily wide.

COMPARISONS

'We have only reached the point where we know what we don't know about comparative patterns' (Hood and Scott, 2000, p. 22).

Undertaking a case study of this depth and detail in a developed country, where substantial prior knowledge and information about governance systems and institutions are readily available is one thing; undertaking a similar exercise in typical developing countries, where such resources are relatively scarce, and often unreliable, is another. We do not even have much in the way of cross-national studies to give a solid grasp of what is often rather loosely referred to as 'international experience' of regulation. Hood and Scott, pointing to the absence of 'any systematic cross-national survey of regulation in government' (2000, p. 18) set out a range of research parameters for such an exercise that is daunting in its requirements, and in any case is aimed at comparison between developed countries. The rigorous benchmark they offer simply could not be satisfied in relation to developing country systems of governance.

Attempts to set up basic research frameworks for regulation and governance in developing countries are being pursued. Levi-Faur agrees that 'the general advance of regulatory reforms . . . is beset by temporal, spatial, sectoral, national and international. . .variations' (Levi-Faur, 2003, p. 2) and proposes that a range of methods to provide systematic analysis of these variations can be extracted from a literature (much broader than that attached to regulation) in international comparative studies. He argues that such methods will give a rigorous research framework for case-oriented analysis. Four methods are identified:

- a *national patterns approach*, comparing national systems, assumes that specific national characteristics exert a major impact on regulatory policies, variations being determined by the embeddedness of specific state traditions;

- a *policy sector approach*, comparing a specific sector (for example, electricity regulation) across national systems, may predict convergence within a sector even where there are significant differences between national systems;
- an *international regime approach* predicts that national and/or sectoral activity will be determined by variations in the strength and scope of international regimes (for example, in trade, finance, labour standards);
- a *temporal patterns approach* suggests that current activity will be best explained by the shaping influence of past events (war, crises, scandals).

While these are suggestive categories, Levi-Faur does not attempt to argue the relative merits of the four approaches to the analysis of regulation, implying that all are equally valid. Nor does he consider specific problems of their application to developing countries. It might be argued that a limiting weakness in this approach is that the choice of any one method would predetermine the findings (in terms of causality) since the researcher would already have decided what was the crucial explanatory variable (sector, nation, international regime, history); while common sense tells us that all of these will be influential, and cannot be neglected in any particular case.

MEASUREMENT

Economists place great emphasis on the need for rigour in methods of analysis. This essentially means quantification as a basis for some kind of modelling, so that models may then provide a template against which to set real-world practice. As with Hood's set of benchmarks for international comparisons, the problematic for this approach to institutional and policy analysis in developing economies is the nature of underdevelopment itself. Characteristically, not only are the institutions of governance themselves 'underdeveloped', but systems for collecting, verifying and presenting data and information are often deeply flawed. There is a real danger then of applying sophisticated tools of analysis to deeply unreliable data. This is not to argue that attempts at rigorous methodology should be abandoned, but to ask for great care in drawing inferences and conclusions.

Interesting attempts have been made to develop ways of measuring institutions in developing country systems. For example, Manning et al. (2000)

try to understand the dynamics of the public sector by measuring the ways in which officials perceive and respond to the incentives and constraints that might be expected to govern their institutional behaviour. On this basis they attempt to develop indicators of institutional environment in terms of the credibility of rules, the credibility of policy, and the predictability and adequacy of resources. They also attempt to construct indicators to measure the performance of public sector organisations, based on the organisational focus on results, and on accountability, and employee morale. Despite the acknowledged difficulties inherent in this exercise, the authors argue that conclusions can be drawn about what can be effectively be done by government, what can be done to make a particular group of people perform more effectively, and how some public sector organisations can be made to improve their performance.

Polidano (2000) examines the problems involved in trying to measure public sector capacity, identified as a gap in current approaches to comparisons of national performance. His 'policy-neutral' index, restricted to central government, concentrates on measures of implementation capacity and effectiveness, rather than policy prescription; but also sets out enabling conditions in the wider institutional environment in which the state operates, and which profoundly affect public sector capacity. For example, ethnic cleavages, political instability, economic crisis.

If we move from these general approaches to the field of regulatory governance, we find some attempts to measure 'regulatory capture'. Hellman et al. (2000) try to estimate how firms exert influence on the state. They analyse the relationship between state and firms in transitional economies within the framework of state capture, defined as the 'capacity of firms to influence the formation of the basic rules of the game (that is, laws, rules, decrees and regulation) through illicit and non-transparent private payments to public officials' (Hellman et al., 2000, p. 2). They assume that firms can interact with the state in three distinct, but potentially overlapping, ways. First, the firms can be the victim of the 'grabbing hand' state where public officials use their position to extract undue economic rents (bribes), called administrative corruption. Second, the firms can attempt to shape the legal and regulatory framework to their own advantage, called state capture; or third, without necessarily resorting to forms of rent-seeking, simply exert influence.

The authors develop a cross-country and multi-pronged measure of the extent of state capture by dividing countries into 'capture economies' where the purchase of state policies and laws is pervasive, and those where it is not. The analysis is based on data from the 1999 Business Environment and Enterprise Performance Survey (BEEPS), a firm-level survey to assess obstacles in the business environment across 22 transition economies. The survey has significant methodological advantages over previous governance and corruption indices in that it relies on the direct experience of firms rather than external assessments and individual perceptions. An index of state capture has been constructed on the basis of the firms' responses on the extent to which different forms of corruption in different categories have had a direct impact on their business:

- sale of Parliamentary votes on legislation to private interests;
- sale of Presidential decrees to private interests;
- Central Bank mishandling of funds;
- sale of court decisions in criminal cases;
- sale of court decisions in commercial cases;
- illicit contributions paid by private interests to political parties and election campaigns.

Finally, an index of the capture economy for each country is constructed by taking the average across all the categories. The authors argue that on this evidence state capture is a strategy of new and dynamic firms trying to compete with powerful incumbents who retain substantial control over state resources. However, state capture for private gains is clearly associated with substantial costs, both in terms of overall economic performance and the capacity as well as commitment of the state to provide critical public goods for the development of the market economy. Kaufmann et al. (2002) support this finding, pointing to a survey where well over 30 per cent of firms in countries such as Moldova, Russia, Ukraine and Azerbaijan reported that they had been significantly or very significantly affected by the prevalence of state capture in their industry.

This approach may be linked to a broader literature on governance–development relationships, which seeks to establish explanatory relationships between high quality of governance and public institutions, and growth in incomes and investment, and other positive development outcomes (e.g. Hellman et al., 2000; Kaufmann et al., 1999a, 1999b, 2000, 2002; Knack and Keefer, 1995). This literature goes beyond analysis of regulatory institutions into whole systems of governance and the relationship to levels of economic development. This is an approach with severe limitations, mainly that it is too highly generalised to produce adequate guidance to specific governance reform agendas; that it often incorporates untested assumptions, for example, that all countries want pluralist democratic governance; and that it fails to account for regional and individual variations. It is an approach that ignores more complex treatments of underdevelopment and its causation, so falling into the trap of asserting that poor development is primarily explained by poor governance, when it is at least as credible to argue that poor governance is a direct result of low levels of development. Such constructs appear to have too many serious limitations to provide an adequate guide to regulatory governance reform policies.

POLICY TRANSFER TO DEVELOPING COUNTRIES

This directs our attention to wider issues of policy transfer. The 'New Public Management' (NPM) model of public sector reform, or versions of it, has been widely imitated in developing countries, by the process we label 'policy transfer', principally through the mediating channels of the international and bilateral aid agencies (Common, 1998). Regulatory reforms are an integral part of the NPM model, specifically in being closely tied to market-oriented institutional changes such as privatisation and contracting. Consideration of the appropriateness for developing countries of developed country models of managerial and regulatory reform must incorporate a critical evaluation of the weaknesses in, and costs of, these models. Second, NPM entails a transformative conception of the state; while it is clear that the state in developing countries is much in need of renewal and reinvigoration, there is very little agreement on what kind of state this should be, or how such a transformation could be achieved. Should we be trying to reduce the scope of that state, or should we be trying to build up its capabilities, powers and resources in order that it may achieve the developmental objectives required by its own citizens? Finally, the most obvious issue is that of cultural difference. Not only are low and middle economies distinctively different in economic, social and political terms from rich economies, but there is considerable variation between national cultures within these broad categories. Taylor (2001) has pointed to the problem that in transferring an NPM model to developing economies, we are making a double transfer, from developed to developing state, then across the public–private boundary. Both types of transfer are culturally problematic, and Taylor stresses the sociological naivety of those who promote NPM managerial practices that ignore or conflict with the social and political dynamics of public service organisations and systems in developing countries, an argument strongly expressed also by a leading practitioner of NPM in developed economies (Schick, 1998).

A related problem arises directly from the condition of underdevelopment itself. It is clear that the economic, social and political conditions for the range of neo-liberal economic and political reforms favoured by the aid donors are rarely present in low and middle income countries. It has been suggested (Cook and Minogue, 2003) that the conditions in which the 'best practice' model of regulation is located include:

- a stable macroeconomic environment, to reduce uncertainty in economic decision making;
- a redistributive tax base, to fund strong social protection arrangements through a well-developed social security system;
- a rules-based system supported by an effective legal infrastructure and the rule of law;
- a transparent and accountable public policy process;
- a clear separation of administrative and political roles within a democratic constitutional framework;
- appropriate financial and human resources to ensure that regulatory agencies can work effectively.

Development agencies are still inclined to proffer models based on conditions and practices such as these in high income economies, then become frustrated when such models do not seem to work elsewhere, or receive little more than diplomatic lip-service. There is a reality gap here between donor ideas of best practice, and the actual legal, administrative, political and economic processes that exist in low and middle income countries. A good example is afforded by the principle of 'independent' regulation.

WHAT IS INDEPENDENT ABOUT INDEPENDENT REGULATION?

'Independent regulation' is a phrase much in use, but is one that appears to produce considerable misunderstanding. Coined in the policy systems of developed economies with apparently well-defined separations between economic, legal, administrative and political institutions, it begins to show strain even in this context when subjected to detailed analysis (see Hood and Scott, 2000). The developed economy literature on regulation generally conceives regulation to be independent where an agency is created with specified powers, and the means to enforce these powers. In many cases such agencies are administratively separated from executive government, as in the USA, or have constitutionally specified powers, as in France. The UK system of 'mixed' executive and legislative powers is altogether more ambiguous and productive of a range of agency types. But even in these developed country systems it is possible to argue that the political executive retains fundamental control through the power of appointment, and that political interventions will always take place in any area of regulation, that is, from time to time, politically sensitive (for example, access to and pricing of significant public services).

If we apply this more political analysis to developing countries we simply cannot expect the creation of arm's-length agencies that can hope to establish any real independence from the dominant political and bureaucratic institutions of the central state, especially where political stability itself may depend on the careful exercise of political patronage. In short, where regulators, and even in many cases judges, owe their positions to the political-bureaucratic elite, the possibilities for the exercise of independent judgement and action are considerably reduced, or may be non-existent. Since privatisation and regulatory reforms are largely concentrated in public utilities where there is a strong public interest factor, and therefore political sensitivity to both policy reforms and to regulatory practice, it is difficult to envisage what 'independent regulation' could possibly mean, or how it might be somehow insulated from overriding political considerations. This factor lies behind the faltering process of privatisation in developing countries, where the persistence of statist values, the resistance of labour unions, and the absence of necessary market conditions, mean that a clear separation between public and private interests and ownership simply cannot be assumed.

It is clear that national political and bureaucratic cultures themselves can and do hinder the release of economic functions from government control, making independent regulation unworkable. Institutional transfers from public to private control may merely offer new opportunities for clientelist patronage, as in the case of the Malaysian power sector, where financial gains went mainly to members of the ruling political parties. In countries such as Sri Lanka and the Philippines, continued political intervention in supposedly independent regulatory bodies has resulted in an acceptance that mechanisms are not working, and a lack of will from either side to do anything about this. In South Africa, privatisation reforms have stuttered in the face of labour resistance, and regulators complain about direct political interventions in regulatory activities.

This may at first glance seem a depressing scenario, but these characteristics may be better understood if we accept the complexity of a development agenda in which political leaders are constrained to place the needs of the poor above the requirements of economic efficiency or emerging markets. The choices involved here are political choices, so it is not surprising that governments so often intervene in nominally independent areas of the economy. This points to the crucial role governance systems play in economic regulation and economic development. In the long run, independent regulation may well be a desirable objective for both developed and developing economies alike, but in the meantime, regulators and donors need to work with, and not against, the political and administrative systems and cultures actually in place.

This may well mean a recognition that corporatisation of economic activities is likely to be a preferred and more effective variant on outright privatisation (Cook and Fabella, 2002) and that regulatory action is more likely to be operated from inside government, rather than in some externalised form. Hood and Scott (2000) see no problem with this, on the grounds that regulators inside government essentially face the same problems as regulators nominally independent of government, that is, information asymmetries, relational distance and compliance costs. While they see an element of autonomy as necessary, this is a matter of organisational separation and formalised authority, rather than positioning across a public–private line. On this view, regulatory reform in developing countries might usefully focus on improvement of regulatory relationships and efficiency inside government, and move away from the current preoccupation with independent regulators external to government. The approach through such methodologies as Regulatory Impact Assessment (RIA) may be valuable here, so long as RIA is treated as a strategic instrument rather than a merely technical tool, and is applied to ex post as well as ex ante situations. It will make little headway if it is merely offered as a perfectible model for the achievement of a preferred 'best practice' when its most significant contribution could be to assess 'regulatory deficit' (for recent work on RIA and its application to developing countries see Kirkpatrick et al., 2004 and Jacobs, 2004).

ACCOUNTABILITY

A central element in regulatory governance is the issue of accountability, since improved accountability and transparency are usually posited as the principal objectives of regulatory reform (assuming this to be defined as re-regulation rather than deregulation). The neoliberal version of accountability with which current regulatory reform is so closely implicated rests on evaluation of performance against pre-set standards or targets, and offers incentives to managers as well as some loosening of the traditional restraints. While financial and procedural accountabilities can be brought within such a framework (and improvements here would undeniably be a gain) it is a framework that sits uneasily with developing country governance (or substantive accountability: see Ogus, 2002). The degree of managerial and institutional autonomy involved, and reliance on a competitive model of public service delivery, assume the existence of market and civil society institutions which in many developing countries are more notable for their absence or deficiencies. Moreover, while the advantages of autonomous regulatory agencies standing at arm's length from state political control and intervention are obvious there are serious disadvantages too, including the reduction of political accountability, and fragmentation at the heart of governments already suffering problems of institutional incoherence. In the political conditions of developing countries we cannot expect significant public agencies to operate as though politics did not exist, as the practice of privatisation has already demonstrated (Ramamurti, 1999; World Bank, 1995). Moreover, giving to the managers of regulated services simultaneously more discretion and more financial responsibility appears to put in place precisely those conditions that may lead to increased corruption (Harriss-White and White, 1996), while giving more autonomy to regulators (by taking them outside government frameworks) is unlikely to reduce regulatory and political capture where constitutional, legal and public interest mechanisms of accountability offer no protection. As limited experiments with executive agencies in developing countries have shown, where there is a conflict between economic efficiency objectives and the internal dynamics of political governance, the imperatives of politics will usually prevail (Harrison, 2001; Therkildsen, 2000). One conclusion we might draw here is that accountability finally is underwritten less by formal institutions than by relations of trust, the argument that now makes the running in the regulatory literature in developed economies (Moran, 2002; Braithwaite, 1999). In this respect, rather than taking the negative, indeed contradictory, attitudes adopted by the aid donors to the social and personalistic networks that characterise the governance institutions of many developing countries (contradictory because political networks are 'bad' while civil society networks are 'good'), we could regard these relations of trust as a foundation on which to build effective regulatory governance.

CONCLUSION

The principal thrust of this chapter has been to rehearse the problematic nature of policy transfer from developed to developing countries in the field of post-privatisation regulatory reform. In the first place, the dominant governance reform model is itself a contested conceptual model, and even in developed economies has produced a contested literature of evaluation and appropriateness. Despite these disputes, reflected in internal debates and power struggles in the major institutions promoting neo-liberal reforms, it is this dominant model that is being 'transferred' to developing economies through aid programmes and by imitation. Problems of adaptation to different economic, social, political, legal and administrative cultures will inevitably arise, and must be the focus of a research agenda concerned to assess policy effectiveness in the context of the stubborn and complex realities of underdevelopment. These have been amply illustrated by Hyden et al. (2004) in a comparative survey of governance in 16 developing countries. They show that:

- most countries scored low on accountability and transparency;
- bureaucracy was generally incompetent, poorly performing, and politically compromised;
- access to public services was largely inequitable;
- judicial systems are slow, captured by the better off, and inaccessible to the poor.

These findings are a reminder of how much has yet to be done to create the essential institutional underpinnings for effective regulatory reforms in developing countries. It is a reminder, too, that the developmental state has an essential role; it will remain both the object and the subject of reform, and is likely to retain considerably greater direct regulatory responsibilities than is now customary in developed countries. Finally, perhaps, we should take note of the warning by Hood (1998) of the importance of cultural and historical variations between national systems, such that the attempt to apply one universal 'ideal type' is likely to produce perverse outcomes, or what he terms 'fatal remedies' (Hood, 1998, p. 208). Above all, the proponents of liberalising reforms need to be reminded that poverty, corruption and bureaucratic pathologies are the products rather than the causes of underdevelopment, and aid donors in particular must learn to accept that local political cultures will shape and mediate externally derived economic and managerial reforms, rather than being transformed by them.

NOTE

1. This chapter is based on a public lecture in the series run by the Centre for Regulated Industries, University of Bath, and given at University College London, on 12 January 2005.

REFERENCES

Black, J. (2002), 'Critical reflections on regulation', Discussion Paper No. 4, Centre for Analysis of Risk and Regulation, London: London School of Economics and Political Science.

Braithwaite, J. (1999), 'Accountability and governance under the new regulatory state', *Australian Journal of Public Administration*, **58**(1), 90–97.

BRTF (no date), *The Better Regulation Task Force*, London: Cabinet Office.

Common, R. (1998), 'The new public management and policy transfer: The role of international organisations', in M. Minogue, C. Polidano and D. Hulme (eds), *Beyond The New Public Management: Changing Ideas and Practices in Governance*, Cheltenham; UK and Lyme, USA: Edward Elgar, pp. 59–75.

Cook, P. and R. Fabella (2002), 'The welfare and political economy dimensions of private vs. state ownership of enterprise', *The Manchester School*, **70**(2), 246–61.

Cook, P. and M. Minogue (2003), 'Regulating for development', *Insights*, **49**, ID21, Institute of Development Studies, University of Sussex.

Dolowitz, D.P. and D. Marsh (1998), 'Policy transfer: A framework for comparative analysis', in M. Minogue, C. Polidano and D. Hulme (eds), *Beyond the New Public Management: Reinventing the Third World State*, Cheltenham, UK and Lyme, USA: Edward Elgar, pp. 38–58.

Guasch, J.L. and R.W. Hahn (1999) 'The costs and benefits of regulation: Implications for developing countries', *The World Bank Research Observer*, **14**(1), 137–58.

Harrison, G. (2001), 'Post-conditionality politics and administrative reform: Reflections on the case of Uganda and Tanzania', *Development and Change*, **32**, 657–79.

Harriss-White, B. and G. White (1996), 'Corruption, liberalisation and democracy', *IDS Bulletin*, **27**(2), 1–5.

Hansher, L. and M. Moran (1989), *Capitalism, Culture and Regulation*, Oxford: Oxford University Press.

Hellman, J.S., G. Jones and D. Kaufmann (2000), 'Seize the state, seize the day: State capture, corruption and influence in transition', Paper presented at World Bank ABCDE Conference, Washington, DC.

Hood, C. (1976), *The Limits of Administration*, London: John Wiley.

Hood, C. (1998), *The Art of the State: Culture, Rhetoric and Public Management*, Oxford: Clarendon Press.

Hood, C. and C. Scott (2000), 'Regulating government in a "Managerial" age: Towards a cross-national perspective', Discussion Paper No. 1, Centre for Analysis of Risk and Regulation, London: London School of Economics and Political Science.

Hood, C., C. Scott, O. James and T. Travers (1999), *Regulation Inside Government: Waste-watchers, Quality Police, and Sleaze-busters*, Oxford: Oxford University Press.

Hyden, G., J. Court and K. Mease (2004), *Making Sense of Governance: Empirical Evidence from Sixteen Developing Countries*, London: Lynne Rienner.

Jacobs, S. (2004), 'Regulatory impact assessment and the economic transition to markets', *Public Money and Management*, **24**(5), 283–90.

Kaufmann, D., A. Kraay and P. Zoido-Lobaton (1999a), 'Aggregating governance indicators', World Bank Policy Research Working Paper No. 2195, Washington, DC, World Bank.

Kaufmann, D., A. Kraay and P. Zoido-Lobaton (1999b), 'Governance matters', World Bank Working Paper No. 2196, Washington, DC, World Bank.

Kaufmann, D., A. Kraay and P. Zoido-Lobaton (2000), 'Governance matters: From measurement to action', *Finance and Development*, **37**(2), 10–13.

Kaufmann, D., A. Kraay and P. Zoido-Lobaton (2002), 'Governance matters 11: Updated indicators for 2000/01', World Bank Working Paper No. 2772, Washington, DC, World Bank.

Kirkpatrick, C., D. Parker and Yin-Fang Zhang (2004), 'Regulatory impact assessment in developing and transitional economies: A survey of current practice', *Public Money and Management*, **24**(5), 291–6.

Knack, S. and P. Keefer (1995), 'Institutions and economic performance: Cross-country tests using alternative institutional measures', *Economics and Politics*, **7**, 207–27.

Levi-Faur, D. (2003), 'Comparative research design in the study of regulation: How to increase the number of cases without compromising the strengths of case-oriented analysis', Working Paper No. 50, Centre on Regulation and Competition, Manchester, University of Manchester.

McGregor, L., T. Prosser and C. Villiers (eds) (2000), *Regulation and Markets Beyond 2000*, Aldershot: Ashgate.

Majone, G. (1996), *Regulating Europe*, London: Routledge.

Majone, G. (1997), 'From the positive to the regulatory state: Causes and consequences of the changes in modes of governance', *Journal of Public Policy*, **17**(2), 139–67.

Majone, G. (1999), 'The regulatory state and its legitimacy problems', *West European Politics*, **22**(1), 1–24.

Manning, N., R. Mukherjee and O. Gokcekus (2000), 'Public officials and their institutional environment: An analytical model for assessing the impact of institutional change', World Bank Working Paper No. 2427, Washington, DC: World Bank.

Minogue, M. (2001), 'Governance-based analysis of regulation', Working Paper No. 3, Centre on Regulation and Competition, Manchester, University of Manchester.

Moran, M. (2001), 'Not steering but drowning: Policy catastrophe and the regulatory state', *The Political Quarterly*, **72**(4), 414–27.

Moran, M. (2002), 'Understanding the regulatory state', *British Journal of Political Science*, **32**, 391–413.

Offe, C. (1984), *Contradictions of the Welfare State*, London: Hutchinson.

Ogus, A. (1994), *Regulation: Legal Form and Economic Theory*, Oxford: Clarendon Press.

Ogus, A. (2002), 'Comparing regulatory systems: Institutions, processes, and legal forms', Working Paper No. 35, Centre on Regulation and Competition, Manchester, University of Manchester.

Polidano, C. (2000), 'Measuring public sector capacity', *World Development*, **28**(5), 805–22.

Ramamuti, R. (1999), 'Why haven't developing countries privatised deeper and faster?', *World Development*, **27**(1), 137–55.

RIU (2003), *A Quick Guide to Regulatory Impact Assessment*, London: Regulatory Impact Unit, Cabinet Office.

Schick, A. (1998), 'Why most developing countries should not try New Zealand's reforms', *World Bank Research Observer*, **13**(1), 123–31.

Taylor, H. (2001), 'Human resource management and New Public Management: Two sides of a coin that has a low value in developing countries?', in W. McCourt and M. Minogue (eds), *The Internationalisation of Public Management: Reinventing the Third World State*, Cheltenham, UK and Northampton, MA, USA: Edward Elgar, pp. 174–95.

Therkildsen, O. (2000), 'Public sector reform in a poor aid-dependent country: Tanzania', *Public Administration and Development*, **20**, 61–70.
Vogel, D. (2001), 'The new politics of risk regulation in Europe', Discussion Paper No. 3, Centre for the Analysis of Risk and Regulation, London: London School of Economics and Political Science.
Wilks, S. (1996), 'Regulatory compliance and capitalist diversity in Europe', *Journal of European Public Policy*, **3**, 536–59.
World Bank (1995), *Bureaucrats in Business: The Economics and Politics of Government Ownership*, Oxford: Oxford University Press.

5. Regulatory governance and accountability: a UK perspective on improving the regulatory state

Peter Vass

INTRODUCTION

Corporate governance has been simply defined as 'how companies manage themselves'. Similarly, regulatory governance is about how regulators, and in a broader context, 'the regulatory state', manages itself. In this respect, therefore, we can talk quite properly of the corporate governance of the regulatory state. Equally, just as we expect directors of companies to treat corporate governance seriously, we should expect politicians to take regulatory governance seriously, and ensure that it is managed properly (Foster, 2005).

These straightforward statements immediately beg two questions. First, to what purpose is the governance directed, and, second, how do we judge whether the governance is good or bad? The first question concerns objectives, or desired outcomes: these provide the benchmark for answering the second question through performance evaluation based on comparing the actual outcome with the expected, hoped for, or forecast outcome. Yet there is another aspect of the second question that goes beyond straightforward comparison of plans with actual outcomes, but concerns internal control by mechanisms and processes that are put in place to help sustain or achieve good performance over time. Conformance (or compliance) with well-designed internal control processes facilitates good performance in terms of achieving desired outcomes (Banaga et al., 1995).

For company directors there are clear disciplines on them to have regard to good corporate governance. Typically, companies operate in a competitive environment. They might go bankrupt, and face the prospect of takeover if shareholders are persuaded that another company can do a better job with the resources than the incumbent management. In this sense, directors are held accountable by the customers and shareholders. But what disciplines are there on politicians and regulators to manage the regulatory state effectively? While voters could be said to be the equivalent of customers and shareholders for the services of the regulatory state, the immediate relationship is, for the most part, less forceful and transparent. For this reason, the state can abuse its monopoly power. The answer is to build up internal control systems in the regulatory state that focus on achieving effective accountability, and thereby create the discipline on regulators, and the regulatory state, to improve its governance and performance.

Characteristics of the Regulatory State

The characteristics of the regulatory state have been well analysed by Hood et al. (2001). They sought to answer the question why regulatory regimes varied, and why some seemed poorly aligned with the arrangements that might have been expected based on an objective (or normative) 'public interest' theory of the regulatory state. This model is typically founded in arguments about market failures, and the methods by which the state can correct for these (hence often judged to be econocentric in outlook), but can be generalised to include both market and non-market failures (Baldwin and Cave, 1999). 'Conduct failures' might therefore be a better description. Inequitable distributional outcomes resulting from the marketplace can be incorporated as a form of 'market failure' because the market has not delivered an outcome acceptable to the community, and thereby the regulatory state seeks to correct for it (e.g. by requiring equal opportunities for the disabled or by lump sum transfers of income through social security and welfare systems).

Hood et al.'s answer was found by asking the question: How does context shape content in risk regulation regimes? They identified three 'shapers':

- 'market failure' pressures (e.g. monopoly power, externalities, missing markets and public goods);
- 'opinion-response' pressures (e.g. public opinion);
- 'interest-driven' pressures (e.g. from organised self-interested groups).

All were found to have significant explanatory power for various extant regulatory regimes, thereby harnessing both normative and positive models in describing the distribution of regulatory regimes (Hood et al., 2001, Chapter 4).

The key question for this chapter is whether the distribution remains essentially static, and subject to all three drivers depending on the circumstances, or whether the regulatory state has mechanisms that promote the 'public interest' drivers and militates against the special interest and 'capture' drivers. The UK perspective is that promoting good regulatory governance through effective accountability processes provides those mechanisms, supported by an 'institutionalised' framework of principles of good regulation and internal checks and controls. Codification of the principles of good regulatory governance is therefore essential to creating a climate of expectations about regulatory conduct that provides a discipline on regulators to operate in the 'public interest', and to develop and reform the regulatory framework as necessary to that end.

UK PERSPECTIVES ON REGULATORY GOVERNANCE

The accountability of regulators in the UK has improved, is improving and will continue to improve. There are many reasons for this, and its effects, particularly over the last ten years, have been beneficial both in redressing the perceived imbalance between the regulators and the regulated with respect to the disciplines imposed on them to achieve good governance, and in improving regulatory outcomes. In short, effective accountability is necessary for effective regulation. It exposes regulators, and thereby undermines arbitrary and irrational regulation by providing a discipline on regulators to seek out, and apply, cost-effective regulation. It also helps avoid regulatory capture. This chapter examines issues of regulatory governance in the light of the recent report of the Constitution Committee of the House of Lords inquiry into the accountability of regulators, which provides a framework for current debates and developments.[1] The governance perspective of this chapter is developed, therefore, from UK experience but the principles are generally applicable, and hopefully persuasive. Nevertheless, their application internationally has to be mindful of the context of each country in question (Kirkpatrick et al., 2005; Minogue, 2005).

Context

The privatisation of the United Kingdom's utilities and network industries (water, energy, transport and communications) from 1984 onwards was accompanied by independent regulators; a new form of regulator to be at 'arm's-length' from ministers (in practice, the powers were vested in individuals as director generals rather than a regulatory authority). Concerns over the democratic mandate for the actions of these technocratic regulators, particularly where they were seen to be trespassing on policy issues, was the first reason for the development of a renewed debate on the accountability of the regulatory state, and its constituent organisations.

Not surprisingly, the regulated were at the forefront of promoting that debate (Vass, 2003). This debate was given a renewed impetus following the privatisation of the regional water authorities in England and Wales in 1989, and the UK electricity industry from 1990. The profits being made, and directors' rewards (including salary, bonuses and share options), grew so dramatically that by 1995 customers and the public generally (or at least their vocal representatives – politicians, the press and the National Consumer Council (NCC)), had become outraged. It was seen as a failure of the regulatory system, and the political consequence was that New Labour's electoral prospectus included a review of utility regulation, with major reforms in prospect, should they win power from the Conservatives in the 1997 election. If regulatory mistakes had been made, then clearly increased accountability was required.

Elected to power in 1997, the Labour government's review of regulation took place almost immediately (DTI, 1998). It turned out, in implementation, to be less radical than perhaps had been hoped for by many – some with their desire to reassert direct state and ministerial control over matters that perhaps had seemed to slip from their grasp with the introduction of the concept of 'public services – privately provided'. This was because, as with any government coming to power, the review gave the opportunity for deeper analysis of the issues than is perhaps available for developing the political rhetoric of a manifesto. New Labour found that the key objectives and mechanisms of incentive regulation (the RPI–X price rather than profit control system), which was policed by independent regulators, were well designed to meet many of the public interest objectives that they espoused. If there had been a failure, then it was a failure of the previous government, just prior to privatisation, in setting insufficiently challenging price controls for the water and electricity industries, rather than a set of post-privatisation regulatory failures. From this realisation came the one-off 'retribution' of the windfall tax; designed to be one-off to avoid erosion of the very incentives to efficiency that the government had found to be such an important characteristic of the regulatory system bequeathed by the Conservatives.

Given that the inherited foundations were found to be 'fit for purpose', the Labour government, having put the past behind it with the imposition of the windfall tax, proceeded to reform the system, in effect, by building on the extant foundations. The results were sometimes surprising, for example, more plans for privatisation and more introduction of competition wherever possible (in part to 'bypass' regulation); and sometimes they appeared to be window-dressing, putting in place reforms that were more political form than regulatory substance (although they were sacred cows for some of the critics of regulation), the three most notable being:

- regulatory boards to replace individual director generals;
- independent consumer bodies to replace the consumer committees of the regulatory bodies;
- promoting customer protection to the formal statutory status of a 'primary' duty on regulators (albeit that regulators had inevitably pursued this objective, it being the primary rationale for their being established in the first place. The original primary duties were retained which had been, typically, the requirement to ensure that 'all reasonable demands for supply were met' and to ensure that 'the regulated businesses could finance themselves').

Unfortunately, of these three, the first two, as noted below, may prove to have a 'downside' of undermining effective regulatory accountability, and hence effective regulation.

A clearer recognition that ministers have to take responsibility for setting social and environmental standards was, however, engendered, particularly as a result of the 'cost of quality' debate taken forward by Ian Byatt, the water regulator, in response to rising water bills driven by a succession of environmental directives from the European Commission. The outcome was to ensure that ministers considered both costs and benefits when setting standards. A new documented process was born – formal 'ministerial guidance' – which reinforces ministers' accountability for defining the 'outputs' to be met by the licensed or contracted private providers.

Real Progress: Better Regulation Not Deregulation

In one respect, however, the results of the review have been a radical development for the regulatory state. These are the 'process reforms' to improve accountability, and hence regulatory governance. Corporate scandals and collapses have contributed over the years to a progressive demand for improved accountability and internal control by company boards, culminating in 2003 with the Combined Code (of Practice) on Corporate Governance, developed first by the Cadbury Committee in 1992 (Financial Reporting Council, 2003). In a similar way, the lack of a demonstrably effective regulatory (and 'providing') state led to calls for improved governance, resulting in a wide range of codes of practice.[2]

Under the Conservatives, regulatory governance was presented as a purely 'deregulatory agenda', but this was inevitably found wanting because some market and conduct failures inevitably call for the attention of the regulatory state. The review of utility regulation was one mechanism for shifting the balance towards a 'better regulation' agenda – regulating where necessary and cost-effectively. It was complemented by a new institutional focus, most notably through the Better Regulation Task Force (BRTF), which published its five 'principles of good regulation', and by a recognition that good regulation requires formal processes, most notably articulation of the objectives and reasoning behind specific regulations (BRTF, 2003a). The BRTF principles of good regulation are:

- transparency;
- consistency;
- proportionality;
- targeting;
- accountability.

These reflect an emphasis on implementation and practice, and can be criticised for an absence of unifying regulatory objectives (such as coherence, objectivity and rationality) or for being opaque. Transparency is perhaps not overly clear (does it refer primarily to clarity of regulatory objectives, for example?), and is consistency about consistency with past decisions, equality of treatment (one person with another) or alignment of regulation with the fundamental objectives of the regulatory system? Hood et al. have also criticised them because 'better regulation principles often turn out to be a set of "contradictory proverbs" . . . without any practical guidance on what to do when one proverb clashes with another' (Hood et al., 2001, p. 180). Nevertheless, the principles have 'delivered' in providing an inescapable cultural context and norms for regulatory governance and practice, and 'guidance and interpretation' is delivered through the central departments of state formally charged with promoting better regulation (including the Cabinet Office, HM Treasury and the Department of Trade and Industry).

Regulatory Impact Assessments (RIAs) were to be the new process tool, and are set to become the foundation stones for regulatory governance and the effective accountability of regulators. To promote and coordinate this, the government established the Regulatory Impact Unit in the Cabinet Office. Accountability has, however, to be set in a context: accountability of regulators to whom, and by what mechanisms? Accountability has been a major concern of parliament throughout its history, and the House of Lords Constitution Committee, in the light of recent developments in the regulatory state, decided to hold an inquiry on these matters during its 2003–2004 session. Its report was published in May 2004, entitled *The Regulatory State: Ensuring its Accountability* (House of Lords, 2004a).

THE CONSTITUTION COMMITTEE'S REPORT

The Committee's report is substantial; a main report of 98 pages with two further volumes of evidence. It states its line of reasoning succinctly: 'Our starting point is that regulation is a means to an end, not an end in itself', and that 'Regulation can only be in the public interest where it serves a clear purpose' (House of Lords, 2004a, p. 5). The problem is crisply set out:

> We have to resist the danger of regulatory creep. . . . This regulatory tendency has to be checked, and the best means is effective accountability. Necessary, and cost-effective, regulation can be properly identified; unnecessary regulation can, and should be removed. (House of Lords, 2004a, p. 5)

The Committee notes in particular the changed context of recent years, identifying, first, the establishment of arm's-length independent regulators and, second, 'the progressive changes to the rights of the regulated in recent years, perhaps most clearly exemplified by the incorporation of the European Convention of Human Rights into UK Law' (House of Lords, 2004a, p. 6). This underpins the idea of appeals against regulatory decisions going beyond the traditional grounds for judicial review, and being allowed on 'the merits of the case' (which looks to the principle of 'reasonable' decisions by regulators, rather than the traditional view that a regulator's decision cannot be overturned unless it was so unreasonable that no reasonable person could have made it – in effect, irrational). Given the higher expectations of those exposed to regulatory decisions about their rights, the Committee observes that 'we can only expect the progressive consolidation of those rights and expectations into law and judicial review procedures to continue' (House of Lords, 2004a, p. 6).

The Committee asked 'who does what and why, and how?' The why and how questions were brought together in the conclusion that 'regulators should be accountable for effective regulation which meets rational, well-defined objectives' (House of Lords, 2004a, p. 6). This defines the purpose of their regulatory governance processes. Regulators must choose appropriate instruments to tackle regulatory problems; not 'sledgehammers to crack nuts'. The who does what questions, however, meant that the issue of effective coordination among regulators had to be addressed, since separate agencies might be established to tackle particular issues of concern to the regulatory state. A broad distinction between economic, environmental and social regulation could be discerned, and the former is reflected in the creation of economic regulators, such as the Competition Commission, the Office of the Director General of Water Services (OFWAT), the Office of Rail Regulation (ORR) and the Gas and Electricity Markets Authority (GEMA), the latter supported by its office, OFGEM. While environmental effects (externalities on third parties) and social concerns (distributional issues such as inclusion, access and affordability) typically require the close involvement of ministers in approving standards and taking responsibility for the 'democratically mandated' judgements involved, normally specialist regulatory agencies are created, such as the Environment Agency, and social security departments, such as the Department of Work and Pensions.

One of the key principles of the regulatory arrangements that accompanied privatisation was the 'unbundling' of the regulatory state, such that independent regulators were put in place at 'arm's length' from ministers (albeit independent within, rather than of, the regulatory state). The advantage was public accountability of the regulator, secured on the basis of their own statutory powers and duties. This gives confidence to investors that they will be protected from arbitrary interventions by politicians (political risk), although it has to be recognised that with independence came discretion (regulatory risk). The pressure for replacing 'individual' regulators (director generals) with 'Authorities' (regulatory boards) has come primarily from regulated companies, arguing in favour of more 'balanced' decision-making. However, given effective accountability mechanisms, it is difficult to see why the decisions of boards should in principle be any better than those of an individual regulator (who normally involved advisory boards in any event). The suspicion is that both governments and regulated companies might feel it is easier to work with authorities than with the high profile, and personally highly accountable, individual directors general.

The Regulatory Framework: Accountability to All Parties

The UK regulatory state is therefore a complex system that has separate regulators addressing different problems, and set within a process that needs communication between the regulatory bodies over time if balanced and cost-effective outcomes are to be achieved. The Committee therefore identified two consequences: first, that regulators must satisfy a '360° view' of accountability to all interested parties, included those regulated (not just formal accountability 'upwards'); and second, the need for a 'whole of government view' of regulation, whereby the government takes responsibility for ensuring an integrated and coordinated design for the regulatory state (perhaps best seen as the regulatory framework or 'blueprint'). The Organisation for Economic Co-operation and Development (OECD) has suggested that a particular department should be charged with this responsibility in order to promote consistency of practice (OECD, 1997, 2002a, 2002b). The Committee's diagram of its 360° view of accountability is shown in Figure 5.1 (House of Lords, 2004a, p. 20).

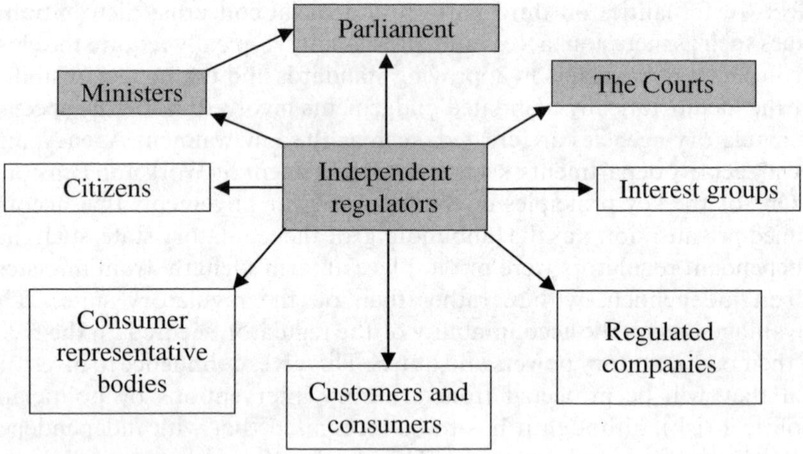

Figure 5.1 360° view of accountability

The consequences are clear. Regulated companies are accountable to regulators for the proper performance of their tasks, but equally regulators are accountable for the proper performance of their own tasks. Nevertheless, the Committee (as the shading in Figure 5.1 shows) 'drew a distinction between regulators exercising a duty to explain' – extending to all the bodies identified in Figure 5.1 – 'and being required to respond to demands made by those who gave them their powers or control of the legal application of their powers' (House of Lords, 2004a, p. 21). Ministers too are directly accountable in this hierarchy, either as direct regulators or as those responsible for operating the regulatory system, including appointing suitable independent regulators.

Parliament does not escape that responsibility either. As the Committee observes, 'improving parliamentary scrutiny is essential', but:

> it is not just a question of the answerability of regulators to parliament, but also one of the duty of parliament to ensure that its scrutiny is effective . . . Scrutiny at the moment is dependent on individual (select) committees deciding that inquiry is necessary into a particular regulator or regulatory decision. It is both fragmented and inconsistent. There is no means of establishing a coherent overview of the regulatory regime operating within the United Kingdom. We believe there should be. (House of Lords, 2004a, p. 7)

The Elements of Accountability

The elements, or steps, by which accountability is given effect therefore required analysis, and the Committee was right to note the insight provided by Sir Derek Morris's evidence (then chairman of the Competition Commission):

> I do think that there are three different and equally important levels of accountability. The first, to give it an epithet, would be transparency. People have to know what you are doing and how you have done it, and in trying to explain that and in being forced to explain there is an element of accountability. . . . The second is more penetrating. It is not just transparency. It is actually being questioned, if you like grilled, on what you have done and how effective have you been in doing it. The decisions cannot be changed but you can be cross-questioned. There, fairly obviously, the role of the select committees is paramount. The third level is where, of course, the decisions can be changed, and that is in our case through judicial review and to the High Court. (House of Lords, 2004a, p. 27)

It identifies the three key elements, all of which are required for effective regulatory governance and accountability:

- the duty to explain;
- exposure to scrutiny;
- the possibility of independent review.

From this it can be seen why the Committee concluded that 'we have not found a conflict between independence and accountability' (House of Lords, 2004a, p. 6). Accountability, like regulation, is therefore not an end in itself, but is there for the purpose of achieving sustainable, effective regulation. In effect, it is a control system – the control system of regulatory governance. The duty to explain incorporates the preparation of regulatory impact assessments (RIAs: Cabinet Office, 2003). As the Committee observes 'Properly done it reveals whether regulators have subjected their decisions to cost–benefit analysis' (where this should be taken to mean costs and benefits in their broadest sense) and 'These RIAs need to be conducted retrospectively as well as prospectively, to ensure that that cost-effectiveness is constantly under review' (House of Lords, 2004a, p. 7). The cost–benefit test is not only concerned with average benefits exceeding average costs, but in ensuring that, at the margin, the incremental benefit of having a standard at the chosen level is approximately equal to the incremental cost of the standard at that level. The methodology of RIAs has therefore to be carefully examined and periodically reviewed (NAO, 2005; OFGEM, 2005a, 2005b).

The Committee drew together these main principles and practices in a table and diagram of regulatory governance, and these are reproduced as Table 5.1 and Figure 5.2 respectively (House of Lords, 2004a, p. 23). They are succinct and self-explanatory.

Table 5.1 The factors effective regulation depends on

Good regulatory design	Control through the processes of accountability	Accountability for outcomes: regulatory performance
Macro (policy) The whole of government view: Encompassed in the regulatory (legal) framework of functions, powers and duties: the division of roles and responsibilities – whether by regulatory sector, theme or hierarchy, e.g. arm's-length independence versus direct ministerial regulation	**Duty to explain** (Provision of information and reasons for decisions) **Exposure to scrutiny** (Use of information – answerability and challenge) **The possibility of independent review** (Complaints, appeals and judicial review – particularly in respect of conformance rather than performance)	**Accountability to whom:** Citizens Parliament Government Ministers Departments of State Regulators Customers Consumers Regulated companies Other interested parties
Micro (implementation) 'Competent' authorities		

Figure 5.2 shows clearly how the process of maintaining an effective regulatory state starts and ends with parliament. The time dimension, shown by moving anti-clockwise around Figure 5.2, not only demonstrates the different, but interrelated, roles that the constituent parts of the regulatory state play at various stages during the regulatory cycle, but also draws attention to the importance of iterative arrangements between regulators if balanced outcomes are to be achieved. Hence, for example, ministers propose initial environmental standards, and the implications of these for costs and customers' bills can then be assessed by the economic regulator, and the implications for affordability taken on board by ministers in making their final judgements. Without this, systemic failure is likely, as exemplified recently by Tom Winsor's excoriating submission from the then Office of the Rail Regulator to the government's rail review (which followed a period of crisis in the rail industry and its regulation following a number of rail crashes attributed in part to the poor performance of the privatised network provider, Railtrack – now Network Rail), and which underlined

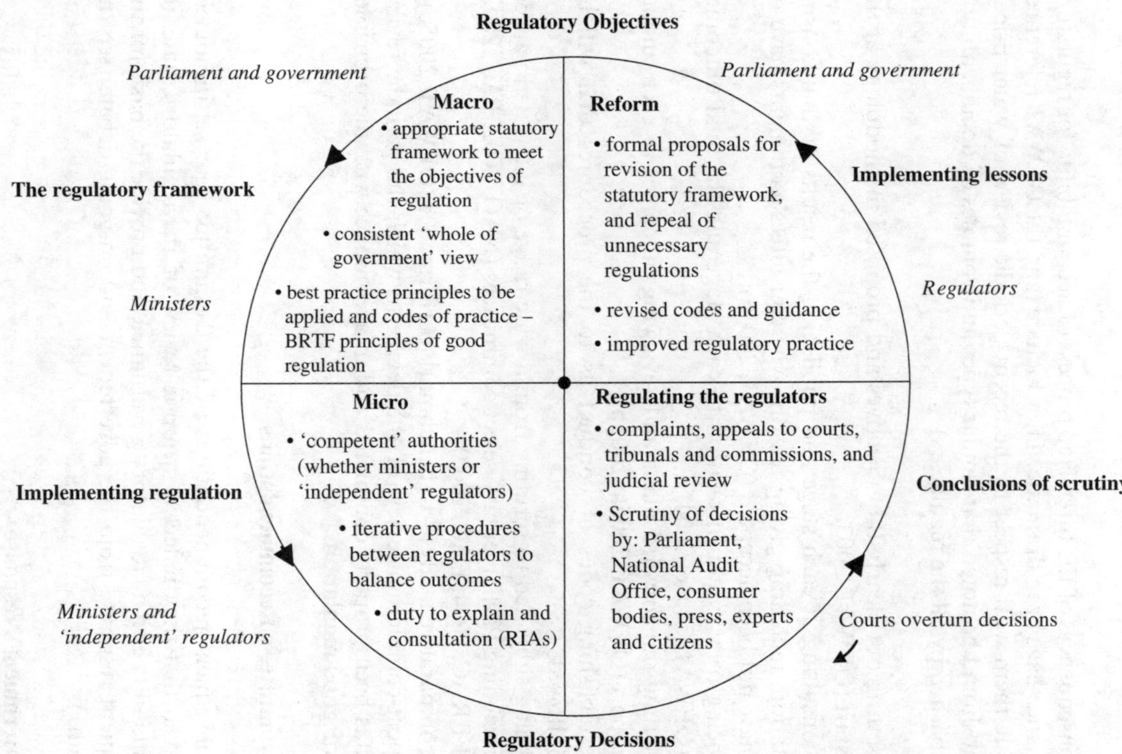

Figure 5.2 The circle of accountability through the regulatory cycle

ministers' responsibilities for properly defining the required outputs of the rail system (Winsor, 2004a).

Regulatory Governance in Practice

The consequences of the three-step process of accountability for regulatory governance have been dramatic. They include (and the OFWAT references illustrate them with respect to the recent periodic review of water prices, while it should be noted that similar types and volumes of documentation are published by all the regulators):

- setting out clearly the objectives and proposed methodology at the start (OFWAT, 2003a);
- consulting at each stage and publishing the results of that consultation, including giving reasons why consultees' comments have or have not been accepted (OFWAT, 2003b);
- being transparent in relation to each stage and the final outcomes (OFWAT, 2003c, 2004);
- setting out forward plans and reviewing outcomes in each annual report (OFWAT, 2005a, 2005b);
- establishing codes of conduct as to the procedures that will be followed;
- being subjected to scrutiny from a wide range of interested parties, including Parliamentary select committees (NAO, 2002; PAC, 2002; EFRAC, 2004; EAC, 2004);
- comparative analysis to benchmark performance (OFWAT, 2005c);
- post-completion review of the degree to which the periodic review has been properly conducted and in accordance with the principles of good regulation.

The Committee's Recommendations

The consequent recommendations of the Committee bear setting out in full, given that they reflect a synoptic review of the regulatory state, its accountability and its regulatory governance, and provide the basis for the subsequent response from the government and on-going debate (see the Appendix).

The government's response

Overall, there were no surprises in the government's response, given the interests involved and past decisions (House of Lords, 2004b). On a positive note, the general welcome for the report gives encouragement to those parties involved in trying to ensure the accountability of regulators that their work will be given progressively more attention, and this adds to the authority and effectiveness of scrutiny. Such bodies are encouraged to tackle their work with more confidence, and to demand the attention that it deserves. This helps provide (or redress) the balance between the regulators and the regulated.

Coherence – the 'Whole of Government View'

The government response is weakest in the area of 'coherence' of regulatory policy and process as a whole. Coherence is a principle that informed the Committee's report and the Committee made reference to it in the context of developing the Better Regulation Task Force's 'Principles of Good Regulation' (see recommendations 10 and 11 in particular). The OECD has placed considerable emphasis in recent years (its 'regulatory project') on the need for member states to manage the regulatory state as a whole, and to provide an appropriate institutional structure for doing that. The Committee referred to that work in its report (see recommendation 8).

The government accepted the need for better communication of the 'whole of government view' (para 34), which is welcome, but its unwillingness to change and enhance the role of the Cabinet Office as the primary coordinator could be said to be a missed opportunity in the light of the overall thrust of the OECD's recommendations cited by the Committee. While the machinery of government proposals and institutional structures often has pros and cons associated with it, it would be too charitable to suggest that the government's view was therefore understandable, if rather inert. The government's response that it should retain the existing 'dispersed' arrangements does not, on the arguments presented, provide a reasoned rebuttal to what should otherwise be considered good practice, being based on the 'one size should not fit all' style of argument (see paras 6 and 34–7 in particular).

Good examples of the weakness with which the government approaches the institutional task of projecting a 'whole of government view', are that:

- No one body is given overall responsibility for coordinating principles and practice, and being the advocate of efficiency and effectiveness in the regulatory state, unaffected by specific departmental interests (as, for example, the DTI has for certain sectors).
- Existing coordinating arrangements are not evidently transparent (see, for example, the recently established panel for regulatory accountability set out in the government's response, para 22).

- The principles of good regulation are not seen as important and generic statutory duties to be applied to regulators.

The arguments in the response seem weak in relation to incorporating the principles of good regulation (para 44), and in particular the second sentence of that paragraph:

> Government does not believe it is necessary to enshrine the principles of good regulation in statute, as a general rule for all sector regulators. Whilst the government is entirely supportive of the 5 principles of good regulation, as noted in response to the BRTF Independent Regulators Report, the principles are not defined in law, so are open to interpretation and potential challenge by judicial review. However, where government departments taking forward amendments to sector legislation consider it appropriate, in particular circumstances, to enshrine the principles within legislation, they will be free to do so. (House of Lords, 2004b, para 44)

Is this saying that the objective is to avoid potential challenge by judicial review, when surely the Committee's recommendation is to give the regulated avenues to improve the reasonableness test of judicial review because judges can refer to the duty and provide a legal interpretation of what the five principles mean? In any event, the principles of good regulation are being enshrined in statute (see, for example, the Communications Act 2003 and the Energy Act 2004).

It is not surprising that the government reports that the BRTF should not want to add to its five principles now that they are fairly widely known and used operationally. However, the requirements for coherence, objectivity and rationality are serious ones, and it is to be welcomed, following the government's discussion with the BRTF, that the BRTF 'will seek to incorporate the Committee's suggestions in the explanation of the 5 principles when the leaflet is next revised' (House of Lords, 2004b, para 33).

An interesting indicator of the overall problem of a lack of strategic leadership for the regulatory state is perhaps illustrated by the fact that the government's response to the Committee came from a DTI minister whose title was Minister for Energy, E-Commerce and Postal Services, which hardly indicates to the wider public a remit for coordination and consistency of the regulatory state.

Representing the Consumer?

Specific examples of incoherence might best be drawn from the development of policy on consumer representation, comprehensive access by the National Audit Office (NAO) to regulatory offices and appeals on the merits of the case.

The government privatised the utilities and network industries with independent regulators. These regulators acted to protect the consumer interest against the potential (or actual) abuse of monopoly power by the industries, and also acted in certain respects to deal with other forms of market and social 'failure' as required by the relevant legislation. The key role of consumer protection was not, however, as explicitly set out in legislation as it might have been (the legislation focusing on such things as the primary duties to ensure that all reasonable demands for supply were met by the industry, and that the companies could finance their regulated businesses). Unfortunately, these 'primary' duties, when contrasted with a 'secondary duty' of customer protection, led to a sense of secondary status for customer interests.

The government has sought to redress this perceived weakness since its review of utility regulation in 1998 with the introduction of, first, primary duties of customer protection (see for example the Utilities Act 2000 with respect to OFGEM and GEMA, and subsequent acts such as the Communications and Water Acts 2003), and, second, the establishment of 'independent' consumer representative bodies, drawing particularly on the model of the pre-existing, independent Gas Consumers Council. The latter policy established specific 'watchdogs' in each industry, most noticeably WaterVoice, Energywatch and Postwatch. In the case of WaterVoice and Energywatch, these replaced statutory representative consumer committee arrangements which had been an integral, but quasi-independent, part of each of the regulatory bodies for water and electricity.

Customer protection by regulators, and accountability for that role, is a key feature of the regulatory system, but at the present time the evidence, contrary in some respects to the above, indicates incoherence in regulatory policy. This is illustrated by the following:

- The Financial Services Authority (from 2000) and the Office of Communications (from 2003) were established with 'consumer panels' integrated within, but quasi-independent of, the regulatory body (contrary as of now to water, energy and posts). This integration is, however, set within a clear primary duty on the regulator (that is, the regulatory board) to protect customers (and hence represent their interests).
- The Department of Trade and Industry, during 2004, developed a new consumer policy (DTI, 2004a, 2004b).[3,4] While these are consultation documents, the emphasis is on potentially consolidating the independent consumer bodies into a prospective national utilities council (and perhaps the NCC could play a host role in this respect), noting that the provisions of the Water Act that will finally empower

WaterVoice were not due to be brought into effect until 2005/6. Also, the role of ombudsmen is given a greater prominence (as in the FSA and OFCOM arrangements).

- The rail review, where the proposals for the Rail Passengers Council in the government's rail white paper were not fully articulated in the context of this evidently ongoing policy debate.

It is unclear therefore why we should have had a policy of independent consumer representative bodies if the regulator is given a primary duty for consumer protection, and it seems that the government is implicitly recognising this policy conflict in its current proposals as set out above, with their emphasis on a revised approach based around the new 'consumer direct' arrangements and ombudsmen. The question for the debate is not so much which policy is right, but that whatever policy is chosen, it should be consistently and understandably applied.

Access by NAO and Appeal on the Merits

In these two cases the government's arguments do not seem to be derived from first principles (comprehensive access and rights of appeal on their merits), other than the acceptable point that there should be a regulatory cost–benefit test of proportionality related to whether there should be extended appeal rights as a subsidiary consideration to the main principle. It is in these two areas that the government's defensive stance seems least satisfactory, albeit understandable.

At present the National Audit Office (NAO) cannot audit and carry out value for money studies on the Financial Services Authority (FSA) and the Civil Aviation Authority (CAA). The special cases of the FSA and the CAA with respect to access by the NAO are argued against by the government purely on the basis of status quo rather than as the outcome of specific reasons which demonstrate that the general presumption of access by the NAO should not be applicable (see recommendation 20 and para 51 of the government's response in particular).

If independent regulatory arrangements are being established by parliament, then the general principle should apply that decisions made by those regulators, where material, are appealable on the 'merits of the case' (that is, a decision for which there is a demonstrable prima facia case that it could be judged to be other than 'reasonable'), and to an appeal body specified in the relevant legislation, being an 'independent tribunal' (see recommendation 22 and para 60 of the government's response in particular).

The government's response is of the 'curate's egg' type: good in parts. There are points that can be debated and rebutted. The important part of the Committee's report relating to parliamentary scrutiny is, as the response notes, for the House Authorities to take forward – but with a word of warning about proportionality, which is useful.

THE HOUSE OF LORDS DEBATE

The debate on the Committee's report took place on 2 December 2004, and gave the opportunity for the government, once again, to argue why it did not accept the most significant recommendations of the Committee (Hansard col. 609: Hansard is the official Record of the UK Parliament). The chairman of the Constitution Committee, Lord Norton of Louth, opened the debate, and had prepared the ground for some of his more trenchant remarks (Norton, 2004a, 2004b). Lord Triesman, responding to the debate on behalf of the government, referred to 'generic' characteristics of the regulatory state by drawing attention to the Committee's statement that:

> regulators have been established at different times and in different ways, but they share a basic model: a sector-specific regulator charged with a responsibility to operate under a hierarchy of statutory duties to achieve a range of public policy objectives. The statutory nature of each regulator's duties, coupled with their independence from government, underpins the successful operation of the regulatory framework. (Hansard, col. 610)

However, rather than focusing on the natural conclusion from this of the need for improved coordination and a lead department to sustain a consistent regulatory model, he chose, first, to question the breadth of definition of regulation adopted by the Better Regulation Task Force: 'Regulation may widely be defined as any measure or intervention that seeks to change the behaviour of individuals or groups' (BRTF, 2003a, p. 1). This, he suggested, is 'so wide as to encompass almost everything' (Hansard, col. 612). He then went on to suggest that as 'knowledge and responsibility is vested in the relevant ministers and department . . . It is crucial that responsibility and authority should not be diluted and disseminated by adding an additional layer of bureaucracy, with the attendant prospect of loss of coherence and clarity which that could entail' (Hansard, col. 612). New 'layers' would create the very danger of regulatory creep that the Committee sought to avoid, and so clear allocation of responsibility for cross-cutting work would ensure effective coordination (as, for example, 'the government believe that the Treasury and the DTI should jointly lead in formulating economic regulation policy and in ensuring that the regulatory framework is fit for purpose' (Hansard, col. 613)).

The other 'rebuttals' were dealt with quite summarily, stating that with regard to access by the NAO to the Financial Services Authority, 'it is worth noting that the FSA has no financial relationship with government or parliament, and it is not to be regarded as acting on behalf of the Crown'. Refusing to extend the right of appeal on the merits was driven simply by the view that 'the consequences seem to be that almost all decisions, particularly decisions on pricing, are likely to be appealed. . . . The processes themselves would begin to take so long that price-sensitive decisions of fundamental importance would take too long to get into the marketplace' (Hansard, col. 615). Neither of these arguments seems to be persuasive practical grounds for resisting the consistent application of core principles for the design of a regulatory state.

THE HAMPTON REPORT

The Hampton report, *Reducing Administrative Burdens: Effective Inspection and Enforcement*, was published by HM Treasury in March 2005 (Hampton, 2005).[5] Curiously, it takes forward for the government some of the agenda on improved regulation and accountability of regulators that the Constitution Committee's report had identified, but that had not been positively embraced by the government at the time. The report identifies the FSA as one of the UK's largest regulators (p. 3) – which should be publicly accountable for its effectiveness – and it focuses on generic frameworks in its recommendations to consolidate regulators: 'regulators should be structured around simple thematic areas' (p. 9). It puts considerable emphasis on the lead department role when it recommends a Better Regulation Executive (BRE). Indeed it states that 'no new regulators [are to be] set up without the approval of the Better Regulation Executive' (recommendation 25, p. 56). Of particular importance in this regard is the recommendation to create a National Regulatory Forum (NRF), to be coordinated (and chaired) by the Better Regulation Executive, and that it should include consumer and business representations, the National Audit Office and the Audit Commission.

As the report states (having focused on risk-based assessment): 'a regulatory landscape which adopts the approaches to regulatory impact the review suggests, which is consolidated, co-ordinated and prioritised, will still need strategic leadership to improve regulators' performance and consistency' (para 4.114). Its vision for the BRE clearly accords with the thinking of the Constitution Committee, it too citing the OECD's work: 'The OECD, in its most recent thinking on regulatory matters, recommends that governments develop a strategic centre for thinking and performance management of regulation' (OECD, 2002c). 'The review's proposed central body (the BRE) could fulfil that role alongside its work in monitoring regulators' performance. . . . The National Audit Office . . . would be the ideal body to carry out this task' (Hampton, 2005, paras 4.117 and 4.118, p. 76). Finally, the report would welcome the setting up of the joint Parliamentary Committee to scrutinise the regulatory state as recommended by the Constitution Committee (para 4.119).

Self and Co-regulation

The Communications Act 2003 incorporated a duty on the regulator to have regard to the principles of good regulation, but at the same time also requires OFCOM to promote self and co-regulation (which some might regard as just one regulatory instrument from which the regulator should choose when seeking to apply the overarching principles of good regulation). Yet if the government seeks to emphasise the deregulatory elements of a better regulation agenda (which is a notable feature of the Hampton report that set the regulatory tone at the start of New Labour's third term), then the question of terminology does need to be addressed if there is to be both public understanding and confidence in the process (NCC, 2000). Self-regulation by an 'industry' or an incumbent in relation to activities for which it has monopoly power will always be viewed sceptically, given concerns over potential abuse resulting from concerted actions or predatory behaviour. The regulatory state can only tolerate self-regulation in these respects where it demonstrably meets public purposes (that is, it substitutes for action that would otherwise be taken directly by the regulatory state). The development of 'co-regulation' is therefore not so much an agreement between equal parties as a delegated relationship, with the principal party being the public oversight body. In this respect, for example, the Advertising Standards Authority – an industry player – is carrying out functions delegated by, and on behalf of, OFCOM. Similar developments can be seen in the legal profession, where traditional 'self-regulation' (termed 'professionally led' regulation) is now to be overseen by a public oversight body, the Legal Services Board.

The new emphasis on promoting self- or co-regulation could, in some respects, be seen as contradicting the progressive decline of self-regulation since the nineteenth century in favour of public regulation. This debate has been well analysed by Moran (2002) when considering the transformation of self-regulation. The reconciliation perhaps is to see two complementary elements. First, a move 'upwards' from self- to co-regulation with public regulatory bodies, but with the emphasis of the public body being on systems control and accountability, so that the detailed implementation and achievement of regulatory outcomes can be delegated ('downwards') to industry bodies and private sector agreements. In this respect, the latter might be seen to be a form of regulatory 'subsidiarity', straddling the public/private sector divide.

CONCLUSIONS ON UK EXAMPLE

During the House of Lords debate, Lord Dahrendorf (formerly the Director of the London School of Economics) noted by way of preamble that 'Even among House of Lords reports, it stands out for its systematic character, the thoroughness of its arguments and the comprehensiveness of the evidence gathered' (Hansard, col. 596). The job it has done might best be described as having revisited the longstanding debates on accountability, and to have 'codified' the principles and practices into a set of conducts that can underpin a modern and effective regulatory state. There is strong evidence to suggest that the government is inexorably moving along the path to full implementation of the vision that the Committee's report has articulated, albeit that 'inertial' forces may slow down the arrival point.

Whether the cement for the new foundations will set is dependent, perhaps, on two key developments. First, that parliament takes this opportunity to focus its attention on improved scrutiny of the regulatory framework and the regulatory state as a whole (to which the recommendation of a joint committee of both Houses is addressed). Second, that select committees focus their attention on Regulatory Impact Assessments as the primary documentation for framing their scrutiny of regulators (and other interested commentators, including judges as part of an improved judicial review process). In this way RIAs will be forced to be 'fit for purpose' by preparers, and the proper balance between the accountability of the regulators and the regulated thereby achieved. This should also focus increased attention on regulatory accounts, too often an underutilised source of information and accountability.

The need to 'entrench' such institutional and process requirements should not be underestimated if we are to achieve overall effectiveness for the regulatory state. Clearly an important start has been made with the BRTF, as evidenced by its outputs (BTRF, 2001, 2003b, 2003c, 2003d, 2004a, 2004b, 2004c, 2005). The BRTF is now to become a 'Commission' with effect from 2006, adding to its authority. Equally, the European Commission is addressing these governance matters in relation to managing its own role as a regulatory 'state' (EC, 2001, 2002).

Only then might we be confident not to have a repeat of the rail debacle (and the danger of mixing roles, as with the integration of economic regulation with health and safety regulation, as has just taken place in rail, given the debates that took place at the time of the Robens Report; see Glaister, 2004; Robens, 1972). The Committee quoted from the evidence of Tom Winsor (the then Rail Regulator) about the problems of maintaining independence from ministers, given his clashes with the Transport Secretary, Stephen Byers, at the time of Railtrack being forced into administration by the government:

> It was an extraordinary episode. I had no expectation that the Minister would ever take the steps that were taken in relation to me. If it was expected that I should be intimidated, I was not. . . . I believe that for an independent regulator to give in to that political pressure, apart from being an irrelevant consideration as a matter of public law, or to resign would have been a very serious and adverse step for the constitutional position of regulators and the relationship between the state and the private sector in areas and in respects going far, far wider than the railway industry. . . . I think it is notable, and I claim no credit for this, that in the bill which is to be brought before parliament in relation to foundation hospitals, the title of the regulator is 'the independent regulator'. (House of Lords, 2004a, p. 41: and see Winsor, 2004b)

Attention to a standard regulatory framework could have both helped to avoid the rather unseemly institutional merry-go-round in rail regulation to date – notably the rise and fall of the Strategic Rail Authority – and helped the government to seek out the most effective structure to result from its review. This would have pointed to a clearer separation of roles between specifying outputs (ministers), providing services (with Network Rail responsible for infrastructure and franchising out rail services), and regulation of those services by the Office of the Rail Regulator either in terms of natural monopoly or of the competitive franchising process. The current policy has an unnecessarily complicated interface between the roles of the Department for Transport and Network Rail. Equally, with entrenched accountability mechanisms, there can be an adequate defence against the possible erosion of accountability that might result from 'faceless' regulatory boards and authorities, compared with the 'identifiable' directors general, when powers were vested in the individual regulator rather than the board.

Relevance of the UK Experience for International Application

The relevance of the UK's experience for the international development of regulatory governance depends most fundamentally on whether generically relevant principles and practices have been identified. If so, then we might have a template of fundamentals that can be mapped onto different cultural and institutional settings, adapted to their particular requirements, and then tested to see if the fundamental principles have been maintained. It is consensus on the fundamental principles that has to come first, before the development of law, processes and institutions in local settings through which the fundamental principles of regulatory governance can be given effect. Simply transferring institutional blueprints and processes, without the prior consensus on objectives and outcomes, is highly exposed to the risk of failure.

By focusing on the development of regulatory governance in the UK this chapter has sought to demonstrate four fundamental lessons. First, that effective regulation is dependent on effective accountability of regulators. Second, that codification of the principles of good regulation is necessary to create the right climate of expectations. Third, that institutionalisation of the processes of accountability has to be secured in order to ensure that the control system works in practice. Finally, that achieving good regulation and an effective regulatory state is an evolving process, where mistakes are made and lessons learned. For this reason the regulatory state must be flexible enough to adapt and develop in the light of the fundamental principles of good regulation.

NOTES

1. The UK Parliamentary system is divided into two Houses: the House of Commons, made up of democratically elected Members of Parliament, and the House of Lords (the 'upper house'), which, among other things, is the revising chamber that scrutinises proposed legislation.
2. The Independent Commission on Good Governance in Public Services (2004), *The Good Governance Standard for Public Services*, Office of Public Management (OPM) and CIPFA.
3. Department of Trade and Industry (2004a), *Consumer Representation in Regulated Industries, A Report by the DTI and HM Treasury*, July.
4. Department of Trade and Industry (2004b), *Extending Competitive Markets: Empowered Consumers, Successful Business, A Consultative Document*, DTI, July.
5. HM Treasury (2005), *Reducing Administrative Burdens: Effective Inspection and Enforcement*, Philip Hampton, March.

REFERENCES

Baldwin, R. and M. Cave (1999), *Understanding Regulation – Theory, Strategy and Practice*, Oxford: Oxford University Press.

Banaga, A., G. Ray and C. Tomkins (1995), 'A Conceptual Framework for Corporate Governance and Effective Management, *Corporate Governance – An International Review*, **3**(3), 128–37, Blackwell.

BRTF (2001), *Economic Regulators*, Better Regulation Task Force, London: Cabinet Office.

BRTF (2003a), *Principles of Good Regulation*, Better Regulation Task Force, London: Cabinet Office.

BRTF (2003b), *Environmental Regulation: Getting the Message Across*, Better Regulation Task Force, London: Cabinet Office.
BRTF (2003c), *Imaginative Thinking for Better Regulation*, Better Regulation Task Force, London: Cabinet Office.
BRTF (2003d), *Independent Regulators*, Better Regulation Task Force, London: Cabinet Office.
BRTF (2004a), *The Challenge of Culture Change: Raising the Stakes, Annual Report 2003–2004*, Better Regulation Task Force, London: Cabinet Office.
BRTF (2004b), *Avoiding Regulatory Creep*, Better Regulation Task Force, London: Cabinet Office.
BRTF (2004c), *Make It Simple – Make It Better*, Better Regulation Task Force, London: Cabinet Office, December.
BRTF (2005), *Regulation – Less is More: Reducing Burdens, Improving Outcomes, A BRTF report to the Prime Minister*, Better Regulation Task Force, London: Cabinet Office.
Cabinet Office (2003), *A Quick Guide to Regulatory Impact Assessment, and Better Policy-making: A Guide to Regulatory Impact Assessment*, London: Cabinet Office.
DTI (1998), *A Fair Deal for Consumers – Modernising the Framework of Utility Regulation*, London: Department of Trade and Industry.
DTI (2004a), *Consumer Representation in Regulated Industries, A Report by the DTI and HM Treasury*, London: Department of Trade and Industry.
DTI (2004b), *Extending Competitive Markets: Empowered Consumers, Successful Business, A Consultative Document*, London: Department of Trade and Industry.
EAC (2004), *Water: The Periodic Review 2004 and the Environmental Programme*, Environmental Audit Committee, 4th Report of Session 2003–04, HC 416, London: House of Commons.
EC (2001), *European Governance – A White Paper*, Com 428, Final, European Commission, Brussels.
EC (2002), *Communication from the Commission on Impact Assessment*, Com 276, Final, European Commission, Brussels.
EFRAC (2004), *Water Pricing: Follow-up*, Environment, Food and Rural Affairs Committee 19th Report of Session 2003–04, HC 1186, London: House of Commons.
Financial Reporting Council (2003), *The Combined Code on Corporate Governance*, London.
Foster, Sir C. (2005), *British Government in Crisis*, Oxford: Hart Publishing.
Glaister, S. (2004), *British Rail Privatisation – Competition Destroyed by Politics*, CRI Occasional Paper 23, Centre for Regulated Industries, University of Bath, Bath.
Hampton Report (2005), *Reducing Administrative Burdens: Effective Inspection and Enforcement*, London: HM Treasury.
Hood, C., R. Rothstein and R. Baldwin (2001), *The Government of Risk – Understanding Risk Regulation Regimes*, Oxford: Oxford University Press.
House of Lords (2004a), *The Regulatory State: Ensuring Its Accountability*, House of Lords Select Committee on the Constitution 6th Report of Session 2003–04, Vols I–III, HL Paper 68 I–III, London: House of Lords.
House of Lords (2004b), *The Regulatory State: Ensuring Its Accountability – The Government's Response*, House of Lords Select Committee on the Constitution, 12th Report of Session 2003–04, HL Paper 150, London: House of Lords.

Kirkpatrick, C., D. Parker and Y.F. Zhang (2005), 'Price and profit regulation in developing and transition economies: A survey of regulators', *Public Money and Management*, **25**(2), 99–105.

Minogue, M. (2005), 'Apples and oranges: Comparing international experiences in regulatory reform', CRI Occasional Lecture 13, Centre for Regulated Industries, University of Bath, Bath.

Moran, M. (2002), *The British Regulatory State – High Modernism and Hyper-Innovation*, Oxford: Oxford University Press. (See, in particular, Chapter 4 'Transforming Self-Regulation'.)

NAO (2002), *Pipes and Wires*, National Audit Office Report HC723, Session 2001–2002, London: House of Commons.

NAO (2005), *Evaluation of Regulatory Impact Assessments Compendium Report 2004–05*, National Audit Office Report HC 341, London: House of Commons.

NCC (2000), *Models of Self-regulation: An Overview of Models in Business and the Professions*, London: National Consumer Council.

Norton, P. (2004a), Professor the Lord Norton of Louth: 'Regulating the regulatory state', *Parliamentary Affairs*, **57**(4), 785–99.

Norton, P. (2004b), Professor the Lord Norton of Louth: 'Who regulates the regulators?', CRI Occasional Lecture, 8 September, Centre for Regulated Industries, University of Bath.

OECD (1997), *Report on Regulatory Reform*, Paris: Organisation for Economic Co-operation and Development.

OECD (2002a), *Regulatory Policies in OECD Countries – From Interventionism to Regulatory Governance, Reviews of Regulatory Reform*, Paris: Organisation for Economic Co-operation and Development.

OECD (2002b), *United Kingdom – Challenges at the Cutting Edge*, Paris: Organisation for Economic Co-operation and Development.

OECD (2002c), *Government Capacity to Assure High Quality Regulation*, Paris: Organisation for Economic Co-operation and Development.

OFGEM (2005a), *A Review of Ofgem's Regulatory Impact Assessments*, Oxford: Office of Gas and Electricity Markets, Regulatory Policy Institute.

OFGEM (2005b), *Guidance on Impact Assessments – Revised Guidance*, London: Office of Gas and Electricity Markets.

OFWAT (2003a), *Setting Water and Sewerage Price Limits for 2005–10: Framework and Approach (Periodic Review 2004)*, Birmingham: Office of Water Regulation.

OFWAT (2003b), *Summary of Consultation Responses and Conclusions (to Setting Water and Sewerage Price Limits for 2005–10: Framework and Approach)*, Birmingham: Office of Water Regulation.

OFWAT (2003c), *Overview of Companies' Draft Business Plans (for Setting Water and Sewerage Price Limits for 2005–10: Framework and Approach)*, Birmingham: Office of Water Regulation.

OFWAT (2004), *Future Water and Sewerage Charges 2005–10: Final Determinations*, Birmingham: Office of Water Regulation.

OFWAT (2005a), *Ofwat Forward Programme 2005–06 to 2007–08*, Birmingham: Office of Water Regulation.

OFWAT (2005b), *Annual Report of the Director General of Water Services 2004–2005*, Birmingham: Office of Water Regulation.

OFWAT (2005c), *International Comparison of Water and Sewerage Service – 2005 Report Covering the Period 2002–03*, Birmingham: Office of Water Regulation.

PAC (2002), *Pipes and Wires*, Public Accounts Committee, 50th Report of Session 2001–2002, HC 416, London: House of Commons.
Robens, (1972), *Safety and Health At Work*, Report of the Committee 1970–72, Cmnd 5034, London: HMSO.
The Independent Commission on Good Governance in Public Services (2004), *The Good Governance Standard for Public Services*, London: Office of Public Management (OPM) and Chartered Institute for Public Finance and Accounting (CIPFA).
Vass, P. (2003), *Accountability of Regulators, in Regulatory Practice and Design – A Collection of Reviews Relating to Utilities and Network Industries*, CRI Collections Series 2, Chapter 1, 1–16, first printed in CRI Regulatory Review 1994, Chapter 12, University of Bath, Bath.
Winsor, T. (2004a), *Department for Transport Rail Review (2004)* – Submission by the Rail Regulator, 6 May, London: Office of the Rail Regulator (ORR).
Winsor, T. (2004b), 'The Future of the Railway Industry Through Effective Independent Regulation', CRI Occasional Lecture 10, 1–26, Centre for Regulated Industries, University of Bath, Bath.

APPENDIX: RECOMMENDATIONS OF THE CONSTITUTION COMMITTEE (House of Lords, 2004a, 8–11)

The Overall Regulatory Framework

1. Independent consumer bodies should be obliged by statute to engage in open meetings and conduct regular surveys of consumers. This has resource implications which should be met out of public funds. Following a review of the budgetary arrangements for each regulator, an appropriate formula should be agreed for calculating this provision and applied to each of these bodies. We believe that these changes will enhance both the accountability and the independence of the consumer bodies. (para 69)
2. We are aware that the government is undertaking a review of consumer bodies, supported by the National Audit Office (NAO), and recommend that the review includes an examination of the relationship between regulators and the related consumer bodies in order to introduce greater clarity in the relationship, if necessary through a statutory provision common to the regulatory regime. (para 70)
3. We welcome the move towards more collective board structures, rather than sole regulators, as one of the principal mechanisms for improving the quality and consistency of regulatory decision-making, and urge that this should be the norm for regulatory regimes. To ensure that there is no loss of accountability we recommend that boards designate one of their number as the public face of the regulator in order not to lose engagement with the public and to perform the role of building confidence and understanding. Normally this should be the Chairman or Chief Executive. Where appropriate open meetings should be held as a means of increasing public understanding and confidence. (para 110)
4. Government should explicitly accept overall responsibility and accountability for regulatory policy and the regulatory framework, while devolving responsibility under defined circumstances to independent regulators. (para 122)
5. Ministers should remain responsible for appointing regulators, subject to Nolan rules, to ensure proper responsibility and accountability. (para 126)
6. Regulatory legislation should normally be drafted in the light of consultation with regulators to achieve clearly defined objectives. The duties imposed on regulators should be consistent with the overall remit of the regulator (for example, economic regulation). They

should make clear the underlying purpose of the regulator's role (such as consumer protection). (para 130)

7. Responsibility for environmental and social standards should normally remain with Ministers as the authority of a democratic mandate is required for decisions in these areas. (para 138)
8. The OECD regulatory checklist should be utilised as standard for legislation, regulatory decision-making and in establishing any new regulator. (para 142)
9. The recommendation of the Better Regulation Task Force (BRTF) that regulators should produce Regulatory Impact Assessments (RIAs) on all new major policies and initiatives has been accepted by the government and should be applied throughout the system. We also endorse the Task Force's recommendations, among others, aimed at increasing the transparency and accountability of regulators, including open meetings and agreeing a management statement with the sponsor Department. (para 146)
10. The BRTF should review its principles of good regulation to ensure that the principles of coherence, objectivity and rationality of approach are incorporated and signalled to the wider public. (para 148)
11. There must be a much stronger communication of the 'whole of government' view of regulation. We recommend that the government appoint a lead Department to be responsible for promoting effective regulation in practice, thereby co-ordinating the various roles currently played by a number of Departments, including HM Treasury, DTI, the Cabinet Office and the Office of the Prime Minister. Logically, the Cabinet Office should assume this role, possibly by expanding the remit of its RIA unit. Its responsibilities should mirror those we outline for a parliamentary committee in paragraphs 199 to 203. (para 152)
12. There should be consistency in applying regulatory models and requirements on a like-for-like basis. (para 153)
13. The move towards self-regulation should be encouraged and co-regulation should, where appropriate, be used as a preliminary to it. (para 157)
14. Regulators should have a statutory duty to have regard to the principles of good regulation and effective accountability. These should include self-assessment of their compliance with the same; the design of effective consultation procedures to engage interested parties; ensuring that redress and compensation procedures are clear and accessible; and incorporating the outturn of plans in their annual reports. They should also include the publication of the following:
    (a) their mission statements;
    (b) codes of practice for the conduct of their regulatory office;

(c) codes of practice for consultation (including the duty to summarise and accept or rebut consultees' comments, with reasons);
(d) their forward plans;
(e) the explanations of and reasons for their decisions; and
(f) all relevant material necessary for their production before and after RIAs. (para 169)

15. Regulators should adopt a structured approach to consultation designed to minimise the burdens on those consulted and to facilitate their engagement with either the principles or the detail as appropriate to the interests of those consulted. (para 173)

Exposure to Scrutiny

16. A dedicated parliamentary committee should be established to scrutinise the regulatory state. (para 199)
17. This should preferably be a joint committee of both Houses and should be given the necessary resources to fulfil its task effectively. (para 200)
18. We recommend that select committees consider expanding their terms of reference to include a requirement routinely to consider and react to regulators' annual reports, and monitor the use of resources. These activities would be in addition to the ad hoc inquiries they undertake from time to time. (para 202)
19. In order that parliamentary scrutiny by select committees can be more consistent and co-ordinated, it should be focused around the annual report and the published RIAs, and with specific attention paid to a harmonised whole of government view of regulation. (para 203)
20. The NAO should have access consistently to all regulatory bodies, including the Financial Services Agency (FSA), with a view to monitoring their cost-effectiveness and budgetary control. (para 212)
21. We welcome the expansion of the role of the NAO and recommend that the annual review of Regulatory Impact Assessments by the NAO be developed. In order to maintain the strict independence of the NAO and its scrutiny role, we recommend that this should not be undertaken as an agency of the Cabinet Office. These RIAs need to be conducted retrospectively as well as in advance, to ensure that cost-effectiveness is constantly under review. (para 218)

Independent Review: Improving Appeals

22. Appeals should provide an opportunity for the regulated to have their objections reviewed on the merits of the case, subject only to the

condition that the appeal body should have the clear ability and power to identify and penalise appeals designed to frustrate equitable regulation. (para 230)

23. Simplified systems of fast track appeals against regulatory decisions and arbitration should be developed for the Competition Commission and the Competition Appeal Tribunal, and made available subject to the agreement of each of the parties concerned. (para 231)
24. We further recommend that a Regulatory Appeals Tribunal should be set up to cover regulatory decisions that do not fall within the jurisdiction of either the Competition Commission or the Competition Appeal Tribunal. (para 232)

PART II

Case studies in institutional reform

6. Regulatory reform in developing countries: designing business set-up processes

Anthony Ogus and Qing Zhang

INTRODUCTION

Business set-up processes are important both because they create opportunities for governments to obtain information about, and where necessary control, commercial and industrial activities; and because, where the process is excessive, ill-targeted or exploited for private purposes, significant harm can be done to the economy. There are two main types of regulatory controls in the set-up process: registration and licensing (Ogus and Zhang, 2005). Registration requires the actor to furnish the public authority with specific information prior to being allowed lawfully to engage in the business activity. The officials merely accept the information and keep it on file; they do not have to determine whether applicants meet substantive conditions for engaging in the activity. In contrast, licensing is intended to test the suitability of applicants and/or their circumstances against substantive conditions and involves some degree of decision-making discretion.

As revealed in a World Bank study (2004a), developing countries tend, by imposing a larger number and a broader range of registration and licensing requirements, to regulate set-up processes for firms more intensively than developed countries and yet the social benefits generated by such heavier regulation are by no means clear. There may then be arguments for developing countries relaxing these regimes provided that the related public interest regulatory functions are not jeopardised.

The different characteristics of these regulatory controls suggest different possible deregulatory measures in developing countries. For registration requirements, a 'one-stop shop' system and/or online registration or data exchange, if available, can effectively reduce the number of registration transactions and the time spent on related processes. An applicant might then submit a single form containing all the information required by various agencies simply to a single agency (Sader, 2000).

Licensing systems may however be too complex for a one-stop shop system to work well, and deregulatory strategies need to be approached with caution. There are two main possibilities. In another paper (Ogus and Zhang, 2005) we focused on the first, abolishing the licensing requirements or replacing them with less interventionist regulatory techniques such as registration or ex post standards if the latter are better able to serve the public interest regulatory purpose. In this chapter we consider the second: where a licensing requirement is justified on public interest grounds, retaining it, but separating it from the set-up process.

Licensing and Set-up Processes: An Overview

When a licensing requirement constitutes part of the set-up process, it must be met before an enterprise can lawfully exist and operate in any respect. Usually, there is at least one procedure in the set-up process to verify that the licensing requirement has been met and thus the authorities are satisfied with the quality of market participants. In contrast, if a licensing requirement is independent of the set-up process, it merely requires authorisation for the particular activities that are to be controlled, and this does not affect the right of the firm to exist and engage in other business activities (Morisset and Neso, 2002). Where the licensing procedure is integrated in the set-up process, we call it 'set-up licensing' (SL); where it is independent of the set-up process, we call it 'independent licensing' (IL).

SL regimes tend to be more widely used in developing countries; IL regimes in developed countries. SL procedures can themselves be classified into two kinds: GSL (general set-up licensing) and SSL (sectoral set-up licensing) (Spall and Szerb, 2004). GSL refers to a licensing requirement imposed on all entrepreneurs before they can establish any kind of business. Some form of GSL regime is imposed in many developing countries (Devas and Kelly, 2001), typically for zoning approval, environmental impact certificates, and approvals relating to working safety, building, fire, sanitation, hygiene, and minimal capital requirements (Djankov et al., 2002). For example, a World Bank (2004b) database reveals that in Gaborone City, Botswana, as part of the application procedure for a trading or industrial licence, all firms must have their premises inspected by the health and environmental authorities to ensure compliance with minimum standards.

In contrast, SSL applies only to those entrepreneurs wishing to engage in specific sector industries. It requires entrepreneurs to obtain approval for a sector business from a sector licensing authority before they complete the set-up procedure. Although not identified as such in the World

Bank study, SSL regimes are often used in developing countries to regulate specific business sectors. Take the case of Costa Rica. All entrepreneurs, in whatever business, must go through at least six procedures, dealing sequentially with the Commercial Registry, Tax Authority, National Insurance Institute, Social Security Institute, Ministry of Health and Municipality (Jansson and Chalmers, 2001). But, in addition, an entrepreneur wishing to operate, for example, a restaurant must comply with the SSL requirement of obtaining clearance from the fire department before registering with the Ministry of Health. In the Philippines, SSL regimes govern, notably, retailers, wholesalers, and manufacturers of veterinary products and of pharmaceutical and food products, feeds and veterinary clinics, custom and real estate brokers, auto, electronic and telecommunication repair shops, and vocational schools (Legaspi, 2004).

LICENSING AND SET-UP PROCESSES: INTERESTING PRACTICES AND DEVELOPMENTS IN PARTICULAR JURISDICTIONS

Before evaluating these regimes, we first flesh out the description of the structure we have given by referring to some interesting practices and developments relating to them that have occurred in particular jurisdictions.

General Set-up Licensing Regimes in the Philippines and Kenya

In the Philippines, obtaining a local mayor's permit is required as part of the general set-up process; and, within that process, it is both the most significant and the most time-consuming (average at 21 days) of the procedures (World Bank, 2004b). Applicants for the permit must normally supply the following documents: a building permit from the Engineering Office for the construction of offices or buildings (if any such construction is desired); a barangay clearance (indicating that the village government approves the business operating in its area); a location clearance (if the business is within an approved zone area) from the Planning and Development Office; a certificate of occupancy from the City Building Office (or a certificate of electrical inspection from the City Engineering Office); a fire safety inspection certificate from the Fire Station of the Department of Interior and Local Government; a contract of lease or proof of ownership; a health certificate for employees and a sanitary permit from the Health Office; a Securities and Exchange Commission registration certificate; the articles of incorporation and a receipt of corporate community tax (for single proprietorship); a trade name from the Department of Trade and Industry; and a receipt of business tax payment (Legaspi, 2004).

These documents effectively represent the licensing criteria for obtaining the mayor's permit. Furthermore, most of these licensing criteria themselves constitute SL requirements. Since these licensing requirements apply to all entrepreneurs and all business sectors, they are GSL procedures according to our definition. In this case, the office responsible for issuing the mayor's permit serves to verify these GSL procedures.

The mayor's permit regime was criticised for its excessive GSL requirements and cumbersome procedures (Legaspi, 2004). Accordingly, some local governments introduced changes, including the computerisation of tax assessment and payment systems, shortening the process time for licensing decision-making and the reduction of an applicant's costs in transacting with various licensing authorities by relocating their offices in one area or establishing a one-stop business centre (Legaspi, 2004). The reforms lowered entry costs imposed on business proprietors and reduced opportunities for licensing officials to receive bribes. However there has been no general shift from a GSL to an IL approach.

In Kenya, before 2000, applicants wishing to set up a business had to demonstrate that they had complied with the planning, public health and safety requirements as prerequisites for obtaining a business licence (Abuodha and Bowles, 2000). These requirements constituted GSL procedures. They could cause lengthy delays and in many cases applicants were incapable of meeting the requirements (Devas and Kelly, 2001). For example, before being issued with a health certificate, entrepreneurs might have to wait for an inspection by health officials but few such officials were available to carry out inspections. Licensing officials could easily find some reasons for rejecting an application.

A reform in 2000 changed these arrangements (Devas and Kelly, 2001). The requirements concerning public health and safety are no longer imposed as a precondition of the (business) licence but rather on an ongoing basis: inspections are carried out on a random basis and, in the event of contravention, the law confers on the authorities the power to revoke the business licence on receipt of a written report stating that the business is jeopardising the community health and safety. It has been said that, 'regular and random inspections are more likely to be effective than the requirements for an approval stamp on a licence application every year. In any case, most public protection issues are already enforced – insomuch as they are enforced – through process separate from local business licensing' (Devas and Kelly, 2001, p. 386).

Set-up Licensing Reform in China

In China, nobody can lawfully operate a new business without a registration certificate from the Industry and Commerce Administration (World Bank, 2004b). If the proposed business is in a sector subject to a licensing requirement, the applicants must obtain this licence from the sector licensing agency and submit a copy of the licence as a supporting document in the application for a registration certificate (Registration Regulation of Business Scope of Enterprises, 2004). This is therefore an SSL regime.

Since 1998, the Chinese government has carried out some reforms of SSL regimes (Zhang, 2004). A number of licensing requirements have been abandoned. In addition, some local governments have altered procedures, involving some shift from SSL to IL arrangements, the use of parallel licensing or joint licensing procedures in case of multiple SSL requirements and a conditional registration certification.

In 2002, in order to reduce the number of SSL requirements and thus improve administrative efficiency, all existing SSL requirements in the Hubei province were categorised into two types: A and B (Hubei Provincial Government, 2002). Type A licensing requirements still have to be met before applying for a registration certificate and thus still constitute SSL requirements. They cover those business sectors affecting national, social and economic security, people's health and safety, exploitation of natural resources, allocation of public resource, and those sectors monopolised or exclusively controlled by the state. The remaining business sectors are subject to type B licensing requirements that can be met after business registration and thus belong to IL regimes. For example, in the agriculture and fisheries industries, after the reform, the sectors subject to type A licensing requirement include: the manufacturing of pesticides, the manufacturing and trading of veterinary medicines, and the purchasing, selling, domesticating and breeding of wild aquatics under first class or second class state protection. The sectors subject to type B licensing control include, for example: seed planting, seed trading, and the purchasing and selling, domesticating and breeding of wild animals under state protection (Jinmen Municipal Government, 2003).

In the case of multiple SSL requirements, parallel licensing and joint licensing procedures have been used to shorten the set-up process. The parallel licensing procedure requires different licensing agencies to engage in processing applications simultaneously instead of sequentially when the exercise of authority by one licensing agency does not depend on a decision from the other agency (Shanghai Municipal Regulation Regarding Adoption of Parallel Licensing Procedures for Business Registration, 2001). If an entry licensing agency's decision is dependent on a decision by another licensing agency, a joint-licensing procedure is used by some local governments.[1] Under this procedure, applicants submit an application and related materials in one transaction, pay a single fee, and obtain the necessary approvals from a single agency (Cui, 2003); *with the coordination of the single agency*, officials from the relevant SSL agencies are then required to meet and make their joint licensing decision.

Further, some local governments have introduced an experimental system called 'a conditional registration with the applicant's promise'.[2] Under this arrangement, an applicant wishing to operate a sector business subject to some SSL regimes can obtain approval from the sector licensing authority and then a registration certificate from the Industry and Commerce Administration even if the substantive conditions required by SSL regimes have not been verified by the sector licensing authorities (Hu, 2004). But these arrangements are subject to two conditions: first, an applicant must acknowledge the SSL requirements and submit a written promise not to operate the sector business until the substantive conditions required by the SSL have been met; second, the sector licensing authority must, within a reasonable period (usually three months) after the registration certificate has been issued, verify that the substantive conditions of the application have been met. If the latter conditions are not satisfied, the firm will be deprived of the right to conduct the business subject to SSL.

This conditional registration system effectively converts the SSL requirement into a registration requirement combined with an ex post standard. This arrangement can effectively reduce the applicant's compliance costs by shortening the time of the set-up process. The applicants do not need to wait for the verification of the licensing authority before they can commence their businesses. But it is worth noting that not all SSL regimes have been reformed in this way. Almost all local governments insist that those businesses related to explosives, dangerous chemicals and important public safety should still be controlled by the SSL regime.

We now compare the cost characteristics of SL and IL regimes and then consider whether the greater use of SL licensing in developing countries can be justified on public interest grounds, or at least explained on private interest grounds.

A COST COMPARISON OF SET-UP LICENSING AND INDEPENDENT LICENSING REGIMES

We begin by noticing important differences between the SL and IL procedures. Since IL is independent of the set-up process, entrepreneurs can choose to engage in the IL procedure before, after, or concurrently with the set-up process. What are the cost implications? To facilitate our analysis, we choose a simplified example, as illustrated in Figure 6.1. We assume that, under an SL regime, the set-up process consists merely of two consecutive procedures. One is the SL procedure (taking 20 days); the other is a registration procedure (taking 10 days), during which the responsible agency ensures that a copy of the set-up licence has been supplied, but has no discretion to reject the registration application once that copy has been scrutinised. If, however, licensing is required under an IL regime, an entrepreneur may choose to engage in the IL procedure concurrently with the registration process, which is also a set-up process. Then we have two parallel procedures: one is the IL procedure (taking 20 days); the other is the registration procedure (taking 10 days). For convenience, we assume that, in respect of matters other than procedure, the substantive conditions under the two systems are identical.

The principal costs can be considered in three broad categories: administrative costs, compliance costs and other, residual, costs incurred by,

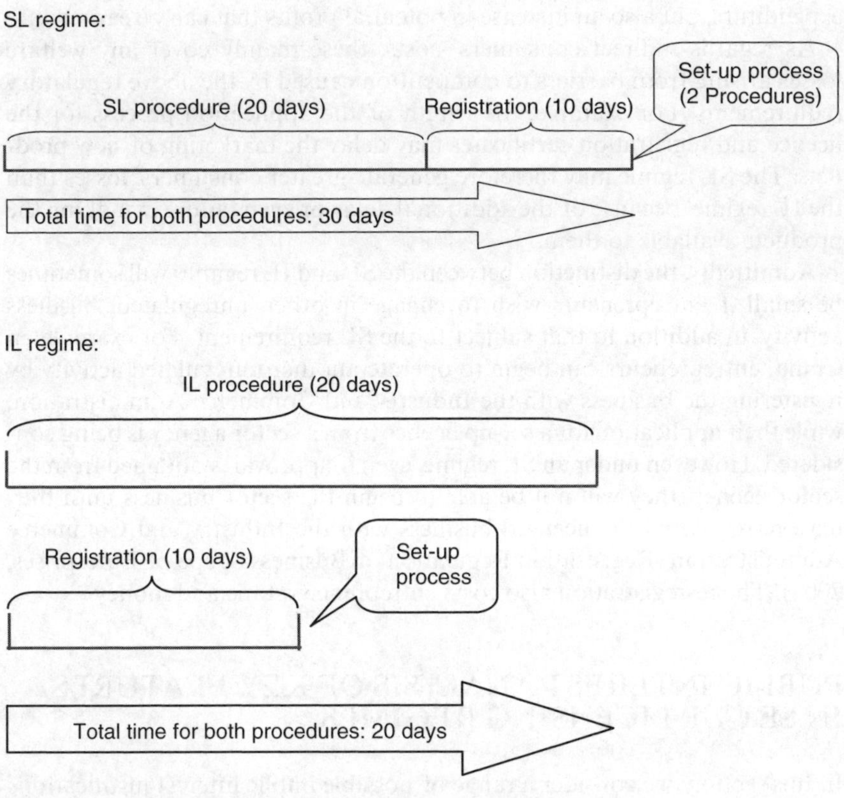

Figure 6.1 The set-up process under SL and IL regimes

respectively, officials, entrepreneurs and consumers. The administrative costs of officials arise mainly from the processing of applications and the inspection and monitoring of entrepreneurs (including detecting and apprehending unlicensed entrepreneurs). Under an SL regime, the costs of processing the applications can be somewhat greater than those under an IL regime, because the SL officials have the additional task of checking that a copy of the licence has been submitted.

The compliance costs to entrepreneurs include direct administrative costs in making their application, other capital investment in meeting both registration conditions and licensing conditions and lost profits resulting from the length of the application process (e.g. losses from delay and failure in marketing new products). Entrepreneurs incur different compliance costs under the two systems. If the SL regime is adopted, it takes entrepreneurs at least 30 days to complete the SL and registration procedures before they can lawfully begin the business. In contrast, under the IL regime, this can be done within 20 days. This shorter period generates not only a saving of direct expenditure, but also an increase in potential profits that can be earned.

As regards indirect consumers' costs, these mainly cover any welfare losses arising from barriers to competition caused by the above regulatory requirements. For example, the length of the application process for the licence and registration certificates may delay the marketing of new products. The SL regime may therefore generate greater consumers' losses than the IL regime, because of the additional delay or even failure in making the products available to them.

Admittedly, the distinction between the SL and IL regimes will sometimes be small if entrepreneurs wish to engage in other, unregulated, business activity, in addition to that subject to the SL requirement. For example, in China, entrepreneurs can begin to operate another unregulated activity by registering the business with the Industry and Commerce Administration, while their application for a set-up licence from a sector agency is being considered. However, under an SL regime, even if approval is obtained from the sector agency, they will not be able to begin the sector business until they have re-registered the licensed business with the Industry and Commerce Administration (Registration Regulation of Business Scope of Enterprises, 2004). The re-registration also costs entrepreneurs time and money.

PUBLIC INTEREST ANALYSIS OF KEY FEATURES IN SET-UP LICENSING REGIMES

In this section, we consider a range of possible public interest justifications for the two types of SL regimes, GSL and SSL, relative to IL regimes.

Justifications for Preferring General Set-up Licensing to Independent Licensing Regimes?

A public interest analysis of GSL regimes mainly involves choosing between an ex ante licensing requirement and regulation that does not control entry but rather is applied ex post, including information regulation (mandatory disclose) and/or ongoing performance standards (Ogus and Zhang, 2005). Few GSL regimes can be justified on public interest grounds since it is almost impossible to identify a licensing requirement appropriate for all sectors, all firms and all activities. To elaborate, the condition for the licensing system to be justified is $C < PL$ where C denotes costs additional to those that would have been incurred with an ex post system, notably the costs of ex ante scrutiny required for the licensing process, P represents the probability of the losses occurring in the absence of such scrutiny and L is the losses that the scrutiny would prevent.

In the light of this reasoning, a licensing requirement can be justified only in some specific business sectors where there is a high value for P and/or for L. For example, a new enterprise may decide to put its business place in a leased office of a building that has passed all fire safety inspections before its completion, and the business in that office involves no significant fire risk; it therefore makes no sense to oblige the new enterprise's office to undergo another fire inspection unless new decoration or an alteration generates significant fire risks. An efficient regulatory system would apply the fire safety licensing requirement only to those business activities with high fire risks, for example running a theatre.

To take this analysis further, we must consider the relative capacity of ex ante licensing regimes and their ex post alternatives to deter activities involving substantial risks. In many cases, even if, for example, there may be substantial health risks caused by employees, usually they cannot be effectively prevented at an ex ante stage; reliance must be placed on ex post control, such as ongoing health examinations to monitor the employees' health condition.

Let us examine another popular GSL example involving the minimal capital requirement imposed on firms. It has been suggested that this requirement aims to protect creditors from the opportunism of some shareholders, especially where they might exploit limited liability (Pistor et al., 2002). However, it is doubtful whether the ex ante minimal capital condition efficiently meets this aim. Opportunist shareholders can easily evade the requirement if they are determined to do so (Jenkins Committees, 1962). For example, they can simply borrow money to meet the condition at the time of registration and then repay it. Moreover, the high compliance costs caused by the requirement can make the corporate form less attractive for small enterprises (Freedman, 1994) or induce them to misrepresent finances to obtain registration. It has been reported that of 201 enterprises inspected by the Shenzhen Municipal Industry and Commerce Bureau (China) in April 1998, at least 130 had forged their investment verification certificate, in order to meet the minimal capital requirement (Sun, 2003). If the market mechanisms or ex post remedies, whether civil remedies or criminal sanctions, are able to prevent or reduce this opportunism at less cost, then the minimal capital requirement as a licensing condition might not be justified. The same reasoning can also be applied to other GSL requirements of public safety and health, such as those imposed in Gaborone City, Botswana.

This analysis reveals the difficulty of justifying GSL requirements. It also lends support to the reforms that we have seen have occurred in Kenya; and it might suggest that the reforms undertaken in the Philippines could be extended by a more general shift from the GSL to the IL approach.

Justifications for Preferring Sectoral Set-up Licensing to Independent Licensing Regimes?

Improving compliance?

For convenience, we assume that, in terms of generating benefits, the SSL and IL regimes would be equally competent in meeting their regulatory aims, for example, reducing health risks, if there were perfect compliance. However, many developing countries are often afflicted by weak regulatory enforcement capacity and the informal economy is typically large and growing (Schneider, 2002). The average size of the informal economy, as a percentage of official GNI in the year 2000, in developing countries was 41 per cent, in transition countries 38 per cent and in OECD countries 18 per cent (Schneider, 2002). There is evidence of large numbers of unlicensed traders operating in the informal economy in some countries (Suhir and Kovach, 2003). For example, it is estimated that there are 30,000–40,000 unlicensed taxis alongside 67,000 licensed taxis in Beijing (Yang, 2004).

As a solution, better regulatory enforcement is often advocated. According to the familiar Becker (1968) model, enforcement may be problematic if potential offenders perceive that formal sanctions and other losses incurred as a consequence of apprehension and condemnation for regulatory contraventions, when discounted by the probability of apprehension and determination of liability, are exceeded by the utility they derive from the contravention. The condition can be expressed by the formula $PD < U$, where P is the potential offender's perceived probability of apprehension and condemnation by a public agency, D represents the costs imposed on the offender, and *U* denotes the latter's perceived own benefits derived from the contravention.

When a licensing requirement is designed as set-up licensing, its enforcement can, at least in theory, be verified by one agency responsible for subsequent procedures. It might be argued that, in comparison with an IL regime, using an SSL system can significantly enhance the value of *P*, the probability of detecting the unlicensed activities;[3] and perhaps the argument has influenced regulatory policy in some countries. Take, for example, the Chinese reforms described above, which involve shifts from SSL to IL requirements. Although the Chinese government has not declared explicitly that type A licensing requirements subject to the SSL regime must generate better compliance than type B licensing requirements subject to the IL regime, some comparison of the sectors governed by the different systems may allow us to draw this inference. Those within the agriculture and fisheries industries subject to type A licensing requirements would generate much larger losses than those subject to type B licensing control, should the regime be subject to inadequate monitoring and enforcement. For example, low quality pesticides might kill people, whereas low quality seeds are likely to lead only to financial losses.

In addition, the concern for ensuring good compliance might help to explain the reluctance of many local governments to apply the conditional registration regime to those businesses involving explosives, dangerous chemicals and important risks to public safety. Perhaps the local governments take the view that SSL regimes would be able to achieve better compliance than the ex post standards arrangements used for conditional registration, and poor compliance by such businesses would generate substantial losses.

However, further consideration suggests that this compliance argument is somewhat problematic. It seemingly assumes that entrepreneurs always complete the set-up process before engaging in any business, which is often not true in practice. The verification procedure designed for SSL regimes will play no role if an entrepreneur decides not to engage in the set-up process, preferring simply to join the underground economy. More entrepreneurs are likely to behave in this way under an SSL regime than under an IL regime, because of the higher compliance costs incurred. Thus the benefits of participating in the informal economy, denoted as *U*, are increased substantially since more costs can be saved by avoiding the set-up process in an SSL regime. According to a survey in 2002, in Shenzhen city, China, there were more than 8,000 business proprietors who operated in the informal economy, without a registration certificate (Wang, 2004 who argues that one major reason for this phenomenon was the existence of SSL regimes).

Let us return to the simplified example in Figure 6.1 and assume there are a number of applicants wishing to operate a sector business subject to the licensing control. Under an SSL regime, applicants have, in theory, three options. Some may go through the whole set-up process, including the SSL licensing and registration procedures (option SSL/1). Some may complete the SSL procedure but not the registration procedure (option SSL/2). However, it is reasonable to assume that an applicant will complete registration once the licensing application has been approved, since the marginal additional costs of doing this are low and the marginal benefits (e.g. lawfully engaging in business) may be high. Finally, due to high entry costs, some applicants may decide not to engage in any procedure and simply operate in the informal economy; or their application for a set-up licence is rejected with the same outcome (option SSL/3). Analogously, under an IL regime, some applicants may complete both the IL and registration procedures (option IL/1); some may complete the registration procedure but not the IL procedure (option IL/2); some may finish the IL procedure but fail to register (option IL/3 – we assume that this will not be chosen because of the low marginal costs of registration and its high marginal benefits); and some will not engage in any procedure but simply operate in the informal economy (option IL/4).

We now consider whether fewer applicants are likely to complete both licensing and registration procedures under an IL regime compared to an SSL regime. We use Figure 6.2 to illustrate our analysis. Some applicants choosing option SSL/3 (avoiding both licensing and registration procedures) would probably decide not to choose option IL/4 (avoiding both procedures) under an IL regime, but rather shift to option IL/1 or IL/2. This is because the benefits to those applicants of avoiding both licensing and registration procedures under an IL regime (saved compliance costs) are less than under an SSL regime. The shift might lead to better regulatory compliance under an IL regime than under an SSL regime. On the other hand, some applicants choosing option SSL/1 would probably decide not to comply with the regulatory requirement under the IL regime, since, to them, the perceived probability of apprehending their contraventions is reduced, owing to the abolition of the verification procedure.

At first glance, it might seem that, under the IL regime, some applicants are likely to complete the registration procedure without attempting to satisfy the licensing requirement; and that this cannot happen under an SSL regime. This would mean that those applicants choosing option SSL/1 now have a new option, IL/2. However, there are arguments why these applicants might not shift to option IL/4: avoiding both procedures is likely to generate fewer benefits (expressed as a smaller *U* figure) under an IL regime compared to an SSL regime; but the perceived probability of apprehension

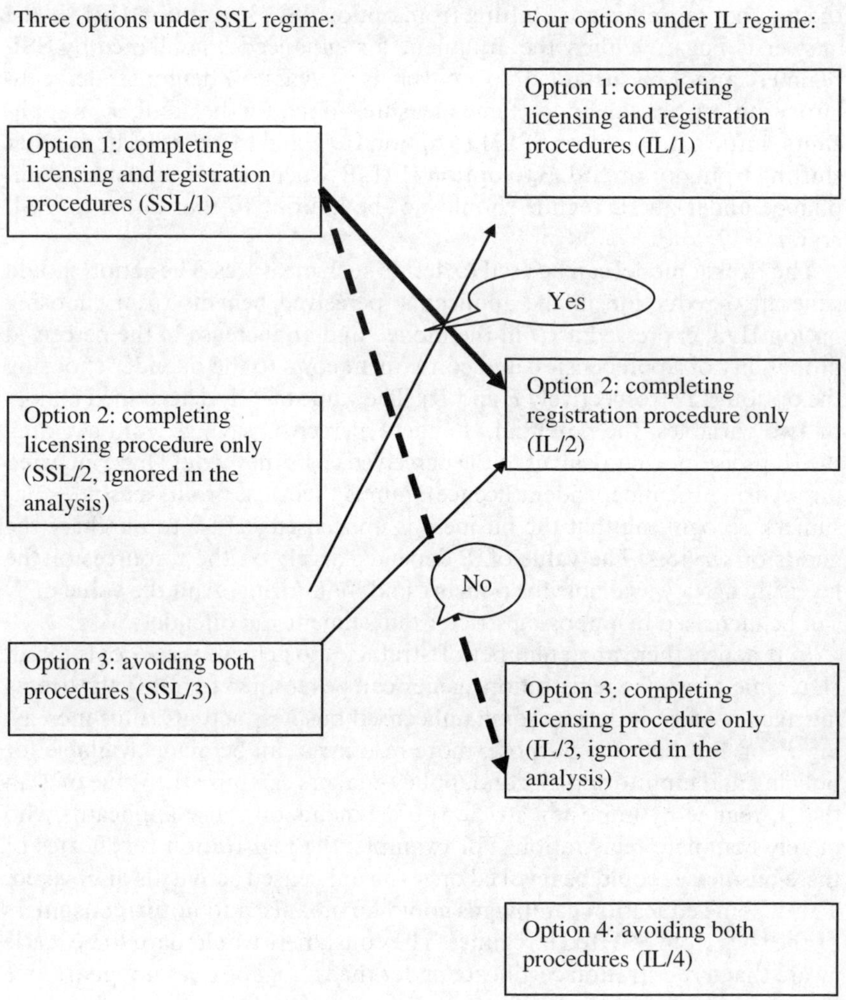

Figure 6.2 Options under SSL and IL regimes

and consequent costs to the offender (respectively, *P* and *D*), are unlikely to differ as between the two licensing regimes (we assume if those avoiding both requirements are detected by one agency, licensing or registration, for one contravention, notification will lead readily to detection of the other contravention).

Whether SSL regimes can generate better regulatory compliance than IL regimes depends ultimately on a balance between two shifts, that is, whether the number of applicants shifting from option SSL/1 to option IL/2 exceeds the number of applicants shifting from option SSL/3 to option IL/1. If the answer is negative, then the argument for enhanced compliance by SSL regimes cannot be sustained. Moreover, as we will now demonstrate, regulatory authorities can adopt some measures to reduce the number of applicants shifting from option SSL/1 to option IL/2, and to increase the number shifting from option SSL/3 to option IL/1. By such means regulatory compliance under an IL regime should not be inferior to that under an SSL regime.

The Becker model can be used to design such measures. The action should generate a reduction in the applicants' perceived benefits from choosing option IL/2, expressed as *U* in the model, and an increase in the perceived probability of apprehension and consequent costs to the offender choosing the option IL/2 (respectively *P* and *D*). The value of *U* is determined mainly by two variables: the potential offenders' perceived savings from avoiding the IL procedure (equivalent to the perceived costs they would have incurred for securing the independent licence), minus their lost profits as some consumers, recognising that the business is unlicensed, refuse to purchase the goods or services. The value of *P* depends largely on the resources of the licensing agency available for policing and monitoring. And the value of *D* can be increased by imposing stricter punishments on offenders.

In practice, there are a number of strategies to achieve these goals for an IL regime. First, the registration agency can be required to notify the licensing agency when it detects some unlicensed business activity, thus increasing *P*; or, for the same purpose, more resources can be made available for policing and monitoring. Second, policy-makers can raise the value of *D* in the IL regime by imposing stricter punishments on those applicants who merely complete registration. For example, the registration certificates of these businesses could be revoked once the unlicensed activity is discovered. Third, some education campaigns could be organised to notify consumers of the shift from SSL to IL regimes. The consumers would have to be made aware that a registration certificate under the IL regime does not guarantee that the holder complies with the substantive conditions of the licensing criteria. This might effectively reduce consumers' purchases from the unlicensed businesses and thus reduce the business profits of the latter. Fourth, the measures reducing *U* and increasing *P* and *D* for applicants choosing option IL/2 may also result in a corresponding reduction of perceived benefits, and increase the perceived probability of apprehension and consequent costs, for those applicants choosing option IL/4. The consequence may be more applicants choosing option IL/1.

Of course, all these policies would increase administrative costs and even consumer costs (receiving information from officials). If any of these policies are necessary to ensure that regulatory compliance under IL regimes does not compare unfavourably with that under SSL regimes, then policy-makers have to make another trade-off. Only if the administrative costs incurred for the suggested policies exceed the additional compliance and other costs falling mainly on consumers and officials under SSL regimes (compared with the IL regimes) can SSL regimes be justified on public interest compliance grounds. Without precise information on this, it is difficult to draw hard conclusions from the analysis, although it may be relevant to the Chinese reform that distinguishes high risk businesses from low risk businesses and then uses a conditional registration or IL regime rather than an SSL regime to control the latter.

Saving compliance costs on other procedures?

It might be argued that, compared with IL regimes, SSL regimes are able to reduce compliance costs arising from other procedures in the set-up process. If entrepreneurs fail to obtain an SSL licence, they will not incur further compliance costs from subsequent procedures. In contrast, under an IL regime, they may well have completed the set-up process and incurred all related compliance costs before being informed of the failure of the licensing application, at least if the licensing procedures take longer than the set-up process. As shown in Figure 6.1, under an SSL regime, entrepreneurs will not incur the costs of registration (at least the administrative costs of making the application) once they are informed of the unsuccessful licensing application. But under an IL regime, they might already, by this stage, have incurred the compliance costs of registration. In the light of this, it is better to slot in the more complex licensing procedure (often with less predictable outcomes) in the earlier stages of the set-up process. If the licensing application is not successful, then it makes no sense to go through subsequent procedures. This argument is particularly strong if the compliance costs incurred for other procedures are substantial, if the rate of rejection of licensing applications is high, and if the entrepreneur only wants to operate the business that is subject to the licensing requirement.[4]

However, the above argument ignores the fact that entrepreneurs can make their own choices to save compliance costs arising under IL regimes. If an entrepreneur is not confident about the success of the application and the compliance costs for the other procedures are high, the decision can be made not to engage in the other procedures until there is information on the success of the licensing application. In theory, at least, the IL regime allows applicants to decide how to minimise compliance costs, notably by balancing savings from the shorter delay in beginning the business operations against possibly irrecoverable compliance costs incurred in completing other procedures. Since the probability of securing the licensing varies from case to case and entrepreneurs bear these compliance costs, it might be better to leave the decision to them. On this ground, IL regimes may be considered preferable to SSL regimes.

Saving monitoring costs for officials?

A third possibility is that SSL regimes generate scale economies of enforcement costs in the case of multiple SSL requirements (Ogus and Zhang, 2005). So, before completing the set-up process, entrepreneurs may be required to demonstrate to an agency that they have already secured all necessary activity licences including, for example, a fire safety permit, a sanitary permit and a location permit. However, the same scale economics can be achieved also by IL regimes, provided that a single enforcement agency is authorised to monitor the various IL requirements. In addition to requiring entrepreneurs to present their licences in its office, the enforcement agency can also carry out investigations on its own initiative. Moreover, IL regimes have the added advantage of reducing the time to complete both the set-up process and IL procedures; under an SSL regime the procedure for checking the multiple requirements constitutes de facto a further barrier to entry.

In summary, the above analysis suggests that the hypotheses favouring SSL on public interest grounds may not always be justified. We turn next to possible private interest explanations for SSL regimes being preferred to IL regimes.

PRIVATE INTEREST EXPLANATIONS

Private interest theory suggests that regulation serves the interest of, and is therefore sought by, particular groups (Ogus, 2004). And there are many studies that purport to show that specific licensing regimes benefit particular interest groups (Svorny, 2000). According to the theory, existing suppliers are motivated to influence the promulgation of licensing requirements that can often limit competition and, in certain circumstances, raise their profits. They are usually able to do this successfully since they typically face lower information and organisation costs than dispersed consumers. Politicians may, therefore, be prepared to meet the demand of suppliers' groups for the licensing legislation in return for campaign contributions, votes and even bribes. Bureaucrats may use licensing regulations to obtain larger budgets, prestige, manpower and further employment conditions. Most importantly, the discretion involved in licensing decision-making creates opportunities for exacting bribes. Moreover, because of their key role in policy-making, such as controlling information, bureaucrats can easily impose licensing regimes. In this section, we explore these hypotheses, to ascertain whether SL regimes can confer more benefits on the interest groups than IL regimes.

Set-up Licensing Agency

Under an SL regime, entrepreneurs who fail to gain approval from the licensing agency should not, at least in theory, engage in subsequent procedures to enter the market. The arrangement might, at least ostensibly, give a good excuse for the licensing agency to rely on verification by other agencies responsible for subsequent procedures and then relax its efforts to police unlicensed activities.

The delay involved in obtaining an SL licence can often impose more costs on entrepreneurs than an equivalent delay under an IL regime. With regard to the latter, as long as it takes the entrepreneur less time to complete the delayed IL procedure than the set-up process, the delay by the licensing agency will not affect the total time for completing both procedures. But under an SL regime, any delay by the licensing agency will directly increase the total time for both procedures. The higher delay costs imposed on the entrepreneur create more opportunities for the licensing officials to extract bribes, because the entrepreneur's benefits from corruption are increased (Rose-Ackerman, 1999).

The pattern of arrangements in the Philippines, where all GSL regimes have been retained, might reflect the influence of SL agencies. Even after the 2002 reform, many business proprietors still complain about the considerable burdens imposed. While the processing time of documents or papers in the Business Permit Licensing Office has been reduced, that of documents in the other departments or offices (SL agencies) has not been shortened. This is particularly true of the GSL regimes for fire safety inspection certificates, sanitary permits and occupational permits (Legaspi, 2004).

In some developing countries, once a licensing requirement has been established, the choice between SL and IL regimes is generally determined by bureaucrats. Even if politicians retain decision-making power, the licensing agency might still be able to persuade them to adopt SL regimes by collaborating with agencies responsible for subsequent checking procedures (ARSCPs). We will now see how those ARSCPs can benefit from SL regimes.

Agencies Responsible for Subsequent Checking Procedures

Under an SL regime, the ARSCPs verify that the SL requirement has been met before the set-up process can be finished. The ARSCPs might be able to obtain power, prestige, and even bribes, since rejection of an application or delay in processing it can cause losses to entrepreneurs. In particular, the entrepreneurs might have invested a significant amount in the SL procedure before applying to the ARSCPs. The investments are generally sunk costs, which will be lost if the entrepreneurs do not engage in the subsequent procedures with the ARSCPs. But, under an IL regime, no agency is responsible for such subsequent checking in the set-up process. This means less power for the agencies in the IL regime to secure bribes or other benefits, than in the SL regime.

Perhaps some benefit to ARSCPs might be inferred from their great enthusiasm for SL requirements when the public interest justifications are not very strong. In China, there were (at least) 146 SSL requirements at the national level in 2000: 29 of these were imposed by the National People's Congress and its standing committee; 79 by the State Council; and 38 by the National Industry and Commerce Administration (NICA) acting as an ARSCP or jointly by the NICA and another ministry (Enterprise Registration Bureau, 2000). It has been suggested that the introduction in 2003 of the Administrative Licensing Act (Articles 14, 15, 16), which abolished rights of central ministries and local governments to impose SL requirements, was, in part at least, to prevent them from establishing the regimes for their own private interest (Qiao, 2003). The NICA seems strongly to have supported the Chinese reforms that retained SSL regimes for some businesses (Wang, 2003). Perhaps the incomplete shift from SSL to IL regimes was able to benefit the NICA and its affiliates more than a complete shift.

Existing Suppliers

Existing suppliers may prefer SL to IL regimes. The longer entry time and higher entry costs can, at least to some extent, protect them against competition from potential or new suppliers. The costs reduce the number of suppliers and thus consumer choice; they may also result in increases in prices and the profits (rents) earned by existing suppliers (Ogus and Zhang, 2005). These latter effects rely on the availability of substitute goods and services in the market: the less willing consumers are to change demand to such substitutes, the higher the price increases and the more the profits to suppliers (Svorny, 2000).

If the costs of coordinating the existing suppliers are low, and there is an effective channel for them to influence policy-makers, the existing suppliers might be able to further their interests very easily. In developing countries, the market is often dominated by relatively few, but powerful, incumbents, including state-owned enterprises, which can easily obtain the government's support in establishing the SL regimes to their advantage. Even if the above conditions do not arise, existing suppliers may be able sometimes to harness their demand for regulation to that of groups that easily obtain public support, for example, those representing consumers, who think they will benefit more from SL regimes than from IL regimes (Ogus, 2004).

Politicians

In developing countries, the distinction between politicians and bureaucrats tends to be blurred and an alliance between the ruling elite and high-ranking officials has often led to an 'oligarchy of power and privilege' (Seidman and Seidman, 1994). These groups may have some common interests in choosing the SL regime. Moreover, perhaps for psychological or cultural reasons, more ex ante prevention might be preferred by the public who are more risk-averse and more likely to accept power inequality between government and individuals (Baptista, 2004). Accordingly, SL regimes might, more easily than IL regimes, enhance the reputation of politicians in developing countries where many people appear to have the above characteristics. This may increase the politicians' prospects of re-election, or facilitate their ruling power.

Finally, it may be that all these interest groups, agencies, existing suppliers and politicians, can secure greater benefits from GSL regimes compared to SSL regimes, because the coverage of the former is wider, imposing licensing requirements on all business sectors.

CONCLUSION

In this chapter, we have investigated the use of licensing procedures in the business set-up processes in developing countries. It seems that some developing countries still widely use set-up licensing (SL) regimes, and although in some jurisdictions there has been a shift to independent licensing (IL) regimes, these reforms have been left incomplete. The SL regimes impose more compliance costs on entrepreneurs, more administrative costs on officials and more welfare losses on consumers than IL regimes. Our principal aim has been to explore the public interest justifications for these SL procedures.

As we have seen, few general set-up licensing (GSL) procedures can be justified since it is difficult to identify a licensing requirement appropriate for all sectors, all firms and all activities. Not all business activities involve substantial potential losses and at least some potential losses can be better addressed by ex post systems of deterrence, including information regulation (mandatory disclosure) and/or ongoing performance standards. In contrast, the sectoral set-up licensing (SSL) regime might, in relation to the sector concerned, be preferable to other regulatory techniques, but it is often difficult to rationalise its role as one step in the set-up process. The argument favouring SSL regimes for their roles in improving compliance ignores the possibility that more applicants might thereby enter the informal economy without going through any official procedures. We have also suggested that, if an IL regime is adopted, effective regulatory compliance can be achieved provided that some necessary measures are taken by government. And we suspect that the related administrative costs of these measures will sometimes be less than the additional compliance costs and welfare losses of an SL regime. We also have reason to doubt the argument that SL regimes may reduce monitoring costs and compliance costs for other procedures.

This analysis lends support to the reform on GSL regime in Kenya but, by the same token, suggests that further reform in the Philippines to replace their GSL regimes with IL regimes or with other less interventionist measures would be justified. The Chinese reform of SSL regimes can be defended as a transitional measure because, while incomplete, it significantly reduces costs on businesses and consumers.

It seems that private interest explanations are more convincing than public interest justifications. The SL agencies, the agencies responsible for subsequent checking procedure, existing suppliers and politicians can all obtain better benefits from SL regimes than from IL regimes. Especially in developing countries, the powerful alliance of politicians and bureaucrats can exploit SL regimes to their own advantage, and at the expense of new suppliers and consumers.

NOTES

1. See, e.g. the joint-licensing centre of construction projects in Harbin City, Heirongjian Province, and the Joint-licensing Service Centre of Ciqi City, Zhejiang Province.
2. For example, Guandong Province, Shanghai City and Fujian Province.
3. A telephone interview between Qing Zhang and an officer (who wishes to remain anonymous) in the State Industry and Commerce Administration, the People's Republic of China.
4. If the registration procedure is not merely for the business subject to the SSL requirement (that is, there exist some businesses not subject to SSL regimes), the losses from the compliance costs might not be so large, because the costs of the registration will be shared with the businesses not requiring licences.

REFERENCES

Abuodha, C. and R. Bowles (2000), 'Business licence reform in Kenya and its impact on small enterprises', *Small Enterprise Development*, **11**, 16–24.

Baptista, R. (2004), 'Culture, institutions and government attitudes towards new firm entry', Max Planck Institute for Research into Economic Systems, Jena, Germany, Entrepreneurship, Growth and Public Policy Discussion Paper No. 39, 2004.

Becker, G. (1968), 'Crime and punishment: An economic approach', *Journal of Political Economics*, **76**, 169–217.

Cui, W. (2003), 'Shenpi (licensing) reform from the perspective of one municipal jurisdiction: Ideologies, institutions, and law', *Hong Kong Law Journal*, **33**, 417–80.

Devas, N. and R. Kelly (2001), 'Regulation or revenue? An analysis of local business licences, with a case study of the single business permit reform in Kenya', *Public Administration and Development*, **21**, 381–91, DOI: 10.1002/pad.195.

Djankov, S., R. La Porta, F. Lopez-de-Silanes and A. Shleifer (2002), 'The regulation of entry', *Quarterly Journal of Economics*, **117**(1), 1–36.

Enterprise Registration Bureau of National Industry and Commerce Administration of P.R. China (2000), *Collection of Laws and Regulations Concerning Prior Approvals for Enterprises' Registry* (in Chinese Pinyin *Qi yie deng ji guan li qian zhi shen pi shi yong fa gui*), Beijing: China Industry and Commerce Association Press.

Freedman, J. (1994), 'Small businesses and the corporate form: Burden or privilege?,' *Modern Law Review*, **57**, 555–84.

Hu, X. (2004), 'Can a conditional registration with the applicant's promise be used in urban construction regulation?' (in Chinese Pinyin 'Shi xi gao zhi cheng nuo zhi zai cheng jian xi tong de ke xin xing'), Published electronically at http://www.zscj.gov.cn/news/shownews.asp?newsid=309 (Accessed on 7 May 2005).

Hubei Provincial Government (2002), *Opinons Regarding Reforms on Prior Approval in Business Set-up Registrations* (in Chinese Pinyin *Guan yu gai ge wo shen gong shan deng ji qian zhi shen pi de yi jian*), Wuhan: Hubei Provincial Government.

Jansson, T. and G. Chalmers (2001), *The Case for Business Registration Reform in Latin America*, Sustainable Development Department Best Practices Series: Reference No. MSM-110, Washington, DC: Inter-American Development Bank.

Jenkins Committee (1962), *Report of the Company Law Committee*, Cmnd. 1749, London: HMSO.

Jinmen Municipal Government (Hubei Province) (2003), 'Implementation opinions concerning the categorization of A and B type licensing for registration of industry and commerce enterprise' (in Chinese Pinyin 'Guan yu wo shi gong shan deng ji qian zhi sheng pi shi xing a b lei de shi shi yi jian'), Published electronically at http://www.jmaic.net/zhengfushenpi.htm (Accessed on 7 August 2004).

Legaspi, P. (2004), 'Reforms and practices in local regulatory governance: The case of Philippines', Centre for Regulation and Competition, the University of Manchester, The 3rd Annual Conference Paper, Published electronically at http://idpm.man.ac.uk/crc/conferences/southafricasep 04/legaspipaper.pdf (Accessed 9 October 2004).

Morisset, J. and O. Neso (2002), 'Administrative barriers to foreign investment in developing countries', World Bank, Washington, DC, Policy Research Working Paper No. 2848.

Ogus, A. (2004), *Regulation: Legal Form and Economic Theory*, Oxford: Hart Publishing.

Ogus, A. and Q. Zhang (2005), 'Licensing regimes: East and West', *International Review of Law and Economics*, **25** (forthcoming).

Pistor, K., Y. Keinan, J. Kleinheisterkamp and D. West (2002), 'The evolution of corporate law: A cross-country comparison', *University of Pennsylvania Journal of International Economic Law*, **23**, 791–872.

Qiao, X.Y. (ed.) (2003), *A Commentary on the Administrative Licensing Act of the People's Republic of China* (in Chinese Pinyin *Zhong hua ren min gong he guo xing zheng xu ke fa shi yi*), Beijing: China Price Press.

Rose-Ackerman, S. (1999), *Corruption and Government: Causes, Consequences and Reform*, Cambridge: Cambridge University Press.

Sader, F. (2000), 'Do "one-stop shops" work?', FIAS (Foreign Investment Advisory Services) Working Paper, Published electronically by the World Bank at http://www.fias.net/documents/ (Accessed 5 January 2004).

Schneider, F. (2002), 'Size and measurement of the informal economy in 110 countries around the world', Published electronically by the World Bank at http://rru.worldbank.org/Documents/PapersLinks/informal_economy.pdf (Accessed 6 August 2004).

Seidman, A. and R. Seidman (1994), *State and Law in the Development Process: Problem-solving and Institutional Change in the Third World*, London: Macmillan.

Spall, H. and L. Szerb (2004), 'The impact of legal rules on the time and capital necessary to organize a new business entity: Hungary, the United States (Washington State) and the countries of the pre-accession EU Compared', *4 Global Jurist Advance* **4**(1), Published electronically at http://www.bepress.com/gj/advances/vol4/iss 1/art3 (Accessed 8 October 2004).

Suhir, E. and Z. Kovach (2003), 'Administrative barriers to entrepreneurship in Central Asia', Published electronically at http://www.cipe.org/pdf/publications/ (Accessed 7 June 2003).

Sun, H.G. (2003), 'Difficulty encountered by entrepreneurs' (in Chinese Pinyin 'Chuan ye nan, nan yu shang qing tian'), Published electronically at http://www.wineast.com./joinmarket/ (Accessed 7 December 2004).

Svorny, S. (2000), 'Licensing, market entry regulation', in B. Bouckaert and G. De Geest (eds), *Encyclopaedia of Law and Economics*, Vol. III, Cheltenham, UK and Northampton, MA, USA: Edward Elgar, pp. 296–328.

Wang, X.D. (2004), 'Untied the tied control: Shenzhen seeking for a new solution to tackle the unlicensed businesses (in Chinese Pinyin 'Kun bang guan li han dai jie kun, Shen Zhen cong qing li wu zao jing ying zhong tan suo jian guan xing mo shi'), Published electronically at http://www.saic.gov.cn/ (Accessed 6 August 2004).

Wang, Z.F. (2003), 'Sticking to comply with "three representatives requirements" and doing a good job in industry and commerce administration' (in Chinese Pinyin 'Jian chi san ge da biao yao qiu zhong lan gong shang guan li gong zhong quan ju'), *China Industry and Commerce Daily*, 7 August 2003, Published electronically at http://www.whhd.gov.cn/news/20030811/092914854.html (Accessed 6 April 2005).

World Bank (2004a), *Doing Business in 2004: Understanding Regulation*, Washington, DC: The World Bank and Oxford University Press.

World Bank (2004b), 'The doing business database', Published electronically at http://rru.worldbank.org/DoingBusiness/TopicReports/EntryRegulations (Accessed 6 June 2004).

Yang, L.M. (2004), 'How many unlicensed taxis in Beijing, and who are engaged in this business?' (in Chinese Pinyin 'Bei Jing hei che you duo shao, shui zai kai hei che'), Published electronically at http://news.xinhuanet.com/fortune/2004-07/20/content_1617780.htm (Accessed 6 August 2004).

Zhang, X.X. (2004), *Research in Administrative Licensing Law* (in Chinese Pinyin *Xing zheng xu ke fa yan jun*), Beijing: Beijing University Press.

The Laws and Regulations Cited

Administrative Licensing Act of the People's Republic of China (in Chinese Pinyin Zhong Hua Ren Min gong he guo xing zheng xu ke fa) (2003), articles 14, 15 and 16.

Pharmaceutical Administration Act of the People's Republic of China (in Chinese Pinyin 'Zhong Hua Ren Min gong he guo yaopi guanli fa) (2001), article 7.

Registration Regulation of Business Scope of Enterprises (in Chinese Pinyin Qi ye jing ying fan wei deng ji guan li gui ding) (2004), articles 5, 8 and 15.

Shanghai Municipal Regulation Regarding Adoption of Parallel Licensing Procedures for Business Registration (in Chinese Pinyin Shanghai shi qi ye zhu ce deng ji bing lian shen pi ban fa) (2001).

7. Reforms and practices in local regulatory governance: the case of the Philippines

Perla E. Legaspi

INTRODUCTION

The emergence of a global economy has considerably affected the role of local government in the governance of communities. Environmental changes and complex demands from the community require the local government to be not only a service provider but also an enabling authority which provides the right kind of environment to facilitate the economic development of the community. This means that local government should take a proactive stance in leading the planning and development of the local economy by providing the necessary framework for the promotion of economic enterprises and activities. The enabling role of local government in economic development emphasizes a two-way relationship between the private sector and local government in addressing concerns in economic promotion. For instance, local government negotiates with the private sector in coming up with planning agreements on how to develop the community. In areas where the private sector is hesitant to come in as investor, local government takes the initiative and risks in developing and diversifying the economic base of the locality. It has to provide the necessary support mechanisms such as infrastructure facilities, efficient and better goods and services, and policy support for the attraction of more investments into the area and to encourage the spirit of enterprise to pave the way for the generation of more economic activities in the locality (Legaspi et al., 1996).

Given its two-way relationship with the private sector, local government is placed at a focal point of relationships and linkages with the private sector (Legaspi, 2001). It is in this context that the local government role on regulation is given focus and emphasis. It is important that the activities of the private sector and other non-government bodies are regulated and monitored to level the playing field as well as to encourage the development and establishment of more economic enterprises and activities in the local area. This role then gives rise to a number of questions, which have to be answered to improve on the regulatory governance at the local level and thus facilitate the economic development of the community. First, what is the state of the regulatory framework at the local level? Second, does the regulatory framework facilitate or hinder economic development? What are the issues and concerns in regulating business or economic activities in the local area?

This chapter attempts to respond to the above questions. It showcases two urban local authorities in the Philippines: Quezon City and Dagupan City. The former is a premier local government authority in the Manila Metropolitan area, while the latter is a second class city in terms of income and is located 200 kilometers north of Manila. The chapter examines closely their business licensing systems. It also looks into the issues, problems and concerns in regulating the operations of business establishments and enterprises in the two cities. This chapter documents actual practices, changes and reforms in the licensing system as well as the effects of the regulatory system on the promotion of business activities in the cities.

CONCEPTUAL FRAMEWORK

The new public administration paradigm emphasizes the shift from government to governance. As broadly defined, governance is the 'system of values, policies and institutions by which a society organizes collective decision-making and action related to political, economic and socio-cultural and environmental affairs through the interaction of the state, civil society and the private sector' (Work, 2003). At the local level, the local government, representing the state, is the principal actor in the local development arena. It is the authority that wields power and influence over the other elements of society. As such, it plays an active role in enabling and facilitating their participation. It thus provides the legal and regulatory framework within which the organizations and institutions plan and implement their programs and activities (Cariño, 2000).

The civil society and the private sector also wield some influence in the decision-making processes in the local community. They may be partners of the local government in policy formulation, service delivery, program implementation, monitoring and evaluation. The local government is no longer the sole source of policies, information and resources. Thus it becomes imperative for the local authority to share with the civil society groups, information, resources, technologies and even personnel to attain development objectives in the community. And it does this through processes of networking and partnership.

In the pursuit of local economic development goals, local government takes a backseat role as it gives primacy to the private sector by being the so-called 'engine of growth' in developing the local economy. This implies that local government views the market as the most efficient and economical mechanism in the provision of goods and services. This does not mean however, that local government abdicates its role in providing a level playing field for those organizations or groups that cannot compete openly because of certain disadvantages and structural disabilities. In other words, the local authority should be able to provide the 'safety nets' for those disadvantaged groups to enable them to compete in the external market.

Although local government plays a residual role in the economy, it can be an interventionist in providing direction in local economic planning as well as in regulating the operations of economic players for the protection of the public interests. Thus it regulates the entry of business through the fulfillment of certain conditions based on legal measures or resolutions passed by the local council. It also conducts post-licensing monitoring to ensure that the license conditions are being complied with. Certain sanctions are then imposed on those who cannot meet the standards or conditions for the entry or operation of business.

DEFINING REGULATION

'Regulation' has varied meanings. According to Baldwin and Cave (1999, p. 2), the term can be viewed as 'a specific set of commands; as deliberate state influence; and as all forms of social control or influence'. In the first sense, regulation involves a set of promulgated rules applied by a body created for this purpose. An example of this would be the set of environmental protection rules implemented by the Environment Management Bureau of the Department of the Environment and Natural Resources (in the Philippines). The second sense of the term, focused on in this chapter, covers actions of the state or local government as used in this chapter that are designed to restrict or influence activities of the various social and economic groups in the community. For instance, local government policies giving economic incentives for the business sector definitely influence the decisions of the private sector regarding their entry into the area or the expansion of their business there. The third sense of the concept involves all those mechanisms affecting behavior, whether these are derived from local government or from other sources such as the market.

The above definitions seem to emphasize the negative implication of the concept, which restricts or constricts activities or behavior of individuals or groups. This implies the occurrence of negative consequences (such as sanctions) if an individual or groups do not follow the given rules. But then, what appears to be important in the state of governance is the facilitative or enabling aspect of regulation (Minogue, 2001). As stated, local government formulates policies and lays down the ground rules for the operations of individuals and groups, most especially the business sector, to promote order and public safety.

THE REGULATORY INSTRUMENTS

There are two main forms of regulatory instruments: economic and social (Ogus, 2001). Economic regulation 'applies to markets which are insufficiently competitive' (Ogus, 2001, p. 10). This means that there is a need to come up with certain measures to make or enhance the competitiveness of the market, such as the formulation of a law on competition and the passage of legal measures on controlling the price and quality of products and services. On the other hand, social regulation deals more with the promotion of public welfare, health and safety. This further implies that rules are applied to the operations of the business firms to control their activities for loss abatement. The activities related to this are: (1) prior approval, where the firms are required to first secure a license or permit to operate from an authorizing agency; (2) mandatory standards, where companies have to meet certain standards, both performance and specification, set by the agency tasked to formulate the standards; (3) information disclosure, where the establishments are required to disclose to the public information regarding harms and risks that may arise from the operational activities and the product; and (4) economic instruments, where local government can offer incentives to the firms in the form of a tax or charge (Ogus, 2001). A local government may also adopt a policy of providing a tax holiday for business firms for a certain tax payment period to encourage more investments into the area.

The more important aspect of social regulation in governance is the control of certain operational activities of the firm for the health and safety of the general public. Thus the enabling role of local government puts a premium on the social aspect of regulation, primarily because of the need to protect the interest of the public and to promote more economic activities in the community for the people's general welfare and well being. However, social regulation may also be viewed as an instrument for the consolidation of the economic and political power of the local leaders or politicians (Ogus and Zhang, 2003; and see their Chapter 6 in this book). By imposing certain regulatory measures on the entry or operations of economic or business firms, the leaders or politicians may be able to block the entry of certain businesses that would run counter to their economic or political interests. This situation is especially true in a third world economy where the distinctions between economic and political elites are blurred. The same case goes for public officials who are tasked to implement the regulatory measures for the entry of business firms. Given certain discretionary powers, they are provided with the opportunity to commit graft and corruption. This may explain their interest to maintain the system of entry controls. Social regulation may then promote public welfare or advance private interests.

The next sections explore the concept of social regulation in local governance in a developing economy like the Philippines, focusing on the business licensing system.

THE LEGAL FRAMEWORK FOR LOCAL REGULATORY GOVERNANCE

Local regulatory governance in the Philippines has its basis in the Constitution and the Local Government Code of 1991. The regulatory and interventionist role of the state is clearly enunciated in the declaration of state policies of the 1987 Constitution (Cariño, 2004), while the Local Government Code provides for the regulatory powers of local governments. Both the Constitution and the Code highlight the role of government in social regulation. They provide the basis for the facilitative or enabling role of government in protecting the public interest and promoting the general welfare of the community.

THE LOCAL GOVERNMENT CODE

A significant provision in the Constitution is the enactment of a local government code which shall provide for a more responsive and accountable local government structure instituted through a system of decentralization. The state has granted the local governments police power through the General Welfare Clause of the Code, which gives them as much power 'as necessary, appropriate, or incidental for their efficient and effective governance and those which are essential in promoting the general welfare' (Tabunda and Galang, 1992, pp. 1–10).

THE REGULATORY POWERS OF LOCAL GOVERNMENTS

Based on the principle and policy of local autonomy, the Code has transferred certain regulatory powers of national government agencies to local governments. This act serves to enhance the police power conferred on local governments by the general welfare clause. These include the power to reclassify agricultural lands, enforce environmental laws and the Building Code, process and approve subdivision plans, inspect food products, and regulate the operation of tricycles. Aside from these expressly devolved powers, local governments may also regulate the provision of health, social welfare, agriculture, public works, and other services already devolved to them.

The power to tax and to impose levies, fees and charges by local governments can be seen likewise as part of their regulatory powers. In terms of economic concerns, they give business licenses and permits to establishments or enterprises before the firms can operate in their respective local jurisdictions. The collection of business taxes can also be viewed as an economic instrument as well as a form of social regulation imposed by local governments.

THE REGULATORY SYSTEMS

The power and functions to regulate are lodged with both national and local governments. Some national laws and executive orders form part of the regulatory regime. Certain national government agencies influence the operations of local governments, particularly their business licensing system, by virtue of their mandated functions. They grant certificates, licenses, or clearances to the business firms or enterprises before they can engage in a business activity in the locality. Among the more important agencies are the Bureau of Fire Protection of the Department of the Interior and Local Government, the Department of Trade and Industry, Securities and Exchange Commission, the Bureau of Food and Drugs of the Department of Health, and the Department of the Environment and Natural Resources.

THE LOCAL REGULATORY SYSTEMS

The local government is the principal institution at the local level, and it provides basic services to the constituencies and regulates the establishment and operations of business enterprises. The executive branch, headed by the mayor, executes policies and implements laws passed by the legislative council, which is presided over by the vice-mayor. There are various departments and offices under the administrative supervision and control of the mayor who serves as the local chief executive. These include the offices of health, agriculture, engineering, social welfare and development, planning, environmental management and protection, treasury, accounting, budget, assessment, and office of business permits and licenses. All of these offices and departments are mandated to provide basic services and functions to the community. As pointed out earlier, local government has been conferred by the general welfare clause of the Local Government Code with regulatory powers to enhance its police power. Part of these powers is the issuance of business permits and licenses to establishments to enable them to operate in the local area.

THE REQUIREMENTS FOR ISSUANCE OF BUSINESS PERMITS OR LICENSES

A business proprietor must apply for a business permit or license each year to be able to operate. A building permit has to be secured from the Engineering Office if the building is not yet constructed. The proprietor has to submit a copy of the contract of lease if the place of business is rented, or proof of ownership if it is owned.

Aside from the national licenses or clearances, the proprietor has to secure the following before the permit is issued: (1) *barangay* (village) clearance from the barangay government where the business is located; (2) locational clearance from the Office of the Planning and Development Coordinator; (3) certificate of electrical inspection from the Office of the Engineer; (4) fire safety inspection certificate from the Fire Station; and (5) health certificate for all employees of the establishment and sanitary permit for the business place.

The establishment has to be inspected by the representatives of the Office of Engineer, Fire Station, and Health Office respectively, to ensure the compliance of the sanitation and safety standards and requirements these offices impose.

The proprietor pays the permit fees based on the revenue code, which specifies the rate of payment depending on the kind of business or the aggregate area utilized by the business.

THE QUEZON CITY EXPERIENCE

Comprising 142 barangays, Quezon City has a total land area of 16,112.12 hectares, representing about 25 percent of the total land area of Metro

Manila. Its population is the largest in the metropolitan area with 2,173,831 people (2000 census) and an average growth rate of 1.92 percent (1995–2000). A large portion of the land area is devoted to commercial and industrial uses. There were 52,245 establishments recorded in 2001. The total income of the city was placed at P3.64 billion (General Fund: about 72,800,000 US dollars) in 2001. The manufacturing sector contributed the biggest share, about 28 percent to the total business tax revenues of the city government. City government expenditures totaled P3.83 billion in 2001. Most of the expenditures (60 percent) went to public welfare and safety. The figures indicate that the city government has given priority to the concerns regarding the promotion of public welfare and safety.

PROBLEMS IN THE SYSTEM OF SECURING BUSINESS PERMITS

When the present political leadership took over the reins of the city government in 2001, many problems were encountered regarding the grant of business permits to establishments operating in the city. Business firms usually complained that there were too many requirements, making it too cumbersome for them to get the necessary permit. It took weeks or months to complete all the clearances needed before they could be issued the permit to operate. The fire safety inspection clearance in particular took a long time. Aside from this, the requirements were described to be inflexible, which made the business proprietors easy prey to fixers. Some business proprietors commented that they tried to meet all the requirements but there were always some loopholes in the system to enable the inspectors to deny the clearance or delay the processing of the document.

The physical set-up or arrangement in the Business Permit and License Office (BPLO) reinforced the above situation. There were no windows for client transactions so people tended to crowd the premises inside the office. Due to the poor recording system in the office, application forms or documents could not be readily found or accessed by the business proprietor when needed. The delay in the issuance of business permits could also be traced to the delay in the conduct of visual inspections by the offices tasked to do this such as the Fire Station, Health, and Engineering. In turn, this could be attributed to the lack of staff in these offices.

Because of the inefficient records management system of the BPLO, data on business establishments and business permits were not accurate. The list of establishments had some double or multiple entries. Also, there were unrecorded permits, fake permits, and fake receipts. This situation made later monitoring and evaluation difficult.

Another problem cited was in the area of assessment and payment of taxes, fees, and charges. There was no networking of data between the BPLO and the Treasurer's Office. Apparently, each office had its own set of data pertaining to business establishments. What seemed to be a problematic area was the discretion given to the assessor in determining the amount of taxes, fees and charges to be paid. Although the amended revenue code of the city government provided for the schedule of minimum gross receipts or sales as a basis for determining the amount of tax to be paid, the assessor still had the leeway to adjust the presumptive income level of the business firm. This could be traced to the lack of available data and information about the operations of the firm. Moreover, business proprietors felt that it was not easy for them to pay because of the lack of a systematic scheme for payment coupled with overcrowding in the offices designated as assessment and payment places. This was especially true during the first quarter of the year when businesses had to renew their permits.

CHANGES IN THE SYSTEM

In line with the policy of making the city more business-friendly, the City Mayor signed two executive orders to facilitate the process of issuance of business permits. The first one provided guidelines on the validity of the annual certificates and clearances issued by the different city offices. It states that the required certificates and clearances must be issued only after the required inspection and/or verification is conducted; that the certificates or clearances issued will have one year validity, to be reckoned from the date of issue; and that the prior year's certificate or clearance shall be used to secure the issuance of the business permit.

The second executive order purports to ensure the early release of renewed business permits to applicants and at the same time to ensure the safety of the public patronizing the business establishments. The order classifies establishments into low risk and high risk. The 'high risk' businesses are those that require the use of equipment and machineries or expose individuals to risk caused by overcrowding, prolonged physical confinement, exposure to toxic, environmental hazards, or similar situations, such as shopping malls, hotels, inns, dormitories, theaters, and the like. For the low-risk business firms, the minimum requirements for renewal of a permit are the barangay and the locational clearances (if there has been a change in location). The other required certificates and clearances can be secured within a 12-month period as spelt out in the first executive order. On the part of the high risk businesses, they have to secure all the required certificates and clearances. Complementing the above executive orders is the computerization of systems. The BPLO and the City Treasurer's Office have started developing a central database for tax assessment and payment. The BPLO is completing the list of business establishments by categories and is networking its data with those of the City Treasurer's Office. A significant change in the system is the computerization of the assessment and payment of fees and taxes. This would help delimit the area for the exercise of personal discretion of the assessor in determining the amount to be paid by the taxpayer.

The City Treasurer has adopted some strategies relative to the problems with the assessment and payment of business taxes. With the discovery of fake receipts, the City Treasurer issued new official receipts with security features to eliminate the issuance of fake receipts. He has also issued a directive to business taxpayers indicating that those with gross income of P500,000 (about 10,000 US dollars) and above shall submit the previous year's financial statement of the firm or company and copies of the monthly payments of value added tax and non-value added tax from the Bureau of Internal Revenue. This would be counterchecked with the declared gross income of the establishment for the year, before the business permit would be renewed for another year.

To make payment of taxes a more pleasurable experience, the City Administration has renovated and opened a comfortable lounge for both assessment and payment of taxes with free coffee and iced tea for taxpayers while waiting. Similarly, with the comfort and easy transaction of the business sector in mind, the BPLO has initiated some physical changes in its office layout. It has provided windows for business transactions to prevent entry of non-employees and thus reduce the use of fixers for transacting business in the office. This would also avoid overcrowding which gives displeasure to the clients.

In the same vein, the City Engineer's Office has begun streamlining the procedures for securing building permits. To shorten the processing time, the City Engineer has designated a documentary officer to be responsible for determining the completeness of documents submitted for processing before these go to the various sections concerned. This should lessen the opportunity for fixers to make their services available to the clients. Further, the physical layout of the office has also been rearranged such that all sections or units performing functions related to the grant of building permits are located in one area.

Another measure adopted is the policy of not allowing non-employees inside the premises. Only building owners, contractors and duly authorized representatives of businesses are allowed to apply. This should prevent the use of fixers in facilitating the processing of papers.

In the case of the City Health Officer's Office, it has likewise started shortening the processing time for health certificates from one week to only four or three days for a fee of P20. This is in response to the problem of the issuance of fake health certificates which can be obtained within five or ten minutes, in comparison with the fixer's fee of P300 to P350 (about 7 US dollars).

SOME EFFECTS OF THE CHANGES

The changes introduced in the system of issuance of business permits and licenses have brought about some positive effects on the city government and the business sector. On the part of the city government, the computerization of the system has sorted out the list of the business taxpayers. As mentioned earlier, the list of establishments was inaccurate due to double and multiple entries, and fake and unrecorded business permits. With computerization, the list has become more reliable as a basis for tax collection. Moreover, the improvement has brought about the networking of data between the BPLO and the City Treasurer's Office. This has also led to better assessment of taxes to be paid by the taxpayer.

The improvement of the system has resulted in an increase in the number of new business permits issued. Statistical data from 2001 to 2002 showed that there was a growth of 69.4 percent. This suggests that more new establishments have been registered formally, doing away with the unrecorded and fake permits. Records also show the increasing trend in the number of registered new businesses in three districts of the city. As indicated by the data, almost all types of business establishments have registered an increase.

Further, with the computerization of tax assessment and payment, the opportunity to exercise personal discretion on the determination of the amount of tax to be paid has been diminished; hence, the opportunity to commit corruption has been lessened. Added to this is the instituting of countercheck measure whereby the taxpayer is asked to present the last year's financial statement of the company or firm plus copies of value added tax (VAT) or non-value added tax payments from the Bureau of Internal Revenue. This has given rise to an increased amount in the collection of business taxes.

Perceptions of the improvements in the system from the business sector, particularly from the manufacturing sector, indicate some mixed reactions. Some have stated that they have been accorded better services. They have been assisted by a sufficient number of city employees while renewing their permits. The construction of an airconditioned lounge for the assessment and payment of taxes has made the payment of taxes very convenient for them. Also, the computerized system has shortened the processing time of papers and documents. However, a number of business proprietors still complain about the many requirements imposed. To them, there is too much paperwork to be done. While the processing time of documents or papers in the BPLO has been shortened, the processing time of documents in the other departments or offices has not been much reduced. This is particularly true in the case of the requirements pertaining to the fire safety inspection certificate, sanitary permit, and occupational permit. One business proprietor commented that it took him three months to get the sanitary permit, and another two months to get the fire safety inspection certificate.

The business sector likewise views the conduct of too many inspections by different city offices as bothersome. Although inspection is recognized to be an important tool for safeguarding public safety, some business proprietors regard this as an opportunity for some inspectors to hassle them and thus delay the processing of the permit if they do not come across.

THE DAGUPAN CITY EXPERIENCE

Dagupan City is located in the province of Pangasinan in Region 1. With 31 barangays occupying a total land area of 44.46 square kilometers, it had a total population of 130,328 in 2000 and an average growth rate of 0.69 (1995–2000). Agricultural uses dominate land use, accounting for around 36 percent of the total land area. Most of these are fishponds (22 percent) and cropland (14 percent). The city is famous for its production of 'bangus' or milkfish. The area used for commercial purposes constitutes about 3 percent, industrial, 1 percent, and institutional, 2 percent. With only a small portion of the total land area utilized for commercial and industrial uses, the commercial activities within the city are not extensive compared with other cities, particularly with Quezon City. As of December 2002, the registered business establishments totaled only 4721.

Classified as a second class city, Dagupan's total income was placed at P260,362,922 (about 5,207,000 US dollars) in 2002. The collections from business taxes and licenses contributed the biggest portion to the local taxes with 67.4 percent. This shows that the city government draws a lot of financial resources from the business sector.

PROBLEMS IN THE BUSINESS LICENSING SYSTEM

When the present City Administration took over the reins of government in 2001, it conducted a review of the management of financial resources of the city government. The review revealed that there was a decrease in the collection of local taxes, which contributed to the overall decrease in the total income of the city in 2001. The decrease could be attributed to the poor tax collection effort on the part of the city government personnel. Partly, this could also be explained by the non-maximization of the proceeds from business taxes and licenses because of the lack of a database pertinent to the total collectibles arising from the existing number of business establishments in the city. What was available then was the list of businesses operating in the city based on the payments made when they went to the Treasurer's Office for renewal of their permits to operate.

It was also a common complaint among the businesses that the procedure of getting a permit was too cumbersome. It took weeks or even months to complete all the requirements or clearances before the issuance of the said permit. This also contributed to the delays in the processing of permits, which often gave rise to opportunities for the commission of graft and corruption. The business proprietors referred to this as the 'standard operating procedure' in the transaction where they are constrained to give 'grease' money to make the process faster. Related to this was the problem aired concerning the payment of license taxes and fees. The assessor had the leeway to adjust the presumptive income level of the business, which gave opportunity for the commission of corruption.

The delay in the conduct of visual inspections could partly be traced to the lack of inspectors in the City Engineering Office, City Health Office, and Fire Department. This has become a great concern during the post-licensing period when the inspectors could not monitor the operations of the establishments. Admittedly, they rarely visit business firms after the issuance of the permit.

Aside from the limited number of inspectors, a complaint among the inspectors was the unresponsive stance adopted by the city government leaders or officials regarding some business firms that did not comply with certain conditions required for entry. Such an attitude could be explained by the influence of the proprietors over the city officials or leaders who may have been recipients of some economic favors from them. Understandably, imposing sanctions on the violators of the set conditions may diminish the officials' economic and political clout in the city.

CHANGES IN THE SYSTEM

The City Administration believes that a way of providing a conducive environment for the business sector to grow and develop is to streamline procedures in the granting of business permits and to provide convenience in transacting business in city hall. Thus a major reform introduced is the establishment of the One Stop Business Center where a taxpayer pays all taxes and fees to the city government under one roof. The payment of all taxes and fees is centered in one office, including the payment of real estate taxes, business taxes, license taxes and fees, permits for the use of government facilities and for the conduct of activities, professional and community tax certificates, and documentary requirements, that is, civil registry certificates.

The Center has been equipped with facilities to make payment of taxes more convenient. The office is airconditioned. It has an information counter to assist taxpayers with their transactions. The collection counters provide for online transactions and payments. The Center has a bulletin board that contains relevant information and regular updates on the city's taxation system. The taxpayers are provided with a water station for their drinking needs and newspapers while waiting for their turn in paying their obligations.

To facilitate the issuance of business permits, representatives of the Engineering and Health Offices and the Fire Department are located in the Center. They are given only three days to conduct inspection of the establishment. This limits the waiting period for the completion of the inspection and, in effect, this lessens the opportunity for corruption where the inspectors demand 'grease' money to complete the inspection in a short period of time.

Before completely computerizing the system, the city government thought it wise to 'tax map' the area first. The process has paid off, producing a list of establishments with and without permits to operate. This provided information to the Center to go after the establishments without permits to operate.

Aside from the changes in the system, the city government has also taken steps towards the promotion of business activities in the local area. Improvements in infrastructure facilities have been made, such as lighting the city streets, most especially in the business section of the city. The city government has encouraged local entrepreneurs to participate in trade fairs where their products could be displayed for promotion purposes. Furthermore, the business proprietors are asked to participate in all the city activities such as the 'Bangus' Festival where they put up streamers advertising their products. In addition, the city government has improved its delivery systems such as its waste disposal and the cleaning of the environment. In a way, this has made the city more business friendly.

SOME RESULTS OF THE REFORMS

The changes introduced into the system increased the city income. In particular, revenues from the business taxes and licenses steadily increased their share of the total income, from 66 to 69 percent between 1999 and 2003. The number of business establishments operating within the city also increased. From 3782 in 1999, the figures jumped to 5545 in 2003. The increase could be attributed to the business tax mapping conducted by the city government.

From the perspective of the business proprietors, the establishment of the One Stop Business Center has made the processing of permits faster and more efficient. It is very convenient for them because they pay all their taxes and fees in one place. The shortened period of processing permits, especially in the conduct of inspection for clearances, has also reduced opportunities for giving 'bribe' money to inspectors.

Moreover, the proprietors appreciate the policy of the city government to assist businesses in the promotion and marketing of their produce or products. To them, this is the right step towards the promotion of more entrepreneurial activities in the city. What they need right now is not only assistance in getting their permit to operate their businesses but also provision of a conducive environment where their business activities can grow and further develop with the proper incentives given by the city government.

THE TWO BUSINESS LICENSING SYSTEMS IN COMPARISON

The two local authorities seem to encounter the same problems in their licensing system. There is a delay in the issuance of permits due to the imposition of too many clearances and due to the lack of inspectors tasked to conduct visual inspections. The delay in the issuance of permits exacts some economic costs on the part of the businesses. To avoid this, the proprietors would readily follow the so-called 'standard operating procedure' where public officials would be bribed to facilitate the issuance of permits. As indicated in the case studies, the cumbersome procedures plus the discretion of public officials to determine the amount of taxes and fees to be paid gave opportunities for the commission of graft and corruption.

What appears to be lacking in both systems is the conduct of post-licensing monitoring. Obviously, the local authorities emphasize more the regulation entry rather than the post-licensing phase of the system. This is validated in the case studies where the inspectors and the interviewed proprietors admitted that they seldom encounter the inspectors after the issuance of the permit.

In responding to the identified problems, both local authorities introduced reforms or changes in the licensing system. They streamlined their procedures to facilitate the issuance of permits; they came up with a new list of establishments for their database; and Dagupan even went further to tax map the business establishments. The process produced a list of businesses with no permits.

Thinking about the convenience of taxpayers, particularly the business sector, in paying their taxes and other obligations to the city government, Quezon City put up its payment and assessment lounges which are airconditioned, with free coffee and iced tea for the taxpayers. Dagupan went beyond this by establishing the One Stop Business Center. The taxpayers need not go from one office to another to pay their taxes and fees. They just go to the Center for all their payments. What is noteworthy here is the presence of all the representatives of the Engineering and Health Offices and the Fire Department in the Center, which facilitates the issuance of permits.

The city government of Dagupan did not just look at the regulation entry of businesses. It also provided assistance to the business sector to enable them to participate in trade fairs; encouraged them to be involved in the city activities where their products would be advertised; and made their environment more business-friendly through the lighting of city streets, and proper waste disposal and collection. To the proprietors, these are promotional activities for their businesses.

SUMMARY

On the whole, the examination of the business licensing systems conveys the fact that the regulation entry of businesses is part of the social regulation instrument of local government. It is aimed at protecting the public interests and welfare by imposing certain conditions for the operation of business firms. However, the case studies show that there are private interests that go with the imposition of conditions. As indicated in the experiences of the two cities, previous city administrations did not attempt to introduce any changes in the licensing system. Any change then could mean a reduction in their political and economic clout in the local area. This is particularly true if the change in the system would affect their political and economic allies. This is validated by complaints from some inspectors whose reports on non-compliance with certain conditions by some business firms are not attended to by the political leaders or officials.

Any change in the system would also be antithesis to the maintenance of the system as far as the public officials are concerned. As shown by the case studies, the imposition of too many requirements, which has caused too much delay in the issuance of permits, has given rise to opportunities for the commission of corruption. The imposition of too many clearances seems to work well with the private interests of the public officials.

ISSUES AND CONCERNS

The above discussions have brought about certain issues and concerns in the business licensing system at the local level. First, is there a need for the regulation entry of businesses? While it is admitted that this is part of social regulation, which is for the protection of the public interests, the case studies have shown that there are also private interests that go with it. As depicted by the experiences of the local authorities, the imposition of too many requirements at the entry level tend to promote private interests more than public interests.

Second, there is the concern regarding the effect of the commission of corruption on the local government system of licensing. The case studies have indicated the opportunities for the commission of corruption in the issuance of permits as well as in the post-licensing phase of the operations of business firms. This deprives the local authority of much-needed resources for the improvement of the community. Besides, the system, which promotes more the private interests of public officials, tends to be very particularistic and may prove disastrous to the interests of the community in the long run.

Third, there is the issue of the exercise of local autonomy by local governments. Regulation of the operations of business enterprises is not the sole responsibility of the local government authority. A number of national government agencies impose certain clearances and licenses on the business firms or companies before they can be granted their permit or license to operate in the local area. And yet, it is the local government that is held accountable for whatever incidents or disastrous events may happen as a result of the operations of businesses in the community. In other words, the decision-making process at the local level is constricted by the imposition of certain requirements by the national government. Shouldn't the responsibility of the local government authority to regulate business operations for the protection of the general public welfare and health, be matched with more regulatory powers and functions to enable the local government to make good decisions relative to the operations of businesses?

CONCLUSIONS

The business licensing systems of Quezon City and Dagupan City have shown how the regulatory regime works at the local level. The cases have indicated the restrictions and constraints faced by a local government authority in regulating the entry and conduct of business at the local level. Aside from the policies, laws or ordinances implemented, and the rules and regulations imposed by local government, there are still a lot of impositions by national government agencies which, overall, have made the entry of establishments into the business or economic arena doubly difficult and cumbersome. Although the main objective of social regulation as a regulatory instrument is to promote general welfare and to protect the public interest, the imposition of too many restrictions on the entry and conduct of business does not provide a conducive environment for the operation of enterprises in the local community. On the other hand, it provides opportunities for the advancement of private interests and the commission of corruption, which negatively impact on the community as a whole. Apparently, the regulatory instrument works the opposite way.

The case studies have also brought to the fore the issue of devolved regulation. Local government does not have complete autonomy in regulating the entry and conduct of business in the local area. The assumption here is that given more regulatory powers and functions, local government would be in a better position to regulate the operations of business establishments than national government agencies, for the simple reason that it is the closest government to the people in the community. As pointed out earlier, the local community holds local government accountable for whatever consequences may result from the operations of said establishments. But then, the fundamental issue here is whether or not the regulation entry is necessary. If so, then it becomes imperative for local government to exercise more powers and authority over the conduct of business in the local area based on the standards set by national government. Policies and laws have to be crafted by national government for universal application but local government, for more efficiency and effectiveness, would do the implementation.

Complementing the need for the grant of more autonomous powers and authority to local governments is the need to develop and enhance further their competencies, most especially in the area of regulatory governance. As depicted by the case studies, local government should have the expertise in monitoring and evaluating the operations of business enterprises. Unfortunately, the local authorities have not really gone deeply into the area of monitoring and evaluation. What has been done so far is to streamline the procedures for the issuance of business permits and licenses with the end view of collecting more taxes from the business sector, rather than facing the issue of how to regulate them better for the public interest.

REFERENCES

Baldwin, R. and M. Cave (1999), *Understanding Regulation: Theory, Strategy, and Practice*, Oxford: Oxford University Press.

Cariño, L. (2000), 'The concept of governance', *From Government to Governance, Reflections on the 1999 World Conference on Governance*, EROPA.

Cariño, L. (2004), 'Regulatory governance in the Philippines: A profile', in Paul Cook, Colin Kirkpatrick, Martin Minogue and David Parker (eds), *Leading Issues in Competition, Regulation and Development*, Cheltenham, UK and Northampton, MA, USA: Edward Elgar, pp. 256–76.

Legaspi, P. (2001), *The Changing Role of the Local Governments Under a Decentralized State: Some Cases in Philippine Local Governance*, Manila: National College of Public Administration and Governance.

Legaspi, P., W. Cabo and M.E. Joaquin (1996), *Local Economic Promotion in the Philippines*, Manila: Local Government Center, UP and German Foundation for International Development.

Minogue, M. (2001), *Governance-based Analysis of Regulation*, Manchester: CRC, University of Manchester.

Ogus, A. (2001), *Regulatory Institutions and Structures*, Manchester: CRC, University of Manchester.

Ogus, A. and Qing Zhang (2003), *Regulating Business Entry East and West*, Manchester: CRC, University of Manchester.

Tabunda, Manuel and Mario Galang (1992), *A Guide to the Local Government Code of 1991*, Manila: Mary Jo Publisher.

Work, R. (2003), 'Overview of decentralization worldwide: A stepping stone to improved governance and human development', in *Decentralization and Power Shift, an Imperative for Good Governance*, Manila: Center for Local and Regional Governance, National College of Public Administration and Governance, University of the Philippines.

Documents on Quezon City, The Philippines

Quezon City, Quality Management for a Quality City, The Belmonte Administration, Year 1, 1 July 2001–30 June 2002.

Quezon City: A Business Destination, City Planning and Development Office, September 2002.

Quezon City, Working in Partnership with the Citizenry in Building a Quality Community, City Planning and Development Office, September 2002.

The Belmonte Administration, Quezon City, Summary of Key Accomplishments, January–December 2002, Office of the City Mayor, 2003.

Documents on Dagupan City, The Philippines

Dagupan City Development Strategy Report, 2003.

State of the City Address, January 27, by Mayor Benjamin S. Lim.

Report on Business Tax Mapping, Task Force on Tax Mapping, January 2003.

Socio-economic Profile of Dagupan City, City Planning and Development Office, 2003.

One Stop Business Center Profile, City Administrator's Office, 2003.

Bangus City Journal, Dagupan City Government, January 2004.

8. The Philippine port sector: a case of regulatory capture

Enrico L. Basilio[1]

INTRODUCTION

The Philippines is an archipelagic country, consisting of more than 7000 islands. Like the various pieces of a jigsaw puzzle, these islands need to be linked together by an efficient and seamless transport system. Unfortunately, the country's sea transport and distribution system, mainly the ports system, is plagued by inefficiency that causes high domestic transport costs. This hampers domestic trade and stymies countryside development, and has had a negative impact on efforts to improve productivity at the farm level, and promote tourism and the global competitiveness of Philippine exports. These inefficiencies have resulted in high costs of transporting goods between islands and the degradation of the quality and quantity of the products being shipped.

The Philippine Ports Authority (PPA), mandated to supervise, operate and regulate the ports system in the country, is endowed with vast powers. But due to a lack of checks and balances, it has become a convenient strategy for vested interests simply to capture the regulator to reap economic rents at the expense of public interest and welfare.

According to Villaseñor (2000), a regulatory agency is said to be under *regulatory capture* when it exhibits any of the following:

- It furthers the industry's interests at expense of consumers;
- It is more responsive to industry pressures;
- It has become too identified with the industry;
- It has become overly protective of regulated firms;
- It is passive, largely rubber-stamping the firms' decisions; and
- It adopts the regulated utilities' objectives as its own.

Simply put, when a regulatory agency undermines the common good in favour of the interest of certain groups, it is guilty of capture. According to G. Stigler (in Villaseñor, 2000) governments do not end up creating a monopoly in industries by accident. Rather, they regulate at the behest of producers who capture the regulatory agency and use regulation to prevent competition.

D. Nikomborirak (1998) has posited that

> years of regulatory experience in many developed countries reveal that regulations, like markets, can also 'fail.' Regulatory failure may occur for two reasons. The first is associated with the 'capture theory' . . . and the second from the fact that the regulator itself is not perfect. We must not forget that by creating a regulator, we entrust an enormous amount of responsibility and power unto a single body. This resembles an autocratic government.

The Philippine ports system embodies these dilemmas and pitfalls. Since the government receives dividends from the PPA's operation, it has also become a party to the ill effects of regulatory capture.

FLAWS IN THE PPA CHARTER

The inefficiencies in port operations and administration are a product of the flaws in the ports policy, embodied in the Charter of the Philippine Ports Authority (PPA), that make the authority very susceptible to regulatory capture.

PPA has Both Developmental and Regulatory Powers

Regulatory capture results from the combination of developmental and regulatory functions in the PPA Charter. The developmental function allows the PPA to work closely with all the operating elements in port development and operations (shipping, cargo handling, terminal operations) – the same parties that it is supposed to regulate.

Conflict of Interest

The PPA's Charter (PD 857) allows the regulator to benefit from its own regulation by allowing it to share from revenues in cargo handling by at least 10 per cent. In the past, the PPA's share from cargo handling revenue even reached a high of 33 per cent. It is therefore not surprising that the PPA almost always approves petitions for a rate increase even when there are no petitioners, no public hearing/s conducted, and/or no financial statements evaluated by the PPA to ascertain the economic or financial justification for the rate increase.[2] In one case, the implementation of a rate

Table 8.1 Annual increases in cargo handling rates (%)

Year	Domestic (%)		Foreign (%)	
	Arrastre	Stevedoring	Arrastre	Stevedoring
1998	12	40	8	40
1999			20	
2000	10	10	8	8
2001	10	10	10	15
2002			10[a]	
2005	38[c]		10[b]	
2006			12[b]	

Notes:
[a] 10% rate increase this year was granted only to the operators at MICT and South Harbour.
[b] Early this year, PPA approved a 2-tiered rate increase to be implemented in 2005 (10%) and 2006 (12%). The private sector will file a complaint questioning the basis of the rate increases.
[c] The cargo handlers operating at the domestic ports have filed a petition to the PPA seeking for a 38% increase in arrastre and stevedoring rates.
No rate increases were approved by the PPA for the period 2003–2004 because of the moratorium ordered by the President. One of the items in the 10-point agenda of the President was to reduce transport cost from Mindanao to Luzon.

increase did not even have Board approval.[3] Table 8.1 shows the rate increases approved by the PPA in recent years.

In August 2002, President Arroyo directed the PPA to adopt a universal rate for collecting the government share from the revenues of cargo handlers – 10 per cent for domestic ports and 20 per cent for international ports. The PPA announced that it had revised its rules on the bidding of cargo handling contracts to comply with the presidential directive. Instead of using 'the highest share to PPA' rule as basis for winning a contract, the PPA will now use 'the lowest service rate' as the basis since its share from cargo handling revenues is already fixed. This is laudable if indeed the award of cargo handling contracts will be done through public bidding. What the PPA failed to mention is that under PPA Administrative Order 01-2001, the renewal of expired and expiring cargo handling contracts will not be subjected to public bidding.

The conflict of interest issue only exacerbates the presence of regulatory capture because the PPA also benefits from the effect of its regulation. Hence, its loyalty to the public diminishes as its loyalty to its partners in development and to itself increases.

The Port is a Huge Government Monopoly

The PPA's Charter provides it with vast powers – that is, the PPA owns, maintains, develops and regulates the ports. It is also vested with taxing powers – to fix rates and collect dues such as wharfage, berthing/usage fees and revenue share from cargo handling. The PPA boasts of the fact that it does not get a single centavo from the national government for its budgetary requirements. In practice, as a government owned and controlled corporation (GOCC), it declares 50 per cent of its net income as dividend to the national government (Table 8.2). This is one of the major reasons why the PPA increases its rates – so that it can generate more revenues for itself and for the national government. But the question is whether the PPA is first and foremost a revenue-generating agency or a service-provider. There is no doubt that the PPA should generate revenues to finance its port development and maintenance activities. But confiscating resources from the business sector and consumers in favour of the government is another story.

Sharing its profits with the government in the form of dividends makes the PPA regulate further against the public interest because now the government also becomes a partner in sharing the returns from the inefficiencies in cargo handling.

Bias Towards Multiple Cargo Handling

Due to the unusual benefit the PPA gets from cargo handling operations, it has encouraged, nurtured, and perpetuated a system based on multiple cargo handling. The more cargoes are handled, the more revenues are generated – thus the higher the share for the PPA (from cargo handling). In 2001, out of the total revenue generated by the PPA from port operations, its share from

Table 8.2 PPA revenues and net income (2000–2002) in million pesos

	2001	2002[a]
Port revenues	4720	3640
• Fixed fee from ICTSI	1400	1230
• Revenue from cargo handling share	837	430[b]
Net income	1640	2120

Notes:
[a] January to September.
[b] ATI only.

Sources: PPA Financial Reports, news reports.

cargo handling accounted for 18 per cent (this figure still does not reflect the share of PPA from the International Ports). Because of this, even shipping companies have gone into cargo handling. Although containerization has brought about positive effects such as reduced breakage/quality deterioration of cargoes, and increased security of cargo/reduced pilferage, the number of steps involved in handling the cargo has remained the same. Self-interest and loyalty to its partners further encourage inefficiency in cargo handling, which gives the PPA more profit.

REGULATORY RISKS

Apart from policy, the PPA's mandate and the current system allow many regulatory risks.

1. *High discretionary power*. The administration of the Philippine port system is highly centralized. All government ports scattered around various parts of the country, with a few exceptions, are managed by the PPA as a centralized port authority. In contrast, none of the successful and well-managed ports cited elsewhere in the world is administered by a centralized system of port administration. Normal practice is that each port has its own authority, whether under the jurisdiction of national or local governments. A decentralized system of local port authorities each operating independently creates the environment for inter-port competition, thereby satisfying one of the important conditions for an efficient market in the port sector. The fact that the PPA owns the public port system and regulates private ports eliminates the possibility of inter-port competition.
2. *Lack of transparency*. Policy formulation and administration in well-managed ports worldwide is carried out by a board dominated by the private sector with a limited degree of government participation. In the Philippines, however, policy formulation and implementation lack transparency and, in most cases, are railroaded. This can be attributed to the virtual absence of participation of other players such as the private sector in policy formulation and implementation. Of the nine board seats in the PPA, for example, only one comes from the private sector. Consequently, public hearings are not conducted properly. Board Resolutions are a product of the decisions of a three-person Board Committee or (BoardCom). In almost all cases, the PPA Board simply ratifies or adopts the resolutions of the PPA BoardCom.
3. *Insufficient autonomy*. Nikomborirak (1998) argues that competent and well-qualified commissioners, assuming they can be found, still do

not guarantee efficient regulation, and that for the regulator to be able to perform its task effectively, a certain degree of independence from the government is required. As a common practice, regulatory agencies are run and managed on a full-time basis by commissioners whose appointments have fixed terms. Unfortunately, the same cannot be said about the PPA Board. As mentioned earlier, the PPA Board is government controlled. Six out of nine Board members are cabinet secretaries who do not have the time to attend all PPA Board meetings.

Regulatory capture is inherent in many Presidential Decrees (PD) issued during martial law because the developmental and regulatory functions were vested in one body with the assumption that the government agency and public interest are one and the same. But public trust was broken once the interests of the private sector, which was supposed to be regulated, began to replace some of the government functions like cargo handling and terminal operations, and the firms also became partners due to the sharing arrangement in cargo handling. This weakens the case for privatizing ports – lest privatization further exacerbate the damage done to public interest.

CASES

There are many examples in the PPA that demonstrate the phenomenon of regulatory capture. For this chapter, the following cases will be discussed to show (a) the close relationship between the PPA and the sector it is supposed to regulate, and (b) the regulatory risks that they exemplify.

Executive Order (EO) 59

Executive Order No. 59 (s. 1998) is a classic manifestation of the misconception plaguing the PPA operation as a developmental and regulatory body. The PPA supported the proponents of a monopoly and excluded the paying public, but nonetheless assumed that it would be the one representing the public interest since it is the regulatory body. However, the regulatory function is completely subdued by the developmental and profit making relationships among the PPA, the port players, and the government that partakes of dividends – while the public continues to pay excessively. It is only through the strong advocacies made by the private sector that the PPA and other government agencies have become conscious of the public interest.

On 28 December 1998, President Joseph Estrada issued Executive Order (EO) No. 59 directing the PPA 'to adopt and implement a programme for further rationalization, modernization, and improvement of port services and facilities in government ports'. Under the existing Charter of the PPA (PD 857), the PPA is mandated to develop sea port terminals, other facilities and ancillary services in the port areas. However, the EO argued that the government does not have sufficient funds to finance the modernization of these public-owned ports. To address this 'constraint,' EO 59 was issued to promote and encourage the 'participation of the private sector by requiring all existing facility operators and service providers such as cargo handling operators, shipping companies and port workers and Labour to unify into *one corporation* by merger, consolidation, buyout, joint venture, or by any other similar means to manage, operate and develop the *entire* government port *without* need of a public bidding' (emphasis added).

While port modernization and greater private sector participation are laudable objectives, the manner by which port privatization and modernization would be implemented as provided in EO 59 is highly questionable, namely:

- *Creation of a big private monopoly*. The contract was supposed to be awarded to a 'consortium' organized two months before the issuance of EO 59. The consortium is composed of terminal operators, cargo handling companies and big shipping lines.
- *Bundling of port services*. This means that all port services, including ancillary services, will have to be provided by the private port monopolist.
- *Negotiated contract*. The operation and development of the ports will be awarded to the port monopolist without the benefit of a public bidding process, contrary to the principle of transparency being promoted by the government.
- *Nationwide coverage*. This is not only a monopoly of one port but of the entire port system.
- *The establishment of a nationwide Portworkers' Social Amelioration Fund (PSAF)*. This issue will be discussed below as a separate example of regulatory capture.

The PPA vigorously supported the consortium, arguing that (a) ports are natural monopolies; (b) the volume at the North Harbour, the biggest domestic port in the country, is even too small to warrant competition (that is, having several terminal operators); and (c) competition will only increase the project cost since there will be duplication of investments in equipment.

There was opposition to EO 59 but the PPA disregarded the evidence presented and arguments raised (see Tables 8.3 and 8.4), saying that the loudest critics of the monopoly scheme have nothing to do with the ports (they are

Table 8.3 Cargo volume at the ports of Manila (1998)

International standard	
– One operator can handle profitably 200 000 TEUs annually	
– One berth with two ship-to-shore gantry cranes	
– Sufficient back-up land	
North Harbour (excluding breakbulk)	706 000 TEUs/year
South Harbour / MICT	1 148 000 TEUs/year
– South Harbour (ATI)	410 000 TEUs/year
– Manila International Container Terminal (ICTSI)	738 000 TEUs/year
ICTSI and ATI are operating profitably	
– ATI Net Income (7/1998–6/1999)	P212 million up 49%
– ICTSI Net Income (1–6/1999)	P251 million up 35%

Note: TEU = Twenty Equivalent Units.

Sources: PPA, Financial Reports, news articles.

Table 8.4 Studies on two operators for the Manila North Harbour

Consultants	Two operators FIRR	Two operators investment
PPA–Halcrow	20%	US$512 million
EMG–ORSP	25%	US$225 million
PCCI–Consilium	30%	US$247 million

Notes:
EMG = Economic Mobilization Group; ORSP = Operations Research Society of the Philippines; PCCI = Philippine Chamber of Commerce and Industry.

It is interesting to note that the project cost based on the PPA–Halcrow study is twice that of the ORSP and Consilium studies. The high cost is a form of entry barrier that the PPA placed to discourage investors and to convince the policy-makers that having two operators, while financially feasible, is costly.

only the port users who have the biggest stake in the modernization of the ports because they are the ones who will pay for its cost and operation). But, during the Economic Mobilization Group (EMG) meeting in Malacañang (the Presidential Offices), the representative of the consortium declared that 'there is no monopoly because we are one big happy family'.

In its obsession to implement EO 59, the PPA rushed the formulation of the Bid Terms of Reference (TOR) under a Single Terminal Operator (STO). In order to project an image that everything was transparent and above-board, the PPA conducted a public consultation. However, it

Table 8.5 Congressional Resolutions related to EO 59

COCAFM Resolution No. 016 (September 1999) – 'Requesting the President to amend EO 59 and adopt a system that requires competitive and transparent bidding among interested service providers.'
House Resolution No. 1659 (August 2000) – 'Requesting the President to rescind EO 59 and direct the PPA to adopt a policy which promotes inter- and intra-port competition and requires competitive and transparent bidding among interested port investors and operators.'
House Resolution No. 1740 (August 2000) – 'Urging the President to direct the PPA to hold in abeyance finalization of the bidding for the privatization and modernization of the Manila North Harbour under a Single Terminal Operator, until such time that His Excellency shall have acted on House Resolution No. 1659 (Requesting the President to rescind EO 59 and declare competition at the North Harbour).'

withheld the dissemination of vital information to the public (by excluding crucial Annexes, thus depriving the public of the opportunity to intelligently comment on the draft TOR).

President Estrada turned a deaf ear to the pleas from Congress to correct the port privatization policy (see Table 8.5). What changed his mind later on was the need to reverse the damage done to his presidency by the exposé of Governor Chavit Singson. Hence, on 30 October 2000, President Estrada in his address to the nation announced a host of policy reforms including the rescission of EO 59 with these words: 'There is a perception that EO 59 will create a monopoly in port services. Thus EO 59 which involves the further rationalization of port services and facilities in government ports is hereby revoked' (Towards a Common Ground). The following day, 31 October, he issued EO 308 formally rescinding EO 59 and directing the PPA to subject the privatization of the Manila North Harbour to competition (by dividing it into two terminals) and public bidding.

But the PPA had a commitment to fulfil. On 7 November 2000, the PPA published in the major daily newspaper a 'Notice of Invitation to Pre-Qualification for the Privatization of the North Harbour under the Single Terminal Operator scheme' – that is, monopoly.

The beginning of 2001 saw a change in government leadership, as Estrada's administration was replaced by that of Arroyo. The PPA, under the new dispensation, presented to the private sector a new Alternative Development Plan for the Manila North Harbour. Under the proposed plan, the North Harbour would be divided into three terminals, instead of two as mandated under EO 308 (s. 2000). The new PPA general manager promised to have the draft Bid Terms of Reference (TOR) completed for comment by the end of August 2001. In the meantime, the PPA started construction at the Marine Slipway (MSW) area of the North Harbour, costing roughly P300 million. The question was, how would this affect the Bid TOR being drafted by the Coordinating Council for Private Sector Participation (CCPSP)? Because of the controversy that erupted as a result of an anomaly in the bidding for the MSW (now the subject of a corruption case filed against PPA officials), the President directed the PPA (December 2002) to stop the modernization of the North Harbour and instead to concentrate on the smaller ports in the regions. Despite this, the PPA presented to the National Port Advisory Council (NPAC) the proposed Bid TOR in October 2003.

Portworkers' Social Amelioration Fund (PSAF)

In April 2003, the issue of setting up a Portworkers' Social Amelioration Fund (PSAF) was, once again, brought to the fore at the National Port Advisory Council (NPAC) Permanent Committee on Port Labour Relations. This is not the first time the issue has been raised. Rate increases in the past were approved by the PPA and paid for by the cargo shippers for the establishment of a Port Labour Trust Fund. The PSAF story highlights the close relationship between the PPA and the cargo handling sector.

Under the Labour Code, employers are required to pay separation and retirement benefits to their employees in cases of termination of employment and retirement from service. Under the law, it is clear that the payment of separation and past benefits is a liability of the employer to his employees. The term 'redundancy or separation benefits for portworkers' first appeared in EO 212 (s. 1994) issued by President Ramos on 28 November 1994: *Accelerating the De-monopolization and Privatization Programme for Government Ports in the Country*. Section 5 of this EO specifically directs the Philippine Ports Authority to adopt measures to protect the interests of redundant and displaced PPA and port personnel resulting from the implementation of the government's de-monopolization and privatization programmes. Towards this end, the EO states that PPA shall provide redundancy or separation benefits *as may be authorized under existing laws*. Likewise, the PPA shall ensure that the welfare and security of tenure of port workers are assured in every port that is privatized (emphasis added).

In January 1995, the PPA issued Memorandum Circular (MC) 05-1995 granting an increase in cargo handling rates for the purpose of raising funds for the Port Labour Trust Fund that was to be established. In this instance, it was the cargo owners/shippers who contributed to the Port Labour Trust Fund. One question that may be asked is, what happened to the Port Labour Trust Fund?

EO 212's implementation was delayed due to objections of the Labour sector, who argued that the privatization of the ports would result in the inability of some cargo handlers to shoulder the retirement requirements of displaced port workers. The Labour sector claimed that:

- The PPA was their main employer and that they were merely subcontracted to perform the services that the PPA was not capable of rendering.
- The cargo-handling contracts granted by the PPA were only for a limited period, a year at most.
- The rate adjustments granted by the PPA were insignificant compared to the rising costs of providing the service. There were even cases where cargo handlers were forced to dip into the retirement fund that they had already established.

In other words, the port workers' bone of contention hinges on the argument that it is not the cargo handler's responsibility to provide for the separation benefits, but that of the PPA. The PPA, on the other hand, argues that the payment of separation benefits is a private liability of the cargo handling operators.

In May 1996, the portworkers staged a nationwide strike to dramatize their concerns and to pressure the PPA to act on them. As a result, a Tripartite Oversight Committee was formed to resolve the problem. The strike ended with the signing of a Memorandum of Agreement (MOA) that addressed Labour concerns such as:

- Security of tenure;
- Recognition of existing collective bargaining agreements (CBAs) and CBA benefits;
- Respect for existing Labour laws;
- The establishment of a Portworkers' Social Amelioration Fund (PSAF);
- Workers' participation in the (cargo handling) enterprise;
- Prohibition against unfair competition in the cargo handling business.

In September 1996, the National Union of Portworkers in the Philippines (NUPP) submitted to the DOTC a proposal for the creation of a Portworkers' Social Amelioration Programme (PSAP). The PSAP is a 'scheme designed to acknowledge the contribution of the port workers in the maritime transport industry to the overall effort to advance the economy by giving them their just share in the fruits of the production and to augment their income, specially during periods of need and distress, as well as to institutionalize the mechanism to implement the program' (NUPW, 1996). The program is said to be a private-sector initiative among the cargo handlers and the port workers. The PSAP aims to augment the income of the port workers by compensating them and their families in cases of death, disability, retrenchments, and retirements; and providing for benefits such as emergency loans, salary loans, educational loans, housing loans, and year-end cash bonuses.

A second proposal was for a Portworkers' Equity Programme (PEP). The idea is for the workers to be co-owners of the company that employs them through the purchase of not more than 25 per cent of the company's shares of stocks. Funding is supposed to be raised by collecting from the shippers an additional cargo handling fee of P1.50 per tonne per port. Given the estimated annual cargo volume of 80 million metric tonnes, total collections for the PSAF would be roughly P240 million yearly (approximately $US4.5m).

Nothing happened to the NUPP proposal to create a PSAP and a PEP. However, the strong objection of Labour to the implementation of EO 212, convinced then President Ramos to rescind EO 212 on Labour Day. The President also issued a Memorandum Order to the Chairman of the PPA Board 'directing the PPA to finalize the implementing mechanisms, including provisions for funding, and ensure immediate implementation of the Portworkers' Social Amelioration Programme (PSAP) which shall provide additional benefits to port workers and their families nationwide . . . not later than May 22, 1997'. Despite this Presidential Order, the PSAP remained a mere concept, since nothing was provided for its implementation. The reason is obvious: 'There was no legal framework that justifies its implementation.'

On 12 November 1997, the Philippine Chamber of Arrastre and Stevedoring Operators (PCASO), NUPP, and the Domestic Shipowners Association (DSA) entered into an MOA for the purpose of 'identifying, pursuing and promoting common business interests and discussing the feasibility and propriety of coming together for the purpose of establishing port service operations . . . which produce mutually beneficial results'. This initial agreement was concretized with the signing of another MOA on 7 October 1998, this time including the big terminal operators, that calls for the creation of a 'consortium' for the purpose of establishing a joint-venture company 'to develop the Manila North Harbour, operate its facilities, improve its efficiency, increase government revenue, [and] reduce government expenditure for port maintenance at the least cost to the users'. To provide the legal framework for this plan, President Estrada issued EO 59 on 28 December 1998. As discussed previously, EO 59 called for the creation of a private monopoly as well as the establishment of a PSAF.

In anticipation of the implementation of EO 59, the Portworkers' Social Amelioration Programme, Inc. (PSAP Inc.) was organized on 30 March 1999. Among the trustees of the PSAP, Inc. are representatives from Labour, shipping and cargo handling sectors.

However, EO 59 was never implemented for lack of an IRR (Implementing Rules and Regulations). This time, it was the private sector (not the Labour sector) that opposed its implementation mainly due to the port monopoly that it sought to create. And because of this, the PPA had to issue, on 16 March 2000, a direction to operationalize the PSAP on the basis of a PPA Board approval. But this direction was also never implemented due to the absence of a legal framework.

In early May, the portworkers at the Manila North Harbour staged a strike over the PPA's failure to address their five-point demand – that is, security of tenure, recognition of existing unions, recognition of existing CBAs, establishment of the PSAF and non-payment of their past benefits. On 8 May 2000, the PPA signed an 'agreement' with the portworkers, confirmed by the Labour Secretary, promising to pay the past service benefits of portworkers whose cargo handling companies were taken over by the PPA Special Takeover Unit (STU). The PPA committed to pay each portworker one month equivalent salary for every year of service. The total amount was estimated at P250 million. In previous instances, the PPA had argued that the past benefits of portworkers were liabilities of the cargo handling operators. This time, the PPA was ready to assume liability. Hence, the PPA management started paying the portworkers their past service benefits on 15 May 2000 even without the benefit of a PPA Board approval. It was only on 23 May 2000 that the PPA Board ratified the actions of the PPA management. During a Congressional public hearing, the PPA argued that it 'merely advanced' the payment of the portworkers' past benefits. The PPA hoped to be reimbursed by the winning bidder in the North Harbour privatization. The private sector objected to the plan of incorporating the 'amount' into the project cost for two reasons: (1) the winning bidder has nothing to do with the liability and (2) incorporating the amount paid to the portworkers as past benefits will unnecessarily jack up the cost of the North Harbour project. In December 2002, President Arroyo ordered the PPA to shelve the North Harbour Modernization Programme and instead use the available fund for the construction of small ports in the countryside. This raises a question as to how the PPA will be reimbursed for the amount it advanced for the payment of the portworkers' past benefits? In any event, if a Port Labour Trust Fund was established as a result of the cargo handling rate increase in 1995, why should the PPA pay the portworkers their past benefits in 2000?

On 31 October 2000, President Estrada issued EO 308 rescinding EO 59. With that rescission went the legal framework for the establishment of the PSAF. With EO 59 gone, the new leadership of the PPA saw the necessity of issuing another directive for the establishment of a Port Labour Trust Fund. This time, however, as part of the PPA's 'heal and build' policy, the requirement of the Port Labour Trust Fund was linked with the renewal of expired and expiring cargo handling contracts. The PPA was quick to pay the unpaid benefits of the workers, claiming this was done because of its subsidiary liability. Perhaps they also construe Labour as their public interest segment rather than the shippers. Again this is because Labour contractors are their 'developmental' partners, like the shipping companies, brokerage and terminal operators.

This PPA directive (PPA AO 01-2001) seeks to grant the renewal of expired and expiring cargo-handling contracts without public bidding, contrary to what the law dictates. The private sector cited EO 40 (s. 2001) and EO 109 (s. 2002) issued by President Arroyo mandating government agencies to subject to public bidding all procurement (including cargo handling) and contract awards. The PPA asked the Office of Government Corporate Counsel (OGCC) for an opinion on the matter. The OGCC in its opinion (No. 234) affirmed that indeed cargo handling is covered by EOs 40 and 109. Instead of implementing the advice, the PPA requested the OGCC to reconsider its opinion, which it did (No. 282). Early that year, Congress passed into law RA 9184 (Government Procurement Reform Act), which defined as a matter of policy, in all cases, the following principles: transparency and competition through public bidding, monitoring, accountability, etc. When the issue was brought up by the private sector at the NPAC for the purpose of making sure that PPA policies are consistent with the law, the PPA said they would seek another legal opinion from the OGCC.

On 2 July 2001, the PPA issued PPA Administrative Order (AO) 01-2001, *Guidelines for the Issuance of Probationary and Long-term Contracts for Expired and Expiring Cargo-Handling Contracts* as part of the government's 'heal and build' policy. A key component of this AO is the establishment of a Port Labour Trust Fund as a key requirement for the renewal of the cargo handling contract/s.

- For the issuance of a two-year 'probationary' contract, the cargo-handling operator must make 'available a port Labour trust fund for the retirement and separation of concerned port workers', among other requirements.
- For the award of a long-term contract (maximum of 10 years), the establishment of a *Port Labour Trust Fund* is required. The amount, to be deposited in authorized bank/s, must be sufficient for the retirement

and separation benefits of individual port workers' employment term, or a programme for the same trust fund secured through an accredited service provider.

The private sector immediately objected to this, citing the benefits to be derived from competition, transparency, and greater private sector participation through public bidding.

Despite the objection, the PPA proceeded with the implementation of AO 01-2001. In an opinion sought by the PPA that year, the Office of the Government Corporate Counsel (OGCC Opinion No. 234 s. 2002) confirmed the private sector's contention that the cargo-handling service is covered by Executive Orders 40 (2001) and 109 (2002) issued by President Arroyo, which require competitive public bidding in the contract award. Instead of following this advice, the PPA requested the OGCC to reconsider its opinion on the matter, which the OGCC did.

One possible explanation for the PPA not wanting to subject the renewal of expired/expiring cargo-handling contracts to public bidding is because of the possibility that the incumbent cargo-handling operator might fail to win in the bidding. If that happens, then the payment of the past benefits becomes due. The problem occurs when the cargo-handling operator does not have the funds to answer for the liability. Hence the need to renew the contract via negotiation and not public bidding so that the liability will not fall due. This probably is a compromise for the inability of the government to establish the PSAF.

Congress has now passed into law Republic Act (RA) No. 9184 *Government Procurement Reform Act*, which requires as a matter of policy, the principles of transparency, competition through public bidding, accountability in government procurement and contract awards, including cargo-handling contracts. It remains to be seen if the PPA AO 01-2001 will be revised to conform to the law.

Harbour Centre

This is a case depicting the PPA as a 'biased referee'. As a regulator, the PPA regulates against competition to protect its own interest over that of the public. The fact that the PPA is vested with proprietary, developmental and regulatory functions makes it favour a scenario that will enable it to benefit from its own regulation, in many cases even at the expense of public interest. This once again highlights the 'conflict of interest' that seems to cloud the PPA's judgement in regulating for the common good.

Competition, privatization, transparency and greater private-sector participation in industry are among the government's declared policy objectives. Ironically, the efforts to meet these objectives in the development and operation of public ports have had mixed results.

The first major initiative at port privatization was the bidding of the terminal operation of the Manila International Container Terminal (MICT) in 1987. In connection with this, a 25-year contract was awarded to the International Container Terminal Services Inc. (ICTSI), a private terminal operator. This was the first successful case of a 'landlord' port model in the country.[4]

This initiative was followed in 1992 by the implementation of the Smokey Mountain Development Plan. In 1992, President Corazon Aquino issued Memorandum Order No. 415 directing the National Housing Authority (NHA) to implement the Smokey Mountain Development Plan and undertake reclamation of the area across Road 10. Smokey Mountain used to be an open garbage dumpsite in Manila. The PPA was directed to assist in evaluating the port-related land issues in the reclaimed area. This effort was continued by the succeeding administration. In 1993, President Fidel Ramos issued Memorandum Circular No. 45 directing all concerned government agencies to liberalize and provide a conducive environment for increased competition in the support service sector, particularly land, air and sea transportation, communication, energy, insurance and port services.

In 1996, the PPA issued a permit to R-II Builders, as part of the Smokey Mountain Development Plan, to construct a 15-hectare private port facility in the reclaimed area. The port facility, named Harbour Centre Port Terminal (HCPT), was envisaged as a private commercial port that would directly compete with the Manila-based ports. In 2001, President Arroyo issued Memorandum Order No. 47 directing the PPA to assist in the technical evaluation of port-related land use in the reclaimed areas and expeditiously process applications for the permits for private commercial ports. Because of this, the PPA issued to HCPT a permanent commercial permit to operate and handle (a) all types of domestic vessels and cargoes and (b) foreign vessels and cargoes chartered by the locators at the Harbour Centre.

Prior to the entry of HCPT, the only competition at the Manila ports was between MICT and South Harbour in the handling of foreign containerized cargoes. While MICT has the permit to handle foreign break-bulk cargoes, it handles mainly foreign containerized cargoes. In the case of South Harbour, it handles both foreign containerized and break-bulk cargoes.

The start of real competition took place when HCPT was issued the permit in 2003 to handle foreign break-bulk cargoes. According to HCPT, it was able to capture 70 per cent of the foreign break-bulk market in a span of one year due to efficiency/better service and lower cost. However, only MICT and South Harbour compete for foreign containerized cargoes despite the capacity of HCPT to compete in this market (Table 8.6). The

Table 8.6 Benefits of competition

Indicators	South Harbour	HCPT
Productivity/ efficiency level	Steel – 6000 mt/hr Cement/rice – 4000 bags per gang/ship	Steel – 7200 mt/hr Cement/rice – 6000 to 8000 bags per gang/ship
Unloading time	8–10 days	5.5 days
Rates	PPA prescribed	30–50% lower

Note: According to HCPT, the port now handles 70% of foreign break-bulk cargoes.

PPA refuses, to date, to issue HCPT a permit to handle foreign containerized cargoes.

It is not difficult to understand the reason behind the position of the PPA in this case. The PPA has nothing to lose by allowing MICT and South Harbour to compete with each other. Both operators pay rent to the PPA, hence any reduction in the share of South Harbour, for example, will be offset by MICT's gains. However, HCPT's gain is a loss not only for the PPA but also for the operators at MICT and South Harbour. Therefore, in spite of the potential benefits full competition would bring to the economy, the PPA has decided to regulate against it:

- Full competition in the foreign containerized market might undermine the income potential of MICT and South Harbour (which was what happened when HCPT was allowed to handle foreign break-bulk cargoes).
- Reduced traffic handled at the PPA port terminals (MICT and South Harbour) has implications for the PPA's income and profitability.
- It will also undermine the ability of the terminal operators to comply with their investment commitments to the PPA.
- A lower gross income will affect the PPA's net income and, consequently, its capacity to declare more dividends to the national government.
- Lower income will also affect the PPA's port development and maintenance activities.
- Competition will also end the economically and financially unjustifiable rate increases.

Manila is the Philippines' major gateway to the world. The ports at Manila handle about 25 per cent of the Philippines' total cargo throughput. Foreign containerized cargoes represent the most lucrative segment of the market (Tables 8.7 and 8.8).

Table 8.7 Statistics on Manila ports (2002)

Port	Cargo throughput (in 000 mt)	Passenger traffic (in 000)*	No. of shipcalls
MICT			
Domestic	7	0	11
Foreign	12 236	0	1 966
South Harbour			
Domestic	0	8 646	113
Foreign	7 298	0	2 105
North Harbour			
Domestic	16 776	3 978	5 891
Foreign	0	0	0
Harbour Centre			
Domestic	323	0	339
Foreign	881	0	68
Manila Ports (Total)			
Domestic	17 606	12 624	6 015
Foreign	20 415	0	4 439

Sources: Master Plan for Strategic Development of the Philippine Port System (JICA Study team, 2003); HCPTI.

WHAT NEEDS TO BE DONE?

Reforming the PPA is a tough act and the enemy of the reform programme is not only the PPA itself but also its so-called *direct* clients. There is an urgent need to correct the flaws in the PPA Charter. Amending the PPA Charter to make it more dynamic and responsive to the needs of the port users and the economy in general requires legislative action. The following principles may be considered in amending the PPA Charter:

- *Separation of the regulatory and development functions of the PPA.* Port administration requires redefining the regulatory as well as the developmental functions of the port authority. The development of general port plans as well as the formulation of broad policies and guidelines in port administration may be given to the DOTC. However, the development of these ports will have to be the domain of the private sector. The independent port authorities, on the other hand, will have to ensure that specific regulations are in place to encourage efficiency, and promote competition and general safety within the port.

Table 8.8 Comparative analysis of North Harbour, South Harbour, and HCPT

Indicators	North Harbour	MICT	South Harbour	Harbour Centre
Area	430 000 sqm	606 740 sqm	200 000 sqm	150 000 sqm
Draft	6.0 m	10–11.5 m	12 m	11.5–12 m
Berths	15 berths	5 berths	3 berths	12 berths
Quay length	–	1000 m	600 m	1 100 m
Container yard	–	322 584 sqm	–	45 000 sqm
Equipment	–	10 gantry cranes 25 rubber tyre gantries 10 reach stackers	8 gantry cranes 9 reach stackers	1 mobile harbour crane 4 rubber tyre gantries 25 forklifts 2 reach stackers
2002 Cargo throughput	16.8 million mt	12.2 million mt	7.3 million mt	1.1 million mt (10% capacity utilization)
Productivity of unloading	–	–	6000 mt/hr	7200 mt/hr
steel @ 40 000 mt/vessel	–	–	8–10 days	5.5 days
Market share (2003)	Break-bulk – 12% Containerized – 49%	Foreign containerized – 80%	Foreign containerized – 20%	Foreign break-bulk steel – 90%

Table 8.8 *Continued*

Indicators	North Harbour	MICT	South Harbour	Harbour Centre
			Foreign break-bulk – 30%	Logs / lumber – 100% Wheat/grain – 50% Domestic break-bulk bottled cargo – 100% Gypsum – 100%
Modernization cost	P3.5 billion	P30 billion (proposed)	P15 billion (as per contract)	P4.8 billion (actual) P1.5 billion (additional equipment and facilities)
Price	PPA prescribed	PPA prescribed	PPA prescribed	PPA prescribed (but has the flexibility to price itself lower being a private port; lower cost since no double handling at the pier side)
2002 net income	Not available	P2.8 billion	P641 million	P1.3 million[a]

Note: [a] This figure is low since prior to 2003, HCPT was only allowed to handle domestic traffic as well as the cargoes of its locators.

Sources: PPA, HCPT.

- *Deletion of the provision authorizing the PPA or the independent port authorities to share cargo-handling revenues.* This will remove the conflict of interest described in the early part of this chapter. This presupposes that the PPA will become regulatory rather than developmental in operation. The development function can be transferred to the private sector.
- *Establishment of more independent port authorities.* To promote inter-port competition and to decentralize port administration, independent port authorities must be established and managed mainly by boards composed mostly of representatives from the private sector. As international best practice indicates: 'A decentralized system of local port authorities each operating independently creates the environment for inter-port competition, thereby satisfying one of the important conditions for an efficient market in the port sector . . . the consistent practice of utilizing competition, whether intra-port or inter-port rivalry, is no accident. Competition is regarded as the primary market force in regulating the operator's business behavior, motivating them to produce higher levels of service quality, disciplining them to reduce costs' (Yee, 2000).
- *Increased private sector representation and participation in the Board of the independent port authority.* Again, successful ports worldwide are run by independent boards (of directors), and professional managers are carefully appointed to represent and serve the interests and aspirations of the local community and industry. Importantly, this form of decentralized administration is predicated on the fact that a local port authority can respond to market conditions more quickly than a centralized authority can. It is no coincidence that a dynamic and responsive board makes a considerable difference in the performance of a port. Although the constitution of a port authority in the international scene offers a diversity of practice, there is invariably a strong commonality among them, such as a strong community and industry representation with a degree of government participation in the board. The utilization of the private sector (or privatization) in port functions has been carefully predicated on the strategy of generating competition among the operators within the port (Yee, 2000).
- *Allow Harbour Centre (HCPT) to handle foreign containerized cargoes.* This is the only way in which the full benefits of competition at the ports of Manila can be realized.

NOTES

1. The author would like to thank Dr Cid Terosa, Senior Economist at the School of Economics, University of Asia and the Pacific.
2. On 26 August 2001, the Distribution Management Association of the Philippines (DMAP) together with the Consumer Complaints Centre (CCC) filed a formal petition to the PPA requesting the PPA to nullify four Memorandum Circulars concerning the cargo-handling rate increases of 2000, 2001 and 2002 for 'lack of due process' in the approval of said rate increases. To date, the only action the PPA made on the petition was to refer it to the Office of the Government Corporate Counsel (OGCC).
3. On 20 December 2001, the PPA Board approved Board Resolution (BR) No. 1987 advising the PPA Management to implement, effective 12 January 2002, the 'additional' 10 per cent rate increase in the cargo handling tariff of the operators at MICT and the South Harbour as previously approved by the PPA Board on 11 January 2001 (PPA BR No. 1858). The 11 January 2001 approval referred to was already implemented on 1 February 2001 and does not speak of an additional 10 per cent rate increase to be granted at a later date to the operators at MICT and South Harbour. What was required of the operators was to comply with the productivity rate of not less than 25 moves per ship hour and to increase it further by not less than 10 per cent (i.e. productivity rate) by 1 July 2001.
4. This model was replicated almost a decade later when the contract for terminal operation of the South Harbour was awarded to Asian Terminals Inc. (ATI).

BIBLIOGRAPHY

Basilio, L. (2004), 'Competition on Manila's waterfront', *UA&P Industry Monitor*, Manila.

Basilio, L. (2002), 'Reforming the port sector', *UA&P Industry Monitor*, December, Manila.

Basilio, L. (2001), 'Port and shipping issues: A sink or swim situation', *UA&P Staff Memos*, Manila.

Basilio, L. (2001), 'Towing the line: Philippine port sector development', *UA&P Industry Monitor*, August, Manila.

Basilio, L. (2000), 'A victory for ports development', *UA&P Industry Monitor*, November, Manila.

Basilio, L. (2000), 'Port operations: Rivalry is the best policy', *UA&P Industry Monitor*, September, Manila.

Basilio, L. (2000), 'The long way to (port) perfection', *UA&P Industry Monitor*, March, Manila.

Basilio, L. (1999), 'Executive Order 59: Still a lot of room for improvement', *UA&P Industry Monitor*, September, Manila.

Basilio, L. and Jennifer C. Llarena (2003), 'Portworkers' Social Amelioration Fund: Another Coconut Levy in the Making?', *UA&P Industry Monitor*, March, Manila.

Basilio, L., Carla G. Grino and Peter Yee (1999), 'EO 59: Forward or aft?', *Philippine Political and Business Monitor*, August, Manila.

National Union of Port Workers of the Philippines (1996), *Concept Paper on the Port Workers Amelioration Program*, A paper submitted to the Philippine Ports Authority: Manila.

Nikomborirak, D. (1998), 'Regulatory dilemmas in Southeast Asia', *TDRI Quarterly Review*, **13**, 1.

Villaseñor, G.B. (2000), 'Understanding and preventing regulatory capture', Congressional Planning and Budget Office (CPBO) Discussion Notes, July, Manila

Yee, Peter (2000), 'Port administration lessons applicable for the Philippines', Unpublished paper.

PART III

Regulation, markets and the poor: cases from South Africa and the Philippines

9. The capability approach and access to information and communication technologies

Erwin M. Alampay

> [F]or many evaluative purposes, the appropriate 'space' is neither that of utilities, nor that of primary goods, but that of substantive freedoms – the capabilities – to choose a life one has reason to value. If the object is to concentrate on the individual's real opportunity to pursue her objectives, then account would have to be taken not only of the primary goods the persons respectively hold, but also of the personal characteristics that govern the conversion of primary goods into the person's ability to promote her ends. (Sen, 1999, p. 74)

Access to information and communication technologies (ICTs) has generally been viewed as critical in society today, largely because of the potential opportunities it provides. ICTs help keep people connected and are crucial in a knowledge-based and information-driven world economy. In turn, universal access to ICT policies can be seen as access to policies that expand people's freedoms. Access to ICTs allows for more opportunities, and provides people with useful knowledge and information for making decisions. However, many of the policies that take into account universal access to ICTs look at ways of providing access without considering the differences in how people value and transform the same bundle of goods, and the goals they have for using them, which is essentially what the capability approach is about (Sen, 1999).

In this regard, this study applies the capability approach to the access and use of ICTs. In particular, it investigates whether people have access to ICTs, the characteristics of people who make use of them, how and for what ends they are utilised. This chapter first discusses the capability approach, and issues pertaining to its operationalisation. Particular focus is given to key concepts in the approach, particularly functioning, capabilities and freedoms. It then looks at how functioning, capabilities and freedoms apply to ICTs and how the concepts are operationalised in the research. Finally it presents findings on how different demographical characteristics affect the access and use of ICTs based on household surveys conducted in Puerto Princesa and Palawan in the Philippines.

SEN'S CAPABILITY APPROACH

In the capability approach (CA):

> the analysis of development . . . treats the freedoms of individuals as the basic building blocks. Attention is . . . paid . . . to the expansion of 'capabilities' of persons to lead the kinds of lives they value – and have reason to value . . . Having greater freedom to do the things one has reason to value is (1) significant in itself for the people's overall freedom, and (2) important in fostering the person's opportunity to have valuable outcomes . . . Greater freedom enhances the ability of people to help themselves and to influence the world. (Sen, 1999, p. 18)

The approach is described as 'a framework for evaluating and assessing social arrangements, standards of living, inequality, poverty, justice, quality of life or well-being' (Comim, 2001, p. 4). It is seen as an improvement on how people have traditionally viewed development, and is central to the idea of human development (Gasper, 2002). Over the years, there has been much discussion on the issues this approach raises and ways for applying its principles. The first step to its practical use is in its operationalisation. One difficulty with this, however, is CA's 'theoretical underspecification and inclusive view of operationalisation which contests not only the evaluative but also the practical foundations of utilitarianism' (Comim, 2001, p. 2). Another problem cited is how its key concepts, namely functionings, capabilities and freedoms are 'obscurely' or interchangeably used (Gasper, 2002). Nonetheless, this has not stopped scholars (Gasper, 2002; Comim, 2001; Biondo, 2002; Wanderley, 2001) from attempting to put a more practical handle on the approach. Below are some of the issues raised.

Functioning

Sen says the concept of functioning 'reflects the various things a person may value doing or being' (Sen, 1999, p. 75). They are 'various components or aspects of how a person lives' (Gasper, 2002, p. 4). Hence, evaluating functionings requires the identification and weighting of valuable things that people are able to be or to do. Individual functionings can be represented by real numbers and a person's actual achievement can be expressed by a functioning vector. This can be operationalised by using an a priori definition of a set of basic capabilities (Comim, 2001).

Capabilities

A person's capability is the set of alternative functioning vectors a person could attain, or in other words the extent of one's positive freedoms

(Gasper, 2002, p. 5). Capabilities could mean actual things that a person has done, as well as things they can possibly do. Furthermore, CA also maintains that people differ in how they transform the same bundle of goods into opportunities for achieving their goals. Differences can be due to people's physical abilities and to the social status different communities confer on people (Biondo, 2002). Sen (1999) identifies the following sources of differences among people: personal heterogenities, environmental diversities, variations in social climate, differences in relational perspectives, and distribution within the family.

Freedom

Freedom involves 'the processes that allow freedom of actions and decisions, and the actual opportunities that people have, given their personal and social circumstances. Unfreedom can arise either through the inadequate processes or through inadequate opportunities that some people have for achieving what they minimally would like to achieve' (Sen, 1999, p. 17). Some see in this discussion of freedom, an extreme emphasis on choice (Gasper, 2002). A person's freedom is seen to have intrinsic value and is part of his or her being. Not only achieved functioning is valuable, but also the capability of choosing and discriminating among possible livings (Comim, 2001). This means that even if someone is provided the opportunity and has the necessary capabilities, he or she still has the freedom to decide whether the opportunity is worthwhile.

How then can CA be used in the area of ICTs? How can capabilities, functioning and freedoms be applied and observed in empirical terms in this field? What are the important differences among people that could affect their capabilities, functioning and freedoms when accessing and using ICTs?

THE CAPABILITIES APPROACH AND THE ACCESS AND USE OF ICTS

There are similarities in how people traditionally measure development and how people conventionally measure progress in information societies. While development was usually measured in terms of gross national products, access to information and communication technologies is often measured in terms of the growth in the infrastructure through teledensities, number of Internet service providers, and number of computers per capita.

However, just as with the human development index (HDI), it is becoming apparent that policies must coordinate the construction of both human and technological capabilities in order to benefit from the potential applications of new ICTs. In measuring indicators for sustainable information societies, the United Nations Commission for Science and Technology for Development (UNCSTD) for instance, aside from infrastructure, includes experience, skills and knowledge as critical components in the development of information societies (Mansell et al., 1998). These components are capabilities that are needed to function in today's information society. Hence, it is easy to see that CA can be applied to ICTs.

In applying this approach, the difference will be more evident in microeconomic studies, wherein people are allowed to discriminate with regard to what they consider as the good life (Comim, 2001). Thus, for research using CA to analyse the use of ICTs, it is important to look at differences at the individual or household level. This was done in this research through household surveys to determine the things people consider important with respect to ICT use.

Functioning, Capability, Freedom and ICTs

Sen says that 'the evaluative focus of this "capabilities approach" can be either on the realized functionings (what a person is actually able to do) or on the capability set of alternatives that she has (her real opportunities). The two give different types of information – the former about the things a person does and the latter about the things a person is substantively free to do' (1999, p. 75). Both versions can be used separately or in combination. If this approach is now applied to the access to and use of information and communication technologies (ICTs), how can realised functionings or the 'capability set of alternatives' be operationalised?

Realised (and Unrealised) Functionings

According to Sen (1999, p. 131) 'the assessment of capabilities has to proceed primarily on the basis of observing a person's actual functionings, to be supplemented by other information. There is a jump here (from functioning to capabilities), but it need not be a big jump, if only because the valuation of actual functionings is one way of assessing how a person values the options he has.' Actual or realised functioning, therefore pertains to actual use of ICTs (see Figure 9.1).

Furthermore, because this research is also specifically concerned with universal access to ICTs, realised functioning with respect to the use of ICTs should consider recent use of ICTs. For the purposes of this research, respondents were asked their use of ICTs over the past year. While it is important to know how people transform a bundle of goods (e.g. ICTs) by

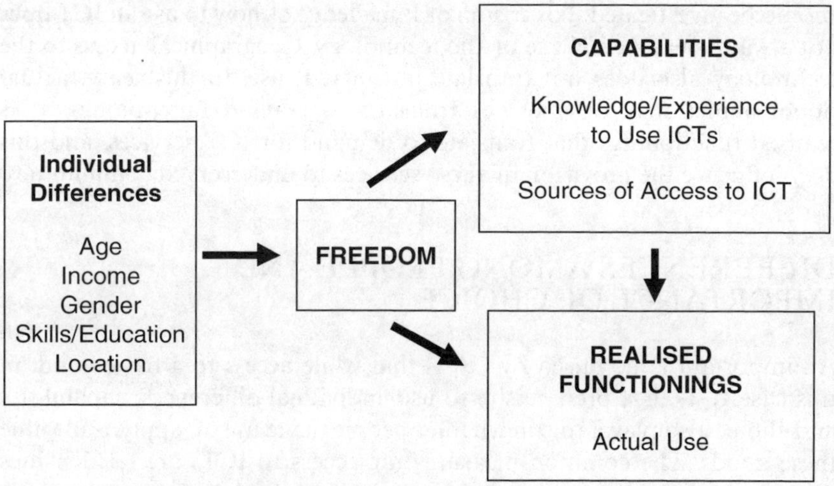

Figure 9.1 The capability approach applied to access to ICTs

knowing how and for what purpose they use them, this was not covered by this investigation.

Capability Set of Opportunities

The difficulty with operationalising CA is that some capabilities are harder to measure than others, which partly explains the limitations to gathering the necessary data to apply this approach. With ICTs, for instance, Mansell et al. (1998) used users' consumption of ICT service and technologies as indicators of the demand potential (capability) for new technology and services. They also used educational attainment in maths and engineering as indicators for the capability to design new applications and artefacts.

Given that a person's capability is the set of alternative functioning vectors a person could attain, or what a person has done, and things they can possibly do, this can be operationalised by asking people whether they know how to use various kinds of ICTs (see Figure 9.1), such as telephones, cellular phones, computers (specifically email and Internet). Real opportunities for using ICTs are also dependent on the availability of technologies in the communities they belong to. As such, sources of accessing ICTs (whether public or private, in school or in offices, through PCOs or telecentres, landline or cellular) need to be identified. Then individuals will have to be asked which of the available service they use.

Finally, in evaluating the impact or improvement with respect to universal access to ICTs, both realised functioning and actual opportunities should be investigated. Possession of knowledge of how to use an ICT does not always mean actual use of the technology. Geographical access to the technology also does not translate into actual use. In this sense, actual opportunities may or may not translate to realised functionings. It is realised functionings that translate to demand for ICT services, and this may influence the provision of these services to underserved communities.

DIFFERENCES AMONG PEOPLE AND IMPORTANCE OF CHOICE

An important issue raised by CA is that while access to a basic good, in this case ICTs, is a prerequisite to use, individual differences, capabilities and choice also play a role in whether people make use of, apply, and value these goods. The common measures for access to ICTs are teledensities (for telephones) or the number of Internet users (for Internet penetration). Traditional measurement of access does not usually look into the variations in the use of these resources by different people. However, Sen argues that 'social and economic factors such as basic education, elementary health care, and secure employment are important, not only on their own, but also for the role that they can play in giving people the opportunity to approach the world with courage and freedom' (Sen, 1999, p. 63). This means that people have different ways of transforming the same bundle of goods into opportunities for achieving their plans in life. These differences may be physically or socially manifested and may be due to differences in: (1) moral and intellectual capacities and skills, (2) physical capacities and skills, (3) conceptions of the good, and (4) tastes and preferences (Biondo, 2002).

In the ICT literature, gender (Colle and Roman, 2002), context (Heeks, 2002), age (Dertouzos, 1997; Delgadillo et al., 2002), social class, race and religion (Gomez and Casadiego, 2002) are some of the factors cited as possibly affecting the ability to take advantage of ICTs. Others also stress the importance of education and skills (Lopez and Villaseca, 1996), which may be indicated through school enrolment and technical training, as being linked to the ability to take advantage of opportunities in the new digital economy (Campbell, 2001). This is echoed by O'Farrell, who adds that aside from education, age, gender and mobility of the community and their proximity to commercial centres, class and ethnic groupings are factors that should also be considered (O'Farrell, 2001). Likewise, the kind of profession and tasks a person does will also dictate their use of or need for these technologies, and the effects on their professional and private lives (Miller and Cardy, 2000; Winter and Taylor, 2000; Rubery and Grimshaw, 2001).

Local language and content are also important (Madhusudan, 2002; Rajora, 2002; Gomez and Casadiego, 2002). Hence, ICT-based systems need to be more indigenised and contextualised to the community they are being situated in (Heeks, 2002). Furthermore, a study by Blanchard and Horan (2000) points to the significant relationship between computer experience, email experience and actual civic engagement of the interest of community members to participate in virtual services offered by government. This suggests that perceived value, motivations and interest are also factors in people's choice and actual functioning.

Given the above differences mentioned in the literature, this research study looked at the differences in access and use in terms of gender, age, education, socioeconomic income and the location of their home (see Figure 9.1). Differences in preferences and perceived value of ICTs were also considered, since individual choice to use a basic commodity can be affected by a person's perceived value for the good: at home or at work and whether positively or negatively. Finally, people may actually know how to use a commodity (ICT), recognise its importance, and value it and want to use it, but be unable to use it. For our purposes, this was defined as 'unrealised functionings'. This is important in this study because people with unrealised functionings are the concern of policies on universal access to ICTs. Unrealised functioning is premised on the fact that lack of access to a bundle of goods inhibits the person from that life choice, consistent with Sen's concept of 'unfreedom'. This was measured by asking people whether they considered certain ICTs to be important at work or at home, why they considered them important, and then comparing this against their actual knowledge and use of the ICT.

THE CASE OF PUERTA PRINCESA CITY

This investigation looked at ownership of and access to ICTs, and mitigating factors for use. It investigated location, gender, educational attainment, income and age as variables that influence the use of certain ICTs, such as telephones, cellphones, text messaging, personal computers (PCs) and email. It is based on a household survey conducted in Puerto Princesa City, Palawan ($n = 269$).

Puerto Princesa is among the larger cities in the Philippines with respect to land area. Its communities are diverse: many are still rural, with some located in the coast, some in farmlands, and others in mountainous areas. In using Puerto Princesa, the research intends to consider various conditions that strategies for universal access should be able to overcome and factor into the application of ICTs for rural poverty reduction.

Table 9.1 ICT ownership (n = 269)

ICT	% who own the ICT
Radio	80
TV	62
Cellular phone	23
Cable TV	13
Landline telephone	7
PC	5

Ownership and Access to ICTs

Table 9.1 shows that radio and television are the ICT most people own in Puerto Princesa, with ownership of cellular phones third. Ownership of radio was higher than TV because of the absence of electricity in some rural communities. That more people own cellphones than landline phones at home is consistent with the national situation where cellphone density has exceeded landline density (NTC, 2003).

Telephone access

While 63 per cent (n = 268) said having a phone in the house was important, only 19 per cent said they had had a landline phone in the house, and only 7 per cent said they still had one. Of those who have had a phone previously or have one currently, 45 said they had Piltel, 2 said PLDT and 1 said Bayantel. Since Piltel and PLDT are actually part of one company, the delivery of landline services in Puerto Princesa remains a virtual monopoly.

There were only 22 people who reported using a landline phone in their own house, even though there were 35 people surveyed who said they currently have a phone (see Table 9.2). This suggests the home phone is not fully utilised. Underutilisation may explain why subscription to landline telephones is generally low in the country even in places where there are available lines (NTC, 2002). Aside from this, those who said they no longer had a phone in the house said the reason they had their line disconnected was because they could no longer manage the costs, or they were unhappy with the service of the provider. Those who didn't have a phone at all said they didn't have any reason to use it anyway, or that they didn't have anyone to call. Some said they simply couldn't afford it, while others said they had a phone in their shop or office. So, it was either they had no use for a phone, or they couldn't afford one, or they had alternatives.

Those who say the phone is not important argue that it is not a necessity since they could personally visit the person they want to talk with. Some

Table 9.2 Telephone access (n = 269), in the past year

	N	%
From friend/neighbour	59	22
Public phone	87	32
Office/school	19	7
Own house	22	8
Has to go to town centre	84	31

cite the problem of monitoring its use, while others say it's only their 'children's friends' who call, which just makes it an added distraction. Some also rank the phone lower in their priorities, especially considering that they might seldom have use for it (if their primary reason is for emergencies and their often being out of the house).

Nonetheless, some people said a phone was important primarily for convenience, especially in situations where there are no public phones nearby. Most said a phone in the house was important, especially in case of emergencies. Some said it could be used to keep in touch with family, while others said it was useful for their business.

Cellphone access

It should also be noted that even though only 23 per cent said they owned their own cellphone, access to a cellular phone at home may be larger if access to the cellphone of another member of the household is considered. Assuming, for instance, that the percentage who access phones from their relatives (23 per cent) do so from cellphones accessible in the same household, then access to cellphones at home is already 46 per cent in Puerto Princesa. One caveat, however, is that cell signals are virtually non-existent in Puerto Princesa's small rural communities (barangays) (see Table 9.3).

In Puerto, 23 per cent of the sample owned their own cellphone, and another 29 per cent borrow the cellphone of somebody else.

The primary reason for not having a cellphone is cost. Either people could not afford one, or could not maintain its regular use. A few argued that they have a cellphone they could borrow or they already have a landline. Only one person said that there was no signal in their area, although in general, many of the rural settlements surveyed really did not have cellular signals, or at best weak signals.

Among those who use a cellphone in Puerto, the majority said they used SMART (80), followed by Globe (20), and then Talk and Text (11). The primary reason is signal quality, the fact that SMART was in Palawan first, and also cost.

Table 9.3 Cellular phone access (n = 269)

	N	%
Own	63	23
Relative	61	23
Friend	14	5
Office colleague	3	1
Office issued cell phone	1	Negligible

Note: Frequencies for other mentions were reclassified into relatives (3) and office colleagues (1).

Of the payment options, 100 said they used prepaid, and only 3 said they had fixed payments. The reason a lot of people prefer prepaid cards is that they feel they have more control over their expenses, and the mode for paying is easier and there's no problem with monthly bills. This explains why prepaid cards have helped in the expansion of the market, especially to lower income groups, since it helps people overcome particular barriers to line ownership. One problem with prepaid cards, however, is that people are less aware of whether they are being charged correctly for their calls.

They consider the cellphone important for the same reasons as the regular landline telephone, for emergencies and convenience. It is easier to keep in touch with friends and loved ones both within the country and abroad, and you can be reached virtually anywhere at any time. But another reason is privacy: with a cell phone, one can keep secrets.

The fact that more people have been able to use a landline telephone at one time or another, versus use of a cellphone, may mean that public access to telephones is better or it may simply imply that landline phones have been around longer and hence people may have been more exposed to them.

Location and Capacity to Use ICT

Table 9.4 shows that as far as ability to use ICTs is concerned, more people use landline phones and cellphones compared to personal computers and email.

It is also apparent that while more recent technologies have yet to take a hold on the population, sending letters via post has already been superseded by voice communications. In Puerto Princesa, where access to the ICT infrastructure is not well developed, access and use are lower for the more modern technologies. Another reason why use of mail is lower than use of phones is because some communities do not have reliable postal services.

Table 9.4 Capability to use communicating media

ICT	% capable
Landline phone	69
Mail	57
Cellphone	52
SMS	42
PC	25
Email	8

Table 9.5 Location and capability to use communicating media

Communicating media know-how	Urban ($n = 120$) %	Rural ($n = 149$) %
Sends post/mail	60	56
Telephone	88	53
Cellphone	72	35
Knows SMS	62	25
Computers	40	12
Has email address	17	1

Location and Capability to Use ICT

The disparity in the capability of people in urban and rural areas to use ICTs is quite pronounced and is indicative of the great disparity in the development of infrastructure in the area (see Table 9.5). In the rural areas, while post may be less reliable, and in some cases non-existent, more people have sent letters/mail rather than using a telephone. This simply shows the inconvenience of accessing a nearby phone for people living in rural areas in Puerto.

The location of the barangay was significant with respect to people's capabilities to use a phone, cellphone, and a personal computer ($p < .05$). People in urban areas have a distinct advantage with respect to capability to use these technologies, as compared to their rural counterparts.

Gender and Capability to Use ICT

Table 9.6 shows that women in Puerto Princesa are actually more capable in using ICTs. The data reveal that women are more likely to be using telephones, cellphones, computers, the Internet and email. Furthermore, by testing whether the relationship between gender and ICT use is significant,

Table 9.6 Gender and capability to use ICT

ICT know-how	Male ($n = 113$) %	Female ($n = 156$) %
Telephone	64	72
Cellphone	43	58
Computers	19	29
Knows about email	9	18
Has email	5	10
Uses Internet	9	10

a chi square test reveals that the differences were significant ($p < .05$) with respect to use of cellphones, computers and knowledge about email. The differences were not significant ($p > .05$) with respect to telephone use. The number of respondents who used the internet and had email accounts was too small to be significant.

That women have more access to ICTs bodes well for development, because women, being the primary caregivers, are more likely to transmit these benefits to the rest of the family and community. This may also have implications for using or tapping women as conduits of information and knowledge, or as intermediaries for spreading knowledge found on the Internet.

The area of gender and communication is a field that is also worth further investigation. Differences in how women and men use the technologies and the kinds of work they are employed in could reflect societal stereotypes. Historically, with the telephone, this was evident with the 'feminisation' of telephone operators (Martin, 1991).

Educational Attainment and Capability to Use ICT

Table 9.7 indicates that education is also a factor in the use of ICTs. Almost all who have finished college (98 per cent) have been able to use a phone, whereas only 55 per cent who have only finished primary schooling have used a phone. The same disparity can be seen with the use of the cellphone and the computer. Sixty-five percent of those who have finished college know how to use a computer, versus only 8 per cent of those who finished elementary schooling.

The data above show that a digital divide exists within communities and not between areas alone. Educational attainment is apparently one of the factors in this. Efforts to bridge the information gap through the access and use of ICTs should begin as early as possible, or else a significant number of people may never gain the knowledge to capitalise on the use of these

Table 9.7 Educational attainment and capability to use ICT (%)

	Capability to use:				
	Landline phone	Cellphone	SMS	Personal computer	Email
Elementary School ($n = 50$)	34	20	12	0	0
High School ($n = 98$)	65	38	30	8	1
College ($n = 105$)	89	77	67	51	19
Vocational training ($n = 14$)	71	64	43	29	7

technologies. This is important because the school system is a logical access point, especially with respect to accessing the Internet.

Income and Capability to Use ICT

Table 9.8 indicates that close to 55 per cent of those with incomes below P5000 per month (one US dollar = 55 Philippine pesos) have used a phone and 35 per cent have used a cellphone. This proves that even poor households have a need for these technologies. In the past, the reason provided by telephone providers for not installing lines in some areas was the argument that there was no market. If market is simply a function of profitability, this may be true. However, there are people who need and use these services; hence there is a rationale for these services to be provided even among the poor communities.

Table 9.8 shows that the use of various ICTs is greatly influenced by income. Telephone use, cellphone use, PC use and the corresponding skills like knowledge of email, ownership of email, and use of the Internet were all significant ($p < .05$) with respect to household income. The data reveal that individuals in households with higher incomes were more likely to have used or to be capable of using ICTs. This indirectly implies that the affordability of these services is still crucial to their use. While competition has brought down prices to some extent, some people still consider the cost of using telephones, cellphones and computers as prohibitive.

It is hoped that with the onset of newer technologies, like cellphones, the cost of providing universal access will become less expensive. However, affordability goes beyond the cost of the technology. There are also some

Table 9.8 Income and capability to use ICT (%)

Monthly household income (P)	Sends mail	Has used a phone	Has used a cellphone	Can send SMS	Has used a PC	Has email account
< 5000 ($n = 117$)	51	55	35	25	11	2
5001–10 000 ($n = 66$)	58	82	56	45	26	6
10 001–20 000 ($n = 26$)	69	92	88	65	46	23
> 20 000 ($n = 14$)	55	55	70	60	45	25
Does not know ($n = 2$)	50	50	100	50	0	0
No answer ($n = 39$)	62	74	51	51	38	13

cost barriers with respect to obtaining a line, maintaining it, and the cost of its use. The increase in cellphone subscriptions as a result of prepaid cards is illustrative of this phenomenon (Celdran, 2002). The use of SMS through cellphones is another reason why it is considered more useful for the poor because SMS is a lot cheaper and can be still be transmitted even in areas with weak signals.

Age and Capability to Use ICT

The older group in the sample were less likely to use telephones, cellphones and computers (see Table 9.9). Some saw these technologies as only for younger people, or felt that they are already too old to use them.

There was significant difference with respect to telephone use, cellphone use, use of SMS, computer use, possession of an email address, and use of the Internet ($p < .05$). In all these cases, the younger groups tend to know more and are more capable of using ICTs. In fact, only one person older than 34 reported having an email address. Clearly, much more can be done considering that those between 35 and 44 years of age are far from being 'untrainable'.

For the elderly and less well educated, what may be key is indirect access to the technology, and to the information and knowledge that comes with it. Indirect access occurs when there are other people in the household who use the ICT and who serve as intermediaries for those who do not know how to use the technology. For example, some people ask their children to email or text for them, and in return some people send messages through these same people who then relay them back to the 'non-users'. In other

Table 9.9 Age and capability to use ICT (%)

	Age in years			
	Age 12–21 ($n = 54$)	Age 22–34 ($n = 102$)	Age 35–44 ($n = 48$)	Age 45 & above ($n = 64$)
Sends mail	50	50	63	56
Telephone	78	74	65	58
Cellphone	74	56	44	31
Uses SMS	74	47	33	13
Computers	43	32	17	3
Used Internet	26	11	2	0
Has email address	20	10	2	0

cases, younger users within the household may actually help bring the elderly to embrace and learn to use the ICTs on their own.

Computer Ownership and Capabilities

Ownership does not guarantee that a person in the household knows how to operate the equipment, and this is evident in the data below. However, ownership makes a person more likely to know how to use a computer than if they do not have a computer in the house.

More people who know how to use a computer, however, do not possess a computer of their own. This may suggest that access to computers is through schools, the office, public Internet cafes or computer rental shops.

Only a slight majority of those who know of email and the Internet possess an email account or have tried using the Internet. However, it is logical that before people start using a computer application, they must first be aware of it and its use.

Perceived Importance of ICTs

Respondents were asked whether they considered the telephone and cellphone important to have at home or at work. They were asked whether it was important to learn to use the computer. Understanding their reasons has implications for how ICTs are used and what prevents utilisation.

Perceived Need for Landline/Cellphone at Work or Home

The proportions of the sample who felt they needed a landline phone or cellphone were approximately the same: two-thirds felt they needed a

Table 9.10 Ownership vs. capability to use a computer

	Can operate a personal computer	
Has own PC	Yes	No
Yes	11	3
No	54	197

Table 9.11 Need for landline phone/cellphone

Need	Puerto Princesa ($n = 269$)
Home landline telephone	63%
Office telephone	23%
Cellphone	61%

landline phone at home; one-fourth saw the need for a landline phone at work; and two-thirds of the samples felt they needed a cellphone for themselves (see Table 9.11).

Regardless of the type of work people had, the proportion who thought they needed a landline phone at home, or needed a cellphone, was consistently higher than the proportion who said they needed a landline phone at work. The lowest proportion who said they needed a landline phone at work were housewives and domestic helpers. It is difficult, however, to determine the reliability of their answers because of the problem of distinguishing between when they are at work and when they are at home. In fact, as the data regarding women and ICT need indicated, most of them considered having a landline at work as 'not applicable' to their situation. If their responses are disregarded, then farmers/fishermen (11 per cent) have the least need for landline telephones in their workplace (see Table 9.12).

However, many housewives and domestic help may have not considered the tasks that they do in the home as work, and hence most did not answer whether the phone was important for the work that they do. But, regarding the question of whether a phone at home was important, 75 per cent of the housewives ($n = 8$) and 59 per cent of the domestic helpers ($n = 29$) in Puerto Princesa said it was important to have a landline phone at home.

Furthermore, two-thirds of the respondents (66 per cent) with 'professional' occupations saw the value of having a landline phone in their place of work. The reverse was true with farmers and fishermen. Only 11 percent said it was important for their work. The reason given by farmers/fishermen who said they do not need a landline phone was that they had no one to

Table 9.12 Work type and % who need ICT

Work type	ICT need		
	Home (%)	Work (%)	Cell (%)
Blue collar ($n = 33$)	63	42	52
Professional ($n = 32$)	75	66	66
Businessman ($n = 47$)	43	38	68
Farmer/fisherman ($n = 28$)	61	11	57
Housewife ($n = 8$)	75	0	75
Housekeeper/domestic help ($n = 29$)	59	3	59

Table 9.13 Gender and landline phone and cellphone need

Gender	ICT need (%)		
	Home telephone	Work telephone	Cellphone
Men ($n = 112$)	64	31	56
Women ($n = 156$)	63	17	65

call, and did not want the added cost. As for having a phone in their line of work, they argue that they have no use for it.

Interestingly, not a significantly larger number of business people in Puerto Princesa considered the landline telephone as important in their line of work. One explanation for this is that some respondents' primary occupation was given as 'store owners'. As store owners, they may not necessarily run or manage the daily operation of their business. Hence, many of them found the question not applicable to their situation. Also, many housewives and housekeepers did not answer whether they needed a phone in their line of work, even though what they did at home was 'housework'.

With respect to gender, the only statistically significant difference was with respect to the perceived need of men and women for a landline telephone in the workplace. This was because most of the women answered 'not applicable' to whether they needed a phone at work. Otherwise, there was no statistical difference between men and women and their perceived need for landlines and cellphones (see Table 9.13).

The reasons why the respondents considered the landline or cellphone important will be discussed next. However, it should be qualified that the reasons that the respondents gave as to why they considered ICT important or not important at work were based on open-ended responses. The themes of their responses were then analysed, and their frequencies were counted.

Table 9.14 Primary reason a phone at home is important (Puerto Princesa, %)

Reason	Urban ($n = 67$)	Rural ($n = 100$)
Emergency	49	39
Efficiency	19	35
Business	16	4
Accessibility	7	6
Social	4	16
Others	3	0

Hence, the answers in Table 9.14 are based on the primary reason people gave, or the first thing that came into their mind, as to why they considered a landline or cellphone important. It does not necessarily mean that if a person said it was important for emergencies that they do not consider it important for work.

Primary Reason for Having a Landline Telephone at Home

In Puerto Princesa, 63 per cent of the respondents said it was important to have a phone at home. Of those who gave reasons why a home phone was important (n = 167), the primary reason given was for emergencies (43 per cent) and for efficiency (29 per cent). Only 8 per cent said it was for work or business. The type or location of the barangay, however, had a significant effect on the reason they gave (χ^2 (5, N = 167) 19.06, p = .002) (see Table 9.14). In both urban and rural barangays, the most common reason given for needing a phone at home was for emergencies (urban = 49 per cent; rural = 39 per cent). What was significantly different, however, was that in rural areas, a higher proportion's primary reason was the landline telephone's part in helping make things run more efficiently in their lives (urban = 19 per cent, rural = 35 per cent), and in maintaining social connections (urban = 4 per cent; rural = 16 per cent). A higher percentage of respondents from urban areas gave having a business as their reason (urban = 16 per cent; rural = 4 per cent).

'Unfreedoms' and Constraints to Using ICTs

Among the reasons given for non-use of the landline telephone (n = 81), the most prevalent was the absence of available lines (51 per cent) and the distance of the facilities (46 per cent). The majority of those whose reason was the absence of lines (95 per cent) or the distance to facilities

Table 9.15 Urban vs. rural comparison – non-use of cellphone due to cost

	Reason of non-use is due to cost		
	Yes	No	Total
Rural	50	34	84
Urban	12	19	31

χ^2 (1, N = 115) = 3.95 p = .047

(94 per cent) were respondents from rural barangays. Cost or lack of money was the reason given by only 4 per cent of those surveyed, as was the lack of knowledge of how to use a phone (4 per cent). Twelve per cent reasoned they had no one to call or did not need a phone. Respondents who had not used a cell phone (n = 129), also cited cost (48 per cent) and lack of knowledge (40 per cent), and motivation (27 per cent) as their primary reasons.

Although cost was the highest inhibiting factor mentioned for not using the cellphone, there were no significant differences with respect to household income ($p > .05$). The significant factor was only between urban and rural residents in Puerto Princesa. Rural residents were more likely to give cost as a reason compared to urban residents (χ^2 (1, N = 115) = 3.95; $p < .05$) (see Table 9.15). However, the absence of knowledge of how to use the cellphone as the reason for its non-use was not significant with respect to the level of education of cellphone non-users.

Finally, the common themes as to why people find it unnecessary to learn the computer were age, motivation and time. Some said that they were too old and that computers were only for the children. Associated with this were the physical limitations of not having good eyesight, or limitations of leaving the house to learn. Those who consider themselves old have many reasons for not using the computer, one of which is where would they apply it if they are old already, and that it is already too late for them to learn. Second, some say that because they are old, they would be hard to teach. Others simply answered that they were not interested, did not have the patience and motivation, and that it's not important for them. Third, some were too busy with work and had no time to learn.

Analysis of Implications

First, the impact of ICTs is dependent foremost on access to them. While access to ICTs is increasing, people must always bear in mind which ICTs are most accessible and used by people in rural communities. It is apparent that radio and TV are more accessible, although cellular technology is quickly gaining prominence.

Second, if access is available, who currently uses it? The data clearly show that the young, the highly educated, people in urban areas and the rich at present are the more likely beneficiaries of access to ICTs. Women, on the other hand, are just as likely, if not more likely, than men to make use of communication technologies. What are the implications therefore for rural poverty alleviation? The fact that more people in urban areas compared to rural areas use ICTs is largely because of the infrastructure availability. That richer households are more likely to use ICTs also has a lot to do with costs. The issue therefore would be how to provide the infrastructure to rural areas and also how to make the cost affordable and manageable. The popularity of prepaid cards for cellphones and the use of SMS show that ordinary households value control over their budgets, and control over the use of ICTs. Since smaller percentages of the population finish high school or higher education, it is important that at the elementary or primary level use of ICTs like the telephone, cellphone and if possible the computer is already taught. The fact that many between 35 and 44 remain ignorant about email goes to show that more effort has to be made to retrain people who did not benefit from computer training in school.

Third, if people have access to and use ICTs, for what purpose do they use them? Some people remain ignorant of the use of ICTs because they do not see how they apply in their situation. Some simply see them as a tool for businessmen without realising their other economic impacts such as savings in time and transportation costs. People still have difficulty identifying the crucial information that runs through their daily lives. If they could see how other people use the technologies then a better appreciation of what they could do for them would develop. With better appreciation will come ideas of how they could be used in their own context.

Finally, ordinary people set priorities based on their own set of values and understanding of what is important in their day-to-day lives. It is important to understand these values in order to increase the positive impact of ICTs in the future.

CONCLUSIONS

Access to ICTs has often been considered simply in terms of geographic access and affordability. However, some argue that access to ICTs is not solely limited to this, but one should also factor in the capabilities of people to make use of these resources (Sen, 1999). As such, some emphasise the need to go beyond the supply of ICTs and focus instead on people and how they use them (Norish, 1998; Soeftestad and Sein, 2003).

Even with liberalisation of the telecommunications industry, universal access is one area that will remain an important regulatory function of government. Recent evaluations of policies connected with the liberalisation of the industry suggest that competition has only occurred within markets deemed profitable, and has resulted in oversupply in selected areas (NTC, 2002). This is not limited to landline phones, but also applies in the cellular market, where competing companies try to steal each others' clients by offering upgraded or free cellphones, rather than actually expanding into other areas by providing more cell sites.

The survey conducted in Puerto Princesa reveals that whether one controls for location, gender, age, income, or educational attainment, the percentage who have used ICTs is highest with respect to use of telephones, and lowest with respect to using email. Landline telephone use being the highest among the ICTs may be because it has been in existence for over a century. The ability to use an ICT may also have more to do with the ubiquity of the technology. Using cellphones and sending SMS is more common, for instance, than using PCs and email, although the latter have been around longer.

In summary, even as newer technologies provide new possibilities for reaching and communicating with people, government should remain vigilant because this is no assurance that the marginalised would gain access to information and new knowledge. It is even likely that those who gain access to them are the same groups who already have access to older technologies. In the end, access to new ICTs could simply mirror the divide that exists with respect to access to older ICTs. The fact that telephones have remained inaccessible to some groups is worth noting. Even though newer technologies are able to overcome some of the technical limitations of the telephone, access to their use is not only technical. For everyone to have equal opportunities to benefit from ICTs, strategies must go beyond access in terms of proximity to the ICT infrastructure, and also look into the socioeconomic and cultural barriers to their use, and build the capabilities of people to use them. People must be made aware of the applications and opportunities that these new ICTs bring. In this way, an integrated approach has to be developed, as to make policies and strategies for universal access to ICTs leads to human development.

REFERENCES

Biondo, F. (2002), '"How can we assess a distributive policy?" Sen and Rawls on the currency of distributive justice' (revised Sept. 2002), *Conference*

Proceedings – Justice and Poverty: Examining Sen's Capability Approach, 5–7 June 2001, Cambridge: Von Hugel Institute, St Edmund's College.

Blanchard, A. and T. Horan (2000), 'Virtual communities and social capital', in E.L. Lesser (ed.), *Knowledge and Social Capital: Foundations and Applications*, London: Butterworth-Heinemann, pp. 159–78.

Campbell, Duncan (2001), 'Can the digital divide be contained? The digital divide: Employment and development implications', *International Labour Review*, **140**, 2, International Labour Organization.

Celdran, D. (2002), 'The Philippines: SMS and citizenship', *Development Dialogue*, **1**, 91–103.

Colle, R.D. and R. Roman (2002), 'Gender as an access issue', in *TechKnowlogia*, July–Sept 2002, Knowledge Enterprise, Inc.

Comim, F. (2001), 'Operationalizing Sen's capabilities approach', *Conference Proceedings – Justice and Poverty: Examining Sen's Capability Approach*, 5–7 June 2001, Cambridge: Von Hugel Institute, St Edmund's College.

Delgadillo, K., R. Gomez and K. Stoll (2002), *Community Telecentres for Development: Lessons from Community Telecentres in Latin America and the Caribbean*, Canada: International Development Research Centre (IDRC).

Dertouzos, M. (1997), *What Will Be? How the New World of Information Will Change Our Lives*, San Francisco: Harper Collins.

Gasper, D. (2002), 'Is Sen's capability approach an adequate basis for considering human development?', Working Paper Series No. 360, The Hague: The Netherlands Institute of Social Studies.

Gomez, R. and B. Casadiego (2002), *Letter to Aunt Ofelia: Seven Proposals for Human Development Using New Information and Communication Technologies*, Canada: International Development Research Centre (IDRC).

Heeks, R. (2002), ' "i-Development not e-Development", Special Issue on ICTs and Development', *Journal of International Development*, **14**.

Lopez, E.J. and M.G. Villaseca (1996), 'IT as a global economic tool', in E. Roche and M. Blaine (eds), *Information Technology, Development and Policy. Theoretical Perspectives and Practical Challenges*, Aldershot: Avebury.

Madhusudan, C.N. (2002), 'India's "Hole in the wall". Key to bridging the digital divide?', *TechKnowlogia*, July–Sept 2002, Knowledge Enterprise, Inc.

Mansell, R., W.E. Steinmuller and U. When (1998), 'Indicators of a sustainable information society: Policy analysis and application', http://www.jrc.es/iptsreport/vol32/english/ISS4E326.html, downloaded 5 June 2003.

Martin, M. (1991), *Hello, Central? Gender, Technology and Culture in the Formation of Telephone Systems*, Quebec: McGill-Queens University Press.

Miller, J.S. and R.L. Cardy (2000) 'Technology and managing people: Keeping the "human" in human resources', *Journal of Labor Research*, **21**(3), 447–61.

National Telecommunications Commission (NTC) (2002), *Assessment of the Implementation of the Service Area Scheme (SAS)*, Manila.

NTC (2003), *NTC Annual Report 2002*, Manila.

Norish, P. (1998) 'Foreword', in D. Richardson and L. Paisley (eds), *The First Mile of Connectivity*, Rome: Food and Agriculture Organisation.

O'Farrell, C. (2001), 'Information flows in rural and urban communities: Access, processes and people', Paper presented at the UDRSA Conference, 2001.

Rajora, R. (2002), 'Assessment and effectiveness of ICT in addressing rural poverty alleviation', Paper presented at the UNESCAP Experts Group Meeting, Bangkok, Thailand, 30 January.

Rubery, J. and D. Grimshaw (2001), 'ICTs and employment: The problem of job quality, the digital divide: employment and development implications', *International Labour Review*, **140**(2), 2001/2 International Labour Organization.
Sen, A. (1999), *Development as Freedom*, Oxford: Oxford University Press.
Soeftestad, L.T. and M.K. Sein (2003), 'ICT and development: East is East and West is West and the twain may yet meet', in S. Krishna and S. Madon (eds), *The Digital Challenge: Information Technology in the Development Context*, Aldershot: Ashgate, pp. 63–82.
Wanderley, L.O. (2001), 'Sen's capabilities approach: A meaningful framework for corporate social responsibility?', *Conference Proceedings – Justice and Poverty: Examining Sen's Capability Approach*, 5–7 June 2001, Cambridge: Von Hugel Institute, St. Edmund's College.
Winter, S.J. and S.L. Taylor (2000), 'The role of information technology in the transformation of work: A comparison of post-industrial, industrial, and proto-industrial organization', in J. Yates and J. Van Maanen (eds), *Information Technology and Organizational Transformation. History, Rhetoric, and Practice. Organization Science*, London: Sage Publications, pp. 7–34.

10. Regulatory governance of the water sector in South Africa

Kobus Müller and Frederik Uys

INTRODUCTION

South Africa is largely semi-arid and prone to erratic, unpredictable extremes of drought and flood. Rivers are the main source of water in South Africa, where the average annual rainfall is in the order of 500 mm by comparison with a global average in the order of 860 mm. Sixty-five per cent of the country receives less than 500 mm precipitation annually, which is generally accepted as the minimum required for successful dry-land farming, and 21 per cent of the country, mainly in the arid west, receives less than 200 mm a year.

It is predicted that in future increasing demands will be made on dwindling water resources and a serious water shortage could be expected by 2025. Not only is primary demand for water a function of South Africa's hitherto rapidly growing population, but the concomitant increase in secondary water demand resulting from expanding requirements for food production and for industry that in turn drives the engine of economic prosperity places limited water resources under increasing stress. South Africa is a water-stressed country where water planners and managers are faced with increasingly complex issues. Water is indeed serious business in South Africa. Prior to the change of government in 1994, an estimated 30–40 per cent of South Africa's population (14 to 18 million people) were without the minimum standard water supply (United States Department of Commerce, 2001). One of the more difficult and pressing challenges inherited by South Africa in 1994, therefore, was that relating to the provision of adequate water services.

Over and above the obvious life-sustaining significance of water in an essentially arid country, South African history and context throw up a myriad of other social, economic and political issues connected to water. In this chapter the focus is on water from the perspective of the way in which the regulatory system for water impacts on the water service delivery system. An attempt is made to link the dynamic developments in respect of the regulatory system to contextual explanations in order to provide an understanding of the regulatory system related to context and changes in context.

POLICY AND LEGAL FRAMEWORK RELATING TO WATER IN SOUTH AFRICA

Brief Legal Historical Context

The water regulatory dispensation moved from the pre-colonial collective realm to become a publicly regulated resource in terms of Roman Dutch law. British colonial rule and Anglo-Saxon jurisprudence, combined with building pressures for settler expansion and economic development, led to a situation where water was gradually captured as a private resource for the benefit of the minority (Muller, 2001, p. 4).

Water law in South Africa dates back to 1894 when the Transvaal (an independent republic at that time) promulgated legislation followed by the Cape Colony, while Natal (a British colony) and the Orange Free State (like the Transvaal, a republic) relied on the common law principles which applied at that time. The Union of South Africa in 1910 brought together the four provinces and, as regards water law, led to the first common legislation, the Irrigation and Conservation of Waters Act, Act 8 of 1912, which was a compromise, as it was largely based on the Cape Act, but with an embrace of certain of the issues introduced from the Transvaal. The broad principles of the Act were that particular rights, relating to public water and surplus water from rivers and streams, relied on common law principles, while the English law tenet that all rights of the owner of the land, including any and all rights relating to water, became the property of the owner due to the 'freehold' principle, was applied to other water rights. One of the major changes brought about by the influence of British rule is that the Court became the final source of interpretation of water rights.

This Act served an initial purpose, but due to the demands of industrial and commercial progress, it was replaced by the Water Act, Act 54 of 1956. The Department of Water Affairs and Forestry (DWAF) was created through this Act. The ever-increasing centralisation of powers and functions that characterised the governmental structures at that time gave rise to the increased authority and powers that the state could exercise over water rights, in addition to dealing with the issues relating to water quality and the awarding of water rights to water users. The functions of the Water Courts, as the institutions to deal with and adjudicate on disputes, were left untouched. Industrial usage of water was given more prominence, while the state was granted more powers over the private rights to public and private water (Thompson et al., 1994, pp. 11–12).

This unfortunately led to the situation where access to water was tipped in favour of a privileged minority of (in the main, white) private land owners. The disadvantaged majority were however in an iniquitous position of not having the resources to approach the courts (Ramazotti, 1996). It however became clear that with the advent of the democratic era in South Africa, it would become necessary to redress many of the imbalances of the past, including access to water and, where necessary, to reinforce the principle as set out in the Water Act, 1956, that the state is the custodian of the public interest, in this case, water.

THE CURRENT CONTEXT

The dawn of the democratic era in South Africa, which began in February 1990 with the release of Nelson Mandela, gave rise to a process of democratic reform that culminated in the first democratic elections in April 1994. The Reconstruction and Development Programme (RDP), which became the manifesto of the government, set out five key areas on which it would focus: meeting basic needs; developing human resources; democratising the state and society as a whole; building the economy; and implementing the RDP (The Republic of South Africa, 1994). Water and the provision of this vital resource were an essential component of each of these programmes (Department of Water Affairs and Forestry, 2002). The RDP iterated the principle that water is a natural resource available to all South Africans in a sustainable manner.

The 1994 elections and the impact on South Africa were not the end of the process, but merely a milestone in the ongoing processes of policy development and reform. The policy and legislative provisions during this phase started early with a White Paper on Water Supply and Sanitation, 1994, which although conceived late in the pre-democratic phase, was initially used in the new democratic dispensation to address the issues of access to water and more especially the principle of right of access to clean water for everyone in the country.

The promulgation of the Constitution of the Republic of South Africa, 1996, Act 108 of 1996, and more especially section 27, specifically addressed the issues of the right of access to sufficient water, while Chapter 3 also looked at the issues of cooperative government and the services that must be delivered by local government in a sustainable manner – water and sanitation services, potable water supply, domestic waste water and sewage disposal systems (The Constitution, Chapter 7 and Schedule 4, part B). Section 1 of the Constitution states that the 'Republic of South Africa is one, sovereign, democratic state founded on the following values – (a) human dignity', an echo to the Universal Declaration of Human Rights (The Constitution, Chapter 1). Chapter 2 of the Constitution contains the Bill of Rights, which entrenches the issues of social, economic and environmental rights. One of the fundamental rights encapsulated in the Constitution (section 27 (1)) states that 'Everyone has the right to have access to – . . . (b) sufficient food and water'. Section 27 (2) further states that 'the state must take reasonable legislative and other measures, within its available resources, to achieve the progressive realisation of each of these rights' (The Constitution, Sections 7–39).

It was however necessary, in the light of the changing circumstances in the country, to revisit and revise the water legislation and the management of water as a natural resource. These aspects were encapsulated in the National Water Act, Act 36 of 1998, while the activities in respect of water supply were set out in the Water Services Act, Act 108 of 1997. The Water Services Act, 1997 provides for the setting of national standards and the establishment of a regulatory framework for water services institutions and water services intermediaries. The establishment and disestablishment of water boards is provided for, in addition to setting out the role of the Minister of Water Affairs to set the requisite standards in respect of water quality and management, while the (always contentious) issue of water service tariffs is dealt with in conjunction with the Minister of Finance. The Act also provides for the creation, management and reporting structures and contractual capacity of the water service authorities.

The National Water Act, 1998 was the result of intense discussion and consultation and formulated a series of key principles that underpinned the legislation. These include the basic principle that the state is the custodian of water, which is a public resource to which all citizens have a right of access, and that the management and utilisation of water resources have to be for the benefit of society as a whole. It is then clear that the purpose of the legislation is to ensure the effective, efficient and economic management of the water resources, the equitable distribution of water, and promoting social and economic development, while also focusing on the protection and conservation of the precious resource.

It is also important to refer briefly to the legislation that has influenced some aspects of water delivery in South Africa. The issues relating to cooperative governance have already been noted, but it should again be highlighted that service delivery is mostly in the sphere of government closest to the people, that is, local government. The Local Government: Municipal Systems Act, Act 32 of 2000, besides setting the parameters by which the performance of a municipality as an organisation can be monitored and evaluated, also deals with the establishment of policies that would ensure the affordability of basic services (including water) for poor households where the combined income does not exceed a pre-determined amount. However the Act does state clearly that any and all charges for the services must reflect the capital costs, in addition to those relating to operating, administration and related costs.

A later policy document is the Strategic Framework for Water Services (2003). This document has, like many of the formal and official documents recently, a focus on the issues of local government and service delivery – in this case the complete responsibility for water and sanitation services, which are now seen as two sides of the same coin in terms of giving effect to the human dignity element of the Constitution, 1996. This focus on local authorities has led to a shift in the roles and responsibilities of DWAF from direct service provider to a supporter of the local authorities in their endeavours to ensure sustainable service delivery. This changing role also reinforces the principle of cooperative government in that the other two spheres of government must provide assistance and capacity to the local government structures.

THE INSTITUTIONAL LANDSCAPE FOR WATER SUPPLY, PROVISION AND REGULATION

The broader institutional context and contextual changes in the broader governance system in respect of water are summarised in detail by Thompson et al. (2001, pp. 24–6). Briefly this governance context provides for the following:

- The structure of government reflects three distinctive, interdependent and interrelated spheres, each of which is assigned its functions in terms of the constitution. This means that provincial and local governments are now, for the first time, governments in their own right and not merely functions of the national government. Other water service provision institutions, such as Catchment Management Agencies (CMAs) and Water Boards that exercise powers and functions are also organs of state, but not part of any sphere of government.
- The allocation of functional areas relating to water cuts across the different spheres of government with *exclusive national government functional areas* (water resources management), *concurrent national and provincial government functional areas* (for example,

agriculture, disaster management, environment, pollution control, regional planning and development), *exclusive provincial government functional areas* (for example, abattoirs, provincial planning and provincial recreation and amenities), and *local government functional areas* (primarily responsible for water services provision).
- National and provincial governments hold regulatory authority to ensure effective performance by municipalities in respect of all their functions, whereas the provincial sphere also has regulatory functions over local government in respect of, inter alia: municipal planning, storm water management systems in built-up areas, and water and sanitation services limited to potable water supply systems and domestic waste-water and sewage disposal systems. The Constitution assigns to local government the executive authority for water supply and sanitation (water services). Nevertheless, national government and provincial government are obliged to support and strengthen the capacity of municipalities, and to see to the effective performance of municipalities via regulation.
- Of particular importance for the governance of the water sector is the fact that the Constitution recognises that responsible governance requires coordination in all spheres of government, and the principles of cooperative government are set out in Chapter 3 of the Constitution. Intergovernmental relations are still evolving, but it has to be noted that the national government is in a powerful position as it collects the majority of taxes and distributes monies mainly according to its determined priorities.

The manner in which the exclusive and concurrent functional areas relating to water have been allocated across all the different spheres of government creates an institutional framework that is not necessarily harmonised and a legislative system that is not necessarily integrated. Such a system opens the door to potential inconsistency and duplication in the regulatory governance of the water sector.

A useful diagram taken from the *Strategic Framework for Water Services* (Department of Water Affairs and Forestry, 2003b) provides a perspective on the water services monitoring and regulatory framework. This framework is depicted in Figure 10.1. With the graphic illustrations as a backdrop, it is now possible to investigate the institutional landscape and process implications of the current policies and legislation. This investigation is based on three questions; namely, who regulates, what is regulated and how the regulation takes place. To enhance the integration of these three elements, the point of departure is taken to be the locus of regulation, or who regulates, and the other aspects are covered from this point of departure.

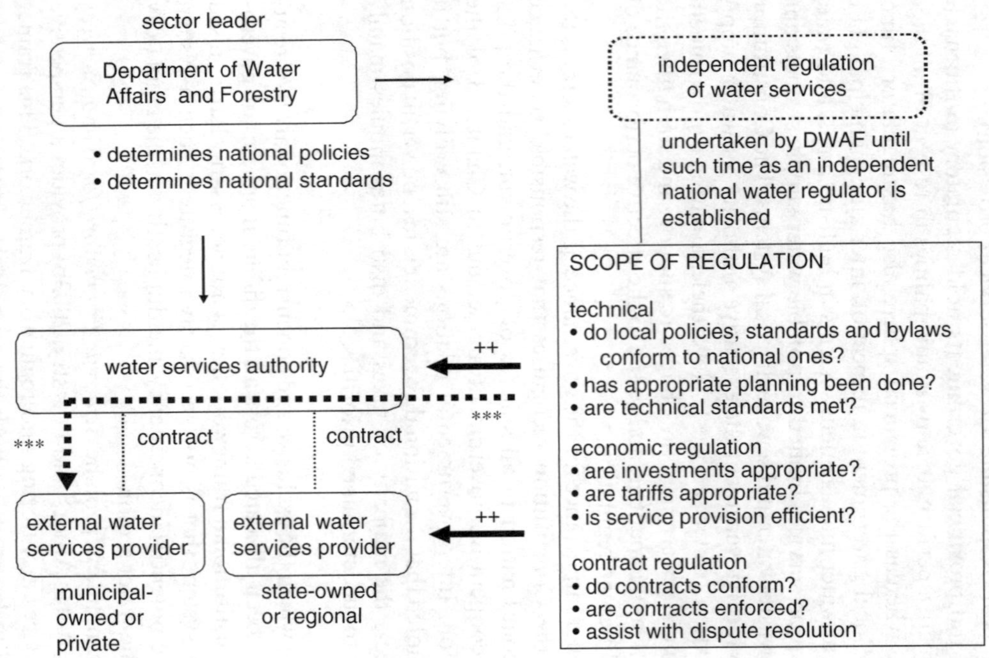

++ Direct regulation of water services authority, state-owned and regional water services providers.
*** Indirect regulation of external water services providers who are not state-owned (via water services authorities).

Figure 10.1 The water service monitoring and regulatory framework (Department of Water Affairs and Forestry, 2003b)

National government is the overall regulator of the water sector. National government regulates through the Minister of Water Affairs who is the executive political office bearer of the Department of Water Affairs and Forestry, which acts on behalf of the Minister in implementation. In the broadest sense, overall, regulation aims to ensure that all role players comply with all the regulatory goals, objectives and measures in respect of the economic, social, political, environmental and technical desirables as provided for in all relevant policy and legislation.

The real and potential complexity of this regulatory mandate, given the context, policies, legislation, institutional complexity and implementation dynamic, is awe inspiring. In order to deal with this complexity the DWAF concretely sees its role as the overall regulator on behalf of national government as:

- setting national norms and standards including planning specification and economic regulation (tariffs);
- the regulation of the water service authorities in terms of the set norms and standards;
- the regulation of contracts in respect of water service authorities and water service providers; and
- the direct regulation of organs of the state, for example, the Water Boards.

In this way the DWAF wants to:

- create macro policy and legislation as a sector leader and oversee the implementation of these policies;
- regulate water service provision, water quality, water tariff structures, planning requirements, water service contracts and the performance in the sector;
- support other spheres of governance as part of cooperative governance and the ideas of developmental regulation;
- serve as a source of reliable and valid information to support the water sector in its management, monitoring and regulatory functions.

The Water Services Act, 1997 provides the Minister and DWAF with real authority to regulate and intervene, but the approach seems to be developmental rather than punitive, which is in line with the ideals of cooperative governance and a developmental state.

The *provincial sphere* of government is involved with regulation of water in accordance with the general principles of cooperative government. Provincial government also fulfils regulatory functions in respect of its other functions such as planning and control, as well as its broad mandate to oversee local government.

In the *local government sphere*, municipalities should be water service authorities (WSA) that fulfil a regulatory mandate in respect of water service providers (WSP). They can, however, also act as water service providers themselves, which may create potential conflicts of interest. As the municipalities have elected councils, these municipalities and their councils are also held accountable to and regulated by their citizens as voters and constituents.

OPERATIONALISATION OF WATER SERVICES AT LOCAL GOVERNMENT LEVEL

The primary responsibility for water services provision rests with local government. In terms of Section 84 of the Municipal Structures Act (Act 117 of 1998), the responsibility for providing water services rests with district and metropolitan municipalities. However, the Act allows the Minister of Provincial and Local Government Affairs to authorise a municipality to perform these functions or exercise these powers. A WSP can be a municipality, municipal-owned entity, water board, community-based organisation, private operator or other types such as water user associations, industries or mines. There must always be a contract between the WSA and the WSP. The district or authorised municipality is the water services authority as defined in the Water Services Act (Act 117 of 1998). There can only be one water services authority in any specific area (that is, water services authority areas cannot overlap).

Water services authorities have the following primary responsibilities:

- Realisation of the right to access to basic water services;
- Planning – preparing water services development plans;
- Selection of water services providers;
- Regulation of water services provision and providers; and
- Communication and consumer education.

A WSA may either provide water services itself (internal mechanism), or contract a WSP to provide water services (external mechanism). For an internal mechanism, the WSA must manage and account separately for the two functions. In practical terms this might mean that a municipal manager, acting on behalf of the municipality, contracts (as the WSA) with the manager of the water services department to provide water services in terms of a performance contract with the municipality. In the second case, the WSA must regulate the WSP according to the contract specifying clearly the allocation of roles and responsibilities between the regulator and the provider.

This ostensible simplicity is, however, hugely misleading. In reality the water system is, or has become, extremely complex. This complexity is clearly illustrated in the *Strategic Framework for Water Services* (DWAF, 2003b) which also represents a first attempt to operationalise regulatory dispensation in respect of water. It is in all probability a valiant attempt, but from the perspective of the authors not successful as it fluctuates between general and specific matters and seems to get caught up in the complexities rather than deconstructing and simplifying it (see section 7 of the *Strategic Framework for Water Services* (2003)).

ACCESS TO AND ECONOMIC REGULATION OF WATER

Fundamental to the manner in which access to water is managed in South Africa is the consideration of affordability of water, and particularly the affordability of a minimum individual quantum of water consistent with constitutional requirements. Access to water as a productive asset is recognised as fundamental to the survival strategies of the poor and the rich alike (Wilson and Ramphele, 1998). What distinguishes between them is the ability to pay for water and the potential herein for effectively (and arbitrarily) curtailing the right of access of the poor through the levying of charges for water that lie beyond their means. High levels of poverty (in the order of 71 per cent of the population in rural areas and 50 per cent of the population overall) and unemployment (at least 38 per cent) exist, making it difficult for most people to pay for even the most basic services (Healthcare in South Africa, 2003).

At a deeper level then and in a country such as South Africa the issue of affordability looms large as a determinant in effect of the means for regulating access to water consistent with the Constitution. In just the final months of 2001, according to the activist group titled the Municipal Services Project (MSP), 700,000 people were affected by water cut-offs for non-payment (Thompson, 2002). The problem of water cut-offs has itself spawned innovative proactive approaches to what in effect is a water rationing system to ensure that consumers do not overreach their capacity to pay. Most recently, in 2002, Johannesburg Water installed pre-paid meters in townships that utilise digital smart card technology to record payments and dispense water from public taps according to the consumer's available water 'credit'.

Economic Regulation of Water in South Africa

Economic regulation of water takes the form of both supply- and demand-side interventions. Pre-eminently the focus of broadly defined 'economic' regulation of water in South Africa has, in varying relative degrees, been on:

- *Supply-side interventions* aimed primarily at the mobilisation of resources for the development of water resources, and distribution and reticulation systems – and particularly financially on making the books balance in the water sector.
- *Demand-side interventions* aimed at managing water demand by means primarily of tariffs and charges, an approach pioneered in Israel (Allan, 1996), and water rationing systems at local level.

The application of demand-side interventions in South Africa has however generally not extended to a fully-fledged economic regulation regime that has set out to bring about fundamental changes in the water economy of the country. Demand-side instruments such as tariffs and charges are still applied primarily in order to 'recover costs' of water provision and therefore in effect to balance the books in a narrower financial sense, rather than to bring about fundamental restructuring of the profiles of supply and demand.

Neither the current legislation in South Africa nor draft regulations and guidelines thereto provide regulatory detail as to the approach that municipalities must take in regard to economic regulation of water and specifically so in regard to (Eberhard, 2002):

- Cost determination of water services provision;
- Guideline rates of return on assets;
- Depreciation of the capital web; and
- The approach to tariff regulation whether by means of rate of return on assets; a cost-plus approach; tariff capping; or capping of 'profits' (i.e. excess of revenues over costs).

This reflects a significant current regulatory deficit in South Africa with many emergent local authorities effectively engrossed in the minutiae of tariff application and in somewhat of a vacuum as regards the objects to be achieved through such regulatory interventions.

In addition, with significant legislative overlap (as for example between the Water Services Act and the Municipal Systems Act) it is not clear which provisions will prevail. In addition contradictory legislative provisions create confusion as to the application of economic regulation (Eberhard, 2002).

Current Water Pricing Policy in South Africa

The stated objective of South Africa's current water policy is the management of the quantity, quality and reliability of the nation's water resources to achieve optimum, long-term, environmentally sustainable social and economic benefit for society from their use. The tensions both in policy and practice between equity and the pursuit of water efficiency are as yet plainly evident. In adopting this policy the South African government appears to be bent on charting a course that takes the country towards commercialisation of the water sector while at the same time maintaining the integrity of the constitutional right to water as a basic need. (See also Brown and Woodhouse, Chapter 11 in this volume, for more detailed consideration of issues of effective regulation, access and affordability based on research in the Mpumalanga Province of South Africa.)

Water Quality and Standards

According to Mackintosh et al. (2000) in almost all South African metropolitan areas, and those areas provided with water by major water boards, the consumer is supplied with high quality drinking water. A recent survey conducted among water boards has shown that South Africa is one of an estimated 12 countries worldwide where water supplied by major water boards is such that it can be drunk with no fear (*Sunday Times*, 2003). The drinking water supply systems are usually well managed, and have water quality monitoring programmes designed to at least meet National Standards for Quality of Potable Water (water supplied by water service providers that is intended to be used for drinking or domestic purposes (potable water) must be of a quality consistent with SABS 241: Specifications for Drinking Water or (in the case of the terms of section 9(1) (b) of the Water Services Act) the South African Water Quality Guidelines published by the DWAF). Efforts have been made by the DWAF and national government to provide water of improved quality through water infrastructure projects. Filtered tapped water has been installed in a number of rural communities around South Africa under the Rural Water Service (RWS) programme. According to DWAF (Naidoo, 2003), some 9 million additional people have been supplied with drinking water. This reduces the backlog from some 14–16 million in 1994 to about 5–6 million. Such progress is indeed impressive.

Nevertheless, attention is now increasingly drawn to the challenge of ensuring that the provided drinking water is of suitable quality. However, despite these concerted efforts to improve water provision, affordability and access, many villages and towns still consume water of very poor quality. Even the DWAF concedes that there has been little improvement in the quality of drinking water supplied to rural and some urban communities (MaConkey, 2003; Department of Water Affairs and Forestry, 2003a). Statistics of deaths linked to water-borne diseases (e.g. 20 per cent of all deaths in the one to five age group are attributable to diarrhoea) confirm that the quality of water provided to communities outside centres serviced by established water utilities is poor (Pegrum et al., 1998).

Clearly regulatory reforms have made water accessible to many South Africans at affordable cost. Implementation of the free basic water policy has helped many poor South Africans and now assists about 70.4 per cent of South Africans and more than 10 million people have been provided with water (Department of Water Affairs and Forestry, 2003a). Reforms, however, have not yet significantly improved the quality of drinking water in most non-metropolitan areas (for more detail on water quality see Mackintosh and Uys, Chapter 13 in this volume, for case studies on the delivery of safe drinking water in non-metropolitan areas of South Africa). The current political debate, driven by the affordability of basic services such as water between the proponents of commodification of water as a private good and its de-commodification as a public good, is analysed in the next section.

POLITICAL ISSUES

The current political issues relating to water are best understood in a historical context that left an inheritance in 1994 of profound inequalities in respect of access to water as a resource and of water service provision (Muller, 2001, pp. 4–5). The policies and legislation in respect of water regulation for the pre-democratisation phase, therefore mostly initially benefited the white minority and their economic interests in agriculture, developing urban commerce and industrial endeavours. With this inheritance the intention of the new government is clear; namely, that benefits should be redistributed from a previously advantaged, mainly urban white minority, to an all inclusive community, including the relatively poor and powerless black rural communities. The current political debate is characterised in particular by the high profile of the affordability of basic services on the political agenda. It throws into sharp relief the tension between the opposing poles of approach to water whether as a public or a private good. Water has been suggested to be a public good in that its benefits and costs extend beyond the direct provision of services to individuals (Eberhard, 2002). Nevertheless to the extent that water may be ‘commodified’ and access to water regulated by the imposition of conditions inter alia of payment, water can indeed be managed as a private good. The inherent tension in the debate in South Africa at present between the proponents of commodification of water as a private good and its de-commodification as a public good derives largely from the perceived difference between these two approaches on the interests and well-being of the poor.

The Case for and Against Commodification of Water in South Africa

For a variety of reasons, not least the importance of water as a staple resource necessary for the maintenance of life, the commodification of water has been challenged in South Africa. The arguments of those favouring all-out commodification of water in South Africa echo those of the World Bank that has routinely included in its structural adjustment loans and water and sanitation loans conditions requiring increased cost recovery, full cost recovery or 'economic pricing' for water services placing increasing emphasis on the consumer to cover water system costs to the extent even of supporting profitability within the sector. It has been successfully argued in South Africa that increased consumer tariffs for water can make safe water unaffordable for poor and vulnerable populations. In particular as water becomes more costly and less accessible, women and children, who bear most of the burden of daily household chores, must travel further and work harder to collect water – often resorting to using water from polluted streams and rivers. Families are forced to make trade-offs between water, food, schooling and health care (Grusky, 2001).

Increased cost recovery is motivated on the grounds that it will improve the economic viability of water utilities for private investors, and contextual experience seems to suggest that these approaches can, all other things being equal, lead to improved water supply. The burden of these arguments is that cost recovery and ultimately privatisation enabled by increased cost recovery, to the extent that it encourages movement of resources into the water sector that government otherwise cannot infuse on a sustained basis, will actually expand access to clean water and sanitation. Where tariff structures are economically inappropriate, middle-class consumers pay subsidised rates that shift the financial burden of the water they use – and often waste – onto the government, with negative spin-offs by way of reduced resources to provide services to the poor.

The problem in South Africa is adduced by some to be less the cost recovery principle itself than the ideology behind its application. From the historical injustices of who receives subsidies to unfair tariff structures, cost recovery on basic services in South Africa has, it is alleged, been largely counter-productive to the goals of equity and environmental sustainability and threatens to undermine post-apartheid reconstruction and development efforts in the country (McDonald, 2002). It is pointed out that cost recovery has not always been the modus operandi of the South African government. During apartheid many South Africans received subsidised services and infrastructure. White suburbanites and white-owned industry benefited the most from these subsidies, with service levels and subsidies in white areas that equalled, and often surpassed, European and North American standards. Much of this subsidisation came at the expense of black workers and consumers who generated the economic surplus necessary, but even black South Africans – to the extent that services were delivered to the townships and rural 'homelands' – received some subsidised service delivery (McDonald, 2002). This ideological argument still features strongly in political rhetoric.

But ideology apart, in the face of the patent inability of government to sustain subsidies to a growing population, few would argue that cost recovery has no place in a highly inequitable country such as South Africa. To the extent that increased cost recovery contributes to improved return on water services infrastructure investment leading to the mobilisation of private sector investment in the water sector and curtails excessive discretionary demand above the minimum necessary, it is generally supported, provided that it does not curtail the constitutional rights of any segment of the population to a basic sufficient supply of water. This can be achieved through an approach that is based on differential tariff structures that progressively penalise high water consumption but enable access to a minimum basically 'sufficient' zero-rated allocation by all South Africans, whether the richest of the rich or the poorest of the poor. Such an approach is dualistic in nature in that while incorporating strong elements of commodification of water for discretionary consumption above a basic threshold necessary to sustain life, it in effect 'de-commodifies' water below that threshold. It represents a practical compromise that accommodates both the proponents of commercialism and those such as organised labour and advocacy groups that have consistently and at times stridently called for the entrenchment of the right to sufficient water consistent with the exercise of constitutional rights.

Privatisation in the Water Sector in South Africa

The at times acrimonious debate on privatisation in South Africa has overflowed to the water sector, as the pragmatic compromise on the imposition of water tariffs by way of a differentiated 'block' tariff structure has suggested. But the predominant issue in South Africa is less *who* delivers the service than *at what price*. Generally the imperative of the South

African government by way of rationalisation of state assets (frequently confused with privatisation per se) has been driven by a complex of considerations including the mobilisation of resources locked up in state enterprises where private sector interests could quite credibly and effectively step into the breach. The dismantling of state monopolies that result in economic inefficiencies has also been a consideration. There is however no evidence at the policy level to suggest any prior preference for 'privatisation' per se on the part of government in the water sector. In the words of the Director-General of DWAF: 'This is not privatising – it is a massive reorganisation of a government and how it provides services. We are still working it out' (Thompson, 2002). There is a stated commitment, certainly on the part of national government, to examine each and every case of restructuring on its own merits. Likewise there is at the policy level no evidence to suggest that the water sector is subject to any different approach save that the fundamental resource or 'asset', namely South Africa's water resources themselves, cannot be alienated. This does however not prevent the privatisation of service provision duly regulated to ensure adherence in both letter and spirit to policy principles.

At present only a relatively few smaller local water service projects are entrusted to longer-term concessionaires and the take-up by the private sector of such opportunities is slow. KwaDukuza became the first municipal authority to enter into a long-term service agreement with a private company. This was concluded in 1999 with Saur who obtained control over the water utility for 25 years. Relatively few other instances are on record, generally affecting smaller to medium-sized authorities although not exclusively so.

CURRENT AND EMERGING ISSUES

The system for regulatory governance of water in South Africa as currently envisaged, is to be found in the policies, legislation and proposals discussed above. At least the intention is that the regulatory system should be effective, productive and efficient, as well as pro-poor and developmental. Whether these objectives can be met jointly or severally as well as the prioritisation thereof in the concrete, practical real world will remain issues with practical consequences for regulatory governance and systems. Given the long-term projections for water availability (or lack thereof) in South Africa over the next quarter of a century, there are a number of current and emerging issues that have come to the fore and in the short, medium and long term will require to be addressed to ensure that the legal structures, institutions and instruments relating to water with specific reference to regulation, provision, commodification and quality are capacitated and sustainable:

- The *plethora of legislation, policies and the institutions* created to deal with the water sector in South Africa has given raise to an extremely complex regulatory and governance system. The overlapping legislation provides some potential for confusion, and declaratory intervention is indicated to head off such confusion.
- The *multitude of regulatory institutions* created in the water sector, with both national and provincial spheres of government having regulatory functions in respect of water and current planning, seems to indicate that each municipality could potentially become a water service authority with regulatory functions vis-à-vis water service providers. This has the potential to create a myriad of close to 300 water regulators in the system with resultant coordination and cost implications.
- Given the institutional complexity and potential diversity, *jurisdictional conflicts* are sure to arise in the regulatory governance system. *Cooperative governance* is essentially positive and value adding, but there will be and is a need to start thinking through the issues of consistent decision-making and action. A set of precedents and conventions will have to be created in theory and practice to ensure inter- and intra-jurisdictional coherence and consistency.
- Although regulatory reforms have made water accessible to many South Africans at affordable cost the reforms have not yet significantly improved the *quality of drinking water* in most non-metropolitan areas, and many villages and towns still consume water of very poor quality.
- Because of the high profile of affordability of basic services such as water, the *political debate* at present is between the proponents of commodification of water as a private good and its decommodification as a public good: the predominant issue in South Africa is less *who* delivers the service than *at what price*.
- With the strong ideological objections from some groups to the principle of *full cost recovery* a practical compromise of *differential tariff structures* that accommodates both the proponents of commercialism and those who called for the entrenchment of the right to sufficient water was implemented.
- There is no evidence at the policy level to suggest any prior preference for '*privatisation*' per se on the part of government in the water sector, and at present the take-up by the private sector of such opportunities is slow with only a relatively few smaller local water service projects entrusted to longer-term concessionaires.

- The generally undeveloped state of formal economic regulation of water usage in South Africa represents a significant current regulatory deficit. This manifests as an (understandable) preoccupation with balancing the books of the water sector while neglecting to bring about a basic remodelling of South Africa's water economy.
- Even in respect of the application of the more modest objectives of tariff recovery for water, regulatory deficits exist more especially in the area of tariff development at municipal level. Emergent municipalities in particular are involved in an area where their experience and expertise generally are in most instances seriously lacking.
- While key developmental decisions continue to be taken on political, ideological and other grounds without full impact assessment on the overall water economy and particularly on the poor that feature high on the socioeconomic agenda, South Africa to all intent and purposes can as yet not lay claim to a fully-fledged economic regulatory regime for water.
- And finally, most of the generic issues previously identified (Schwella, 2002; Ackron et al., 2002) relating to the emerging competition and regulatory governance system in South Africa (e.g. resource and capacity constraints, systems of democratic control and public accountability, the state of consumer constituencies and their actions) are also applicable to the water sector.

SUMMARY AND CONCLUSION

Water, a life-supporting resource as well as a social and economic good, creates a formidable platform for issues to develop. This general proposition is even more acutely manifested in South Africa, given its history and limited water sources. It is therefore not surprising that many hard battles are fought in respect of all aspects of water in this country. These battles are premised on the multitude of large and small issues pertaining to water. At the most basic level the issue with water is its scarcity and the provision of access to water. Ostensibly there is agreement that water should be for the benefit of all and therefore provided to all. The methods for such provision are, however, subject to serious debate between marketisation of water and prices that recover full costs from all consumers in an equitable way and its 'de-commodification' (Bond, 2002, pp. 2–4) as a public good.

As neither of these two extreme positions is attainable, the compromise positions are open to debate and the influences of power and economics in any given reality. In the South African reality the current position (since July 2001) involves a lifeline supply of 6000 litres of free water to all residents, with a commitment to continue cost recovery even if it results in excluding access to those who do not meet the obligation to pay for water used in excess of the free provision. This position, of course, necessitates a system of regulation. The system currently envisaged is to be found in the policies, legislation and institutions discussed above. At least the intention is that the regulatory system should be effective, productive and efficient, as well as pro-poor and developmental. Whether these objectives can be met jointly or severally as well as the prioritisation thereof in the concrete, practical real world will remain issues with practical consequences for regulatory governance and systems.

BIBLIOGRAPHY

Ackron, J.C., J.J. Muller, K. van der Molen and F.M. Uys in association with E. Schwella (2002), *The Institutional and Policy Framework for Regulation and Competition in South Africa: A Preliminary Map*, Centre on Regulation and Competition Working Paper Series; No. 47, Manchester: University of Manchester.

Afrol News (2002), 'Ten million water cuts after South Africa's water privatisation', Afrol News, 4 November 2002 (Online news agency), Retrieved from http://www/afrol.com/News 2002/sa024_water_private.htm

Allan, J.A. (1996), 'Water use and development in arid regions: Environment, economic development and water resource politics and policy', *Water Use and Development*, **5**(2), 107–15.

Bond, P. (2002), 'Principles, strategies and tactics of decommodification in South Africa', *LINKS International Journal of Renewal*, **22** (September to December 2002) (Online journal), Retrieved 26 March 2003 from http://www.dsp.au/links/issue22/Bond.htm

Bourne, D.E. and N. Coetzee (1996), *An Atlas of Potentially Water-related Diseases in South Africa*, WRC Report No. 584/1/96, Pretoria, South Africa: WRC.

Department of Water Affairs and Forestry (1994), *Water Supply and Sanitation Policy White Paper – Water an Indivisible National Asset*, Republic of South Africa, Cape Town, Retrieved from http://www.dwaf.gov.za/Documents/Policies/WSSP.pdf

Department of Water Affairs and Forestry (1997), *National Water Policy White Paper*, Retrieved from http://www.dwaf.gov.za/Documents/Policies/nwpwp.pdf

Department of Water Affairs and Forestry (2002), *National Water Resource Strategy* (Proposed First Edition), Republic of South Africa.

Department of Water Affairs and Forestry (2003a), *Directorate: Water Conservation – Questions and Answers*, 8 September 2003, Retrieved from http://www.dwaf.gov.za/WaterConservation/QA.htm

Department of Water Affairs and Forestry (2003b), *Strategic Framework for Water Services*, September 2003, Pretoria, South Africa, Retrieved from http://www.dwaf.gov.za/Documents/Policies/Strategic%20Framework%20approved. pdf

Eberhard, R. (2002), *Economic Regulation of Water*, Draft discussion document prepared for the WRC, Palmer Development Group, Retrieved from http://www.tips.org.za/events/event_details/papers/Eberhard.pdf

Grusky, S. (2001), 'Privatization tidal wave, IMF/World Bank water policies and the price paid by the poor', *Multinational Monitor*, September 2001; Globalization Challenge Initiative, Retrieved from http://www.thirdworldtraveler.com/Water/Privatization_TidalWave.html

Hall, C.G. (1939), *The Origin and Development of Water Rights in South Africa*, Oxford: Oxford University Press, p. 11.

Healthcare in South Africa, Poverty and Unemployment (2003), 'Essential information: South Africa at a glance: health', p. 3, Retrieved from http://www.safrica.info/ess_info/sa_glance/health/923087.htm

Kasril, R. (2002), 'Budget vote No. 33: Water Affairs and Forestry', 10 May 2002, Republic of South Africa, Cape Town, Retrieved from http://www.dwaf.gov.za/Communications/Minister%20Speeches/Kasrils/2002/Budget%20speech%2010%20May%202002.doc

Kasril, R. and G. Gosh (2001), Press release, 'Launch of South African chapter of Vision 21'.

McDonald, D.A. (2002), 'No money no service: South Africa's poorest citizens lose out under attempts to recover service costs', *Alternatives Journal*, **28**(2), Retrieved from http://216.239.53.104/search?q=cache:1aPwfnE8C28J:qsilver.queensu.ca/~mspadmin/pages/Project_Publications/Journals/Money.pdf

Mackintosh, G.S., M. Ramba, E. Delport and B. Genthe (1999), *Drinking Water Quality Management Procedures for Rural Communities. South African Case Studies*, Conference Proceedings, IWSA World Water Congress, Buenos Aires, Argentina.

Mackintosh, G.S., E. Delport, N. Smith and J. Mansfield (2000), *Considerations regarding South Africa's Draft Compulsory National Water Standards*, Conference Proceedings, IWA Conference: Managing Water and Waste in the New Millennium, 23–26 May 2000, Mid-Rand, South Africa.

MaConkey, G. (2003), Personal communication, Department of Water Affairs. Johannesburg.

Muller, M. (2001), *Transforming Water Law to Achieve South Africa's Development Vision: A Case Study in National Law*, South Africa: Department of Water Affairs and Forestry; 21 January 2003, Retrieved from http://www.dwaf.gov.za/communication/DepartmentalSpeeches/HAGUELWF.doc

Naidoo, D.P. (2003), Personal Communication, Department of Water Affairs, Johannesburg.

Pegrum, G.C., N. Rollins and Q. Espey (1998), 'Estimating the cost of diarrhoea and epidemic dysentery in KwaZulu-Natal and South Africa', *Water SA*, **24**(1).

Ramazotti, M. (1996), *Readings in African Customary Water Law*, Rome: FAO.

Schwella, E. (2002), *Regulation and Competition in South Africa*, Centre on Regulation and Competition Working Paper Series, No. 18, February 2002, Manchester: University of Manchester.

South African Bureau of Standards (2001), *South African Bureau of Standards 241:2001: South African Standards for Drinking Water*, Pretoria, South Africa.

Sunday Times (2003), 'Cheers! South Africa has it tapped', *Sunday Times*, 27 April 2003.

The Constitution of the Republic of South Africa (1996) (Act 108 of 1996) as adopted on 8 May 1996 and amended on 11 October 1996 by the Constitutional Assembly: annotated version (Christina Murray, Friedrich Soltau).
The Republic of South Africa (1994), *The Reconstruction and Development Programme: A Policy Framework*, Retrieved from http://www.polity.org.za/govdocs/rdp/rdp.html
The Republic of South Africa (1997), Water Services Act, 1997 (Act 108 of 1997), *Government Gazette*, 19 December 1997, 390 (18522).
The Republic of South Africa (1998), National Water Act, 1998 (Act 36 of 1998), *Government Gazette*, 26 August 1998, 398 (19182).
The Republic of South Africa (2000), Local Government: Municipal Systems Act, 2000 (Act 32 of 2000), *Government Gazette*, 425:21776, Cape Town: Government Printers, Retrieved from http://www.gov.za/acts/2000/a32-00.pdf
Thompson, G. (2002), 'Apartheid gone, new challenge is water', *The International Herald Tribune*, Monday 23 December 2002, IHT online, Retrieved from http://iht.com/cgi-bin/generic.cgi?template=articleprint.tmplh&ArticleId=81150
Thompson, H., C.M. Stimie, E. Richter and S. Perret (2001), *Policies, Legislation and Organizations Related to Water in South Africa, with Special Reference to the Olifants River Basin*, International Water Management Institute Working Paper 18, South African Working Paper No. 7, Retrieved from http://www.iwmi.cgiar.org/pubs/working/WOR18.pdf
United States Department of Commerce (2001), *South Africa Water Management*, Strategis Collection: Market Research Reports, STAT-USA on the Internet, Retrieved from http://strategis.ic.gc.ca/SSG/1/dd72506e.html
Vidar, M. and M.A. Mekouar (2001), 'Water, health and human rights', Article prepared for the World Water Day, Legal Office, Food and Agricultural Organization (FAO), Retrieved from http://www.worldwaterday.org/2001/thematic/hmnrights.html.
Wilson, F. and M. Ramphele (1998), *Uprooting Poverty: The South African Challenge: Report for the Second Carnegie Inquiry into Poverty and Development in Southern Africa*, Cape Town: David Philip.

11. Pioneering redistributive regulatory reform: a study of implementation of a Catchment Management Agency for the Inkomati Water Management Area, South Africa

Julia Brown and Philip Woodhouse

INTRODUCTION: GUIDING PRINCIPLES ON WATER RESOURCE MANAGEMENT AND SOUTH AFRICA'S 1998 NATIONAL WATER ACT

Following constitutional reform and the establishment of majority rule in 1994, the South African government embarked on legislative reform to provide the basis for more equitable development. The legislative framework for water was established through the Water Services Act (1997), concerned with provision of water supply and sanitation services, and the National Water Act (1998), which covers the broader management of water resources. While the two elements of water management are linked, this chapter is primarily concerned with the implementation of the National Water Act.

South Africa's National Water Act of 1998 (Act No. 36 of 1998) is widely regarded as a pioneer of an international wave of reform in the water sector, including the EU Water Framework Directive (EU, 2000) and Mexico's National Water Plan (2001–2006), which embodied a set of guiding principles agreed at the 1992 International Conference on Water and the Environment (ICWE) in Dublin (Calder, 1999; Heathcote, 1998; World Bank, 1993, 2003). The key ICWE principles are:

1. The river basin is a natural unit of analysis and management. A holistic approach to water management is advocated, that is, *integrated catchment management*.
2. Action should to be taken at the lowest appropriate level (subsidiarity). This will necessitate the *devolution/decentralisation* of management.

3. Water has an *economic value*. Economic instruments should be used to encourage the efficient use of the resource.
4. A *participatory* approach is advocated – all stakeholders (with particular reference to women) should be involved in the planning and management of water resources.

From a regulatory perspective, the first three principles are primarily concerned with environmental (natural resource management) efficiency whereas the fourth principle (participation) emphasises equity and issues of redress, whereby previously unheard voices are to be included in decision making. This is a particularly important consideration in post-apartheid South Africa. There are tensions between these objectives, however. There is, first, a tension between environmental and equity goals, in particular with regard to subsidiarity, the most appropriate level at which decisions should be taken. Devolution may enable better use of local knowledge to manage water, but not result in redress where the process becomes co-opted by controlling local elites whose interests are best served by maintaining the status quo. A second tension arises between equity of access to water for individuals and the principle of economic value of water. Broader access to irrigation, for example, may result in increased water use by inexperienced or inefficient irrigators, since within South Africa at present water management expertise is concentrated within white-dominated commercial agriculture. Thus increasing water access for previously disadvantaged groups is likely, in the short term at least, to reduce efficiency.

South Africa's National Water Act of 1998 explicitly seeks to implement environmental efficiency principles as well as to regulate water use in a way that is socially fair by seeking to redress past inequalities. The purpose of the Act is stated (section 2) as:

> 'to ensure that the nation's water resources are protected, used, developed, conserved, managed, and controlled in ways that take into account . . .
>
> - meeting basic human needs of present and future generations;
> - promoting equitable access to water;
> - redressing the results of past racial and gender discrimination;
> - promoting the efficient, sustainable and beneficial use of water in the public interest
> - facilitating economic and social development;
> - providing for growing demand for water use;
> - protecting aquatic and associated ecosystems and their biodiversity;
> - reducing and preventing pollution and degradation of water resources;
> - meeting international obligations;
> - promoting dam safety;
> - managing floods and droughts.

> And, for achieving this purpose, to establish suitable institutions and to ensure that they have appropriate community, racial and gender representation.

The four ICWE principles are manifest in the National Water Act in the ways described below.

Integrated catchment management is pursued through redefinition of water property rights and, in particular, the abolition of the distinction between 'private' and 'public' water recognised by earlier legislation (the 1956 Water Act), and, in consequence, effective extinction of water rights tied to ownership of riparian land. Under the 1998 Act, water is 'an indivisible national asset' and the national government will act as the custodian in the public interest (DWAF, 1997). The 1998 Act also broadened the definition of water use to include any activities that result in a reduction of stream flow (for example, forest plantations), a deterioration of the water resource (for example, waste, effluent, or cooling water disposal), or the removal and disposal of underground water (for example, mining). The 1998 Act also requires the definition of a 'Reserve': the guarantee of water to meet basic human needs and to maintain environmental sustainability.

Integrated catchment management is to be achieved following the principle of *devolution/decentralisation of water management*. The new legislation divides South Africa into 19 Water Management Areas (WMAs), each of which will be managed by a single Catchment Management Agency (CMA), representing the interests of different water users at the catchment level. Central government (the Department of Water Affairs and Forestry – DWAF) will not delegate all its current water resource functions to the newly established CMA; rather, the delegation of functions will be phased in over time as and when the CMA is deemed a 'responsible authority'. According to section 80 of the National Water Act, the CMAs will have three initial functions:

- To investigate and advise on the protection, use, development, conservation, management and control of water resources in its WMA.
- To develop a catchment management strategy.
- To coordinate the related activities of water management institutions within the WMA.

Over time, the DWAF may delegate far-reaching powers to the CMA. For example water allocation to different users could be determined by the decentralised CMA, which may require all water users to apply for a licence to continue using water so as to achieve a fairer allocation of water, to improve the efficiency of resource management or to protect water quality (section 43).

The operation of the CMA is conceived as *participatory*, both through representation of the different water users on the CMA governing body, and through the more local engagement of those interests in Water Users' Associations (WUA). Under the National Water Act, the governing board of a CMA is to be appointed by the Minister of Water Affairs 'with the objective of achieving a balance among the interests of water users, potential water users, local and provincial government and environmental interest groups' (section 8.1 of the Act). The Minister must also appoint an advisory committee, which will make recommendations on which sectors and interests within the WMA should be represented on the CMA governing board. The composition and balance of the CMA Governing Board is of crucial importance because it is a likely indication of the future commitment of the CMA to a redistributive agenda.

Chapter 8 of the 1998 Act outlines the establishment of WUAs as water management institutions that operate at a restricted local level and are effectively 'cooperative associations of individual water users who wish to undertake water-related activities for their mutual benefit' (section 92). Irrigation Boards, which currently manage water resources at the local level on behalf of the commercial agricultural sector, are to be transformed into more inclusive WUAs (section 98). The Act also envisages situations whereby the management of smallholder schemes in former homeland areas will be devolved to the users, who would then form WUAs to manage their particular schemes (DWAF, 2002, p. 1), according to the powers and duties that are assigned or delegated to them.

The fourth of the ICWE principles, that water has an *economic value*, is reflected in the provision of the National Water Act (chapter 5) that all water use, regardless of where it occurs in the water cycle, is now subject to a Water Resource Management Charge. The charge will fund the prototype CMA (generally the local DWAF technical staff), and ultimately the full CMA's activities. The charge may vary across the 19 WMAs and different tariffs may be levied for agriculture, domestic/industrial use, and forestry. Some or all charges may be waived for disadvantaged groups to promote equitable access for productive purposes such as agriculture (Woodhouse and Hassan, 1999, p. 30). The economic valuation of water is also expected to result in more efficient water use, as allocations of water to users will not be permanent, but for a 'reasonable' period, and may be traded with other users, subject to ministerial consent.

Implementation of the National Water Act remains at an early stage. In the years that have elapsed, it is clear that the establishment of CMAs is very uneven across the 19 WMAs in South Africa. The CMA process is most advanced in the Inkomati WMA, where the CMA was officially launched on 30 March 2004. It is an opportune moment to explore how implementation of the different elements of the Act has altered the prospects of access to water for South Africa's poorer social groups.

THE INKOMATI WATER MANAGEMENT AREA

General Characteristics

The Inkomati WMA is located in north-eastern South Africa and borders Mozambique to the East and Swaziland to the South-East. Administratively, the majority of the Inkomati WMA falls within Mpumalanga Province, with a portion within Limpopo Province. Three principal river catchments make up the Inkomati WMA: the Sabie-Sand, the Crocodile and the Komati (top to bottom on Figure 11.1). All drain in an easterly direction and eventually flow into Mozambique. The Great Escarpment, which divides the WMA into the Highveld plateau area in the west (2000 m above sea level) and the Lowveld to the east (140 m above sea level) is the most striking topographical feature of the Inkomati WMA. Rainfall, which is strongly seasonal, occurs mainly in the summer months and ranges from 400 mm to 1000 mm over most of the Lowveld through to 1500 mm in mountainous reaches of the escarpment. Annual evaporation rates vary across the WMA, from less than 1400 mm on the Highveld to more than 1900 mm in the Lowveld, and as a result irrigation requirements vary (DWAF, 2003 p. 1), with high demand in the drier and hotter Lowveld. Water resource infrastructure is well developed in the majority of the Inkomati WMA reserved for the white population under apartheid. Major dams have been constructed on many of the rivers in the WMA, including the Driekoppies (237 million m^3 capacity) and Maguga (303 million m^3 capacity) dams built in the past decade to provide water for irrigated agriculture, although the most recently constructed (Maguga) has never been filled to capacity due to persistent drought in recent years. The recently constructed Injaka dam (120 million m^3 capacity) on a tributary of the Sabie, was built to augment domestic water supplies.

Main Water Users in the Inkomati

Data for water use within the Inkomati WMA are widely disputed but figures published by the DWAF (Table 11.1) show that *irrigated agriculture* dominates water use, accounting for 57 per cent of the total requirements of the WMA, and up to 73 per cent of water demand in individual catchments. The geography of irrigated agriculture still largely reflects its development under the apartheid era, almost entirely in white farming areas.

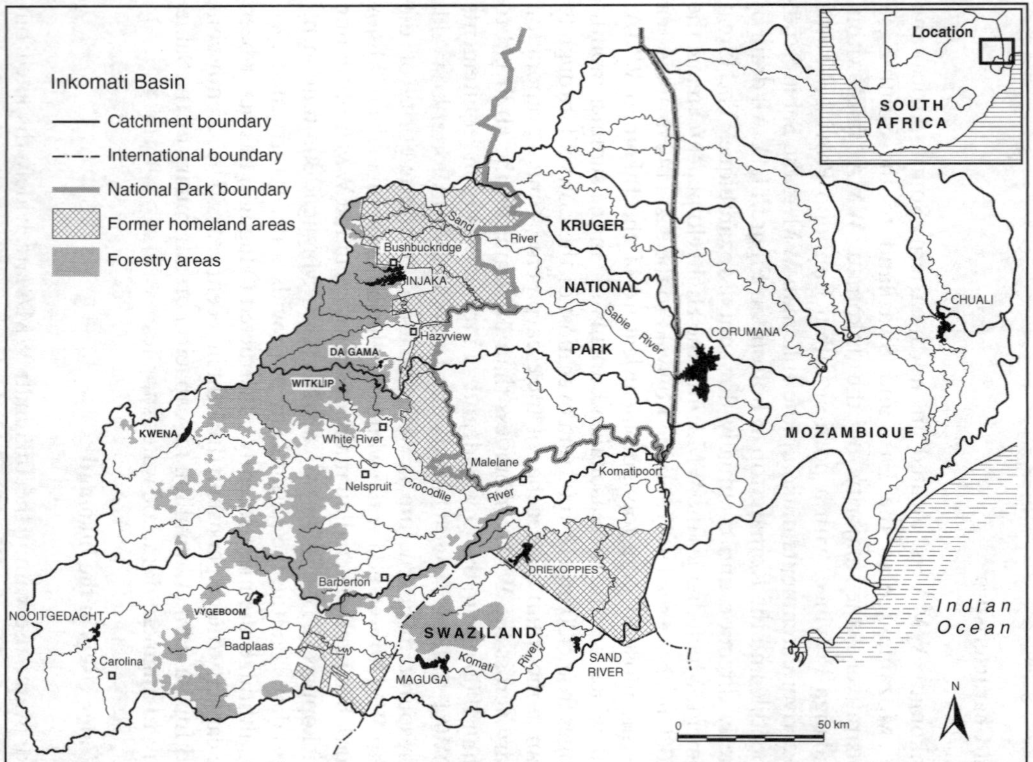

Figure 11.1 Map showing the location of the Inkomati WMA

Table 11.1 Water requirements for the various water users in the Inkomati for the year 2003 (million m³/annum), 2004

Catchments	Komati (West of Swaziland)	Komati (North of Swaziland)	Crocodile	Sabie/Sand	**Total Inkomati WMA**	%
Irrigation	21	222	257	65	565	*57.0*
Urban	2	3	35	22	62	*6.3*
Rural	4	6	7	4	21	*2.1*
Mining	–	1	23	0	24	*2.4*
Afforestation	23	12	42	37	114	*11.5*
Total requirements	**50**	**244**	**364**	**128**	**786**	
International requirements	–	60	49	0	109	*11.0*
Transfers	97	–	0	0	97	*9.8*
Grand total	**147**	**304**	**413**	**128**	**992**	

Source: DWAF (2004, p. 55).

Irrigation development opportunities in the former homeland areas of the Inkomati WMA have been far more restricted; Woodhouse and Hassan (1999, pp. 10–11) identified five categories of irrigation activity by black farmers: (1) smallholder sugar cane (average 7 ha) in the Nkomazi area; (2) smallholder irrigation of maize and vegetables on formal schemes built by homeland administrations; (3) non-formal smallholder irrigation for commercial vegetable production; (4) 'community gardens' microplots irrigated by buckets or gravity tanks supplied from streams; and (5) 'backyard irrigation' using water from household supplies.

Commercial *forestry* plantations, primarily eucalyptus and pine, cover an area of 3357 km², dominating the upper reaches of catchments. They account for an estimated 11 per cent of total water requirements in the WMA, under the terms of the 1998 Act, through intercepting rainfall and reducing streamflow. Forestry is a major water user in the Sabie catchment (29 per cent) and to a lesser extent the Crocodile catchment (10 per cent). The DWAF (2004) has indicated that no further expansion of forestry plantations will be permitted.

While not differentiated by the DWAF in their figures, *industry and manufacturing* are significant users of water. The manufacturing sector, which in 1997 accounted for 24.6 per cent of the WMA's GGP, is based around Nelspruit, the Inkomati's largest urban centre (DWAF, 2003, p. 9). However, the single largest water requirement, amounting to 66 per cent of water use in the Komati (West of Swaziland), is for 97 million m^3/annum transferred (Table 11.1) into the adjacent Olifants WMA for cooling Eskom's (electricity company) coal-fired power stations. 'Water will continue to be transferred' (DWAF, 2004, p. ix) for this 'strategic' water use. Other industrial users of water include the Sappi Kraft paper mill at Ngodwana in the Elands Valley (upper Crocodile catchment) and the two TSB sugar mills in the Lower Crocodile. In the Crocodile catchment, mining and quarrying activities account for 5.5 per cent of water use.

Primary water use (for drinking, washing and other domestic purposes) reflects the population distribution in formerly white towns such as Nelspruit and White River and in the densely populated black former homeland areas of Ka Ngwane, Lebowa and Gazankulu. The Injaka dam was constructed to augment supplies to the large black population on the Upper Sabie and Sand catchment (Bushbuckridge area), estimated at 0.5 million in 1995, and expected to reach 0.93 million by 2010. The provision of domestic water is governed by separate legislation, the 1997 Water Services Act, but the high level of assurance of supply required to meet domestic demand (an allowance of 25 litres per person per day) as part of the 'Reserve' under the 1998 National Water Act, means that growing primary water use may reduce availability for other uses, particularly during drought periods. However, even these legal requirements are not yet being met in many of the former homeland areas, and even historically 'white' towns such as White River experienced shortages during the recent drought period.

In addition to primary use, the water requirements of the 'Reserve' will need to cover flows to sustain ecology. These are complicated to determine, but are likely to be significant in the Inkomati WMA. The Kruger National Park (KNP) and Sabie-Sand Game Reserve lie downstream of the main (irrigation and forestry) users on the Sabie-Sand and Crocodile, and if flow levels entering the KNP are too low the ecological functioning of the park will be affected.

South Africa also has to meet international agreements (for example the Interim IncoMaputu Water Use Agreement) with Mozambique on cross-border flows. *International requirements* are therefore an important water use in the Crocodile (12 per cent) and Komati (20 per cent) catchments.

The *water balance* (the reconciliation of water requirements and water availability) for the Inkomati indicates that with the exception of the Sabie, projected to have a surplus of 31 million m^3/annum (DWAF, 2004, p. 38), there is a shortfall: 41 million m^3/annum in Komati West of Swaziland (DWAF, 2004, p. 31), 6 million m^3/annum in Komati North of Swaziland (DWAF, 2004, p. 37) and 149 million m^3/annum in the Crocodile (DWAF, 2004, p. 42). During the recent drought period, the WMA experienced severe water shortages, despite the construction of two major dams (Driekoppies and Maguga) within the last decade.

INSTITUTIONAL FRAMEWORK

The formal roles of the various actors and agencies with an interest in water resource management and the CMA will now be outlined.

The DWAF

Under the terms of the 1998 Act, the Minister for Water Affairs is responsible for water resources in South Africa, and the Department of Water Affairs and Forestry (DWAF), based in Pretoria, is responsible for implementing the National Water Act, including approval of all CMA proposals. The Mpumalanga DWAF Regional Office, in Nelspruit, is charged with managing water resources in the Inkomati WMA and the adjacent Olifants WMA, effectively undertaking the CMA functions until the CMA is deemed to have sufficient capacity and expertise. At the time this study was undertaken, DWAF Mpumalanga had four subdirectorates: Forestry, Planning and Development, Water Quality, and Water Resources Management. The last of these is responsible for reviewing all water licence applications, registration of licences, verification of registered water use, maintenance of dams and other infrastructure, and compliance with international obligations. The Nelspruit office began engaging stakeholders in the CMA process in 1997 (Woodhouse and Hassan, 1999), as outlined in Figure 11.2 and discussed more fully later in the chapter.

Municipalities

From 1 July 2003 municipalities, the lowest tier of local government, became the Water Service Authority (WSA – as defined in the 1997 Water Services Act), with a regulatory responsibility for domestic water supply and sanitation services under the DWAF's supervision. The responsibility for the former Homeland schemes (taken on by the DWAF when the areas were reincorporated into South Africa in 1994) was also transferred to municipalities. While municipalities are WSAs they do not necessarily have to be the Water Service Provider: the 1997 Act (No. 108 of 1997) provides a framework that allows municipalities to enter into a variety of partnerships for the provision of water services (for example public/public, public/private or public/NGO/community).

As indicated earlier, the Inkomati WMA does not correspond with political boundaries. Although it is mostly within the Ehlanzeni District Municipality of Mpumalanga Province, it also extends into Limpopo Province. Ehlanzeni District contains the local municipalities (WSAs) of Mbombela, Nkomazi, Thaba Chweu and Umjindi. Two municipalities included in this study were Mbombela (covering Nelspruit and the area bounded by the Kruger Park to the east and the Sabie river to the north), and Nkomazi (lower Crocodile and Komati North of Swaziland). In the latter the municipality (WSA) was also the Water Service Provider, responsible for delivery of water supply and sanitation. In Mbombela, the provision of water services is more complicated due to a series of municipal boundary changes. Following the democratic elections of 1994, new municipal boundaries amalgamated relatively prosperous white towns such as Nelspruit with neighbouring black townships and densely populated former homeland areas. Relative to the old Nelspruit local council, the population of the new Nelspruit Transitional Local Council (NTLC) increased tenfold and its responsibilities mushroomed.

In 1999, the NTLC decided to award a 30-year contract to a private company, the Greater Nelspruit Utility Company (GNUC), in which the British company BiWater has a majority shareholding, to supply water and sanitation services to the greater Nelspruit area. In further boundary changes following the December 2000 local government elections, Nelspruit TLC became Mbombela municipality and WSA, with a greatly increased area, incorporating large swathes of former Ka Ngwane homeland. For roughly half of the newly expanded municipal area Mbombela is the WSP, while GNUC remains the WSP for the greater Nelspruit area.

Transfer of the operation and maintenance of the water supply schemes in the former homelands is currently under way in Mbombela and Nkomazi. The obligations of municipalities have also grown further following the introduction of the Free Basic Water Policy (FBW) in February 2001. This commits water providers to providing free to poor households 6000 litres of water per household per month. The responsibility of municipalities for water supply means that, as well as being the elected representative of the local population, they are important stakeholders in the management of water resources in the Inkomati.

Traditional Leaders

Traditional leaders (Tribal Authorities), particularly after the promulgation of the Communal Land Rights Act, represent an important and influential body over the development and management of communal lands in the former homeland areas. Tribal Authorities are officially an institution of local government; however, they do not sit easily in this role. Tensions between democratically elected municipal representatives (councillors) and traditional leaders are often high and working relations between the two authorities are frequently strained. The large swathes of former homeland areas in the Inkomati, where the majority of the poor population reside, render traditional leaders an important stakeholder in the CMA process.

Commercial Farmers

With the exception of small schemes run by homeland administrations, irrigated agriculture in the Inkomati has historically been the preserve of white commercial farmers producing irrigated sugar cane and high value fruit and vegetable crops. A highly organised lobby represented nationally by Agri SA, commercial farmers promote their interests locally through local action committees and lobbying campaigns, and their own legal advisers. They also have a long tradition of organisation to secure access to water through local irrigation boards (IBs), and most of the government's investment in storage dams in the Inkomati WMA has been designed to serve their needs (Woodhouse, 1995).

Irrigation Boards

Under the 1956 Water Act, large parts of the Inkomati WMA were designated Government Water Control Areas, within which it was mandatory for irrigators to belong to Irrigation Boards (IBs) delegated by government to undertake the day-to-day management of water at the local level, including scheduling irrigation, operating water works, and prosecuting members who are found to be stealing water. IBs constitute the main body of expertise and information about water use in their locality, and many IBs have invested in infrastructure through construction of canals, weirs and other water management systems. Control of water resource management in the Inkomati WMA is therefore highly decentralised, but also often locally concentrated, with, for example, the Nkomazi Major IB and the Crocodile River Main IB, each of which covers three minor IBs, sharing a single office and secretary. Under the terms of the 1998 Act the IBs were expected to form broader, more inclusive Water User Associations (WUAs). This issue is explored later. However, except in areas of expansion of sugar-cane production by black smallholders (the Nkomazi Irrigation Expansion Programme: NIEP), notably the Lomati and Komati IBs, few IBs in the Inkomati WMA have any black farmer members. Through their detailed local technical knowledge of water use by agriculture, commercial farmers and the IBs they control are in a potentially strong position to influence the future direction of the CMA. Further, as the largest water user, commercial agriculture will contribute the largest proportion of the Water Resource Management Charge and therefore the CMA will be largely financially dependent on this sector.

Black Farmers

A consequence of the labour and land policies under apartheid is that black farmers do not have a long history of irrigated farming in the Inkomati WMA. The expansion of irrigation for black farmers under NIEP was part of the South Africa–Swaziland treaty to build the Driekoppies and Maguga dams, with water allocated by the DWAF to the Ka Ngwane administration and distributed by the Department of Agriculture among tribal authorities in the Nkomazi. The first phase of the NIEP scheme, between 1993 and 1998, saw 7094 ha of sugar planted (NOWAC, 1999, p. 10). Funding difficulties stalled the scheme between 1998 and 2000, but development of a second phase from 2000 has been funded through the LRAD programme (Land Redistribution and Agricultural Development), a sub-programme of Department of Land Affairs' Land Redistribution programme.

Government agencies generally recognise three different sub-categories of black farmers: 'land claim' farmers, 'emerging' farmers and 'potential farmers'. Access to water rights varies between these three groups. In recent years there have been a small number of successful land claims in traditionally white farming areas made by black communities (for example in the Burgers Hall area of the Sabie catchment). These land-claim farms are often run as cooperatives, have irrigation rights and are usually members of local IBs. However, they constitute a tiny proportion of all black farming activity in the Inkomati area.

The Inkomati CMA Advisory Committee differentiates between 'existing agriculture' (so called 'emerging' farmers) that is, small-scale farming activity with irrigation rights (for example, in NIEP areas), and 'potential' farmers, that is, individuals with access to land (typically those engaged in dry land farming or beneficiaries of land reform), but who currently have no entitlement to water. These two categories are important when considering representation and ultimately water allocations.

The majority of black farmers in the Inkomati are still relatively inexperienced in the day-to-day operations of high input farming, and they have yet to develop strong networks. The Mpumalanga African Farmers Union (MAFU) represents black farmers in the province but, with the exception of those in the NIEP, few are members of irrigation boards, and their understanding of quantitative aspects of water resource management is often low. Overall, the black farming sector is therefore potentially in a weak negotiating position vis-à-vis commercial farmers and other sectors. The issue of representation of the interests of black farmers in the CMA and WUA is explored later in the chapter.

Industrial Interests

Sappi Kraft paper mill and the Transvaal Sugar Limited (TSB) mills are the main industrial users of water in the Inkomati WMA and as such are important stakeholders in the CMA process. TSB processes all the sugar produced in the area and provides technical support to emerging sugar cane growers in the Nkomazi area. TSB therefore wields considerable power over its growers and the irrigation boards, and TSB managers sit on the governing boards of the IBs, often being the chairmen of several IBs. TSB also has a potentially powerful position in the Inkomati CMA because sugar accounts for over a third of the land irrigated in WMA.

Forestry

Downstream users, especially commercial farmers and their irrigation boards and environmental interest groups, have for many years been highly critical of what they see as forestry plantations' pre-emptive water use on the upper catchments, and particularly the planting of eucalyptus, a heavy water consuming species.

The 1972 Forestry Act, through the introduction of a permit system, regulated forestry for the first time, effectively halting its expansion. Since the change of government in 1994, there has been tighter monitoring of the system and, under the 1998 National Water Act, stream flow reduction caused by forestry is designated a water use, and is subject to a Water Resource Management Charge.

The forestry companies have sought to rehabilitate forestry's image as a 'good citizen' (Woodhouse and Hassan, 1999, p. 44) through a number of initiatives: increasing the number of environmental managers; establishing a Forest Environment Liaison Committee to deal with public complaints; supporting the government's 'Working for Water' programme to clear exotic vegetation from water courses; establishing a Stream Flow Reduction Committee to liaise with the DWAF on permits and criteria for protecting watercourses and wetlands. These efforts, which the Department of the Environment (Mpumalanga) acknowledges demonstrate environmental responsibility, have not placated downstream users and environmental NGOs, who remain critical of the role of forestry, particularly in times of drought, and continue to exert pressure for the removal of all exotic trees. Despite these problems, commercial plantations are a stakeholder group with considerable influence as a result of their economic significance and employment generating potential through a large number of wood-using industries in South Africa.

Environmental Interests

The sector is well represented by local government departments, the KNP, environmental NGOs, and local conservancies established by farmers seeking diversification into wildlife-based enterprises. The Mpumalanga Parks Board is in charge of assessing and protecting the biodiversity of the whole province, but it does not have any regulatory function. The Department of Environmental Affairs and Tourism has some regulatory functions. It produces the State of the Environment report and is the lead provincial agency for Environmental Impact Assessments. The Kruger National Park (KNP) is probably the most important and influential environmental interest in the Inkomati, and has been instrumental in developing ideas on integrated catchment management. KNP initiated the Sabie River Working Group in 1992, and the Save the Sand integrated management project in the Sand sub-catchment run by the Association for Water and Rural Development (AWARD). However, the KNP has in the past been viewed as obstructive to the development of water infrastructure, particularly in the homeland areas on its boundaries (Woodhouse, 1995). Recently it has shown itself more willing to negotiate, for example on the building of new weirs. A new Crocodile Catchment Forum was set up with the DWAF in February 2004, which placed the KNP in an important and potentially influential position in this catchment. Overall, the environmental sector, through the government agencies and NGOs, has considerable technical expertise and therefore potential to counterbalance the commercial farming sector in the CMA in terms of water resource management issues. The environmental sector is also likely to play an important role in the determination of the ecological reserve.

IMPLEMENTING INSTITUTIONAL REFORM

Introduction

The following section charts the process of institutional changes envisaged under the 1998 Act (Section 1), as they took place in the Inkomati WMA. Two new institutions were to be created: at the WMA level the CMA, in effect replacing the DWAF regional office, and at the local level a series of WUAs, replacing the IBs.

The CMA Process

The Inkomati CMA was formally launched on 30 March 2004, but engagement of stakeholders in the CMA proposal process began before the 1998 Water Act was promulgated (see Figure 11.2). This process culminated in a 'reference group' (representatives from three catchment forums) and submission of a finalised CMA proposal to the DWAF in September 2000 (MBB, ACER and AWARD, 2000), since when the reference group has not met and there has been little activity. There followed a delay, attributed in part to the lack of specific criteria to evaluate CMA proposals under the 1998 Act, and the Inkomati proposal was shelved for 18 months. The lack of progress in actually establishing the CMA is of concern to many of the

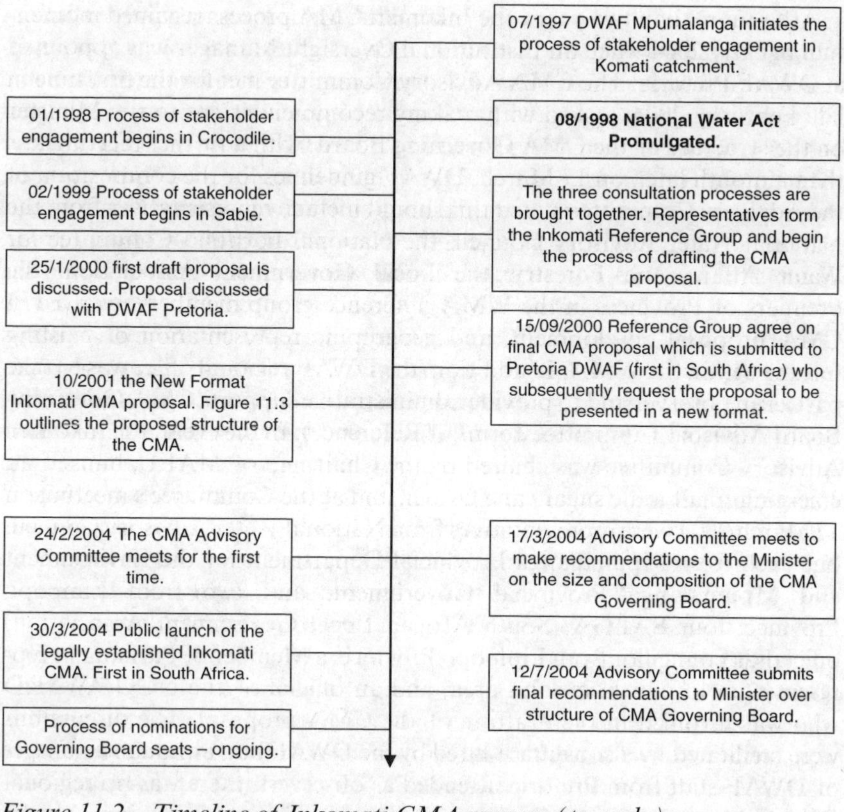

Figure 11.2 Timeline of Inkomati CMA process (to scale)

stakeholders, and the DWAF's Institutional Oversight Directorate in Pretoria has commented that initially the DWAF was 'too optimistic' in believing that the Act could be implemented quickly.

DWAF Mpumalanga's Chief Engineer (Water Resources Directorate) believes that the DWAF 'should not have tackled the Inkomati first' because it is the 'most controversial' and complicated WMA in South Africa. This challenge was compounded by the severe shortage of DWAF personnel at regional level, let alone any with experience of institutional change. In the event, the Water Quality Directorate Deputy Director championed the CMA proposal process, making extensive use of external consultants to facilitate the institutional process (Woodhouse and Hassan, 1999, p. 34). However, when this official relocated to DWAF Pretoria, the role was not taken on by the remaining staff, who felt uncomfortable about moving outside their engineering background to deal with institutional matters. As a result, a lot of CMA institutional memory was lost and a vacuum created in the regional office that has yet to be filled.

After more than two years, the Inkomati CMA process regained momentum in early 2004 when an Institutional Oversight Manager was appointed at DWAF Pretoria. The CMA Advisory Committee met for the first time in late February 2004, tasked with making recommendations to the Minister on the structure of the CMA Governing Board, with a further meeting less than a month later, on 17 March. DWAF guidelines for the composition of the Advisory Committee stated this should include representatives from the National Water Advisory Council, the National Portfolio Committee for Water Affairs and Forestry, the Local Government Association, the Premiers of Provinces in the WMA, reference group members involved in CMA proposal development, and geographic representation of existing forums within the WMA. In addition, the DWAF regional office was to take part as an observer and to provide administrative support (CMA Governing Board Advisory Committee Terms of Reference). In the event, the Inkomati Advisory Committee was chaired by the Chairman of MAFU, himself an emerging small-scale sugar cane farmer, and at the Committee's meeting on 17 March 2004 were representatives from National Water Advisory Council, one each from Mpumalanga Provincial Department for the Environment and Mpumalanga Provincial Government, and two from Limpopo Province; four SALGA (South African Local Government Association) officials, a councillor from Limpopo Province, a Member of Parliament representing a former homeland area, and an official of the NGO AWARD who was involved in the drafting of the CMA proposal. The discussions were facilitated by a consultant hired by the DWAF but, although a number of DWAF staff from Pretoria attended as observers, there was no regional DWAF Mpumalaga representative on the first day of discussion. On the meeting's second day, all observers, bar key DWAF officials from the Institutional Oversight Directorate, were excluded.

Despite a series of further meetings, the CMA Advisory Committee had not agreed the composition of the CMA Governing Board by the time the CMA was formally launched on 30 March 2004. In early June 2004, Inkomati stakeholders were given an opportunity to comment on the proposed structure (Table 11.2) of the Governing Board, which differed significantly from that submitted in 2000 in the CMA proposal (Figure 11.3). In particular, representation through geographical sub-committees had been replaced by representation according to 'sectors'. Four seats are specifically for black stakeholder groups: 'emerging' farmers, 'potential' farmers, productive use by the poor and traditional leaders. Environmental interests also have three seats: Civil Society ('environmental interest in the

Table 11.2 The structure of the Inkomati CMA Governing Board as recommended by the Advisory Committee, July 2004

	Sectors represented on the Governing Board	Number of seats
Major existing water users	Commercial Agriculture	1
	Streamflow Reduction Forestry	1
Industry	Industry, Mining and Power Generation	1
Previously disadvantaged (black) groups	Existing Agriculture (HDI) Emerging Farmers	1
	Potential Agriculture (HDI)	1
	Potential Productive Use of Water by the Poor	1
	Traditional Leaders	1
Environmental groups	Tourism and Recreation	1
	Conservation	1
	Civil Society	1
Local government	Local Government Integrated Planning	1
	Local Government Water Services Authority	1
Provincial government	Mpumalanga Provincial Government	1
	Limpopo Provincial Government	1
Total seats		**14**

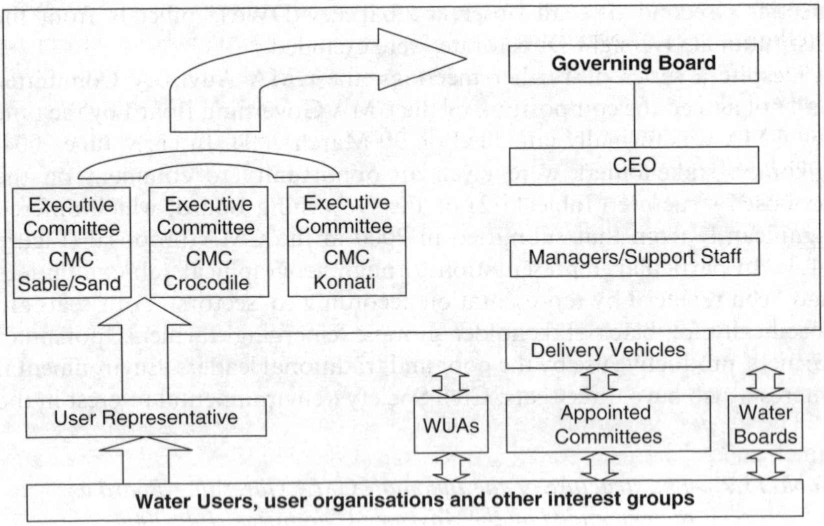

Figure 11.3 *Proposed CMA structure (surrounded by box), as outlined in the 2000 proposal*

protection of water resources, for ecological sustainability and sustainable utilisation of water and associated resources by local communities', Recommendations to the Minister by the Advisory Committee, July 2004, p. 6), Tourism and Recreation (including fishing and aquaculture) and Conservation (KNP, private and community conservancies) and this indicates that environmental interests have a high priority. Provincial governments and municipalities have two seats each. However, Commercial Agriculture, the single largest water use in the catchment, has been allocated just one seat on the Governing Board. Not surprisingly, some stakeholders, notably commercial forestry and commercial farmers, were unhappy at their level of representation, and in the light of the forestry's comments, the Advisory Committee modified their recommendations and gave forestry a seat on the Governing Board. The Advisory Committee reported to the Minister in mid-July 2004, and its proposal was subsequently approved.

After the process of nominating Governing Board members was launched in late 2004, the DWAF reported receiving nominations from most of the sectors, but not from the Historically Disadvantaged (HDI) sector ('emerging' farmers, 'potential' farmers, and representatives for 'productive use by the poor'). In some senses this is not surprising, particularly for the latter two groups, who by definition are not organised into clearly identifiable groups.

Although local interest groups were given an opportunity to comment on the Advisory Committee proposal before they were sent to the Minister, local stakeholders had less say over the direction and representational makeup of the Governing Board than would have been the case if the Advisory Committee had followed the 2000 proposal. It is also likely that had the original proposal been followed, well-organised groups such as commercial farmers could have had a strong representation on the Catchment Management Committees Executive Committee (Figure 11.3) and would thereby have had their interests reflected on the CMA Governing Board more strongly than in the Advisory Committee's proposal. This raises a question of whether local processes are conducive to redistributive reform, or whether 'outside' (for example, national level) intervention is needed to pursue equity goals.

The DWAF has announced plans to establish a further three CMAs in quick succession over the next two years. The experience in the Inkomati WMA indicates that a lot of the momentum of the consultation process depended on individuals, not just institutional structures. The loss of impetus during 2002 and 2003 meant the continuous dialogue with stakeholders on the CMA process ceased, and the forums and reference group fell apart. In the interim, many stakeholder contact details changed and several representatives, particularly in industry, left the area. This has created difficulties when trying to re-engage the stakeholders now that representation from poorer social groups is needed. The DWAF's experience from other WMAs is that a forum that is formed around the CMA proposal tends to fall away once the objective is achieved, whereas a forum that is formed to address a more locally important issue, and which subsequently works on the CMA proposal, is more likely to continue. The dissipation of public awareness – already weak – of the CMA in the Inkomati WMA (Q&A, 2004) presents serious problems for involving poorer and disadvantaged stakeholders in further steps, of which the most immediately important is public consultation on the Catchment Management Strategy.

Transformation of Irrigation Boards into Water Users' Associations

The 1998 Act envisaged that WUAs would come about as the result of the transformation of existing organisations, in this case Irrigation Boards (IBs) into more inclusive organisations. In addition the Act requires the formation of WUA in areas where there were not previously water management organisations. All 27 IBs in the Inkomati WMA submitted proposals to transform into WUAs during 1999/2000, and all were rejected by the DWAF, on the grounds that they were insufficiently representative of different water users. As of March 2005, just one WUA had been formally

Table 11.3 Selection of Inkomati Irrigation Boards, their Government Water Control Status and transformation scenario

Inkomati sub-catchments	Irrigation Board	Government Water Control Area (1956 Water Act)	IB scenario
Sabie	Sabie Valley Irrigation Board (SVIB)	No	1
	White Waters / Burgers Hall Irrigation Board (BHIB)	No	2
Crocodile	Elands Valley Irrigation Board (EVIB)	No	1
	White River Valley Conservation Board (WRVCB)	No	1
	Crocodile Main Irrigation Board (CMIB)	Yes	1
Komati	Komati Irrigation Board (KIB)	Yes	2
	Lomati Irrigation Board (LIB)	Yes	2

established – the Upper Komati WUA, covering the Komati West of Swaziland (see Figure 11.1). Elsewhere in the WMA the difficulties over the creation of WUAs by transformation of existing IBs has raised questions about how WUAs are conceptualised within the new legislation. While it is not disputed that IBs have previously been the preserve of white commercial farmers, the process of transforming them into more inclusive WUAs needs to recognise the important differences in the powers hitherto exercised by different IBs and the ways these differences inform the type of transition to be achieved.

This study interviewed members of seven IBs (Table 11.3) to obtain their views of the proposed transformation to WUAs. An important difference between IBs is whether, under earlier (1956) legislation they were within a Government Water Control Area (GWCA). Within such areas, the state asserted control over all water abstractions, generally delegating management to the local IB. Therefore, the Crocodile (CMIB), Komati (KIB) and Lomati (LIB) Irrigation Boards had delegated powers to control all water abstraction from the rivers under their jurisdiction. In the case of rivers not within a GWCA, such as the WhiteWaters or the Sabie, membership of an

IB was not compulsory and the powers of an IB were limited to regulating water use by its members (often linked to managing specific infrastructure such as a dam or a canal) and did not extend to non-members drawing water from the same river (Woodhouse, 1995). This (GWCA) distinction has a perceptible influence on the expectations that different IBs have of their role following transformation to WUAs.

A first scenario, common in non-GWCA areas where irrigation by black farmers is not yet significant (for example, SVIB, the EVIB, the WRCB and the CMIB), is a fear among IB officials that they will have to involve groups with whom they have little in common. These IBs appear to be reconciled to 'arms-length' discussions with representatives of municipalities about water supply to towns, but reluctant to engage with any management of water outside the dams/canals/networks they operate. The Chairman of the SVIB typifies this view, being 'Quite unhappy about the whole set-up' because they now have to 'accommodate people who have no interest in the canal' (Chairman of the SVIB).

In a second scenario, those IBs accustomed to working under a GWCA regime have been concerned about a more 'inclusive' WUA resulting in a dilution of their control of water use. They have been quick to bring black farmer representation into the IB (for example, the KIB and LIB in the NIEP areas): half the LIB is made up of emerging sugar farmers who receive a transport allowance to attend meetings and are exempt from capital repayments for equipment. The vice-chairman of the KIB is a black farmer and the meetings are held in English and SiSwati.

However, these IBs had their WUA proposals turned down by the DWAF for failing to achieve representation of municipalities. A similar judgement confronted the (non-GWCA) BHIB, where successful land claims have been made and black farmers are running commercial enterprises and receiving their water as members of the BHIB. In this scenario it is possible to see existing IBs assimilating black farming interests essentially within an unchanged management regime, and correspondingly reluctant to engage with municipalities who are more likely to challenge existing allocation principles and processes. Thus the BHIB was unhappy that they were expected to include 'outsiders that are nothing to do with the Irrigation Board', while the KIB maintains it was difficult to get non-agricultural sectors to attend transformation meetings.

A third scenario is exemplified by the Upper Komati, where the highveld (fodder and cattle) farmers extracted water independently and never paid levies. It is interesting to note that this is the first WUA to be established in the Inkomati, doubtless because it confers legitimacy on water use that was previously not formally recognised, and indicates that reforming existing institutions such as IBs is more complicated than forming a new institution.

An underlying theme in the difficulties of transforming IBs is the ambiguity of whether membership of a WUA is compulsory for all water users. The IBs included in this study point out that, under the terms of the 1998 Act, WUAs are classed as an association of members, interpreted as meaning that water users are free to be associated to the WUA or not. The wording of the Act is vague on this point and IBs argue they can see no incentive for water users to join voluntarily: 'Why should you join because if you join you have to pay money?' The collection of the WRMC is another concern of the IBs; they argue that there have no 'hold' or'teeth to force payment' from WUA members: this has financial implications for the CMA. For IBs in GWCAs, accustomed to control over all water use in their area of jurisdiction, and normally under conditions of water shortage, the absence of a measure of control over water users through compulsory membership undermines their ability to regulate water use.

Acknowledging these concerns, local DWAF officials concede that IBs are not resisting transforming into WUAs, but are 'uncomfortable over what is expected of them', and that it is 'too easy [for DWAF Pretoria] to say they are holding onto the past' (DWAF Mpumalanga official). Under considerable pressure from IBs and Agri SA (commercial farmers' union) to reconsider the transformation issue, the DWAF established a National Steering Committee to review the WUA process. The Committee considered the possibility of keeping IBs in their current form, but as members, along with other users such as municipalities, of an umbrella WUA organisation. Thus IBs, rather than transforming and leading the process, would have less institutional responsibility than currently, but would continue to manage water extraction and flows in defined stretches of rivers and to prosecute infringements. DWAF Mpumalanga believes this is the only model that will work, for otherwise the IBs will 'run away', leading to a loss of continuity and expertise. Building on this model, two rounds of negotiations between the DWAF and the Irrigation Boards reached agreement in principle on consolidation of the 27 existing IBs into '6 to 8 multi-sectoral WUAs based on geographical positions, similar climate and crops and to get the benefit of scale for more effective IWRM'.[1] There are still discussions over the boundaries of the WUAs, however, and this is a source of tension, compounded by what the IBs see as a failure of the DWAF to reimburse them for legal fees and administration costs for new WUA constitutions already drawn up. It remains to be seen, moreover, which other sectors would take on the responsibility for leading the WUA process if the IBs do not, and how these proposals will overcome the problem posed by voluntary membership of WUA, and associated difficulties in enforcing the payment of the Water Resource Management Charge, both still major areas of concern to the IBs.

The new model of WUA establishment in effect means that IBs are not being forced to make radical changes by becoming more inclusive representative bodies. In effect they will continue to represent the interests of the commercial farming sector they currently serve.

ISSUES IN REDISTRIBUTIVE REGULATORY REFORM

Introduction

This study suggests a number of issues relating to the establishment of the CMA that affect its operations and ultimately the achievement of the goals of the legislative reform. We have reviewed the process by which the Inkomati CMA has been established, and are now able to identify a number of key challenges.

Lack of Transparent and Reliable Figures on Water Use

It is important to note that there is a high level of uncertainty over the exact amount of water used by the irrigation sector (Woodhouse and Hassan, 1999, p. 11). Although the IBs supply information about how much water their members are using, the DWAF suggests the numbers are 'conflicting' and there are 'inconsistencies'. The DWAF's 2004 Internal Strategic Perspective document stresses that a lack of confidence over the exact quantity of water used in the WMA, and by irrigation in particular, is still an issue requiring immediate attention. The DWAF is currently engaged in an exercise using satellite telemetry and field measurements to verify the water use earlier registered by water users. Within a year this should provide a set of more transparent and reliable figures. Only then will it be possible to consider increasing the allocation of water rights to black farmers and communities. However, a more equitable distribution of access to water is likely to result in reallocation of water licences away from commercial farmers because water demand already exceeds supply (see earlier), with few opportunities to increase supply from new dams. International obligations to allow water to neighbouring Mozambique and shortage of water in neighbouring South African WMAs further restrict the possibilities of increasing the available water for agriculture.

Compulsory Licensing was planned to be piloted in 2005 in the Lower Crocodile sub-catchment where water shortages are acute. It is possible that the whole of the Inkomati WMA could become subject to Compulsory Licensing because it is such a stressed catchment. As envisaged by the 1998

Act, a future role of the CMA could be the provision of licences to water users, giving the CMA considerable redistributive powers. However, the pilot Compulsory Licensing in the Nkomazi will be undertaken by DWAF Pretoria, who will contract consultants. This demonstrates the recurring tension between centralised and decentralised decision-making in relation to redistributive goals. On the one hand the national political agenda of redistribution is pursued through central intervention: the role of allocating and reallocating water will be undertaken centrally, not by the locally based CMA. On the other hand, lack of central government capacity to implement those interventions means ceding control to agencies that may be linked professionally, politically, and socially to the local water users and entrenched local mechanisms of control of water use.

Black Representation and Participation in the CMA and WUAs

Despite the DWAF's attempt to act as 'honest broker' and encourage black representatives to overcome historical disadvantages to attend CMA consultation meetings, awareness of the CMA has not been disseminated among the black constituent population. Even emerging farmers interviewed as part of this study had virtually no knowledge of the CMA and the consultation process, although there are differences in awareness according to location: sugar farmers involved with Irrigation Boards have learnt something of the CMA, while black farmers and community members in areas without IBs knew nothing about the CMA. The long interval since the initial CMA consultation process may be a contributing factor but, notwithstanding the four seats allocated to black interests on the CMA governing board, the evident low level of awareness among the black population raises questions over the legitimacy of the CMA as an organisation that represents the interests of all water users in the area. The failure to nominate representatives to these seats on the governing board also echoes claims of IBs, as well as other forums such as the Crocodile Catchment Committee, that they have experienced difficulties in getting black representatives to attend the meetings. Possible deterrents include the use of English (though more familiar/acceptable to them than Afrikaans) rather than African languages, and meetings at hotel venues that could prove intimidating and difficult to reach for poor people. There is also a perception that some groups who currently do not pay IB levies or the WRMC are nervous that attending meetings could result in them being charged for their water.

A further difficulty is that effective participation is not achieved simply by black stakeholders being physically present in meetings, but through their active involvement in discussions and decisions. This is not to understate the importance – not least in the aftermath of apartheid – of legitimating stakeholders' claims by simply making them 'visible' through invitations to meetings. However, the widely supported participation principle (see the Introduction) assumes that stakeholders are willing and able to participate in the management of the resource, whereas South African society is marked by a legacy of gross discrimination and inequality, not least in terms of access to water. The study of the Inkomati demonstrates quite clearly the importance of this legacy in terms of asymmetries of knowledge and expertise, as between black farmers on one hand and commercial farmers or environmental organisations on the other, in relation to quantities of water supply and demand. The KIB Chairman is adamant that emerging farmers are not merely spectators at the meetings, and the former Chairman of the LIB suggests emerging farmers have 'as much to say as anyone else' though he admits that they are at a disadvantage: 'technically it is very difficult for them to understand'. Therefore, despite the Chairman of the CMA Advisory Committee being a black MAFU official, the question of black representation and participation remains a concern.

The CMA process in the Inkomati WMA suggests that where asymmetries are least, as between commercial and environmental stakeholders, there appears more effective pressure for existing water use to change. Where asymmetries are stronger, as between black farmers and communities and commercial farmers, there appears least prospect of change in established, inequitable, water use. Thus for participatory approaches to generate change an 'honest broker' must achieve a reduction in these asymmetries of knowledge about the water resource among stakeholders. In this respect the water use verification exercise being undertaken by the DWAF with the aid of digital imaging and positioning technologies is a vital step in changing the terms of negotiation.

The CMA Financial Model

Bound up with many decentralisation models is the idea that the funding for devolved management institutions needs to be locally generated. As with the ICWE guidelines, the 'user pays' principle at the heart of the CMA financial model has significant implications, especially with regard to the representation of interests.

The source of money to maintain the CMA operations, after an initial one-off allocation from central government, will be the Water Resource Management Charge (WRMC) that all water users should pay under the 1998 Act. The Inkomati CMA experience suggests that the largest users of water thereby become the principal funders of the CMA. Thus, despite having only one of the 14 seats on the CMA governing board, commercial farmers have considerable financial leverage over the CMA process, and indeed over the WUAs. This possibility is increased by the difficulties being experienced in collecting municipal water charges. This is partly a question of affordability, since about 46 per cent of households in Mbombela have monthly incomes below the poverty line of R800 (Brown, 2005). However, non-payment is also a legacy of political protests during the apartheid era, and in this study avoidance of water charges was often cited as the reason stakeholders do not participate in WUAs. If some stakeholders opt out, then water management institutions will be undermined, and clearer statements are needed than in the 1998 Act that both water charges and membership of the WUA are mandatory. However, in parallel with the water services sector, if an orthodox 'user pays' model is adopted in areas with extreme poverty differentials it is likely that a proportion of users (assuming they have been allocated water rights) will be unable to afford water. So how are indigent 'emerging' farmers and potential water users to pay the WRMC? DWAF officials point to a centrally funded subsidy system, but to date neither IBs nor black water users have been sufficiently informed of this to overcome their misgivings over WUA and CMA discussions.

The relationship between funding contribution and representation is interesting. The IBs consulted felt that from the beginning of the CMA consultation process, commercial farming interests have been excluded: despite lengthy consultation, it was not a truly participatory process and DWAF 'bulldozed through' the proposal without 'people on board'. Commercial farmers, seemingly in a powerful negotiating position, being the largest water users with the best knowledge of the resource situation, feel that they are inadequately represented and thus do not see the CMA process as having legitimacy. The Advisory Committee's decision to award the commercial farming sector just one of the 14 seats has added to this feeling.

As a protest against what they see as 'taxation without representation', most of the IBs contacted were withholding payment of the charge. If the CMA cannot be made financially viable, then its operations and functions will be severely limited. The stance of the IBs presents a dilemma for the DWAF, who may be forced to reach a compromise, or the CMA may have to look for alternative funding arrangements. It is also clearly undesirable to alienate such a large, powerful and technically experienced user from the CMA process.

DYNAMICS FOR CHANGE: LESSONS FOR REGULATORY REFORM

This section is concerned with identifying the forces driving and resisting change in the current context of the Inkomati WMA. It also identifies some lessons in relation to the internationally recognised principles for water management identified at the beginning of the chapter.

An initial lesson is that there are tensions between environmental objectives and the objective of more equitable access to water, and between economic pricing of water and equity of access. A further lesson is that assumptions about the advantages of decentralised decision-making structures need to be scrutinised critically for the specific objectives they are expected to achieve. Although decentralisation and participation of different stakeholders may plausibly be proposed as a means to achieve integrated water management in the Inkomati WMA, this seems much less likely for redistribution of access to water. This is because, although the need for improved access to water is acutely felt by many black people within the Inkomati WMA, the principal underlying driver of redistribution of water rights is the national political consensus seeking redress of historical disadvantage in access and use of natural resources, and the DWAF, as the central government department responsible, is therefore a key agency of change.

It is important to recognise that this is a role for which the structure and personnel inherited by the DWAF from the apartheid era were not always well suited, necessitating the creation of new structures and competencies as indicated by the seven years delay between promulgation of the Act and the – still incomplete – launch of the first CMA. Through its Institutional Oversight Directorate (IOD), DWAF Pretoria sees its role as 'levelling the playing field' by reducing asymmetries of power between stakeholders and acting as an 'honest broker' in the CMA process. This is consistent with Hildyard et al.'s conclusions, from India, that until the relative bargaining powers of stakeholders are factored into participatory approaches, they 'are in danger of merely providing opportunities for the more powerful' (2001, p. 9), and that a failure to engage with the 'distribution and operations of power within local communities and the wider society in which they live is likely to offer little to marginalized groups' (Hildyard et al., 2001, p. 57). Thus Pretoria officials claim they were protecting the rights of the disadvantaged when they rejected local CMA proposals because they were not representative enough.

It is important to recognise differences in the contexts of central and local state agencies, and the tensions to which these may give rise. It is not surprising that officials of the DWAF's regional office had close links to the Irrigation Boards in the apartheid era, symbolised by the transfer of key infrastructure to IB ownership immediately before the end of apartheid in 1994 (Woodhouse, 1995). However, it is also clear that many of today's DWAF regional staff feel uncertain about their prospects when the CMA takes over water management, and unprepared to be thrust into the front line of a struggle with commercial farming interests whose influence extends beyond the local level. As a consequence, local DWAF input to driving a redistributive agenda in the CMA has depended on the agency of particular committed individuals, and has stalled when they transferred elsewhere.

The development of the CMA in Inkomati can be seen as a series of engagements in which a national agency, the DWAF, has tested the capacity for change among the principal existing local water users (commercial farmers/IBs). We return to these below, but first we review the local constituencies for redistribution.

Municipalities are not only the locally elected representatives of the people, but also, as Water Service Authorities, are responsible for primary water – access to which remains the most urgent concern for many of the poorest people. With a couple of exceptions, municipalities so far have had little involvement with the CMA process, and municipal officials are worried that politicians have not yet recognised that the CMA is where the discussions to increase primary allocations need to take place, and that it is the municipalities' role (not the DWAF's) to negotiate these. That such discussions are long overdue is underlined by the fact that the allocation for Nelspruit has not increased in 20 years despite a tenfold increase in the population for whose water supply the municipality is responsible (see earlier.). The municipalities' future role in shaping water allocations within the WMA is indicated by the two seats allocated on the CMA governing board.

Black farmers in the Inkomati WMA do not yet have the organisation to mount effective pressure for re-allocation, and where they are most organised, as in the NIEP areas, they are also most likely to be closely bound to commercial farming agendas via the IBs and the sugar industry. Manzangu (2002), commenting on stakeholder representation in catchment management in Zimbabwe, argues that weak stakeholder groups need to act strategically, either by forming alliances or by withdrawing from the participation process, thereby delegitimising it. We question whether withdrawal from the participation process is an effective strategy, insofar as it is as much an option for commercial interests as it is for disadvantaged groups, and argue that emphasis should be on identifying alliances and incentive structures that support redistribution of water to disadvantaged groups that minimise reductions in water use efficiency. Potential allies are government agencies closely involved with black farming, such as the Department of Land Affairs (DLA) and the Mpumalanga Department of Agriculture (DoA). Neither department has been allocated a seat on the CMA, nor yet shown itself to be an effective advocate for black farmers, however. DLA only belatedly acknowledged the 'problem of water is a concern for land reform' and was absent from the early CMA consultation process (Woodhouse and Hassan, 1999, p. 36). The DoA, although lobbying for improved water rights for black farmers in the Nkomazi area, and leading a campaign for construction of a new dam for black farmers (at Gutshwa on the Nsikasi tributary of the Crocodile) has yet to establish its credentials as an effective provider of support to black farming. One role such departments could play is ensuring that black farmers and poor people take up the opportunity of representation on water management decisions offered by the seats allocated to them on the CMA governing board.

Black water users may find other potential alliances, with industrial and environmental interests, more ambiguous. TSB sugar provides an example where industry sees an advantage in increasing black farmers' access to irrigation. However, the industry's willingness to further the development of black irrigated farming, with the prospect of diversifying into higher value crops and possibly competing for water with existing commercial farms, is questionable. The *environmental lobby*, as a longstanding and increasingly successful critic of existing water use by commercial agriculture and forestry, stands as an influential potential ally to initiatives for change. However, despite projects working to reconcile the needs of forestry, black communities and ecology, such as the Save the Sand Project run by AWARD, it cannot be assumed that environmentalists will always find common cause with disadvantaged communities, as indicated by the often conflictual relations over water rights between the KNP and black communities on the park fringes (Woodhouse, 1995). It may be difficult for environmentally focused organisations to acknowledge redistributive (equity) priorities on a par with those of conservation (ecology).

The DWAF's concern over the prominent role of the IBs in the CMA process led to the rejection of a locally designed CMA structure built around three catchment executive committees. The structure proposed by the CMA Advisory Committee provided the principal existing water users with only one of the 14 seats on the CMA governing board. On the transformation of IBs into 'more inclusive' WUAs, however, the DWAF appears to have allowed IBs to retain their existing structure and governance. The IBs are now proposed as members of WUAs, now reconceptualised as fewer, larger, umbrella organisations. If implemented, this compromise may be viewed as recreating the WUAs as the kind of multi-sectoral 'catchment executive committee' structure of the original CMA proposal. In that sense, it may be interpreted as a success for the IBs, but one that was made possible by the vagueness of the 1998 Act over whether membership of WUAs should be compulsory. Defining who has access to a common property resource is one of Ostrom's (1992) eight design principles for the management of common pool resources (resource and user-group should be well defined), which suggests the IBs' concerns were well founded. Moreover, it is not clear which other sector has the resources to take the lead within WUAs. It seems possible that if membership of a WUA were to be made compulsory for all water users, IBs would feel more inclined to take greater responsibility for the broader management of water, rather than focusing on retaining the water they currently have.

The next round of struggle between the DWAF and the IBs will arise over the moves, currently being piloted in the Komati catchment, to verify registered water use and introduce compulsory licensing for future water use. Yet again, however, the DWAF's recourse to consultants to implement the verification and permit process underlines the limited capacity of a central government agency to intervene at the local level.

The struggle over the Inkomati CMA raises a question of whether, failing complete dismantling of local power structures, central government can provide stronger incentives to existing local water managers, such as IBs, to align themselves to a redistributive agenda. Decentralisation is not a selling point, since many IBs see the CMA process as a centralisation of power. The most important incentive is arguably increasing commercial farmers' security. Following verification and licensing, the CMA could legitimise commercial farmers' water, replacing their interim 'existing lawful use' status under the 1998 Act that allows continuity of past water use but is also a source of suspicion about commercial farmers in the eyes of the DWAF and other users. It seems possible, therefore, that a redistribution in water could be traded off against greater legitimacy and security of water use for commercial farmers.

NOTE

1. DWAF Mpumalanga note to authors, 20 October 2004.

REFERENCES

Brown, J. (2005), *Water Service Subsidies and the Poor: a Case Study of Mbombela Municipality, South Africa*, Report to Centre on Regulation and Competition, Manchester: University of Manchester.

Calder, I.R. (1999), *The Blue Revolution. Land Use and Integrated Water Resources Management*, London: Earthscan Publications.

DWAF (1997), *White Paper on a National Water Policy for South Africa*, Pretoria, South Africa: Department of Water Affairs.

DWAF (2002), *Establishing A Water User Association*, Guide 3 in the CMA/WUA Guide Series, Pretoria, South Africa: Department of Water Affairs.

DWAF (2003), *National Water Resources Strategy. Inkomati Water Management Area: Overview of Water Resources Availability and Utilisation*, Pretoria, South Africa: Department of Water Affairs.

DWAF (2004), *Inkomati Water Management Area: Internal Strategic Perspective*, Pretoria, South Africa: Department of Water Affairs.

European Union (2000), 'Water Framework Directive', http://europa.eu.int/comm/environment/water/water-framework/index_en.html

Heathcote, I. (1998), *Integrated Watershed Management – Principles and Practices*, New York: John Wiley.

Hildyard, N., P. Hegde, P. Wolvekamp and S. Reddy (2001), 'Pluralism, participation and power: Joint forest management in India', in B. Cooke and U. Kothari (eds), *Participation the New Tyranny?*, London: Zed Books.

Manzangu, E. (2002), 'More than a headcount: Towards strategic stakeholder representation in catchment management in South Africa and Zimbabwe', *Physics and Chemistry of the Earth*, **27**, 927–33.

MBB, ACER and AWARD (2000), *Proposal for the Establishment of a Catchment Management Agency for the Inkomati Basin (New Formant)*, prepared on behalf of the Inkomati Catchment Management Agency Reference Group and DWAF, Nelspruit, South Africa.

NOWAC (1999), *The Contribution of Irrigation to the Nkomazi/Onderberg Region of Mpumalanga*, Malelane, South Africa: Nkomazi/Onderberg Water Action Committee.

Ostrom, E. (1992), *Governing the Commons: The Evolution of Institutions for Collective Action*, Cambridge: Cambridge University Press.

Q&A Research (2004), Prepared for DWAF: *Phase 1 Findings of a Research Study to Determine the Existing Levels of Awareness and Participation for Developing a Suitable Framework for Efficient and Sustainable Public Participation to Draft a CMS for the Inkomati WMA*, Johannesburg, South Africa.

Woodhouse, P. (1995), 'Water rights and restructuring in South Africa: A case study from Eastern Transvaal', *Water Resources Development*, **11**(4), 527–44.

Woodhouse, P. and R. Hassan (1999), *Implementation of the National Water Act. Catchment Management Agencies: Interests, Access and Efficiency. Inkomati Basin Pilot Study*, Prepared for DWAF and DIFD-Southern Africa, Pretoria, South Africa.

World Bank (1993), 'Water resources management policy paper', www.worldbank.org

World Bank (2003), 'Water resources sector strategy: Strategic directions for World Bank engagement', http://lnweb18.worldbank.org/ESSD/ardext.nsf/18ByDocName/TheWorldBankWaterResourcesSectorStrategyentiredocument255MB/$FILE/WaterStrategy-FullDocument.pdf

12. Pro-poor water services in Metro Manila: in search of greater equity

Jocelyn C. Cuaresma

INTRODUCTION

This chapter examines the water and sewerage service delivery programs for the poor residents within Greater Manila service area. Specifically, it analyzes the pro-poor water programs of the two private water concessionaires operating in this metropolitan area, by looking into the mechanisms adopted to expand access of the poor to water and sewerage services, to raise the number of hours that water is made available, and to keep the price of water affordable. Lessons are drawn from the experience for informed and improved regulation of the water concession.

Water tariffs in Metro Manila have increased nine times (or by more than 500 percent) since the private water concessionaires took over operations of the Metropolitan Waterworks and Sewerage System (MWSS) service area on 1 August 1997. In the first seven years of the concession, water coverage expanded in both zones – to 82 percent in the East and to 78 percent in the West – but with the West Zone Concessionaire missing its target.

Despite the expansion of the service coverage, 2.4 million of the 12.4 million people remain without access to piped drinking water, and only 8 percent have sewerage services. The Concession Agreement (CA) contains no specific service commitments to improve service delivery to the poor and low-income households in the MWSS service area. Except for the requirement to maintain existing public faucets, it is discretionary on the part of the concessionaires to develop their own pro-poor water services delivery programs.

This chapter examines the water services delivery programs of MAYNILAD (West Zone concessionaire) and MWCI (East Zone concessionaire) for the poor residents living within the MWSS service area. Specifically, it looks into the approaches adopted by the two water companies in expanding water coverage and enabling the poor to have access to piped drinking water. A brief introduction and description of the regulatory framework for water are presented. This is followed by a discussion of the pro-poor water distribution programs of the two concessionaires for informal settlers within the MWSS service area and an assessment of the equity aspects of the prevailing water tariff structure and pricing policy. Finally, the issues and lessons learned on the impact of water regulation on service delivery to the poor customers of MWSS are summarized.

PRIVATIZATION AND REGULATION

The privatization of the MWSS in August 1997 was conceived as the solution to the government corporation's poor service delivery performance and huge foreign debt. Prior to privatization, the MWSS has been criticized for its highly deficient operation indicated by a low service coverage (serving only 7.32 million population, or 66.5 percent of the potential service population), a billing rate of only 42.7 percent of its 3000 million liters daily water production, water availability averaging 17 hours daily, and non-revenue water of 56 percent of actual production. The lack of access to water generally afflicts the 1.27 million poor and informal residents of Metro Manila who live below the poverty threshold level of income. About 80 percent of Metro Manila's urban poor have no legal water connection mainly because they have no legal claim over the land they occupy (Yu, 2002).

The regulation of the water sector, whether in the hands of government or the private sector, has been justified on various grounds, that is, it is a natural monopoly; water has no close substitutes; customers and service providers do not exercise equal bargaining power (Mitlin, 2002). Indeed, the water and sewerage services sector, whether in public or private hands, is subject to a monopolistic market and must therefore be met with appropriate government regulation to ensure efficient provision, with protection for the most vulnerable sectors of society (Gleick et al., 2002). Necessarily, price, water quality, and manner of provision, among other things, must be the subject of regulation.

Regulation has been defined as 'the sustained and focused control exercised by a public agency over activities that are valued by a community' (Cariño, 2002; Minogue, 2001, and Baldwin and Cave, 1999, p. 2, both cited in Cariño). Under the framework of governance, government exercise of regulatory powers is understood to mean a deliberate attempt not only to steer, but also to enable and facilitate private sector investment. There are sets of rules justified by the need to protect the public interest and the need for the creation or facilitation of conditions for effective markets (Cariño, 2002). In effect, government has to be able to balance the promotion of the interests of the private sector with that of the general public. The experience in the regulation of privately operated water utilities shows that privatization can work well in some cases, but can lead to mixed or problematic results in others.

THE MWSS TERRITORIAL JURISDICTION

The 1940 square kilometer MWSS service area was divided into the East and West Zones as a result of the 1997 privatization. The Manila Water Company, Inc. (MWCI), and the Maynilad Water Services, Inc. (MAYNILAD) won the 25-year water concessions for the East and West Zones,[1] respectively. The MWCI is a consortium of four companies with 60 percent ownership by Ayala Corporation. MAYNILAD is owned by two companies led by the Benpres Holding Corporation.[2] Refer to Table 12.1 for a brief profile of the East (MWCI) and West (MAYNILAD) Zones.

The Pro-poor Water Programs

Water and sewerage service obligations

The Concession Agreement (CA) is basically neutral in its treatment of service obligations for the poor customers of MWSS (Cuaresma, 2003). The provisions on water and sewerage service obligations contained in Article 5 of the CA contain no direct mandate that obligates the concessionaires to provide water services specifically to the poor. In the absence of any compelling provision in the CA to undertake pro-poor service delivery, it took MAYNILAD and MWCI more than a year to draw up their respective pro-poor programs. MAYNILAD introduced the Bayan Tubig program in 1999, while MWCI started its Tubig Para Sa Barangay program in 1998.

MWCI's Tubig Para Sa Barangay (TPSB)

The MWCI introduced the Tubig Para Sa Barangay (TPSB) program (or Water for Depressed Communities) in response to the clamor for water service connections in poor areas. The TPSB was described by Rivera (2001)

Table 12.1 Profile of the East and West Zones

	MWCI (East Zone)	MAYNILAD (West Zone)
Population	4.96 million (40% of the total service population)	7.4 million (60% of the total service population)
Service area	1400 sq km	540 sq km
Assumed debt	US$80 million	US$800 million
Bid rate*	2.32 pesos per cubic meter	4.96 pesos per cubic meter

Note: * Peso–dollar exchange rate in 1997 was 26 Philippine pesos to one US dollar.

Source: Cuaresma (2003, p. 3).

as an innovative scheme, introduced to provide legal water connections to poor communities who live in crowded, densely populated areas where it is often difficult to install conventional water pipes. MWCI waived the land title requirement to enable informal settlers to obtain an official connection.

The TPSB offered a menu of three different schemes (Dumol, 2001):

1. *Individual metered connection*, or Level III connection, refers to individual piped connections. This service is traditionally provided to businesses and households not classified as informal settlers;
2. *Group taps* – one metered connection serving two to five households (HHs); and
3. *Community taps* – an entire community is served with one metered connection.

Under the group taps scheme, a group of three to five households is connected to the main pipe through a mother meter to which they all connect and put up their own sub-meters. Some groups composed of relatives may opt not to install sub-meters to avoid incurring extra costs. Each group of HHs is responsible for paying the connection charge and monthly bills. For every official (mother meter) connection, a group pays an installation charge of 5850 pesos (as of October 2003) to cover the cost of installation (a fixed amount to cover the cost of pipes within 25 linear meters and an additional amount beyond the 25 linear meters), cost of laying a water mainline extension, value added tax, meter deposit guarantee, and other incidental charges. The total installation charge is payable in 3 to 6 months to be shared by all HHs connected to a mother meter.

The scheme requires the households to form a group and choose a leader/treasurer who is tasked to collect and pay the water bill for the group. The leader pro-rates the cost to each household based on the individual sub-meter readings, where sub-meters are installed. The group taps scheme leads to the generation of only one bill, computed on the basis of the total consumption of three or five households, as the case may be.

MAYNILAD's Bayan Tubig (BT) Program

MAYNILAD's water policy for depressed areas in its service area offers three levels of services:

1. *Public faucet level I* – the request to put up a public faucet is endorsed by the local government unit
2. *Public faucet level II* – the NGO or community association request a public faucet
3. *Level III* – individual metering scheme.[3]

The policy was formalized through the Bayan Tubig (BT) program launched in February 1999 to provide low-income communities in the West Zone with potable and cheap water primarily through individual water connections. The BT was MAYNILAD's strategy to expand service coverage and reduce the incidence of non-revenue water. MAYNILAD charges an installation cost of 4800 pesos within a minimum distance of 25 linear meters from a water main, value added tax, and a guarantee deposit payable within 6 to 12 months. A set of criteria are followed in establishing a BT scheme in a community (Rosenthal, 2001):

- The area is reasonably close to the primary network;
- Beneficiaries are not located in an area liable to flooding;
- The scheme is technically feasible; and
- The site is not on private land where the question of tenure poses problems.

To ensure the participation of informal settlers, the land title requirement was waived and people were allowed to pay the installation charge in installments of up to 12 months.

TPSB and BT compared

Table 12.2 compares the features of the TPSB of MWCI and BT of MAYNILAD. The pro-poor programs differ from the regular method of obtaining a service connection on the following points: (1) households served by both programs have to pay a connection charge; (2) the cost per connection in the East Zone is higher and is payable within a shorter time period. In the case of the West Zone, the connection charge is nominally less and payment can be extended up to one year; (3) both the BT and the TPSB suffer from a lack of equity because of the wider application of the group taps scheme; and (4) both programs waived the land title requirement, enabling informal settlers to apply for a formal connection even if they do not own the land where they have built their house. However, the waiver of the land title requirement applies only to informal settlers occupying public lands.

ASSESSMENT OF THE WATER SERVICES DELIVERY MECHANISMS

Water services delivery mechanisms have taken many variants since the privatization of the MWSS in 1997, allowing the private sector and community organizations to participate in water distribution. These mechanisms include: (1) direct, individual water connections, (2) public faucets,

Table 12.2 Features of the TPSB of MWCI and BT of MAYNILAD

	Tubig Para Sa Barangay of MWCI	Bayan Tubig of MAYNILAD
Policy	• To improve service connections in depressed communities by providing properly connected water services, where each service connection with a water meter is shared by a cluster of up to a maximum of 5 households • Land title requirement is waived	• To provide low-income communities with potable and cheap water through individual water connection • Land title requirement is waived
Metering scheme	1 meter serves several dwellings for a maximum of 5 families	1 meter per 1 house connection
Service connection/ installation charge (per connection)	• Installation cost (minimum for within 25 linear meters (lm) and at cost beyond 25 lm) • Meter deposit • Laying of water mainline extension • Value added tax • Guarantee deposit • Other incidental charges Total charges of 5850 pesos (as of October 2003) payable in 6 months	• Installation cost (minimum for within 25 lm and at cost beyond 25 lm) • Value added tax • Guarantee deposit • Total charges in the amount of 4730 pesos (as of October 2003) payable in 6 to 12 months
Customer classification	Residential or the highest rate classification in case of mixed usage.	Residential or semi-business in case of mixed usage.
Estimated number of persons per connection	Approximately 17.8 persons per connection (based on 6 persons per household connection being used by MWCI)	Approximately 9.2 persons per connection

Source: MWSS-RO.

(3) vendors who have individual MWSS connection, (4) group taps with shared mother meters, and (5) bulk buying of water by private subcontractors, and community associations (David, 2000, p. 27; Inocencio, 2001a; Mitlin, 2002, p. 15).

Individual Household Water Connections (Level III)

Level III is the most desirable, cheapest and most convenient way of providing piped water to consumers. Both concessionaires pursued the installation of individual water connections, with MAYNILAD being more explicit in its policy of using the Level III scheme under the BT program. As of 5 July 2003, MAYNILAD had installed at least 71 323 individual household connections under the BT program. In the case of MWCI, it completed 309 TPSB projects from 1998 to June 2003, benefiting a total of 81 538 households.

Group Taps

The MWCI used the group taps scheme in the TPSB program more widely than Level III. The group taps scheme enabled the MWCI to significantly expand service coverage through local water resellers who operate piped water networks within the service area. The scheme entailed the involvement of household associations, community groups, and local subcontractors specializing in water distribution who buy large quantities of network water and sell to households in low-income neighborhoods via sub-networks. Operators of water tanks and handcarts were allowed to continue servicing off-network markets (Dumol, 2001).

The group taps scheme as a mechanism was found to be advantageous to the MWCI. It enabled the company to rapidly expand water service coverage, meet obligation targets, and respond to consumer demand. Thus from 1998 to June 2003, the MWCI was able to cover a total of 81 538 households, and to pass on directly to households, and indirectly to water subcontractors, the cost of connection and network laying, and maintenance of pipes beyond the water main. Overall, the group taps approach fast-tracked the achievement of the MWCI's coverage target. On the part of informal settlers, the group taps scheme is a better arrangement than buying water from public faucets wherein they have to physically carry water from the faucet to their houses, or buying vended water, which is much more expensive.

Public Faucets

The old MWSS operated 130 public faucets in squatter areas prior to privatization. The maintenance of public faucets, however, was problematic with the failure of communities to pay water bills on time. This reason provided a strong impetus for a Level III connection and led either to the conversion of public faucets into individual connections or to their decommissioning (Rosenthal, 2003).

Despite the difficulty in maintaining public faucets, the two concessionaires continued the public faucet tradition. As of March 2003, MAYNILAD maintains a total of 402 public faucets; MWCI has 533. Installed without extra charges to the community, every public faucet covers 475 people or up to 50 households. Both the MWCI and MAYNILAD required the community to have the public faucet managed by a person in the community as determined by the community association or barangays officials primarily to ensure the timely payment of water bills.

For a community with no piped water, a public faucet is certainly a better arrangement, although it is more expensive than individually piped water, especially when households have to pay somebody to fetch water. Similarly, a 'public faucet manager' is usually assigned to manage the public faucet. In practice, the public faucet manager charges an extra fee for services rendered including that of ensuring that queuing is followed, collecting payment per container, and remitting the collection to the barangay or directly to the MWCI or MAYNILAD, as the case may be. The experience of Barangay Parola in the West Zone shows that public faucets tend to be mismanaged. The public faucet manager may have efficiently manned the sub-connections to the public faucet, collected payments from residents, and remitted collections to the Barangay Chairman, but the latter did not remit the payment to MAYNILAD, amounting to 2.4 million pesos (or US$48 100). The public faucet in Barangay Parola was disconnected in late 2000 (Inocencio, 2001a).

Vended Water

Vended water is a mainstay in the way water is delivered in the MWSS service area. Water is bought from households with official connections or from public faucets. In both cases, households usually pay other people to fetch water for them, who in turn carry water in gallon containers or cans using a wooden pole, pushcart, or motorized vehicle (Inocencio, 2001b). Households who have to buy water from vendors usually keep water in two to three drums to have a ready supply for two or three days. Vended water is more costly than individually piped water, but less costly than bottled water.

Bulk Water Supply

Bulk selling of water is a major strategy employed by the MWCI to drastically expand water coverage. Under the group taps scheme, the MWCI sells bulk water to a water sub-contractor, household associations, or water cooperatives. In turn, the sub-contractor directly distributes water to households. The MWCI sells bulk water in cases where a connection is: (a) community managed, and (b) privately managed.

Community Managed Water Connection

In this category, a whole community forms an organization to deal directly with the concessionaire, pays its bulk water bill, and sets up its own mini-distribution system, billing and collection. This strategy is similar to the group taps scheme, where the combined water consumption is billed as a single account under one mother meter for the entire community. Sub-meters are usually installed to pro-rate individual household consumption. Like in group taps, the community is in charge of meter reading, billing and collection from member households, and pipe maintenance beyond the water main.

The 228 informal households in Durian Street, in Barangay Pasong Tamo, Quezon City have opted for a community managed water connection. The Samahan is not charged the special rates for bulk water, but is charged according to actual consumption multiplied by the applicable tariff rates for a residential connection. The residents of Durian agree that the water access situation is much better now than before even if they have to pay more than twice the bill of a household with an individual connection. Added costs to the Durian community members are the honoraria of the meter reader, the area coordinator and treasurer, totaling 3000 pesos per month (Inocencio and David, 2001, p. 17).

Privately Managed Water Distribution

A well-known example of water sale by a private sub-contractor is that by Inpart Engineering, a steel fabricating company that branched out into the construction and operation of local water systems (Philippine Center for Water and Sanitation, 2001, cited in Rosenthal, 2003).

Inpart is a local contractor supplying water to a particular area. It entered into a Memorandum of Agreement (MOA) with the local government, community residents and the MWCI for it to operate a water system under a build–operate–transfer arrangement for more than 24,050 households in six low-income communities in the eastern part of Metro Manila. Inpart invested in a water distribution system, buys bulk water from the MWCI, and charges consumers a single fixed rate of 1.50 pesos per 20-liter container or 75 pesos per cubic meter. About 40 percent of the revenue of Inpart goes to the income of water tenders and to a community fund. Part of the remaining 60 percent is paid to a meter reader and electric bill, and the difference serves as the return on investment. While Inpart cannot increase rates without prior consultation with representatives of households, there is no government agency that supervises its operation, except for the water quality monitoring being done by the municipal health department (Philippine Center for Water and Sanitation, 2001).

The MWCI classifies water sold to customers under a privately managed water distribution as 'bulk water' and charges them the highest rate for residential customers. The advantage to the MWCI is that with one mother meter (one official connection), it is able to cover many households. The management of sub-meters and sub-connections is the task of the subcontractor. On the other hand, customers are disadvantaged by having to pay more than the cost of water from individual connections.

In a TPSB project in Addition Hills in Mandaluyong City, the MWCI permitted a private contractor to invest in and operate a water distribution system with bulk water from the MWCI. The contractor entered into a contract with the MWCI and an MOA with the barangay to be allowed to retail water to households at 1.50 pesos per 20-liter container or roughly 75 pesos per cubic meter. The contractor, with 60 paid water tenders, operates a number of taps with long hoses to convey water. The water tenders get 0.50 pesos per container, while the barangay gets 10 percent of the gross water revenues (Inocencio and David, 2001).

Impact on Water Service Coverage

Water service coverage is a basic indicator of performance subject to monitoring by the MWSS-Regulatory Office. Information on service coverage is also used to derive other performance indicators, such as the percentage of the population with piped water supply. The service targets have been set in the CA expressed as percentages of the total projected service population (except those connected to a piped source of water other than the MWSS) for the particular year.[4] Referring to Table 12.3, MAYNILAD fell below its water service coverage target in 2001 and 2002 by as much as 11 percent. On the other hand, the MWCI exceeded its target by 1.5 percent.

Based on similar data gathered from the MWSS-RO, 100 percent coverage had been achieved in 8 out of 37 localities within the service area. The town of Imus is only 7 percent covered; Muntinlupa City, 8 percent; Antipolo City, 17 percent; Taguig Municipality, 20 percent; and Las Piñas Municipality, 29 percent. Caloocan City, Valenzuela City, and Navotas Municipality were at least 68 percent covered. Otherwise, nine municipalities have not yet been reached by the water system (Cuaresma, 2003).

Table 12.3 Water supply coverage targets, East and West Zones, in percentage

Zone and year	2001		2002	
	Target	Actual	Target	Actual
East	77.1	76	80.5	82
West	87.4	79	89.34	78

Source: Concession Agreement; MWSS-RO.

Table 12.4 MAYNILAD water service coverage, 1997–2002

Year	Official connections	Total connections	Total service population based on MAYNILAD's business plan	Percentage coverage using official connections	Percentage coverage using total connections
1997	449 234	467 205	7 263 606	65.41	68.02
1998	449 144	468 645	7 356 124	64.45	67.25
1999	498 051	518 399	7 452 470	70.41	73.29
2000	547 880	571 281	7 553 627	76.27	79.53
2001	577 637	602 424	7 640 714	79.37	82.77
2002	573 194	598 316	7 736 026	77.65	81.05

Source: MWSS-RO.

Interestingly, the two concessionaires use different labels to represent the existing number of water service connections. The MWCI uses the terms 'regular connections' and 'equivalent household connections', while MAYNILAD uses 'official connections' and 'total connections', respectively, to mean the same thing. The terms are defined as follows:

- *Regular/official connections* – include billed services including metered regular connections, bulk-metered connections (excluding connections downstream of the bulk water and connections under special billing, e.g. raw water, water district, sea transport).
- *Equivalent household connections or total connections* – include official connections plus connections downstream of bulk-metered connections.

Referring to Tables 12.4 and 12.5, the difference between the 'official connections' and the 'total connections' of MAYNILAD is narrower by 25 122

Table 12.5 MWCI water service coverage, 1997–2002

Year	Official connections	Total connections	Total service population based on MWCI's business plan	Percentage coverage using official connections	Percentage coverage using total connections
1997	310 682	325 527	4 543 886	80.48	84.32
1998	323 533	340 037	4 722 645	79.81	83.88
1999	332 582	390 349	4 901 396	78.31	91.92
2000	339 491	408 894	5 080 150	76.46	92.09
2001	352 982	427 755	5 258 906	76.17	92.30
2002	369 699	470 522	5 139 030	82.02	100

Source: MWSS-RO.

in 2002, compared to 100,823 difference for the MWCI in the same year. This confirms earlier findings that MAYNILAD relied more on individual connections, while the MWCI had more of the group taps and use of subcontractors and homeowners associations to expand service delivery.

The distinction between official connections, equivalent household connections and the average household size multiplier used is important in determining the actual number of service connections, and whether the concessionaires have actually complied with their water service coverage target. The concessionaires insist on counting the sub-metered connections even though residents have to shoulder the cost of their individual connections.[5]

IMPLICATIONS FOR WATER REGULATION

The success of the policies of privatization and regulation can only be measured by the extent to which these have improved the quality of life of Filipinos (National Economic and Development Authority of the Philippines, 2000, p. 1). In the case of MWSS, its privatization acquires meaning only when the problems of inefficiency, limited access to water by customers, and intermittent water supply are being addressed or have been achieved.

The preceding sections discussed and analyzed the pro-poor programs introduced by the MWCI and MAYNILAD to meet their service obligations. The CA imposed no clear and specific service obligations on the concessionaires to meet the demand of poor residents in the service area. As observed, the two concessionaires came up with their own pro-poor water service delivery programs. In comparing the service obligations of the concessionaires to their performance, the following observations are made.

1. On a positive note, the pro-poor programs have benefited the poor. Access to water has significantly expanded. Through the pro-poor programs, access to water services by the poor and informal settlers living within the MWSS service area expanded significantly. The means by which the poor obtain potable water was improved from buying water from vendors to either buying from public faucets, or having a shared connection, and at best having their own individual connection.

   In both BT and TPSB programs, there is ample evidence to show that the members of poor communities have significantly benefited. Access to water has resulted in improved living conditions, more time for work resulting in higher income, increased water consumption, and other related benefits from an improved water system. The removal of the land title requirement is highly laudable.
2. People participated in the administration of public or communal faucets. The people became more aware and vigilant. The participation of the people increased, and so did their awareness of their responsibility for ensuring the integrity of their own water connections. The level of responsibility of households increased depending on the kind of water connection they have. In the shared connection or group taps scheme, the households became partly responsible for managing their pipes, protecting the system from illegal connections and pilferage, religiously paying their bills, policing their members, and seeing to it that the appointed overseer remits the payment to the concessionaire.
3. People are willing to pay extra costs. The urban poor proved willing to shoulder connection charges for as long as they are formally connected to piped water. Indeed, as it turned out, the poor are willing to pay extra costs. Their main concern was to have access to piped water; the cost of access and the resulting mechanism through which water would be provided became secondary.
4. Water tariffs are higher. The distribution of water through homeowners' associations and small sub-contractors resulted in water tariffs three to four times higher than the concessionaire regulated tariff rates. Further, such private water suppliers are not regulated by the MWSS-RO in their pricing and service performance. The increasing block tariff failed to ensure that low-income consumers pay less per cubic meter since the schemes used in poor areas, i.e. group taps, sub-contractors, bulk water, etc., effectively result in a reclassification of households from 'Residential' to 'Semi-Business' customer, which means they are charged the highest rates.

   To illustrate (refer to Table 12.6), the monthly bills of two households are compared where: (1) they share a connection; and (2) each is individually connected. Assume that they have a combined consumption of

Table 12.6 Classification of MWSS customers and of water sold

Classification of customers	
Residential	Domestic / sanitary use
Semi-Residential	Sari-sari (convenience) stores, food stall, vulcanizing shops, small bodega except bonded warehouse, seasonal business, etc.
Business Group I	Bakery, car assembly, construction activities, cottage industry, ice plants, glass / handicraft / knitting / plastic factories, printing press, soft drinks manufacturing
Business Group II	Combination of industrial, commercial and/or residential activity
Classification of water sold	
Raw water	Water which did not undergo any purification or treatment
Sea transport	Water directly sold to ships or to any sea transport
Bulk water	Water sold in bulk at some withdrawal point

Source: MWSS-RO.

32 m^3 – Household (HH)-A is a family of five and consumes 18 m^3; HH-B has four members and consumes 14 m^3. Under a shared connection, their shared bill amounts to P253.15 or P323.98 under TPSB or BT, respectively. If they are individually billed, HH-A will pay only 107.63 pesos or 81.98 pesos under the TPSB, and HH-B pays 147.91 pesos or 112.32 pesos under the BT. On this basis, households with a shared connection tend to pay more.[6]

5. There is high dependence on group taps, sub-contractors, homeowners' associations, community organizations, and public faucets. The private sector played a key role in fast-tracking access by the urban poor to piped drinking water through group taps, community-shared taps, and privately managed water distribution systems. Consequently, private sector participation meant higher costs for their services.

   Of the low-income households, only 20–25 percent have individual water connections. The majority are connected through group taps, or buy vended water from bulk buyers of water, or public faucets.
6. The classification of customers has no pro-poor bias. Classification is done in the presentation of the water tariff schedule, wherein customers are classified into Residential, Semi-Business, Business Group I and Business Group II. Residential consumers are imposed the lowest tariff

rates. Aside from the classification of customers, water sold is also independently classified. As shown in Table 12.6, the classification of customers does not seem to promote social equity. For instance, 'sari-sari' (convenience) stores are listed under the category 'Semi-Residential' as against well-to-do households with swimming pools, listed under the category 'Residential'. Under the pro-poor water programs, a group of five households sharing a connection would be classified as 'Semi-Residential' for billing purposes if one of the households has a sari-sari store. A sub-contractor who buys bulk water from the concessionaire and resells to a community is classified under 'Business Group I' and billed as such.

The point being emphasized is that the classification of customers and the increasing block tariff (IBT) structure are inherently weak in equity considerations. The rich households tend to be better subsidized since they usually have individual connections and fall under the 'Residential' category, while the poor tend to share a connection or obtain water from bulk selling, so they tend to be classified under the 'Semi-Residential' or 'Business Group I' category and, thus, pay more.

7. Households shoulder the cost of connection. The rule on charges for connection or reconnection to a water main or a public sewer is governed by Section 9.5 of the CA. Section 9.5(i) prescribes a fee not to exceed 3000 pesos for connection or reconnection by residential customers to a water main or a public sewer that are both located less than 25 meters from the connection point. The connection fee is adjusted annually by the percentage change in the Consumer Price Index. Beyond 25 linear meters, customers pay an additional connection charge equal to the costs reasonably and efficiently incurred by the concessionaire, including the costs of upgrading or restoring existing connections or metering facilities to acceptable technical standards.

   As of October 2003, the MWCI charged 5850.89 pesos per connection within 25 linear meters from a water main, while MAYNILAD charged 4730.89 pesos for the same connection. The components of the connection charge are shown in Table 12.7. The connection charge of the MWCI is higher than that of MAYNILAD because of the meter deposit and metering charge in the amount of 1020 pesos. Back in 1997, the MWCI was charging 750 pesos for meter deposit. The fact that the cost of the meter itself is already part of the installation cost further makes the meter deposit as well as the metering charge an overcharge.

   In terms of the period of payment of connection charges, the MWCI allows only a maximum period of 6 months compared to 12 months in the case of MAYNILAD. This is contrary to the CA, which provides

Table 12.7 Water service connections within 25 linear meters, as of October 2003 (in pesos)

Connection charges	MWCI	MAYNILAD
1. Installation cost*	4118.99	4118.99
2. VAT (10% of 1)	411.90	411.90
3. Guarantee deposit	300.00	300.00
4. Meter deposit and metering charge	1020.00	none
Total	5850.89 pesos	4730.89 pesos

Notes: * The installation cost in 1999 = 3473.15 pesos; 2000 = 3718.58 pesos (Consumer Price Index or CPI = 6.6%); 2001 = 3889.63 pesos (CPI = 4.6%); and 2002 = 4118.99 pesos (CPI = 6.0%).

that payment of connection charges can be extended to a period of five years.

Overall, it is not very obvious that it costs the poor and low-income consumers more to obtain a water connection. High-income households usually have their houses located beside a road, which means they do not pay any connection charge, unlike the poor and informal settlers whose houses are located mostly at some distance from a main road.

Moreover, concessionaires leave it to a community association, homeowners' association, or sub-contractor to install and maintain the pipes connecting the households. In terms of reporting, the concessionaires count each household to determine service coverage and the number of connections.

CONCLUSION

The governance framework brings the government, private sector and civil society together to respond to the challenges of development. In the case of water and sewerage services delivery in the MWSS service area, the national government as well as the MWSS have provided a very conducive political, legal and business framework to make privatization and private sector participation work.[7]

However, self-regulation, or for that matter self-governance, does not seem to work even within a framework of good governance. Therefore, the government, whose roles were identified to be an enabler, facilitator, and partnership builder, must continue to regulate. The market cannot be totally left to itself. Regulation must be undertaken by an independent and trusted institution of the government with the participation of the public and civil society groups. This is strongly called for to regulate private sector participation in water distribution given the monopolistic nature of water provision, and the tendency of the private sector to put its profit-maximizing motive first without due regard for the welfare of people.

The regulation of the privately owned water concessionaires has so far generated very modest gains as well as disadvantages to the poor. Population served increased by an additional 1.5 million people within the first five years of MWSS privatization. The numerical increase in the number of connections including that for the urban poor was, unfortunately, accompanied by significant increases in water tariffs, below minimum capital investments, and costly arbitration procedures. Water coverage improved by 12 percent, but still remains very low in certain areas, particularly those that are farthest from the network's center in Balara and La Mesa Dam in Quezon City.

The private concessionaires have not fully performed as expected. They have failed to achieve their service targets. Much remains to be desired in terms of expanding water and sewer services coverage, and keeping water tariffs affordable. The average number of hours that water is available improved from 17 to 21, but not in all areas. In addition, the concessionaires have yet to drastically reduce non-revenue water, which still ran to about 69 percent in the West Zone and 53 percent in the East Zone as of 2002, or about the same level as it was before privatization.

Lessons Learned

What lessons can be learned from the regulation of water in the MWSS service area (see also Nickson and Vargas, 2002)?

First, commitment to water tariff increases must be accompanied by concrete commitments to improve service targets for the poor and disadvantaged sectors. A detailed statement of service targets must be required from concessionaires in relation to petitions for tariff increases.

The CA and its amendments contain no clear commitments that would directly promote the welfare of poor and low-income constituents living in the MWSS service area. We can only allude to the mandate on the provision of public faucets, and a provision in Amendment No. 1, where concessionaires were required to study means to improve cross-subsidy in favor of poor households, and to accelerate the delivery and provision of water services to the poorest barangays. In fairness to the concessionaires, the BT and the TPSB manifest the concrete implementation of this provision.

Second, a desirable balance between promoting concessionaire interests vis-à-vis that of consumers must be achieved. Private sector participation in the delivery of water services within the MWSS service area hastened the delivery of water services and revolutionized the way in which water is delivered, although not all schemes are advantageous to customers. While water from public faucets is better than having no water at all, water from this source tends to be more expensive than water from individual water connections. In instances when water has to be rationed, the public faucets are the first ones to run dry or experience reduced supply.

In relation to water tariffs, the block tariff structure per se is not a problem, although it has its own defects. The problem is the actual classification of customers and the classification of water consumed by them. Households using water for purely residential purposes tend to be charged higher tariffs in cases where they share a group tap, buy water from the community or sub-division association or from a private service provider, or from public faucets. In effect, they pay up to three times more than households with a single connection.

The group taps scheme under the TPSB program turns out to be more expensive than an individual connection. Households have to pay out an extra amount of money to cover the cost of pipes and water meter to connect to the water main, and other installation costs. The implementation of the TPSB and BT pro-poor programs can be improved by lengthening the payment period of the connection charge to five years, as the CA provides.

Third, there is a need to regulate sub-contracted water, and to ensure the accountability of private contractors. The regulatory structure should ensure that the service providers are made accountable for their actions by involving the public in auditing the companies' performance through information dissemination. As it is, the sub-contractors are not regulated. The accountability of private contractors is not covered by any provision of the CA.

Fourth, the regulatory structure could enjoin the concessionaires to have a plan of converting group taps, sub-contracted water, public faucets, and so on, into individual connections. This would solve the problem of having to regulate smaller units supplying water, and technically reduce the bill of consumers. Prior to conversion of all communal means of water service delivery, there is a need to develop criteria for the regulation of sub-contractors of water. The bottom line here is to monitor the operations of local sub-contractors and community water associations whether by the MWSS-RO or by the local governments, or both jointly, to ensure accountability in water pricing and quality.

Fifth, the regulatory structure should require the concessionaires to provide detailed reporting on the accomplishments of the pro-poor programs, including the agreements entered into with private sub-contractors and community associations. It should also do its own monitoring of the performance of sub-contractors/community associations, especially where residents have in particular clamored for the MWCI or the MAYNILAD to take over water distribution.

In relation to this, it is suggested that the RO maintains a database of small water service providers and sub-contractors of the MWCI and MAYNILAD, and draws up the rules and regulations that they are subject to. The rules and regulations should be published so people may know and participate in the monitoring of performance. The RO could further improve its accessibility to the customers of MWSS by creating a web-based system of reporting complaints.

Sixth, the RO should promote transparency and accountability to customers. Mechanisms could be put in place through which the customers of MAYNILAD and the MWCI can participate in the performance audit of the companies. To ensure accountability, the RO could render public reporting of performance, organize water consumer forums, and publicize dispute resolution processes. The RO could tap community or people's organizations or non-government organizations, tasked with a clear mandate for monitoring water distribution and related problems in assigned areas.

The RO may, through the media, educate water consumers of the tariff setting process and provide mechanisms for consumer/client participation to raise the level of accountability of service providers and help the RO implement the provisions of the CA. The RO may consider coming up with a systematic program for raising public awareness on how to make water service providers more accountable. For instance, people should be taught what aspect of performance to monitor and how to monitor this, how and to whom to report (see Gotelli, 2004). Popular versions of the CA and its amendments may be printed for dissemination to the public, particularly the provisions on the monitoring of performance of concessionaires. This adds to transparency and can generate support and build consensus from and among stakeholders, customers and concessionaires included, and facilitate the enforcement of the CA as amended.

SUMMARY

In the absence of clear provisions in the Concession Agreement on providing services to the poor, on the one hand, and how private water sub-contractors may participate in water services delivery, on the other, both concessionaires have developed their respective pro-poor water services delivery programs. The programs are commendable, having connected more than 152,000 households to the piped network as of mid-2003. A closer look at the programs, however, shows elements of inequity. The regulatory structure should take appropriate action to maintain a desirable balance between promoting the interests of concessionaires vis-à-vis that of consumers, especially the poor. The tariff structure, the cost of connection, and the actual manner by which water is delivered, among others, should be re-examined with regard to equity considerations.

The return to the MWSS in March 2004 of the West Zone concession offers an opportune time to reflect on the experience of water privatization and regulation. The government takeover (pundits call it a 'bail out') of the West Zone is indisputable proof of the failure of privatization and regulation. The experience should compel the government to revisit its policy of regulation of water services delivery by the private sector, and the privatization of basic sectors.

NOTES

1. The East Zone covers the towns of Marikina, Mandaluyong, Makati, Pasig, Pateros, San Juan, Taguig, parts of Quezon City and Manila; Antipolo City, Angono, Baras, Binangonan, Cainta, Cardona, Jala-Jala, Morong, Pililia, Rodriguez, San Mateo, Tanay, Taytay and Teresa all in Rizal Province. The West Zone services the municipalities of Malabon, Navotas, Muntinlupa, Caloocan, Pasay, Parañaque, Las Piñas, Valenzuela, and parts of Quezon City, Manila and Makati; Imus, Bacoor, Kawit, Noveleta, Rosario (all in Cavite Province) and Cavite City.
2. MWCI is owned by the Ayala Corporation (60%), United Utilities (20%), Bechtel Corporation (10%), and Mitsubishi Corporation (10%). MAYNILAD is owned by the Lopez-led Benpres Holding Corporation (60%), and Ondeo (subsidiary of Lyonnaise de Eaux (40%).
3. Level I water supply services are directly from existing shallow wells, deep wells or springs. Level II water supply service is characterized by a communal faucet system where houses are densely clustered enough to justify a piped distribution system. Level III water supply service provides an individual faucet system.
4. Service coverage is determined by dividing the total population, less the number obtaining water from an alternative legal source, by the total number of individuals served by the concessionaire.
5. The concessionaires used a multiplier of 9.2 households per person. Thus MAYNILAD reported that it was serving 1.7 million people in Manila as of the end of 2001, based on 184 782 connections (or an average 9.2 persons per household). Using figures from the Bureau of Census, the total service population would amount to 1.4 million potential beneficiaries in MAYNILAD's section of the city (or an average of 7.6 persons per household). Similarly, MWCI had estimated its total number of customers in Makati City to be more than 450 000, based on 47 178 connections (or an average of 9.5 persons per household). MWSS argued that the figure should only be 250 000 potential customers using census data. Overall, there is bloating in the reported covered population. If official census data are followed, MAYNILAD's coverage at the end of 2001 would fall to 76 percent, while the MWCI's coverage rate would drop to 65 percent.
6. Table 12.8 gives an illustrative computation of the monthly bills of two households under a shared connection and an individual connection (not connected to sewer). The amounts are expressed in Philippine pesos.

Table 12.8 Comparison of monthly bills

Charges	Shared connection		Individual connection – Household-A		Individual connection – Household-B	
	TPSB	BT	TPSB	BT	TPSB	BT
1. Basic charge	168.95	191.95	66.85	75.79	50.33	57.07
2. CERA	32.00	32.00	18.00	18.00	14.00	14.00
3. FCDA	6.91	68.58	2.73	27.08	2.06	20.39
4. EC	20.78	29.25	8.76	12.09	6.64	9.15
5. MSC	1.50	2.00	1.50	1.50	1.50	1.50
6. VAT	23.01	29.45	9.78	13.45	7.45	10.21
Total bill	253.15	323.98	107.63	147.91	81.98	112.32
Pro-rated bill:						
Household-A	142.40	182.24				
Household-B	110.75	141.74				

Notes: CERA – Currency Exchange Rate Adjustment; FCDA – Foreign Exchange Differential Adjustment; EC – Environmental Charge; MSC – Maintenance Service Charge; VAT – value added tax; TPSB – Tubig Para Sa Barangay of MWCI; BT – Bayan Tubig of MAYNILAD.

Source: Computation based on tariff structures of the MWCI (dated October 2003), and MAYNILAD (dated 1 January 2002).

7. Five months prior to the August 1997 privatization, President Fidel V. Ramos raised water tariffs to 8.78 pesos per cubic meter (or by 38 percent) to enable the bidding companies to bid low and ensure the success of the bidding process. Then, within the first five years of the concession, the CA was amended mainly to introduce other ways to adjust water tariffs and enable the concessionaires to recover foreign exchange losses in the aftermath of the 1997 Asian Financial Crisis. Amendment No. 1 to the CA dated 5 October 2001, introduced three water tariff adjustment mechanisms, each with specific provisions applicable for each of the concessionaires: (1) Accelerated Extraordinary Price Adjustment (AEPA); (2) Special Transitory Mechanism (STM); and (3) Foreign Currency Differential Adjustments (FCDA).

   The FCDA is a quarterly rate adjustment to be made depending on the concessionaire's declared FOREX losses. In July 2002, the FCDA was computed at 35.73 percent of basic water charges for MAYNILAD customers and 49.593 percent for MWCI customers. On 7 October 2003, an FCDA of 4.09 percent of basic charge for MWCI took effect.

   The AEPA is a mechanism used to recover foreign exchange (FOREX) losses incurred from 1 August 1997 to 31 December 2000. The AEPA rate adjustment of 1.00 pesos/m^3 is retroactive from 25 October to 31 December 2002 or up to the next immediate rate rebasing period.

   The STM is used to recover FOREX losses for the period from 1 January to 31 December 2001 and FOREX losses incurred from 1 December 1997 to 31 December 2000, which are unrecovered as of 31 December 2002. The STM was implemented from 1 July 2002 up to the first rate rebasing on 1 January 2003.

   Amendment No.1 practically resulted in reduced water and sewer service targets (e.g. water pressure level will be maintained at the current level of 7 pounds per square inch (psi) instead of the original target level of 16 psi; the sewerage coverage target of 66 percent for 2021 to be reduced to only 31 percent for MAYNILAD and from 55 percent to below 15 percent for the MWCI).

BIBLIOGRAPHY

Ayala Now, **5**(4), July to August 2002, Manila.

Baldwin, Robert and Martin Cave (1999), *Understanding Regulation Theory, Strategy and Practice*, Oxford: Oxford University Press.

Cariño, Ledivina V. (2002), 'Regulatory governance in the Philippines: A profile', Paper for Session 4: Country Studies, Centre on Regulation and Competition International Workshop, 4–6 September 2002, University of Manchester, Manchester.

Cuaresma, Jocelyn C. (2003), 'Water in private hands: Impact on governance and the urban poor', Paper presented at the International Conference on Challenges to Development: Innovation and Change in Regulation and Competition, 14 October 2003, Manila, Philippines.

David, Cristina C. (2000), 'MWSS privatization: Implications on the price of water, the poor, and the environment', Philippines Institute for Development Studies, Discussion Paper Series No. 2000-14, Makati City, Philippines, Manila, Philippine Institute for Development Studies, April.

Dumol, Mark (2001), 'The design of the Manila concessions and implications for the poor', PPIAF/ADB Conference on Infrastructure Development – Private Solutions for the Poor: The Asian Perspective, adb.org.

Gleick, Peter H., Gary Wolff, Elizabeth L. Chalecki and Rachel Reyes (2002), *The Risks and Benefits of Globalization and Privatization of Fresh Water*, Oakland, California: Pacific Institute for Studies in Development, Environment and Security.

Gotelli, Ilze (2004), *Changing Regulation: From Independent to Credible Regulator. Water for the Poor: Setting the Rules, Finding the Money*, Manila: Asian Development Bank.

Inocencio, Arlene B. (2001a), 'Partnerships in urban poor water supply and sanitation: The case of Metro Manila', Paper presented at the Asian Development Bank Forum on Services for the Urban Poor, Manila, June.

Inocencio, Arlene B. (2001b), 'Serving the urban poor through public–private–community partnerships in water supply', *PIDS Policy Notes*, No. 2001-10, September, Manila.

Inocencio, Arlene B. and Cristina C. David (2001), 'Public–private community partnerships in management and delivery of water to urban poor: The case of Metro Manila', Philippine Institute for Development Studies, Discussion Paper Series No. 2001-18, Manila.

Manila Water Company, Inc. (2002), *4th Quarter Service Performance Report for the Year 2002*, Manila.

Manila Water Company, Inc., *Financial Statements December 31, 2002 and 2001 and Report of Independent Auditors. SGV & Co*, Manila.

Manila Water Company, Inc., *Service Performance Report, August 1, 1999–August 1, 2000*.

Manila Water Company, Inc., *Audited Financial Statements, 1997–2000*, Manila.

Maynilad Water Services, Inc., *Financial Statements December 31, 2002 and 2001 and Report of Independent Auditors, SGV & Co*, Manila.

Maynilad Water Services, Inc. (2000), *Water Supply in Low-income Areas, West Zone, Metro Manila*, Manila.

Minogue, Martin (2001), 'Governance-based analysis of regulation', Centre on Regulation and Competition, Working Paper No. 3, University of Manchester, Manchester.

Mitlin, Diana (2002), 'Competition, regulation and the urban poor: A case study of water', CRC International Workshop, 4–6 September 2002, University of Manchester, Manchester.
MWSS Board, *Resolution No. 487-2001 dated September 3, 2001*, Manila.
MWSS Board, *Resolution No. 512-2001, dated 12 October 2001*, Manila.
MWSS, *Amendment No. 1 to the Concession Agreement dated October 5, 2001*, Manila.
MWSS, *COA Annual Audit Reports, 1991–2000*, Manila.
MWSS, *Concession Agreement, August 1, 1997*, Manila.
MWSS-RO, *Customer Service Regulation Complaints Services Monitoring Department. Five (5) Year Accomplishment Report 1997–2002*, Manila.
National Economic and Development Authority of the Philippines (NEDA) (2002), *A snapshot of Philippines Governance: Status Programs and Guidelines.*
Nickson, Andrew and Claudia Vargas (2002), 'The limitations of water regulation: The failure of the Cochabamba Concession in Bolivia', *Bulletin of Latin American Research*, **11–19**, **21**(1), 128–49.
Philippine Center for Water and Sanitation (2001), 'Vendors and small scale independent providers: 30 years of urban water experiences in the Philippines', Paper prepared for the Water and Sanitation Program, East Asia Regional Office, Jakarta.
Rivera, Virgilio C. (2001), 'How private sector involvement can help the poor: Lessons from Manila (East)' Conference on From Private Sector Participation in the Urban Water and Sanitation. Managing the Process and Regulating the Sector, 5–6 December, Manesar, Haryana, India.
Rosenthal, Shane (2001), *The Manila Water Concessions and their Impact on the Poor*, New Haven: Yale School of Forestry and Environmental Studies.
Rosenthal, Shane (2003), 'The design of the Manila concessions and its implications for the poor', Manila.
Yu, Sandra O. (2002), *Infrastructure Development and the Informal Sector in the Philippines*, Geneva: International Labour Organization.

13. Climbing South Africa's water services ladder: safe drinking water through regulatory governance

Grant Mackintosh and Frederik Uys

INTRODUCTION

Of the many challenges inherited by the new South Africa, one of the more difficult and pressing was that relating to the provision of adequate water services. Prior to 1994, an estimated 30–40 per cent of South Africa's population (approximately 14 to 18 million people) were without adequate water supply services and some 21 million people were without adequate sanitation (Van der Merwe, 2003). Furthermore, in those rural areas where water supply existed, drinking water quality was often poor and could not be considered safe. The resulting impact on primary health was (and remains) significant, with diarrhoea being responsible for some 25 per cent of all deaths in the one to five age group (Bourne and Coetzee, 1996) and an annual estimated 43,000 deaths and 3 million incidences of illness, with an associated treatment cost of some R3.4 billion (Pegrum et al., 1998). Not surprisingly, the water services sector received significant government attention, and the introduction of a new municipal system, new water policies and a new financial framework have resulted in landmark changes in the approach to water services delivery in South Africa.

In addressing this challenge, the Department of Water Affairs and Forestry (DWAF) introduced the concept of a 'water ladder'. The provision of access to a basic level of safe drinking water is the first rung on the 'water ladder', and as the ladder is climbed so people will experience better standards of supply and service (Kasrils, 2003). Progress achieved to date has indeed been impressive, and as of 2004 some 10 million additional people had been supplied with access to drinking water, thereby reducing the drinking water supply backlog to some 4 million. As regards drinking water, of critical consideration is the actual quality of the drinking water being provided at point-of-distribution for consumption. Current investigations indicate that the actual quality of drinking water is unacceptably poor, and furthermore that Water Services Authorities fail to comply with compulsory national standards for the quality of potable water.

This chapter provides background on ruling legislative requirements, and then demonstrates by way of a series of abbreviated case studies how the introduction of both regulatory and cooperative governance within the different tiers of government (local, provincial and national) has been shown to bring about the delivery of safe drinking water in non-metro areas of South Africa. Insight into the challenges regarding the rollout of such governance-driven initiatives throughout South Africa's non-metro water services is also provided.

LEGAL AND INSTITUTIONAL OVERVIEW

The legal framework and institutional arrangements relating to water services provision are complicated and can be somewhat daunting to the uninitiated. This section provides a summary thereof (a more detailed account is in Müller and Uys, Chapter 10 in this volume), with particular consideration as to applicability towards drinking water quality.

Since 1994 various pieces of legislation concerning the water and local government sectors have been finalised. The most important are:

- The Constitution of South Africa, 1996, assigns responsibility of ensuring access to water services to local government. The role of the national and provincial spheres of government is to support, monitor and regulate local government.
- The Water Services Act, 1997, further defines the municipal functions of ensuring water services provision.
- The National Water Act, 1998, defines a new way of managing South Africa's scarce water resources. This Act states that water is an indivisible national resource for which national government is the custodian.
- The Local Government: Municipal Demarcation Act, 1998, provides a legal framework for defining and implementing a post-transitional system of local government.
- The Local Government: Municipal Structures Act, 1998, defines types and structures of municipalities. Three categories of municipalities exist in South Africa after demarcation: Category A (Metropolitan), Category B (Local), Category C (District).
- The Local Government: Municipal Systems Act, 2000, defines how

local government should operate and allows for various types of partnership arrangements a municipality may enter into to ensure delivery of services, for example water.

- The Local Government: Municipal Structures Amendment Act, 2000, places the function of ensuring access to water services (as well as Health and Electricity) at a district level, unless a local municipality is authorised to perform this function

The New Municipal System

The second democratic local government elections held on 5 December 2002 heralded the introduction of the new local government municipal system. The new system reduced the number of local government structures from 843 to 284:

- 6 metropolitan municipalities (Metros – 'Unicities' with no sub-structures);
- 47 district municipalities covering the whole country; and
- 231 local municipalities located within the areas of the district municipalities.

A district municipality may typically contain three to six local municipalities. A local municipality usually includes two to three towns as well as surrounding rural areas.

The new local government structures are faced with many challenges, including amalgamation of old administrations, as well as the challenge posed by rural areas and parts of the former homelands. The division of powers and functions between district and local municipalities has been, and still remains, a major issue to resolve.

Institutional Arrangements for Water Services

The primary responsibility for water services provision rests with local government. In terms of Section 84 of the Municipal Structures Act, the responsibility for providing water services rests with district and metropolitan municipalities. However, the Act allows the Minister of Provincial and Local Government Affairs to authorise a local municipality to perform these functions or exercise these powers. The district (or authorised local) municipality is the Water Services Authority (WSA) as defined in the Water Services Act. There can only be one WSA in any specific area (that is, water services authority areas cannot overlap).

Duties of Water Services Authorities

WSAs have the following primary responsibilities:

- Realisation of the right to access to basic water services: ensuring progressive realisation of the right to basic water services subject to available resources (that is, extension of services), the provision of effective and efficient ongoing services (performance management, by-laws) and sustainability (financial planning, tariffs, service level choices, environmental monitoring).
- Planning: preparing water services development plans (integrated financial, institutional, social, technical and environmental planning) to progressively ensure efficient, affordable, economical and sustainable access to water.
- Selection of water services providers: selection, procurement and contracting of water services providers (including itself).
- Regulation: of water service provision and water services providers (by-laws, contract regulation, monitoring, performance management).
- Communication: consumer education and communication (health and hygiene promotion, water conservation and demand management, information sharing, communication and consumer charters).

A WSA may either provide water services itself (internal mechanism), or contract a water services provider (WSP) to provide water services (external mechanism). For an internal mechanism, the WSA must manage and account separately for the two functions. In practical terms this might mean that a municipal manager, acting on behalf of the municipality, contracts (as the WSA) with the manager of the water services department to provide water services in terms of a performance contract with the municipality. In the second case, the WSA must regulate the WSP according to the contract, specifying clearly the allocation of roles and responsibilities between the regulator and the provider. In all circumstances the WSA is the regulator of the service and is responsible for ensuring that services are provided effectively, efficiently, sustainably and affordably.

Duties of Water Services Providers

The main duty of WSPs is to provide water services in accordance with the Constitution, the Water Services Act and the by-laws of the WSA, and in terms of any specific conditions set by the WSA in a contract. A WSP must publish a consumer charter that is consistent with by-laws and other regulations, is approved by the WSA, and includes the duties and responsibilities of both the WSP and the consumer, including conditions of supply of water services and payment conditions.

LEGISLATION RELATING TO DRINKING WATER QUALITY

A useful and necessary means for tracking water services delivery is via the monitoring of the quality of drinking water. Drinking water quality monitoring allows the correct interpretation of simple and readily measurable analytical determinants, gives insight into the operating state of water services provision, and draws attention to Operations and Maintenance requirements. Most importantly, drinking water quality monitoring is also necessary in that poor drinking water quality has a direct impact on the health of the community. In South Africa, all water services authorities are legally required to monitor drinking water quality on a monthly basis. The Water Services Act introduced a compulsory national standard for drinking water quality. The Compulsory National Standards for the Quality of Potable Water, as published in *Government Gazette* No. 22355 of 8 June 2001, reads as follows:

Quality of Potable Water

5. (1) Within two years of the promulgation of these Regulations, a water services authority must include a suitable programme for sampling the quality of potable water provided to consumers in its water services development plan.

(2) The water quality sampling programme contemplated in sub regulation (1) must specify the points at which potable water provided to consumers will be sampled, the frequency of sampling and for which substances and determinants the water will be tested.

(3) A water services institution must compare the results obtained from the testing of samples with SABS 241: Specifications for Drinking Water; or the South African Water Quality Guidelines published by the Department of Water Affairs and Forestry.

(4) Should the comparison of the results as contemplated in sub regulation (3) indicate that the water supplied poses a health risk, the water services institution must inform the Director-General of the Department of Water Affairs and Forestry and the head of the Provincial Department of Health and it must take steps to inform its consumers:

(a) that the quality of the water that it supplies poses a health risk;
(b) of the reasons for the health risk;
(c) of any precautions to be taken by the consumers; and
(d) of the time frame, if any, within which it may be expected that water of a safe quality will be provided.

The guiding drinking water quality document is SABS 241-2001, which specifies three classes of water in terms of physical, microbiological and chemical quality, as follows:

- Class 0: an ideal standard that is closely comparable to current international standards.
- Class I: water that is known to be acceptable for whole lifetime consumption.
- Class II: water considered to be maximum allowable for short-term consumption (usual and continuous daily consumption for periods not exceeding one year).

Class 0 is largely based on present first world standards such as those pertaining to the European Union and the United States of America; even South Africa's largest water boards would be hard pressed to satisfy Class 0 with regard to some of the determinants. Class I is known to be acceptable for whole lifetime consumption, and is therefore the objective of most South African WSAs and WSPs. Class II is an acknowledgement that, at present and for the foreseeable future, in many cases South Africa' s piped drinking water will not satisfy the previous existing Maximum Allowable Limit (Class I); and yet there is a risk to condemning as 'unfit for human consumption' piped municipal drinking water that only marginally fails Class I, and thereby driving consumers to a potentially worse quality and possibly 'illegal' source. It is acknowledged that it is more prudent to allow consumption of the delivered drinking water at a relaxed level for short-term consumption (Class II), where risk is quantifiable and understood and it is acknowledged that urgent actions are required to improve quality to Class I. Where water fails Class II, and in particular with regards to bacteriological quality, it should be regarded as unfit for human consumption and urgent attention and mitigative action are required.

While the Water Services Act does not criminalise non-compliance with the national standards (and this is in keeping with the phased approach contemplated in the Act), it does make it an offence for any person to 'fail or refuse to give information or to give false and misleading information when required to give information in terms of this Act'. As such, as long as the WSAs comply with the peremptory obligation under sub-regulation 5(4) above and inform the Minister and the Province, as well as its consumers, of its inability to meet its obligations under the law, it faces a vastly reduced risk of incurring penalties under the Act.

Clearly, a regulatory governance requirement therefore exists for local government to monitor drinking water quality, and for both provincial and national government to ensure that such is taking place. Where local government lacks the resources to carry out such monitoring, a co-operative government requirement would require provincial and/or national government to ensure that monitoring takes place.

RECENT SURVEYS REGARDING DRINKING WATER QUALITY

National Strategic Survey on Drinking Water Quality

In order to determine the compliance by local government (LG) to drinking water standards a Strategic Survey on Drinking Water Quality was undertaken by DWAF's Chief Directorate: Water Services: Directorate Planning and Information (DWAF, 2004b). More specifically the survey set out to determine the likely status of drinking water quality management by assessing drinking water quality monitoring, service quality and service reliability. The methodology used was one of 'self-assessment' via a survey questionnaire. This approach has the benefit of providing insight into how those tasked with service delivery perceive themselves, and how well they understand their roles, responsibilities and accountability. A referenceable cross-check review based on drinking water quality analyses was also conducted to assess the relative accuracy of information presented via comparison with current field circumstance. Data from the Free State DLG&H monthly water quality audit and other drinking water quality audits in the Western Cape and Eastern Cape were used to cross-reference the survey findings. This field experience could then be used, in conjunction with the survey findings, to develop an appropriate strategy to improve drinking water service delivery. A total of 155 municipalities were canvassed in the Strategic Survey on Drinking Water Quality.

In determining whether acceptable water quality service delivery is occurring (see Table 13.1), the following assumptions were made regarding monitoring practices:

1. Laboratories must be used for testing.
2. Monitoring of water samples should be continuously carried out at several points within the water distribution system, documented and communicated as per the Compulsory National Standards for the Quality of Potable Water.
3. Consumers should receive drinking water of acceptable quality (satisfying SABS 241-2001 Class I).
4. Monitoring of certain basic water variables should be undertaken regularly, and guidelines for these are specified by SABS 241-2001.

Table 13.1 Estimate of local municipalities (LMs) adhering to drinking water quality issues

Province	Number of LMs	Number of LMs complying	Percentage
Eastern Cape	25	5	20
Free State	7	3	43
Gauteng	9	5	56
KwaZulu/Natal	34	13	38
Mpumalanga	15	4	27
Northern Cape	19	7	37
Limpopo	14	7	50
North West	11	8	73
Western Cape	21	14	67
South Africa	155	66	43

While the limitations of the Strategic Survey are clear, its findings had a good correlation with other initiatives, and were in agreement on causative issues. Key observations included that LGs are not familiar with drinking water service requirements, and that inadequate monitoring of water quality results in services that regularly fail legislated requirements.

Western Cape Survey on Drinking Water Quality

In the Western Cape, a Masibambane–DWAF project was carried out to assess the current status quo regarding drinking water quality at all 24 non-metropolitan Water Services Authorities (Emanti, 2004) and included both:

- Interviews with technical directors (or delegated staff);
- Collection of drinking water samples and testing of drinking water quality at CSIR's SANAS accredited laboratory in Stellenbosch.

The objective of the survey was to use the information gathered to assess (a) the current status of drinking water quality and (b) the quality of drinking water services in the Western Cape. The outcomes of the study would be used to guide future assistance to Water Service Authorities (capacity, infrastructure, operation and maintenance).

Summary of key issues identified from interviews
The following key drinking water issues were identified from the interview process:

- Most local municipalities are not sufficiently aware of their legislative and regulatory governance requirements regarding effective drinking water service delivery:
  (a) Lack of understanding of legislative requirements, water quality standards/guidelines, requirements for effective monitoring, etc.;
  (b) Service delivery to smaller towns/communities is not as effective and efficient as that in the larger towns of the same local municipality.
- Inadequate monitoring (and associated proactive management) of drinking water services consistently results in drinking water quality that fails legislated requirements:
  (a) Lack of drinking water quality data;
  (b) Lack of basic laboratory equipment;
  (c) Drinking water quality is not always ideal or good;
  (d) Through monitoring water quality issues are identified;
  (e) Accurate laboratory analysis is essential to enable informed decision-making.
- Inadequate infrastructure management results in premature failure of drinking water services:
  (a) Maintenance budgets are not adequate to ensure sufficient asset maintenance;
  (b) Appropriate and sustainable technologies are not always implemented.
- Present Water Service Authority institutional capacity (staffing, funding, expertise, education) is limiting adequate service provision:
  (a) Constant restructuring leads to staff being stressed, demotivated, with poor attitudes, no initiative;
  (b) Staff numbers are not adequate; too many ghost posts;
  (c) Skilled staff leave for higher paying jobs, away from small towns;
  (d) Water Service Authorities have difficulty in attracting suitably qualified staff;
  (e) Not sufficiently supported by LGWSETA in training and capacity-building requirements.

Summary of water quality results from one-off sampling

The drinking water sampling programme was such that samples were collected in one major town, two smaller established towns, and two small communities within each district council of the Western Cape. In most instances, six treated drinking water samples were collected in each town/community. Samples were collected from the water treatment works (where applicable) and from household taps throughout the water distribution network of the town/community. Samples were analysed for the

Table 13.2 Western Cape bacteriological drinking water quality results (February to June 2004)

Western Cape, February to June 2004	Total samples	Total coliform % samples failing	Faecal coliform % samples failing
All samples	162	42	19
Major town samples	30	7	0
Smaller established town samples	94	41	20
Village/community samples	38	71	32
SABS 241-2001 Class I allowable compliance*		4% of samples, max	

**Note:* Although the objective of disinfection should be to attain zero total coliform bacteria and zero faecal coliform bacteria, the SABS 241-2001 Class I allowable compliance is a maximum of 4 per cent to have total coliform bacteria count greater than 10 per 100 ml and faecal coliform bacteria count greater than 1 per 100 ml.

minimum determinants as outlined in SABS 241-2001 Drinking Water Specification, namely: total coliform bacteria, faecal coliform bacteria, electrical conductivity, pH, turbidity, appropriate residual treatment chemicals (iron, aluminium) and disinfectants (free chlorine residual). A summary interpretation of bacteriological drinking water results as compared to SABS 241-2001 Class I standards (the required quality standard for WSAs) is shown in Table 13.2. (Bacteriological results give an indication of the potential risk of contracting waterborne diseases and as such can be considered to have a direct and acute health impact.)

The Table 13.2 shows that:

- Significant failures with regards to both total coliforms (42 per cent failure) and faecal coliforms (19 per cent failure) were recorded in the towns/communities sampled (maximum 4 per cent failure allowed).
- The percentage total and faecal coliform failure in villages/communities (71 per cent and 32 per cent failure, respectively) was significantly higher than that recorded in the major towns (7 per cent and 0 per cent failure, respectively).
- The percentage total and faecal coliform failure in smaller established towns (41 per cent and 20 per cent failure, respectively) was also significantly higher than that recorded in the major towns (7 per cent and 0 per cent failure, respectively).

Although not presented here, suffice to note that physico-chemical determinant analysis also showed significant failures with regards to turbidity (33 per cent failure) and iron (31 per cent failure).

REGULATORY GOVERNANCE CONSIDERATIONS

Within the concept of cooperative government there is also the recognition that performance by the different spheres of government (that is national, provincial and local) needs to be monitored and regulated. The functions of the various spheres of government with regard to regulatory governance are described briefly below.

Local government is an independent sphere of government that is assigned (by the Constitution) the executive authority for water supply and sanitation (water services). The WSA (municipality) is the local regulator of water services. It determines local policies and standards (which must conform to national minimum norms and standards), promulgates by-laws, plans the provision of water services (water services development plan), determines how investments in water services are undertaken and sets tariffs. Where the water services authority is also the water services provider, then there is self-regulation. The Strategic Framework for Water Services (DWAF, 2003) notes that the accountability of the WSA to the local electorate is an effective regulating mechanism for the provision of water services in this context.

Provincial government is involved in the regulation of water in accordance with the general principles of cooperative government. Provincial government also fulfils regulatory functions in respect of its other functions such as planning and control, as well as its broad mandate to oversee and assist local government. Provincial government is tasked with directing national programmes to assist local government, such as the Municipal Infrastructure Grant and the Capacity Building Grant.

National government is both the sector leader and the overall regulator of the sector. National government regulates through DWAF. In the broadest sense, regulation aims to ensure that all role players comply with all the regulatory goals, objectives and measures in respect of the economic, social, political, environmental and technical desirables as provided for in all relevant policy and legislation.

In essence, national and provincial government are therefore obliged to support and strengthen the capacity of municipalities and hold regulatory authority to ensure effective performance by municipalities in respect of all functions. Although the above mandated responsibilities are well documented, the existing situation in South Africa is that regulation of local government by national and provincial government is generally poor in the water sector. The result is that in many cases drinking water does not meet the required standards. In many cases Water Services Authorities are not familiar with the Compulsory National Standards for the Quality of Potable Water, and inadequate monitoring of water quality and/or inadequate interventions to address poor drinking water quality result in services that regularly fail in the provision of safe drinking water.

Considering the above, the ideal situation would be where consistently safe drinking water is achieved through adherence to legislation and good management practice by WSAs and the effective regulation thereof by DWAF. Provincial government should play a cooperative and regulatory role and assist WSAs to fulfil their obligations.

Furthermore, DWAF could introduce supportive measures towards WSAs such as the development of a national drinking water quality strategy; provide generic and appropriate drinking water quality management systems for use by WSAs; maintain a database of the state of WSA monitoring systems; work to support the identification and verification of simpler and more affordable testing methodologies for WSAs and updating SABS 241 to include these. Finally, as sector regulator, DWAF should track and review the adherence of WSAs to their mandated requirements. Where there is lack of adherence to requirements, DWAF should intervene in a proactive manner.

CASE STUDIES DEMONSTRATING THE ROLE OF GOVERNANCE IN DRINKING WATER QUALITY

The following section presents two successful case studies where the implementation of fairly simple drinking water quality management procedures has resulted in a significant improvement in drinking water quality.

Self-regulation by the Water Services Authority: Stellenbosch Municipality

Stellenbosch Municipality is a Water Services Authority (WSA), and is part of the Boland District Council of the Western Cape. In 1997, Stellenbosch Municipality (as WSA) introduced a proactive drinking water quality management (DWQM) programme for the town of Stellenbosch. This DWQM programme provides the necessary self-regulation of the service Stellenbosch Municipality provides, and ensures that services are provided effectively, efficiently, sustainably and affordably. The programme includes the communities of Pniel, Johannesdal, Kylemore, Klapmuts and Franschhoek. At present approximately 90 samples are collected on a monthly basis from source, through the treatment chain, reservoirs and distribution network to the consumers' taps. These samples are analysed at CSIR's SANAS Accredited Analytical Laboratory in Stellenbosch. The following two historical case studies highlight successes achieved through the self-regulatory practices of Stellenbosch Municipality:

- During 2001, the town of Franschhoek was included within the areas of responsibility of Stellenbosch Municipality as WSA. An initial investigation at Franschhoek in October 2001 found that the drinking water quality within the town was very poor, often failing SABS 241-2001 standards. In particular, it was noted that 95 per cent of all samples collected failed required levels for total coliforms, while 88 per cent failed required levels for faecal coliforms. Subsequent interventions resulted in 100 per cent compliance with required drinking water quality standards (see Figure 13.1) within a reasonable time frame.
- An investigation in 2002 of residual aluminium concentrations (following treatment where aluminium sulphate is used as a coagulant) revealed that aluminium concentrations in excess of the SABS 241-2001 Class I (Acceptable) Limit of 0.3 mg/l (and sometimes in excess of the SABS 241-2001 Class II (Maximum Allowable) Limit of 0.5 mg/l) were recorded in those reservoirs receiving water from the Paradyskloof Water Treatment Works. Subsequent interventions

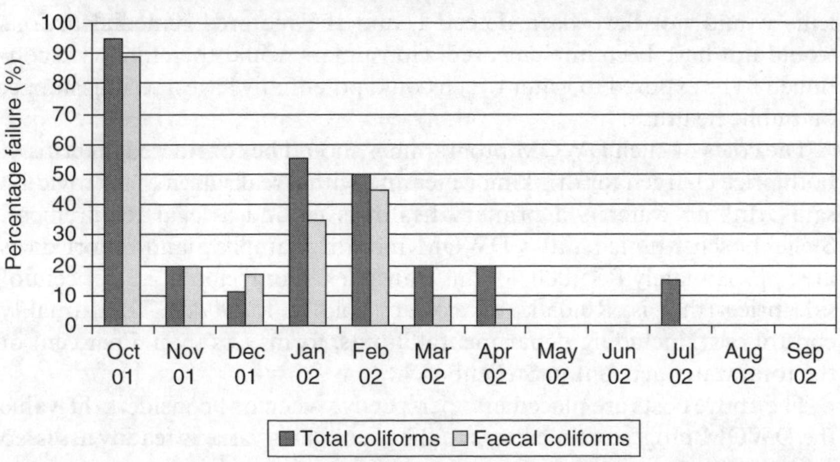

Figure 13.1 Franschhoek Year One: percentage failure of drinking water with regards to SABS 241-2001 for total coliforms and faecal coliforms

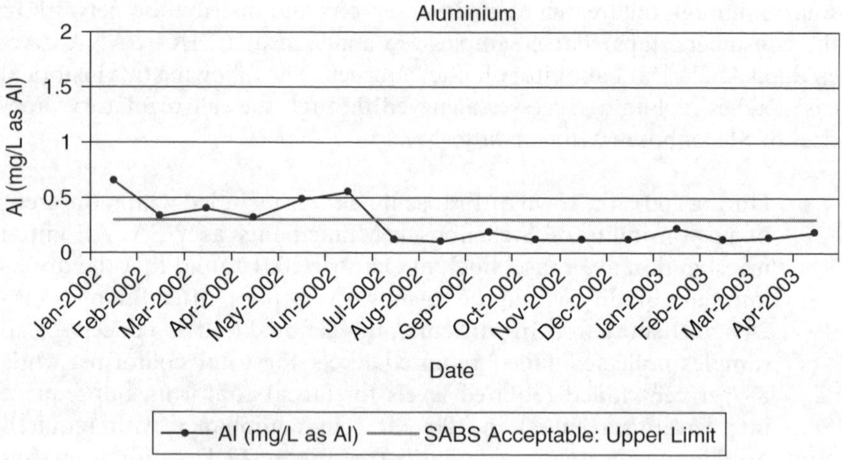

Figure 13.2 Aluminium residual monitoring at Paradyskloof Reservoir #1, Stellenbosch

resulted in 100 per cent compliance with required drinking water quality standards (see Figure 13.2) within a reasonable time frame.

These simple examples show the powerful value of adherence by a WSA to the Compulsory National Standards for the Quality of Potable Water. Without adherence thereto, and the associated monitoring, the above problems would not have been detected, and the required remedial actions would not have been implemented. Consumers would therefore have continued to be exposed to water which could potentially have a serious impact on public health.

The costs of such DWQM programmes should be considered in terms of both price charged for drinking water and with a realisation that providing safe drinking water is a primary health issue and a legal requirement. Stellenbosch Municipality's DWQM monthly sampling and report costs are approximately R35,000.00; this translates to only about 2.5 per cent of sale price (that is, R0.05/kl of a water sold at R1.90/kl). Total quality control cost, including departmental inputs, forms less than 5 per cent of the total water account in Stellenbosch.

The above costs are placed into perspective when one considers the value the DWQM programme delivers to the client. This value is readily assessed using a quantitative technique, termed 'Value Impact Assessment' (using a Net Present Value (NPV) approach). The NPV assessment captures both the costs and income (or benefits) arising from a project, and relates these as one financial sum in terms of today's money. If the NPV is positive, the value impact to the client is positive by the amount of the NPV. In the assessment conducted for Stellenbosch Municipality both improvements in operational efficiency (reduction in treatment costs, optimisation of chemical addition, and reduction in pipe bursts) and personnel efficiency (reduced manpower requirements via improved efficiency of network management and water treatment processes) were considered (Moorgas, 2004). Using various inputs for operating and maintenance costs, DWQM programme costs, inflation, risk, and so on, cash flows were developed that were then translated into a Net Present Value for Stellenbosch Municipality. Using a Monte Carlo simulation technique (with 300 NPV simulations) a frequency distribution was developed.

The Value Impact Assessment results showed that it was highly likely that DWQM-related efficiencies would result in substantial savings to Stellenbosch Municipality (as indicated by the highly positive NPVs). Importantly, the distribution showed that there was no probability that a negative NPV would result. That is to say, at all times the DWQM service at least pays for itself; and in all likelihood delivers an attractive positive NPV to the client. For the purpose of debate, even discarding expected benefits from the DWQM programme, the cost of the consultative auditing process that assures the drinking water quality of Stellenbosch translates to R5/person/year or R0.42/person/month. A very nominal price indeed for ensuring the delivery of safe drinking water!

A current challenge faced by Stellenbosch Municipality is the expansion of the DWQM programme to smaller communities/hamlets that are within the municipal area but fall outside the formal town boundaries (including Devon Valley, Faure, Lanquedoch, Raithby, La Motte, Wemmershoek). A status quo assessment of these areas is currently underway. This assessment will assist Stellenbosch Municipality in deciding the required courses of action and guide the way forward.

Cooperative Governance: The Free State Water Quality Management Initiative

While it is a non-transferable legislated responsibility of WSAs (local government) to ensure the provision of adequate services, the supportive and regulatory role of provincial and national government is crucial. The Free State Department of Local Government and Housing (DLGH) operates a far-sighted cooperative government initiative to assist local government in the delivery of water services.

The basis of the initiative is a monthly Consultative Audit of both drinking water and treated wastewater across all communities in the Free State (approximately 85 communities/towns/cities). During the audit, drinking

Table 13.3 Summary of bacteriological water quality in surface water based systems

Source	Total analyses	Total coliforms percentage failure (i.e. > 5 per 100 ml)		Faecal coliforms percentage failure (i.e. > 0 per 100 ml)	
	2004	2003	2004	2003	2004
Surface water based systems	1741	6.2%	3.4%	2.7%	1.9%
SABS 241-2001: Class I (acceptable)	–	4% maximum		4% maximum	

water samples are collected from both the water treatment works and points of use in the distribution network, while treated wastewater samples are collected from wastewater treatment works. The collected water samples are analysed for various microbiological and physico-chemical parameters (depending on the water in question) utilising internationally accepted methods. Water quality data are then collated, verified and interpreted according to required standards (for example, SABS 241-2001, DWAF General Authorisation), which helps to identify issues of concern that require attention and highlights improvements made in service delivery. Water quality results are then presented/reported to local and provincial government via monthly fax reports; quarterly and annual reports, and monthly, quarterly and annual feedback sessions. Through this audit, and despite a past general failure of WSAs to carry out their own legally required DWQM programmes, a progressive and considerable improvement in drinking water quality has resulted. Summarised results obtained for both the period 1 April 2002 to 31 March 2003 and the period 1 April 2003 to 31 March 2004 are shown in Table 13.3.

Table 13.3 shows that:

- 3.4 per cent of the 1741 drinking water samples collected from surface water based systems failed required SABS 241-2001 limits for total coliforms, while 1.9 per cent of the samples collected failed required SABS 241-2001 limits for faecal coliforms (a maximum failure of 4 per cent is allowed).
- Comparison of the drinking water results obtained in 2003 with those obtained in 2004 indicates that an improvement in bacteriological water quality occurred, with both the total coliform and faecal coliform percentage failures in 2004 satisfying the SABS 241-2001 Class I (acceptable) limit of 4 per cent maximum failure.

These compliance figures are significantly better than other areas of the country (where such programmes are not operated – see earlier). As such, this programme is regarded as a national best practice. Importantly, DLGH is now using the Water Quality Management programme to:

- Guide WSAs to become legislatively compliant through the introduction of their own Water Quality Management procedures.
- Direct and assess infrastructural and capacity building support to local government, including funds from the Municipal Infrastructure Grant (MIG) and the Capacity Building Grant.

The monthly consultative auditing process for the Free State translates to approximately R1/person/year or R0.08/person/month. Again, this is a nominal sum indeed if it results in a significant improvement in drinking water quality, and the associated primary health benefits.

A current challenge faced in the Free State is that despite considerable progress, serious problems still exist. At a number of municipalities, no progress has been made for periods exceeding six months. Through the introduction of an easily accessible web-based water quality management system (currently in progress), it is anticipated that clearer insights into water service delivery in the Free State will be provided. The web-based system will enable easy identification of issues and will assist with prioritisation (ranking) of these issues. Once water quality data are accessible to all stakeholders via the internet, the onus will be on municipalities to provide evidence of steps attempted in trying to improve water service delivery and (if applicable) why these steps have not been successful.

CONCLUSIONS

It has been shown that considerable national progress has been made since 1994 in ensuring the provision of adequate basic drinking water services delivery (the first step up the 'Water Ladder'). However, it has also been shown that most non-metro Water Services Authorities in South Africa are failing in their compliance with the Compulsory National Standards for the Quality of Potable Water, and that in many instances this failure in regulatory governance is resulting in the provision of drinking water of unacceptably poor quality. A direct associated impact on primary health can be expected.

It has also been shown that implementation by Water Service Authorities of simple regulatory governance methodologies such as adherence to the Compulsory National Standards for the Quality of Potable Water via a simple, well-structured, sustainable DWQM programme will make considerable difference to ensuring the provision of safe, good quality drinking water. It is further shown that, where Water Service Authorities lack capability, a provincially based cooperative government programme such as that of the Free State, results in considerable improvement in drinking water quality. In determining the way forward and ensuring sustainable progression up the Water Ladder (that is, ongoing improved standards of supply and services), the following multi-pronged approach can be considered:

- Special efforts need to be made by WSAs to become legally compliant with regard to the compulsory standards.
- Provincially based Consultative Audits of drinking water quality provided by WSAs should be introduced; and used both to intervene in acute and chronic drinking water failures, and to direct provincially based national assistance programmes such as the Municipal Infrastructure Grant and the Capacity Building Programme.
- The National Department of Water Affairs and Forestry (as sector leader and sector regulator) needs to create a supportive environment for improved services delivery by Water Services Authorities and also to act effectively as overall sector regulator, intervening in those cases where the aforementioned initiatives are not sufficient to ensure the delivery of safe drinking water.

Finally, it can be expected that any initiatives that provide transparency regarding drinking water quality to consumers and other stakeholders (such as user-friendly web-based reporting systems) will contribute greatly to a cycle of continuous improvement with regard to the delivery of acceptable drinking water quality in the non-metro areas of South Africa.

BIBLIOGRAPHY

Bourne, D.E. and N. Coetzee (1996), *An Atlas of Potentially Water-Related Diseases in South Africa. WRC Report No. 584/1/96*, Pretoria, South Africa.

DWAF (2002), *Guidelines for Compulsory National Standards – Regulations under Section 9 of the Water Services Act (Act 108 of 1997)*, Pretoria, South Africa.

DWAF (2003), *Strategic Framework for Water Services, September*, Pretoria, South Africa.

DWAF (2004a), Advertorial – *Water, Sewage and Effluent*, **24**(3), 64–65, May.

DWAF (2004b), Chief Directorate Water Services, *Survey Report on the Quality of Water Services in Local and Metropolitan Municipalities, 12 May*, Pretoria, South Africa.

Emanti Management (Pty) Ltd (2004), *Drinking Water Quality Management System for the Western Cape*, Submitted to Stellenbosch Municipality for Masibambane Western Cape, July.

Kasrils, R. (2003), 'Statement by Minister Ronnie Kasrils on the celebration of the 9 millionth person to receive safe water since 1994, 5 July', South Africa.

Moorgas, S. (2004), Personal communication.

Pegrum, G.C., N. Rollins and Q. Espey (1998), 'Estimating the cost of diarrhoea and epidemic dysentery in KwaZulu-Natal and South Africa', *Water SA*, **24**, 1.

SABS: South African Bureau of Standards (2001), SABS 241-2001: *Specification for Drinking Water*, Pretoria, South Africa.

Van der Merwe, L.H. (2003), In *Water Sewage and Effluent*, **23**(5), 50–51. September.

PART IV

Capacity building for regulation

14. A diagnostic model for capacity building in regulatory agencies and competition commissions: an empirical study based on the ICT sector, Southern Africa

Derek Eldridge and Brian Goulden

INTRODUCTION

This chapter reports on a research study to build a new concept of capacity building relevant to the needs of regulatory agencies and competition commissions. The justification for a new approach for capacity building was established through discussions with regulators and other senior/professional staff in a range of countries on how regulatory effectiveness could be increased. In this initial study (Eldridge, 2004) respondents suggested that many regulatory bodies still had not reached optimum performance in:

- seeking to understand how to fully convert defined regulatory intentions into the required actions, particularly in terms of transition factors affecting their particular sectors and stakeholder relationships;
- trying to establish ways of working conducive to regulatory effectiveness, particularly where agencies had been separated from or were still part of the mainstream public service;
- understanding how to build collaborative relationships and to invoke appropriate management styles.

The comments gathered suggested an organising concept for the research study incorporating three components:

- regulation is an intention which results in outputs and impacts that can be monitored as to their effectiveness;
- regulation is also a process whereby individuals cooperate to deliver flows of work that affect the well being of regulatees/stakeholders across traditional administrative/professional boundaries;

- quality outcomes in regulation depend on the effective and efficient management of people and processes.

Further, these components could be incorporated into a diagnostic model (see Figure 14.1) and the possibility existed of utilising it as a capacity building tool for analysis that allows interactions between parameters within the system to be recognised and explored qualitatively as to their contribution to the regulatory process. Thus the model could be applied in a practical way to enable regulators to explore the possibilities for performance improvement. Such an application is presented in CRC Policy Brief No. 4 (2004).

This chapter concentrates on a presentation of the research aimed at justifying the form and content of the model and proceeds through the following sections:

- Form of the model and its conceptual justification;
- Description of the main components of the model and their connection with the management of regulation;
- Design of the research study and its regional/organisation context;
- Research methodology;
- Data analysis;
- Discussion of findings;
- Concluding remarks on the value and use of the model.

FORM OF THE MODEL AND ITS CONCEPTUAL JUSTIFICATION

The model, shown in Figure 14.1, provides a systemic framework (Beer, 1985) to demonstrate how intervening parameters affect the progress of regulation from its inception to delivery and subsequent evaluation. Models of this type are common within management literature and provide a means by which the main forces for and against organisational change can be identified along lines suggested by Pollitt and Bouckaert (2000, p. 21). If it is possible to visualise the management of regulation in this way then a systemic understanding can give rise to actions that are coordinated and consistent in improving performance and less randomly chosen (Asch and Bowman, 1989, p. 404). Of particular importance is the model's ability to describe how actions embodied in the management components may support or inhibit capacity building as represented in four variables, namely:

- Key skills provision;
- Effective group/institutional learning;

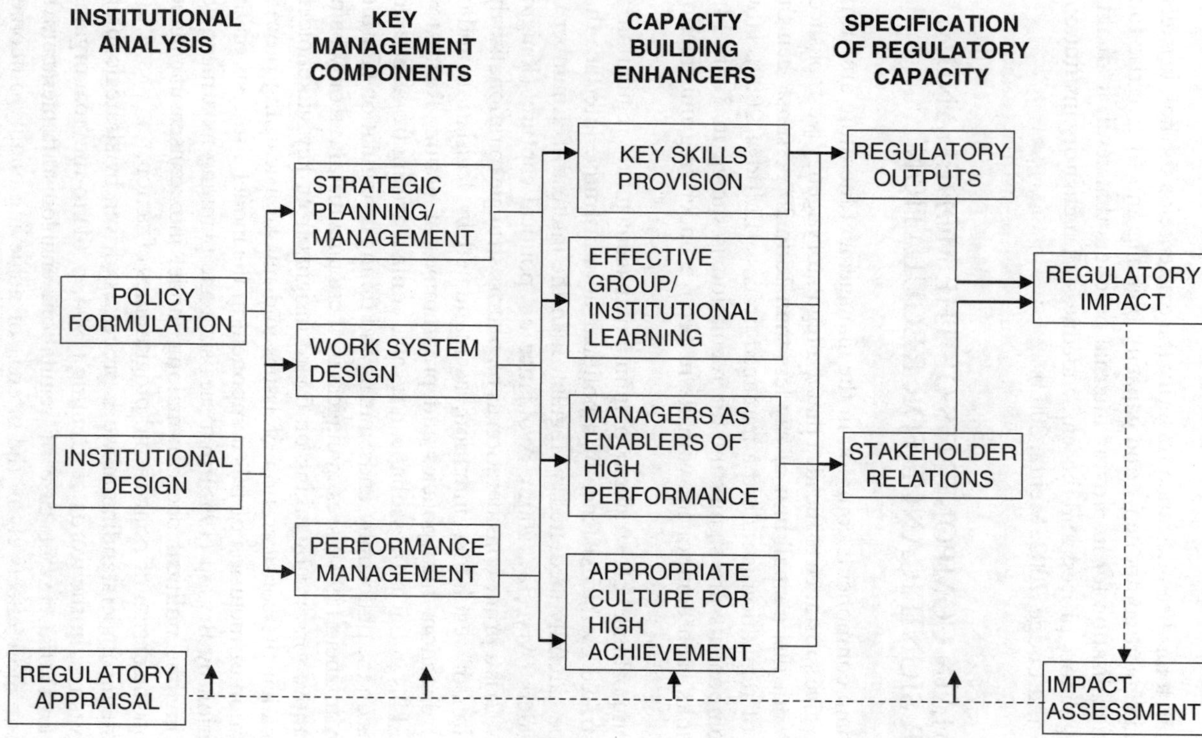

Figure 14.1 The diagnostic model for capacity building

- Managers as enablers of high performance;
- Appropriate culture for high achievement.

The research has been designed to verify the existence of the link between the management components and capacity building and to give rise to a practical realisation for improving internal practices that result in quality in the regulatory process and the 'embeddedness' of regulatory institutions (Stirton and Lodge, 2002; Mehta, 2002).

THE MAIN COMPONENTS OF THE MODEL AND THEIR SIGNIFICANCE FOR REGULATION

Three main components common in the management literature are introduced to give substance to the idea that if a regulatory agency is established, and it is not just a small unit of say less than 15 to 20 persons, then the process of regulation is indeed a managed process (Eldridge, 2002). How these components are significant for regulation is shown in Table 14.1 which links each component with its respective underlying information source.

The importance of strategic planning/management to regulation is demonstrated by the existence of a political–administrative interface that has to be carefully mediated by regulators in the interest of a number of stakeholders (Aryeetey, 2002). Avoidance of 'political capture' (Knight-John, 2002) is a prime consideration as regulators struggle to rationalise the translation of regulatory intention, as mandated by legislation and/or political direction, into policies and programmes of action. Regulators require skills in this process that can resolve conflict arising from different opinions on the philosophy, ends, means and timing of regulation (Cariño, 2002). Mintzberg (1994) sees managers in these circumstances only being able to move forward by taking on board insights from key stakeholders that broaden the consideration of issues and invoke a learning process. Justification of inclusion of this component in the model also rests on the proposition by Bryson (1995) that sees strategic planning as a means of translating the political decision-making model into consensual agreements on the design of policies and programmes of action.

A systemic understanding of work processes, driven by strategic intention, gives rise in the words of Deming (1994, p. 61) to the 'real organisation chart' that, in the case of regulation, enables staff members to interrelate more effectively in the interest of achieving quality outcomes. Such interrelationships are also able to stimulate a learning climate that furthers progress on specific elements of regulation and builds knowledge vital

Table 14.1 Key organisation and management components in a regulatory agency

Component	Likely source for information vital to component function (aims and content)
Strategic planning/ management	• The stated political aims of regulation • Legislation, including definition of the 'regulatory space' for intervention • Evaluation of previous regulatory practices in the sector concerned • Political climate for regulation including degree of emphasis on pro-poor provision • Views of key stakeholders including those of consumers • Financial/market performance of major private companies in sector • The type of relations expected between the regulatory agency and key stakeholders • Conditions under which 'regulatory capture' can be avoided
Work system design	• Nature and scope of the regulatory system implied by legislation and political objectives • Identification of supplier/client relationships in the regulatory system • Views of key stakeholders • Interpretation of key effectiveness criteria in regulation
Performance management	• Definition of the above components – strategic business plan – system development needs (regulatory system) • Choice of management inputs – managerial style – culture – feedback mechanisms for increasing effectiveness • Knowledge of current skills and potential of the workforce • Views of staff and other stakeholders, such as human resource specialists

for system functioning and improvement among those involved. Achieving this type of learning synergy involving knowledge and associated actions is at the heart of consistency within regulation and contributes to an enhanced awareness of transparency (Minogue, 2004b).

Central to the achievement of quality outcomes for regulation are the skills and attitudes that staff in an agency can bring to bear on the complexity of processes. Without sufficient attention to the human dimension, regulators cannot expect to bring their organisations to a peak of effectiveness. Hence the need for a sound system of performance management, whose form is influenced by the strategic planning/management and work system design features adopted as appropriate for the type of regulation in question. Choice on the form of a performance management system adopted also rests to some extent with a regulator, dependent on her or his preferred managerial style, the type of internal culture promoted, the extent of team working to be encouraged and the degree to which staff members are to be empowered as individuals and in teams in securing effective processes of regulation. Approaches are likely to reflect good governance measures already applicable to the public sector in a specific context (Minogue, 2004a) and encompass these types of question:

- How far is appraisal of performance related to what people are expected to achieve rather than to the behavioural attributes they possess?
- Should there be a recognition that the development of staff is very much linked to the task demands they face and the nature of the systems they operate in, rather than purely to their own specified career choices?
- How far is there to be a consideration of the fact that no one individual is likely to be responsible for the quality of what is being achieved, and that performance has to be undertaken and reviewed as a joint responsibility among the relevant staff?
- Is it possible that any formal written appraisal and subsequent discussion are always based on regular and informal reviews of the progress in a prior period?

Organisations will evolve the form of the management components according to their own needs and circumstances, but their formation is always likely to be an interrelated process to ensure a congruency of efforts in respect of regulatory intention, actions, and outcomes and their evaluation. The major concern of the diagnostic model is the potential to achieve cohesiveness of the management components within capacity building efforts, and the possibility of this is a main concern of the research project.

DESIGN OF THE RESEARCH STUDY AND ITS REGIONAL/ORGANISATION CONTEXT

Specifically the research is designed to understand:

- Whether the management components identified in the model are operative within the survey organisations.
- How these management components activate capacity building as represented by the four enhancers of the model.
- If the overall form of the model offers a viable representation of the management of regulation within the organisations.

The ten organisations subject to the research are ICT regulatory agencies of member states in the Southern Africa Development Community (SADC). They are also members of the Telecommunications Regulators' Association of Southern Africa (TRASA) who facilitated much of the access to relevant people for the purposes of data collection by interview, questionnaire and workshop participation. The organisations represented in the research are in Botswana, Lesotho, Malawi, Mozambique, Namibia, Seychelles, South Africa, Tanzania, Zambia and Zimbabwe. All have their origins in the last ten years in response to privatisation and liberalisation within the telecommunications sector, which as a result has seen the entry of new service providers particularly with the growth of the mobile market. Seven of the organisations are the result of legislation for the sector within their respective countries that has resulted in independent public bodies headed by chief executives. While most stand as independent entities outside the mainstream public service, controlling ministries have a role in their conduct, which in the case of three agencies has led to a blurring of the lines of accountability. The impact of technology within the sector has also led to the redesignation of three agencies in recent years to include broadcasting as an integral part of their affairs. Other agencies are likely to have to consider this change within coming years.

Most of the agencies are subject to the influence of some form of advisory board usually appointed through the relevant ministry and usually giving a brief to a wider group of stakeholders to influence internal affairs. Boards also ensure that organisational and management matters are subject to scrutiny as to their efficacy in supporting regulatory outcomes. While most of these boards apparently fulfil their expected roles well and advise from 'outside' with part-time members, for one survey organisation the board is appointed on a full-time basis. Some evidence suggests that for this exceptional situation decision-making is potentially problematic for the chief executive and senior personnel due to the 'top heavy' nature of the organisation and what is seen by many senior personnel as undue interference from board members.

Staffing of key skills in most of the ten agencies has been difficult at one time or another in the last five years. While for most of the agencies remuneration packages for professional and technical staff have been advantageous as compared to the mainstream public sector, there has been a constant problem to retain vitally needed staff. On the whole the agencies attract very good candidates but in many cases fail to keep them, with many departing to work for the service providers. In one organisation virtually all key professional service resigned in a one year period while this research was proceeding.

Chief executives appointed to the agencies have usually had sound careers within the public sector or other large organisations. While they usually bring sound managerial competence it is apparent that the decision-making styles in some organisations result in able senior personnel being excluded from strategic decision-making. Such styles also create an internal culture that may not generally be an inducement to high organisational performance.

Being members of TRASA since its formation, all of the ten organisations represented in the research have engaged in an extensive regional exchange of views, particularly on technical matters, resulting in the furtherance of ICT progress within the SADC. Chief executives have also regularly shared opinions, and other senior personnel responsible for human resource development have collaborated in workshops to assist in the building of their respective organisations. This climate of cooperation has furthered access to the ten organisations and enabled the range of methodologies adopted for this research to be reasonably successful in implementation and outcome. No significant barriers to access or to obtaining relevant information were encountered by the authors apart from the usual slow responses on requested data found generally in research projects of this type. Indeed all chief executives and senior staff were highly cooperative and open in expressing their views and in providing key information.

INFORMATION-GATHERING METHODOLOGIES

Varying approaches were taken to understand:

- The degree of regulatory effectiveness being achieved in the survey organisations.
- The key factors in building regulatory effectiveness in the organisations concerned, referred to as the capacity building enhancers.

- The nature of the underlying management initiatives that would activate the capacity building enhancers to a sufficient degree for regulatory effectiveness.

Information was gathered from a range of regulators as follows:

- Chief executives and other senior personnel of the agencies on an individual basis and usually within their own location or in regional meetings (20 in number).
- Senior officials of the relevant overseeing ministries usually in their own location (18 in number).
- Key informants considered expert on the ICT sector with a deep knowledge of the organisations, through either consultancy/donor advice inputs or employment within the sector, on an ad hoc basis according to location at the time of the study (12 in number).
- Members of the workshops referred to below (28 in number).

One important consideration prior to any investigation of how well management actions supported capacity building was establishing a measure of the degree of regulatory effectiveness being achieved in each of the survey organisations. It was important for the purposes of the research that the diagnostic model should be verified in a situation where organisational effectiveness was being achieved. To do this the majority of the respondents in the research were asked to measure on a four point scale the degree of effectiveness being achieved in the organisation(s) they had an interest in according to the criteria listed in Table 14.2.

Note that this is a somewhat limited list as against wider measures of regulatory effectiveness as, for instance, listed in Eldridge (2003), but in the absence of a full regulatory impact assessment for the survey organisations it was difficult to move beyond interpretations of current legal and administrative conditions which are more easily reportable. However, comments were made in many interviews and questionnaires that suggested that some

Table 14.2 Criteria utilised to establish degree of regulatory effectiveness achieved

- Legal powers of the agency clearly defined and enacted
- Clearly defined roles for the agency vis-à-vis parent ministry
- Clearly defined roles for the agency vis-à-vis sector suppliers (the regulated enterprises)
- Clearly defined roles for the agency vis-à-vis consumers

of the wider impacts expected within the ICT sector are being experienced, such as licensing incentives for wider penetration.

The degree to which capacity building enhancers and the associated management practices, as portrayed in Figure 14.1, were present in the survey organisations, and at what level of quality, was established through a number of methodologies:

- Three workshops involving between three or four senior professionals from each of the organisations.
- Interviews with chief executives and other senior professionals of all the organisations.
- A questionnaire survey of senior personnel within the ICT sector in the country/region with an interest in regulation.
- Interviews with consultants directly involved in assisting the organisations towards effective performance.

The workshops included senior staff from the ten organisations who were mainly concerned with organisational and human resource development. The first workshop had as its main aim the creation of understanding on how to build internal capacity through an analytical dialogue and the preparation of action plans for improvement to which all participants were committed. Second and third workshops after periods of 6 and 16 months respectively allowed a reporting back on the progress made in the action plans and discussion in general on capacity building methodologies. Diagnostic techniques applied in the workshops produced many views that coalesced around the possibility of improvement through the capacity building enhancers that would need to be supported by management actions. Techniques used generated views on the performance of each organisation and comparisons between them in respect of capacity building initiatives. This feature was necessary in order that each organisation could gain ideas from others, and from the research perspective a picture of similarities and differences in practice built up. The following methodologies were applied in the workshops:

- SWOT analysis for each organisation (giving rise to debate on the quality of strategic planning).
- Hierarchic task analysis on the job of each participant to allow an assessment of the respective design of work systems for which they held responsibility.
- The production of questions from each organisation which when answered would allow an assessment of the quality of performance management it was achieving (these were discussed by a group of

participants experienced in the topic, so increasing the understanding of the role of performance management).

- An analysis of skill deficiencies in each organisation and a related diagnosis of the respective training and learning systems (the latter conducted as a consultancy exercise led by a small group of participants experienced in the area).
- A cultural diagnosis of each organisation to assess current values and associated management styles with personal/group views established on the shift necessary in organisations if effectiveness was to be increased.
- A force field analysis for each organisation, and on a comparative basis, to look at the forces operative for change and the constraints faced in moving forward with capacity building.

All the above information was collected in written form in terms of records of sessions, participants' views recorded on flip chart paper and completed pre-prepared proforma designed to assess the group in knowledge and understanding related to workshop aims. As the workshops progressed written records were made available to all participants to enable comparative dialogues to take place to feed ideas for either the preparation of the action plans (first workshop) or the review of their progress (second and third workshops). The action planning process itself produced further documented evidence in both the planning and review stages of how management processes support capacity building.

The multifarious perspectives produced by the sequence of methodologies enabled a comprehensive picture to be built up of the connection between management processes and capacity building. In particular, a provisional picture of the interrelationship arising from data collection and analysis in the first workshop was utilised to identify how further information could be derived from the second workshop.

DATA ANALYSIS

Regulatory Effectiveness

Regulatory effectiveness in each of the survey organisations is said to be present if three or four of the criteria in Table 14.2 are rated 'high' or 'medium' by its respective respondents. To achieve a result in this respect required a triangulation of data from respondents reporting on the same organisation, typically along the following lines depicting one of the organisations shown in Figure 14.2.

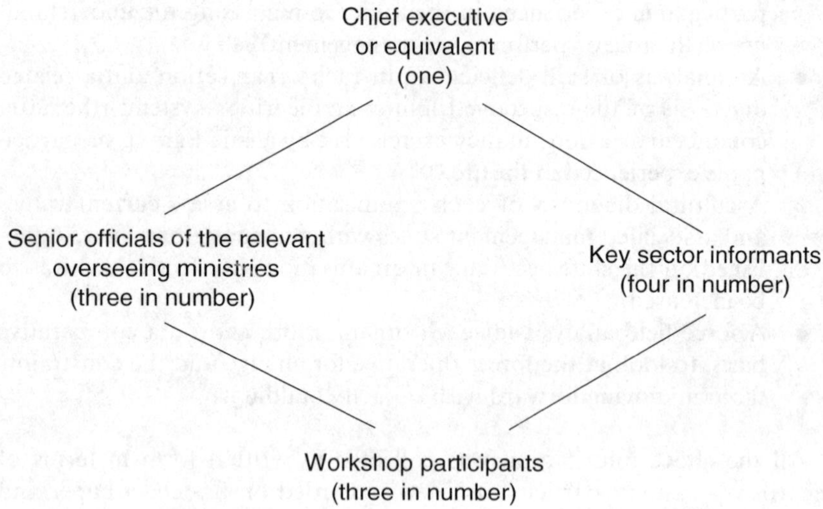

Figure 14.2 Example of triangulation of data for one of the survey organisations to establish the extent of regulatory effectiveness

Thus it was possible to disaggregate the organisations surveyed into two groups considered effective and non-effective. It has to be said that this is a somewhat crude separation given a possible continuum of progress of organisations, some only established in recent years, towards becoming effective in their domain of influence. However, it enables in a simplified way a connection to be made between degree of effectiveness and the force of the capacity building enhancers and their underlying management components.

Of the ten organisations surveyed, eight were considered effective on the basis of the criteria adopted. The two not measured as effective had major issues related to their legal enactment, organisational structures or senior staffing, and of the ten are two of the most recently set up bodies. They were therefore excluded from the next part of the analysis, which proceeded on the basis of the eight remaining agencies.

The Capacity Building Enhancers and Underlying Management Components

An analytical record based on the format of the diagnostic model was prepared for each organisation, bringing together data from the various sources so that organisational experiences could be classified according to links in the model, such as whether recognition of skill development needs takes place within performance appraisal. Examination of the analytical records enabled a view to be taken on the way in which management components were supporting the development and implementation of the capacity building enhancers for each of the organisations.

Given that none of the organisations were optimum in their performance and that weaknesses were being identified and rectified, very much as part of 'growing pains' of the regulatory process, information was drawn out on current deficiencies. These deficiencies were classified according to the operative influence of capacity building measures undertaken, classified as:

- Key skills provision;
- Effective group learning;
- Managers as enablers of high performance;
- Appropriate culture for achievement.

For each of these four sets of deficiencies a link was identified to the management components of the model. What the organisation was planning or doing to rectify deficiencies through actions was summarised from the raw research data and classified under the management components of strategic planning, work system design and performance management. These were listed as 'good practice' measures. 'Good practice' refers to the ability of each of the organisations to identify measures appropriate to its own needs and circumstances and not imposed, for instance, from the general pool of 'best practice' contained in management textbooks. Each of the organisations was finding its own way towards a level of performance by choosing actions appropriate to its own Specification of Regulatory Capacity that it had set for itself, and the primacy of this process was reflected in the information collected from the various sources. The analysis is shown in aggregated form for eight of the organisations in Table 14.3. As previously mentioned two of the ten organisations were excluded from the analysis on the basis it was difficult to make the connection from the data collected between actions under the management components and a strengthening of the capacity building enhancers, as reflected in the failure of the organisations concerned to pass the effectiveness test as described in the first part of the research analysis.

DISCUSSION OF FINDINGS

The study has proven the central hypothesis that strategic planning/ management, work system design methodologies and performance management are important in the development of regulatory agencies, and that

Table 14.3 The link between needed capacity building and the measures adopted to achieve it

Deficiencies recognised	Adopted 'good practice' measures as related to the management components
Key skills provision	
• No strategic approach for forecasting and resourcing key skills in future periods • Lack of correlation between senior management's priorities and requirements established by the human resource department • Training needs not adequately defined so unfocused training undertaken • Lack of a performance management system means no review undertaken of learning needs and how to address them • Outside training undertaken for personal rather than organisational needs • Biased approach to the selection of staff for training reflecting seniority, gender and affiliations • Reliance on outside training when in-house learning events or attachments would suffice • Expensive technical training overseas supported when it is not really affordable • Local training providers not optimally used • No database available to list skills resourced through training	• Strategic human resource development strategies and plans drawn up directly in relation to overall strategies • Strategic planning used as a coordinating influence on what work units do and how they develop • Chief executive 'drives' the strategic planning process, which leads to a focus on learning needs for the organisation • Robust human resources department set up to enable a fully professional approach in training • Training is based both on projected skills deficiencies as well as on learning needs currently arising among staff • Reviews of performance include an assessment of learning needs and how they might be met • Training plans are fully budgeted for within the financial projections • A recognition that all training should be evaluated to assess the extent to which learning acquired is applied in the workplace • An ability to draw on regional expertise and resources when investigating learning needs, and matching them with training resources available
Effective group learning	
Deficiencies recognised	Adopted 'good practice' measures as related to the management components
• Poor internal communication on the progression of work	• Job analysis used to generate relevant job descriptions and to focus on learning needs

Table 14.3 Continued

Effective group learning	
Deficiencies recognised	Adopted 'good practice' measures as related to the management components
• Too much 'informality' affecting consistency of work procedures • Staff experience limited autonomy in what they do and are unable to discuss problems arising • Teamwork is just 'mouthed' with limited actual practice • More emphasis is required on the processes of work as against the results required • No staff meetings are organised to discuss work issues arising • The absence of a performance management system means there is no focus on required learning needs and how these may be met	• Decentralised approaches used to harmonise work flows, enhance collaboration between units and build up team spirit • Understanding established among staff of the need for deliverable service to the public through team effort • An action plan approach utilised based on staff feedback and a performance tracking exercise • Staff meet twice annually away from their jobs to review objectives and address problems arising
Managers as enablers of high performance	
Deficiencies recognised	Adopted 'good practice' measures as related to the management components
• Unpredictability of political appointments that affect the strategic planning process and leadership style • Failure to sensitise stakeholders to participate actively in consultative meetings to generate critical feedback for the regulator and government • Outputs of the strategic planning process are 'not strategic' but purely current needs focused and passive • The current staff attitude towards customers (internal and external) is not right • Senior and well qualified staff not included in strategic decision making	• Sound strategic planning has been nurtured by a conducive 'policy environment' • The value of strategic planning as a coordinating influence on what work units do recognised and acted on • The regulator recognises that the organisation is different to the public sector and value is given to accumulated experience among staff • In one department managers meet twice a year to review progress on current objectives and set new ones • Steps have been taken to introduce a performance management system that will focus on key needs of the regulatory process • A performance management system is in operation but will be further

Table 14.3 Continued

Managers as enablers of high performance	
Deficiencies recognised	Adopted 'good practice' measures as related to the management components
• 'Firefighting' prevails and not 'fire prevention' • Involvement of full-time board members has confused management efforts	developed to focus on career development and succession • The regulator's management style has encouraged recognition of each others' efforts and generated respect in the workforce.
Appropriate culture for achievement	
Deficiencies recognised	Adopted 'good practice' measures as related to the management components
• Remnants of the 'old public sector culture' still around, which impede performance • Staff identify more with their professions than with the organisation as a whole • Lack of awareness of the external environment and the need to have a capacity to respond to changes in it • Staff unable to talk about problems and conflicts • Senior manager unable to receive criticism	• The regulator recognises that the organisation is different to the public sector and value is given to the accumulated experience of staff • A culture of innovation with decisions based on risk assessment is seen to be important by the regulator • The new performance management system emphasises values required in the organisation as well as ways of improving effectiveness

they are required areas of action to further capacity building. However, the original conceptual model for capacity building (Eldridge, 2004) has been amended as a result of the issues and organisational responses listed in Table 14.3 and the associated discussions with respondents. The primary change is in the definition of the capacity building enhancers that categorise the responses to the issues. These have been redefined as indicated in Table 14.4.

While the transition of (a) and (b) to (d) and (e) respectively in Table 14.4 represents to a large extent a redefinition of focus, (c) has evolved into areas of action and responsibility subsumed in (f) and (g). Both 'managers as enablers of high performance' and 'organisation culture' underpin the degree of accountability and transparency desired in a Specification of Regulatory Capacity (see Figure 14.1), for example, what form does

Table 14.4 The identification of the capacity building enhancers

As originally conceived	As a result of the study
(a) Adequate staff resourcing and development	(d) Key skills provision
(b) Individual, team and organisational learning capabilities	(e) Effective group/institutional learning
(c) Owned accountability and transparency components	(f) Managers as enablers of high performance
	(g) Appropriate culture for high achievement

Key skills provision ↓	Having on board the baseline technical, operational and managerial skills
Effective group/ institutional learning ↓	Building on baseline skills through an internal learning process that focuses on quality responses in terms of both technical and institutional needs
Managers as enablers of high performance ↓	Building on the skills and experiences of managerial staff so that they understand how to support the learning of others towards high performance
Appropriate culture for high performance	As managers and others evolve the best ways forward to support learning, development and achievement, an appropriate culture is identified

Figure 14.3 The interconnection of the capacity building enhancers

'transparency' take in the intended experience of recipients of the regulatory process. The results of the research summarised in Table 14.3 not only confirm the validity of the inclusion of (d), (e), (f) and (g) in the model but also suggest a sequencing of capacity building effects that is shown in Figure 14.3. Thus a failure to recruit and develop needed baseline skills for an organisation may inhibit appropriate developments in the other three enhancers.

Turning now to the diagnostic model as a whole, what do the research results imply? First of all the survey organisations all utilise actions that can be defined under the management components listed. They all recognise capacity building as being influenced by actions in the areas defined and recognise consequences that can be categorised according to the capacity building enhancers defined for this study. As a result the 'heart' of the diagnostic model can be said to offer an explanation of how regulation is managed and enhanced. The 'peripheral' elements of the model, namely, institutional analysis, institutional design and the specification of regulatory capacity also represent activities that all organisations have undertaken (Goulden, 2001), as clearly recorded in interviews and questionnaires utilised in the research. The diagnostic model is therefore confirmed as a viable conceptual explanation of how regulation is furthered from intention to outcome. The only element that is portrayed in the model but is apparently absent from the practice of the ten organisations is regulatory impact assessment, which in many respects is in its infancy as a viable methodology in most countries and sectors.

CONCLUDING REMARKS ON THE VALUE AND USE OF THE MODEL

While confirmation is now established of the usefulness of the diagnostic model for capacity building within the ICT agencies included in the study (apart from two excluded on the basis of inadequate internal development and lack of effectiveness), the question arises as to its possible wider use, particularly for agencies outside the regional context of the study and in other sectors. A number of developments can be cited to suggest the possibility of a wider use of the model for capacity building activities, as follows:

- Outside this particular study, interviews have been held with a number of senior regulatory staff across all sectors in a range of developing countries, and evidence gathered to suggest the model represents a viable framework for analysis and action.
- Very experienced international consultants have incorporated the diagnostic model within their own portfolio of analytical methods appropriate for regulatory bodies.
- The diagnostic model has been presented at numerous conferences, seminars, workshops and gatherings of key people concerned with capacity building in regulatory agencies and their response has been a positive one at both the conceptual and action orientated levels.

On the basis of this cross-relationship between the empirical findings and evidence drawn from elsewhere it is possible, we believe, to recommend the inclusion of the diagnostic model in capacity building deliberations outside the ICT sector represented by the survey organisations. We feel reasonably safe in this respect as the model is not presented as a 'best practice' one, that is, things should be done in this specific way. It is presented as an approach designed to stimulate the identification of questions on what might constitute 'good practice' for *any* regulatory body. 'Good practice' represents a situation in which regulatory and associated management practices reflect:

- Context: What are the political, legal and administrative inheritances that influence the ability to regulate?
- Experience: What has been the experience to date in the enactment of management of regulation?
- Culture: What overriding values govern the way people think and act both as deliverers and recipients of regulation?

These are broad points that obviously break down into more detailed questions that, when answered, guide the development of 'good practice' for a regulator. Such discussion encompasses the use of the model, whose overall purpose is to stimulate understandings and activities to improve performance. Thus at one level as both a visual representation and a description of systematic connections it can be introduced into workshops involving regulatory staff to induce thinking on the key capacity building issues faced. In this respect it represents a 'thinking tool' to pose whether the variables (management components and capacity building enhancers) included in the model are identifiable in the agency concerned along the lines of:

- What form do the key variables take?
- To what extent do they interact with one another within management processes?
- What is the quality of the interactions if they are vital in achieving high performance?
- What actions are necessary to improve capacity building through new/enhanced managerial actions?

Through such a process in a workshop, for instance, a regulator can achieve a more sophisticated picture of the situation in which an agency finds itself and be able to describe this. Thus the introduction of the model involves language built in terms of the management and organisational concepts described and moves the regulator to the primary question 'how

Table 14.5 Primary questions arising in the diagnostic model

Institutional analysis/design	
Policy formulation	What strategic intentions and legal enactments give rise to the regulator's work?
Organisation diagnosis	What are the current strengths/weaknesses of the regulatory agency?
Regulatory design	What are the key features of the regulatory system and its decision-making needs?
Organisation design	What do the key features of the regulatory system imply for organisation and management in the agency?
Key organisation components	
Strategic planning	What are the specific purposes of regulation and outputs expected?
Work system design	What are the key work processes to achieve the desired regulatory outcomes?
Performance management	What management processes enable the purposes and processes of regulation to proceed?
Critical capacity building enhancers	
Key skills provision	How can staff resourcing and development be geared to priority needs?
Effective group/institutional learning	How can individual, team and organisational learning capabilities be enhanced for effective and efficient regulation?
Managers as enablers of high performance	How can managers best support the quest for achievement through the learning and development of staff?
Appropriate culture	How is an appropriate organisation culture created for high performance?
Specification of regulatory capacity (impacts)	
	Structural factors What is planned in terms of the impact on recipients/stakeholders in terms of: • the system of regulation • its outputs and delivery • competences displayed • quality of information provided • who is accountable for what?
	Cultural factors What is the intended experience of recipients/stakeholders in terms of how regulation is perceived vis-à-vis:

Table 14.5 Continued

	• values promoted • sensitivity to the interests involved • quality of communication channels • transparency of operations?

can the management of regulation be improved – what is "better" in this respect?' Absence of any part of the model in the reality of the organisation is not a fault in itself but a stimulation to further discussion to discover why this is so. Such an approach seeks 'critical adaptation' early in the discussion among the regulator and others concerned to ensure the consequences of 'imported' practices are analysed as to their usefulness to the country/organisational circumstances faced (Minogue, 2002). Examples of the types of question likely to be stimulated by the model are shown in Table 14.5.

The use of the management components is more fully explored in CRC Policy Brief No. 4 (2004), that aims to take the agenda for capacity building beyond purely prescriptive measures to a systemic view of internal processes that can be understood and positively influenced by organisational members. It is a contribution that promotes the ownership of the identification of learning needs and consequent actions for improvement, thereby removing any undue influence on institutions from consultants and donors.

Also reflected in the approach is the urgent need for regulatory agencies, if they are to succeed, to be sharper in internal performance than the market suppliers that they are dealing with, and to be crucially aware of how to handle effectively the multiplicity of stakeholder influences and needs. All this suggests the creation of organisations that have antennae hanging out of them in respect of receiving information, processing it and responding in appropriate ways through their internal mechanisms, a level of performance being required that in many cases is beyond what traditionally organised public sector organisations can offer.

BIBLIOGRAPHY

Ackoff, R.L. (1999), *Re-creating the Corporation*, New York: Oxford University Press.

Aryeetey, E. (2002), 'The institutional and policy framework for regulation and competition in Ghana', Centre on Regulation and Competition, Working Paper No. 46, University of Manchester, Manchester.

Asch, D. and Bowman, C. (eds) (1989), *Readings in Strategic Management*, Basingstoke: Macmillan.

Beer, S. (1985), *Diagnosing the System for Organisations*, Chichester: Wiley.

Better Regulation Task Force (2003), *Principles of Good Regulation*, London: Cabinet Office, Regulatory Impact Unit.

Boschken, H.L. (1994), 'Organisational performance and multiple constituencies', *Public Administration Review*, **54**, 308–12.

Bowman, J. (1994), 'At last an alternative to performance appraisal: Total quality management', *Public Administration Review*, **54**(2), 129–36.

Brigham, B.H. and L. Fitzgerald (2001), 'Controlling managers and organisations: The case of performance measurement in a regulated water company', Centre for Management Under Regulation Research Paper No. 01/1, Warwick.

Bryson, J.M. (1995), *Strategic Planning for Public and Non-Profit Organisations*, San Francisco: Jossey-Bass.

Bryson, J.M. and B.C. Crosby (1992), *Leadership for the Common Good: Tackling Public Problems in a Shared Power World*, San Francisco: Jossey-Bass.

Cabinet Office (undated), 'Objective setting in personal review', Main Report, London: Cabinet Office, Office of Public Service and Science.

Cariño, L.V. (2002), 'Regulatory governance in the Philippines: A profile', Centre on Regulation and Competition, Working Paper No. 44, University of Manchester, Manchester.

Cook, P. (2001), 'Privatisation and regulation in developing countries', in W. McCourt and M. Minogue (eds), *The Internationalisation of Public Management, Reinventing the Third World State*, Cheltenham; UK and Northampton, MA, USA: Edward Elgar.

CRC (2004), 'Capacity building for regulation', Manchester: Centre on Competition and Regulation, Policy Brief No. 4

Deming, W.E. (1986), *Out of Crisis*, Cambridge, MA: MIT Institute for Advanced Engineering Study.

Deming, W.E. (1994), *The New Economics for Industry, Government, Education*, Cambridge, MA: MIT Press.

Deming Society (1994), *Performance Appraisal and All That*, London: Deming Society.

Eldridge, D. (2002), 'Raising the agenda for capacity building in the CRC', Centre on Regulation and Competition, Working Paper No. 19, University of Manchester, Manchester.

Eldridge, D. (2003), 'Exploring the inter-relationships of strategic planning, work system design and performance management in regulatory agencies', Centre on Regulation and Competition, Working Paper No. 49, University of Manchester, Manchester.

Eldridge, D. (2004), 'A diagnostic model for capacity building in regulatory agencies', in P. Cook, C. Kirkpatrick, M. Minogue and D. Parker (eds), *Leading Issues in Competition, Regulation and Development*, Cheltenham, UK and Northampton, MA, USA: Edward Elgar, pp. 182–201.

Goulden, B. (2001), *Bridging the Digital Divide: The Regulatory Environment in Southern Africa*, London: The Commonwealth Telecommunications Organisation.

Guth, W.D. and I.C. MacMillan (1989), 'Strategy implementation v. middle management self interest', in D. Asch and C. Bowman (eds), *Readings in Strategic Management*, Basingstoke: Macmillan.

Knight-John, M. (2002), 'The institutional policy framework for regulation and competition in Sri Lanka', Centre on Regulation and Competition, Working Paper No. 40, University of Manchester, Manchester.

Lewis, C.W. (1991), *The Ethics Challenge in Public Service: A Problem Solving Guide*, San Francisco: Jossey-Bass.

Majone, G. (1999), 'The regulatory state and its legitimacy problems', *West European Politics*, **22**(1), 1–24.

Mehta, P.S. (2002), 'Friends of competition', Capacity Building for an Effective Competition Regime in Developing Countries, Jaipur, CUTS.

Minogue, M. (2002), 'Public management and regulatory governance: Problems of policy transfer to developing countries', Centre on Regulation and Competition, Working Paper No. 32, University of Manchester, Manchester.

Minogue, M. (2004a), 'Public management and regulatory governance: Problems of policy transfer to developing countries', in P. Cook, C. Kirkpatrick, M. Minogue and D. Parker (eds), *Leading Issues in Competition, Regulation and Development*, Cheltenham, UK and Northampton, MA, USA: Edward Elgar, pp. 165–81.

Minogue, M. (2004b), 'Regulatory governance and the improvement of public services', Centre on Regulation and Competition, Working Paper No. 64, University of Manchester, Manchester.

Mintzberg, H. (1983), *Power In and Around Organisations*, Englewood Cliffs, NJ: Prentice Hall.

Mintzberg, H. (1994), 'The fall and rise of strategic planning', *Harvard Business Review*, January–February, 107–14.

Osborne, D. and T. Gaebler (1992), *Reinventing Government*, Reading: MA: Addison-Wesley.

Parker, D. and C. Kirkpatrick (2003), 'Regulatory impact assessment: Developing its potential for use in developing countries', Centre on Regulation and Competition, Working Paper No. 56, University of Manchester, Manchester.

Paton, R.A. and J. McCalman (2000), *Change Management. A Guide to Effective Implementation*, London: Sage.

Peters, G. (1995), *The Politics of Bureaucracy*, New York: Longman.

Pfeffer, J. (1992), *Managing with Power: Politics and Influence in Organisations*, Boston, MA: Harvard Business School Press.

Pollitt, C. and G. Bouckaert (2000), *Public Management Reform: A Comparative Analysis*, Oxford: Oxford University Press.

Stirton, L. and M. Lodge (2002), 'Embedding regulatory autonomy: The reform of the Jamaican Telecommunications Regulation, 1988–2001', London School of Economics, Centre for Analysis of Risk and Regulation.

Vass, P. (2002), 'The principles of "better regulation" – separating roles and responsibility', Centre on Regulation and Competition International Workshop, Manchester, September 2002.

Index